Revolution

Revolution

An Intellectual History

Enzo Traverso

VERSO

London • New York

First published by Verso 2021
© Enzo Traverso 2021

1 3 5 7 9 10 8 6 4 2

Verso
UK: 6 Meard Street, London W1F 0EG
US: 20 Jay Street, Suite 1010, Brooklyn, NY 11201
versobooks.com

Verso is the imprint of New Left Books

ISBN-13: 978-1-83976-333-5
ISBN-13: 978-1-83976-360-1 (UK EBK)
ISBN-13: 978-1-83976-361-8 (US EBK)

British Library Cataloguing in Publication Data
A catalogue record for this book is available from the British Library

Library of Congress Cataloging-in-Publication Data
Library of Congress Control Number: 2021941136

Typeset in Fournier by MJ&N Gavan, Truro, Cornwall
Printed and bound by CPI Group (UK) Ltd, Croydon CR0 4YY

Contents

Abbreviations

MECW = Marx, Engels, *Collected Works*, London: Lawrence & Wishart, 1975–2005, 50 vols.

LCW = Lenin, *Collected Works*, Moscow: Progress Publishers, 1960–70, 45 vols.

WBSW = Walter Benjamin, *Selected Writings*, Michael Jennings (ed.), Cambridge, MA: Harvard University Press, 2003–06, 4 vols.

List of Illustrations

Acknowledgements

T his book has greatly benefited from a sabbatical year at Cornell University. The Covid-19 pandemic changed my plans and I had to cancel several research-stays in Europe, notably in Paris and Berlin, but in the end the isolation I was forced to endure in Ithaca, New York, proved a fruitful retreat, profitable to introspective meditation and writing on history. It was a good opportunity for 'working through' many ideas and experiences: the ideas I have encountered, adopted, defended or criticized in the past; and the experiences I have accumulated in my life, from my first political commitments in the 1970s to the intellectual debates of the twenty-first century. I never participated in a revolution – except for having lived during a time when revolution was in the air – but many questions and dilemmas which I try to reconstitute and analyse in this book have also been mine. Thus, if my views have changed on many issues, there is no doubt that writing this book solicited my recollections and frequently resonated with my lived experience. However, I have not written it as a 'witness' or in order to come to terms with the past; I am not adopting any apologetic posture or trying to settle my accounts with adversaries or critics. I simply feel part of the history I tell, burdened as it was with utopias, generosity, fraternity, and greatness, but also with mistakes, illusions, deceptions, and sometimes monstrosities. Writing on the history of revolutions requires awareness of the dangers of subjectivity, which cannot be repressed but needs to be managed, controlled, and mastered. I remember an interesting conversation with Tzvetan Todorov — a thinker I respected, despite our considerable disagreements — in which we both admitted that Italians and Bulgarians cannot look at the history of communism through a similar lens, simply because they are located in very different observatories and communism does not mean the same thing in their respective countries. I do not know whether I have been able to make a proper and fruitful use of my existential background, which is limited and emphatically particular, by both keeping it at a necessary distance and mobilizing it as an analytical tool, but I do know that this exercise requires humility and modesty. With regard to revolution, too often critical understanding has been replaced by naïve enthusiasm, moral judgement or ideological stigmatization. These are not the options I have chosen, and my book does not pretend to transmit the lessons of the past; it is simply an attempt at critical knowledge and interpretation. This is the main task that my generation can accomplish today.

Writing this book, I realized how much I was indebted towards friends, comrades, scholars, and authors: those with whom I have had fruitful discussions, as well as those whom I have never met but whose works have nonetheless accompanied me on my intellectual journey. Classical thinkers and original scholars, but also unknown, rank-and-file activists whom I encountered in several countries and at several different times: all of them mattered to me. It would take too long to mention them here, but I am grateful to all of them.

This book was born from a couple of graduate seminars which I had the pleasure to teach in recent years at Cornell University and, in a more condensed form, at other universities in both Europe and Latin America, notably the University of San Martín and the CeDInCi in Buenos Aires, Argentina, in November 2018; and the University of Valencia, Spain, in January 2020. I am very grateful to my students, as well as to the colleagues and good friends who invited me to share and discuss my ideas: Horacio Tarcus and Nicolás Sanchez Durá. Singular chapters have been presented as lectures, keynote speeches, or discussed as papers in seminars at several universities and cultural societies: the University of Rome 3, in January 2018; Jour Fixe Lectures, Berlin, June 2017; the Free University of Brussels, October 2017; the University of Texas, Austin, April 2019; the University Rio

Piedras of Puerto Rico, May 2019; the University Pompeu Fabra of Barcelona, June 2019; the UNAM in Mexico City, October 2019; and the Fondazione Feltrinelli in Milan, January 2020. For these opportunities, I would like to express my gratitude to Chiara Giorgi, Gabriele Pedullà, Elfi Mueller, Mateo Alaluf, Jean Vogel, Benjamin C. Brower, Carlos Pabón, Antonio Monegal, Esther Cohen, and David Bidussa. A first, much shorter version of Chapter 6 appeared in *South Atlantic Quarterly*, 116/4 (2017), with the title 'Historicizing Communism: A Twentieth-Century Chameleon', and was subsequently translated into Spanish and German, where it appeared in two collected books: *1917: La Revolución rusa cien años después*, ed. Juan Andrade and Fernando Hernández Sánchez (Madrid: Akal, 2017), and *Anti!Kommunismus: Struktur einer Ideologie*, ed. Jour Fixe Initiative Berlin (Muenster: Edition Assemblage, 2017). I also summarized some ideas of Chapter 1 in 'Las locomotoras de la historia', included in Esther Cohen (ed.), *Imágenes de Resistencia* (Mexico: UNAM, 2020), where they are followed by Aureliano Ortega Esquivel's critical commentaries ('Del progreso a su nemesis: Metáforas del ferrocarril'). A first, very short version of Chapter 5 appeared in Spanish with the title 'El tortuoso camino de la libertad' in *La Maleta de Portbou*, 38 (2019). Written in English, this book benefited significantly from the linguistic revision and critical reading by Nicholas R. Bujalski and William R. Cameron, my valuable research assistants at Cornell University, whom I thank. At Verso, Lorna Scott Fox was a remarkable copyeditor, and I am very grateful to her. The support from my editor, Sebastian Budgen, was essential from the beginning.

Ithaca, NY, April 2021

Introduction

Interpreting Revolutions

Proletarian revolutions ... constantly engage in self-criticism, and in repeated interruptions of their own course. They return to what has apparently already been accomplished in order to begin the task again; with merciless thoroughness they mock the inadequate, weak and wretched aspects of their first attempts; they seem to throw their opponent to the ground only to see him draw new strength from the earth and rise again before them, more colossal than ever; they shrink back again and again before the indeterminate immensity of their own goals.

Karl Marx, *The Eighteenth Brumaire of Louis Bonaparte* (1852)

Many years ago, leaving an exhibition at the Louvre Museum just before closing time, I suddenly found myself in an empty room – all other visitors had already left – in front of Théodore Géricault's *The Raft of the Medusa* (1819). The impact of that striking moment has endured, and I still have a clear memory of what I felt. Of course, I knew this painting, one of the most famous works of nineteenth-century romantic art, but this unexpected meeting revealed to me a completely unknown piece: I was admiring one of the most powerful allegories of the shipwreck of revolution. Not only the French Revolution, the only one the painter could think about when making his masterpiece, but also – and above all – the revolutions of the twentieth century, which had just passed away at the time of

Théodore Géricault, *The Raft of the Medusa* (1819).
Canvas. Musée du Louvre, Paris.

my Louvre visit. Many details of this monumental canvas achieved a
clear meaning to me when related to modern revolutionary history.

Images look at us. As Horst Bredekamp has magisterially explained,
they are not passive or dead objects delivered to our interpretive gaze.
They are living creations whose meaning transcends the purposes and
intentions of their authors, thus taking on new reality and significance
with the passing of time. Far from being frozen, their meaning changes
diachronically, insofar as their potential is permanently renewed.
Like literary texts, they live in a dialogical relationship with their
observers: 'Images are not passive. They are begetters of every sort of
experience and action related to perception. This is the quintessence
of the image act.'[1]

Unlike Paul Klee's *Angelus Novus*, which Walter Benjamin interpreted by envisaging a landscape of ruins not included in the canvas
itself, Géricault's work offers an astonishingly rich collection of allegorical elements that insistently interrogate the historian of revolutions
two centuries after its completion. The history of this canvas is too

---

1   See Horst Bredekamp, *Image Acts: A Systematic Approach to Visual Agency*
(Berlin, New York: De Gruyter, 2018), 283.

well-known to need any considerable explanation. Originally titled *Scene of a Shipwreck*, it was first exhibited at the Salon of 1819, achieving international celebrity after its display in London the following year.[2] Its inspiration comes from an event that made a great impression a few years earlier: the shipwreck of the French frigate *Medusa* in July 1816, during a journey to Senegal, where it was transferring officers, soldiers, and materials for the new colonial administration. Led by an incompetent captain appointed under the Restoration because of his conservative views and his connections to the Bourbon family, it ran aground off the coast of North-Western Africa. Whereas half of the crew managed to escape on light sailboats, 147 people were abandoned on a makeshift raft quickly built by the sailors. When the brig *Argus* finally rescued it, two weeks later, only fifteen survivors remained. They bore witness to the death and despair that had seized men completely starved and dehydrated, driving some of them to throw their comrades overboard and even, seized by ethylic intoxication after consuming two barrels of wine, to cannibalism. The object of a trial, many testimonies, and a successful chronicle written by two survivors, this shipwreck rapidly became a major event at the end of Louis XVIII's reign. Géricault met the survivors personally and asked them to pose; he devoted many studies to the sea, the waves and the wind; and he frequently visited the morgue, taking corpses into his studio to capture the colour of their skin. His painting, however, is not realist. Rather than a truthful picture of the shipwreck, it is the representation of a human tragedy that respects the aesthetic codes of Romanticism and neoclassical painting. What significantly changes in his canvas are the subjects portrayed: instead of kings and aristocratic figures, *The Raft of the Medusa* displays the affliction of ordinary people. Its characters are sailors, soldiers, workers, carpenters, the representatives of the lower classes who found no place aboard the sailboats and the brigs that left the frigate.

Depicting this raft in a stormy sea, the canvas focuses on the contrast between despair and hope: the despair overwhelming the crew

---

2   On the history of both the shipwreck and Géricault's painting, see Jonathan Miles, *Medusa: The Shipwreck, the Scandal, the Masterpiece* (London: Jonathan Cape, 2007).

and the hope of a few among them who discern the silhouette of a sail on the horizon, the sail of the brig *Argus* that will rescue them. This spark of hopefulness is embodied by a black sailor who, hauling himself up onto an empty barrel of wine, waves a red rag, probably a piece of his own clothing. The entire crowd is surmounted by this figure that, expressing muscular energy and physical presence, clashes with the exhaustion of his companions. Indeed, the actual raft included a black survivor, a sailor named Jean-Charles, and Géricault gave him the features of Joseph, the best-known black model of his time in Paris.[3] This choice, which clearly mirrored the abolitionist views of the painter, alluded to his project of an ambitious canvas against the slave trade that he never completed. Exhausted by the realization of *The Raft of the Medusa* and weakened by tuberculosis, he died in 1824.

In contrast to this black sailor who scans the horizon in front of him and whose back alone is visible to us, a second central figure of this painting shows his face. Older than the other characters, he seems indifferent to both the agony of the wreck surrounding him and the breath of hope spread by the sight of the *Argus*'s sail. Clearly reminiscent of the Damned Man who appears in the *Last Judgment* of Michelangelo (1534–41), and already anticipating Auguste Rodin's *The Thinker* (1904), this figure is passive, static, and meditative. His face is quietly untroubled; his white beard highlights his maturity and gives him the cast of wisdom. He does not hide his face and, unlike those of Michelangelo's Damned Man, his open eyes are not frightened; they rather reveal a feeling of resignation. His left hand curls around a pale corpse and in front of him lies the trunk of a legless man, which evokes the episode of cannibalism mentioned above. If the raft is a metaphor for a shipwrecked humanity, he stoically observes it as an ineluctable event. There is no rescue. Any search for salvation is meaningless.[4]

---

3   See Laurent Martin, 'Le modèle noir de Géricault à Matisse', *Sociétés et Représentations*, 49 (2020): 235–8.

4   The Damned Man in Michelangelo's Last Judgment was interpreted by Detlev Peukert as an allegory of Max Weber's resignation in front of the 'iron cage' of modernity. See Detlev Peukert, *Max Webers Diagnose der Moderne* (Göttingen: Vandenhoeck & Ruprecht, 1989), 27.

Many features of *The Raft of the Medusa* would become the sources of allegorical interpretations or be invoked as examples of historical prefiguration. In 1848, Jules Michelet saw in Géricault's painting the mirror of a society torn between death and hope, past and future: 'This is France herself, it is our society whole and entire that he puts to sea on this raft.'[5] No longer externalized or displaced to an exotic or mythological realm, violence crosses through French identity itself, akin to what happens in a revolution or a civil war.[6] In more recent years, art historians have detected in this masterpiece, as a message piercing the conventions of neoclassicism, the premonition of anticolonialism and black liberation. According to Hugh Honour, this painting is the most effective claim for the right of blacks to liberty and equality ever made in the whole history of Western art; a visual claim in which, for the first time, blacks are freed 'from the stigma of inferiority implicit in straightforward abolitionist iconography'.[7] From a different perspective, Linda Nochlin caught in Géricault's work the signs of a 'femininity without women': a depiction of the feminine 'detached from the representation of the actual bodies of women' but rather evoked through the display of an ensemble of 'castrated' and 'disempowered' male bodies. In other words, this 'symphony of masculine desire' and intermingled men is the exact opposite of a triumph of virility.[8]

The towering figure of this canvas is a black man – a symbol of the most oppressed and disparaged members of the human race at that time – who is waving a red rag or handkerchief like a flag. He is the harbinger of something that in 1819 has just appeared – the Haitian Revolution – or that does not yet exist: an insurgent movement of ruled races and classes. At that time, the red flag had not yet become a

5   Quoted in Lorenz E. A. Eitner, *Géricault's Raft of the Medusa* (London: Phaidon, 1972), 56.

6   See Ralph Hage, 'Protecting Identity: Violence and Its Representations in France, 1815–1830', *Contagion: Journal of Violence, Mimesis, and Culture*, 25 (2018): 49–77.

7   Hugh Honour, 'Philanthropic Conquest', in David Bindman and Henry Louis Gates Jr. (eds), *The Image of the Black in Western Art* (Cambridge, MA: Harvard University Press, 1989), vol. 4.1, 125.

8   Linda Nochlin, 'Géricault, or the Absence of Women', *October*, 68 (1994): 51.

universal symbol of rebellion. However, the socialist and communist iconography of the early twentieth century, with its muscular proletarian bodies waving red flags and breaking the chains of oppression, undoubtedly comes from this neoclassical tradition of the representation of naked bodies. This is one of the reasons for which, two centuries after the Paris Salon of 1819, *The Raft of the Medusa* can be seen both as a powerful allegory of the shipwreck and as a harbinger of revolution. How not to see the raft as the remains of a movement that – like the frigate sailing the ocean – aimed to conquer the future and ended as wreckage? How not to see in the incompetence of the captain an allusion to the mistakes and betrayals of Stalinism? How not to catch in the frightening testimonies to the cannibalism in the raft a metaphor for revolutions devouring their own children? How not to compare the raft mutinies with the rebellions against the authoritarian turns of socialism, from Kronstadt in 1921 to Budapest in 1956, from Prague in 1968 to Gdansk in 1980?

On the other hand, the impactful contrast between the old man passively contemplating the catastrophe and the young black man energetically waving a red handkerchief suggests another widespread dilemma of our time: the conflict between resignation and hope, between capitulation and the obstinate search for an alternative, between abandonment and rebirth, between impotence and despair before a landscape of defeats and the desperate effort to resist. The brig *Argus* is not a guarantee of rescue: several witnesses said that it disappeared for two hours before joining the raft. In Géricault's painting, it is a tiny point just detectable on the horizon. Liberation is not an ineluctable happy ending, but a remote possibility, a chance to be taken without any predictable outcome. Lucien Goldmann depicted socialism as a 'wager', a wager based on 'the risk, the danger of failure, and the hope of success'.[9] The *Argus*'s sail is 'the *weak* messianic power' that, in Walter Benjamin's words, 'we are endowed' with, 'like every

---

9   Lucien Goldmann, *The Hidden God: A Study of Tragic Vision in the* Pensées *of Pascal and the Tragedies of Racine* (London: Routledge, 1964), 301. See also Mitchell Cohen, *The Wager of Lucien Goldmann: Tragedy, Dialectics, and a Hidden God* (Princeton: Princeton University Press, 1994).

V. V. Spassky, *To the Lighthouse of the Communist International*
(1919). Soviet Poster. Lenin Library, Moscow.

generation that preceded us'.[10] A weak messianic power that socialism
seized and transformed into a lever to change history. In the twentieth
century, this lever became so powerful that many fighters mistakenly
held it for an irrefutable historical telos; but socialism was *Argus*, a
potential rescuer, not *Medusa*, the conquering frigate, and revolution
reeled like a raft in the middle of a stormy sea.

To tell the truth, Géricault's painting had already inspired an allegorical representation of socialist shipwreck. In 1919, the Soviet artist
V. V. Spassky realized a propaganda poster for the Communist International that almost explicitly cited the masterpiece of his illustrious
French predecessor. Produced by the government – the header mentions the Russian Socialist Federative Soviet Republic – the placard
shows a small raft which, by struggling against the waves not far from
a wrecked ship, tries to reach a dark coast where one bright light is

---

10   Walter Benjamin, 'On the Concept of History', *WBSW*, vol. 4, 390.

shining. It is a book-raft built from *The Communist Manifesto*: the left page reads 'Workers of the World Unite!', and on the right is written its author: Karl Marx. The single castaway who appears in this poster is white, but he shows his naked back and, much like in *The Raft of the Medusa*, he holds a red handkerchief. The inscription under the image is a dedication: 'To the Lighthouse of the Communist International.'

It is difficult to say what this wrecked ship is supposed to symbolize: either the collapsed Tsarist empire, as suggested by the yellow strip of its torn flag, or, more probably, the Second International, which destroyed any form of proletarian solidarity during the Great War. The message of the poster is clear nonetheless: the socialist future is not compromised, since the Communist International embodies a light of hope. And the instrument of this salvage is a text: *The Communist Manifesto*. At the end of the twentieth century, we have experienced a similar revolutionary shipwreck, but there is no visible lighthouse yet.

Without referring to *The Raft of the Medusa*, Walter Benjamin sketched a comparable image in 1936, when he edited in exile, under the nom de plume of Detlev Holz, a collection of letters from the foremost thinkers of the Enlightenment with the title *Deutsche Menschen* (*German Men and Women*).[11] In the copies he dedicated to his sister Dora and his friend Gershom Scholem, he presented the book as a an 'ark, built after a Jewish model', which he lowered 'when the fascist flood started to rise'.[12] Benjamin's purpose was the salvage of German culture threatened by Nazism, and the Jewish prototype of this ark, Scholem suggested, was a textual heritage: Benjamin alluded to the fact that, throughout the centuries, 'the Jews took refuge from the persecutions in the Writ, the canonical book.'[13] From this point of view, Spassky's book-raft was also built 'after a Jewish model', since it depicted Marx's writings as an ark allowing the revolutionary left

---

11   Walter Benjamin, *Deutsche Menschen: Eine Folge von Briefen* (Frankfurt: Suhrkamp, 1980 [1936]).

12   Gershom Scholem, *Walter Benjamin: The Story of a Friendship* (New York: New York Review of Books, 2003), 255.

13   Ibid. See also Albrecht Schöne, '"Diese nach jüdischem Vorbild erbaute Arche": Walter Benjamins *Deutsche Menschen*', in Stéphane Moses and Albrecht Schöne (eds), *Juden in der deutschen Literatur: Ein deutsch-israelisches Symposion* (Frankfurt: Suhrkamp, 1986), 350–65.

to resist both the nationalist wave of 1914 and the betrayal of social democracy. The shipwreck of the twentieth-century revolutions, however, is still waiting for an ark or a book-raft. Its salvage does not require the fetishistic preservation of an untouched legacy of experiences and texts. On the contrary, it means a critical working through of the past that can spare neither theory nor canonical texts, but without an ark or a raft this work cannot be accomplished.

The method inspiring this historical essay on revolution owes much to both Karl Marx and Walter Benjamin. Faithful to their intellectual tradition, it approaches revolution as a sudden – and almost always violent – interruption of the historical continuum, as a break of the social and political order. Against the 'revisionist' narrative that has proliferated after the collapse of real socialism, the profound wisdom of which argues that changing the world means building totalitarianism, it aims at rehabilitating the concept of revolution as an interpretive key to modern history. It departs from classical Marxism, however, insofar as it does not adopt a historicist gaze. First of all, it does not depict revolution as the result of a deterministic causality, or the outcome of a kind of historical 'law'. In many texts, Marx and Engels transform Hegelian historicism into an evolutionary theory of history as a lineal succession of modes of production going from primitive to modern socialism throughout centuries of oppression: slavery, feudalism, and capitalism. According to Marx, this historical progression arises from the clash between, on the one hand, the development of the productive forces (the complex articulation of human labour, machines, technology, and science applied to the economy) and, on the other, the property relations of a given mode of production to which corresponds an ensemble of ideological and political superstructures. A famous passage of his Preface to *A Contribution to the Critique of Political Economy* (1859) summarizes quite clearly this deterministic vision of revolution:

> At a certain stage of development, the material productive forces of
> society come into conflict with the existing relations of production
> or – this merely expresses the same thing in legal terms – with the

property relations within the framework of which they have operated hitherto. From forms of development of the productive forces
these relations turn into their fetters. Then begins an era of social
revolution. The changes in the economic foundation lead sooner or
later to the transformation of the whole immense superstructure.[14]

But there is a second view of revolution that runs through Marx's
political writings. It focuses on human agency and depicts the past
as the realm of class struggle. Without neglecting the material basis
of social conflicts, this approach avoids economic determinism and
emphasizes the transformative potentialities of political subjectivity.
Mostly relegated to the background of his economic works, class
struggle pulses on every page of his political essays, from those on
the revolutions of 1848 to those on the Paris Commune. In these texts,
history is no longer the result of 'a process of natural history' but
rather the outcome of collective action, passions, utopias and selfless
impulses that merge with egoistic interests, cynicism and even hate.
As Marx and Engels write in *The Holy Family* (1844), 'History does
nothing, it "possesses no immense wealth", it "wages no battles". It
is man, real, living man who does all that, who possesses and fights;
"history" is not, as it were, a person apart, using man as a means
to achieve its own aims; history is nothing but the activity of man
pursuing his aims.'[15]

In short, history is a permanent process of production of subjectivities. Class struggles engender historical turns that transcend their
premises and cannot be explained exclusively through economic
necessity or the mechanical submission to structural factors. In Marx's
view, both revolutions and counterrevolutions reveal the 'autonomy
of the political'.[16]

The entanglement of causality and agency, structural determinism
and political subjectivity – two explanatory keys that tend to remain

---

14   *MECW*, vol. 29, 263–4.

15   *MECW*, vol. 4, 93. See Sandro Mezzadra, *In the Marxian Workshops: Producing Subjects* (London: Roman & Littlefield International, 2018).

16   See Mario Tronti, 'Sull'autonomia del politico' (1972), *Il demone della
politica* (Bologna: Il Mulino, 2017), 285–312.

separated in Marx's writings – has produced the best achievements of Marxist historiography, from Trotsky's *History of the Russian Revolution* (1930–32) to C. L. R. James's *The Black Jacobins* (1938); from Daniel Guérin's *Bourgeois and 'Bras Nus'* (1947) to Adolfo Gilly's *The Mexican Revolution* (1971).[17] Here, I would like to devote some additional observations to Trotsky's historiographical masterpiece, which probably constitutes the paradigm of this methodological entanglement.

There is no doubt that the chief of the Red Army wrote his book as a work of art. In the preface to the second volume, he quotes Proust and Dickens and claims the right of the historian, beyond analysing the sequence of events and interpreting the actors' roles, to depict their sentiments. In order to understand the past, the historian does not need to submit it to an 'anaesthetic' procedure, neutralizing the feelings of the protagonists and removing their own emotions. Laughter and crying are a part of life and cannot be erased by the collective dramas that mark the rhythm of history. The moods, passions and feelings of individuals, of classes and of the masses in action deserve the same attention with which Proust probes, in dozens of pages, the state of mind and the psychology of his characters. A faithful account of the Napoleonic battles, Trotsky writes, should go beyond the geometry of the camps and the rationality and effectiveness of the strategic and tactical choices of the Staff. The account should not overlook misunderstood orders, generals' inability to read a map, or the panic and even colic of fear that seized soldiers and officers before the assault.[18]

The salient features of *History of the Russian Revolution* lie in its narrative power, in its ability to revive events in all their intensity, to reconstruct the overall picture through the intertwining of the action of the protagonists and the breadth of the collective groups in movement. The book's ambition is stated from the beginning: 'The history of a revolution is for us first of all a history of the forcible entrance of

---

17 Leon Trotsky, *History of the Russian Revolution*, trans. Max Eastman (Chicago: Haymarket, 2008); Daniel Guérin, *Class Struggle in the First French Republic: Bourgeois and Bras Nus 1793–1795* (London: Pluto Press, 1977); and Adolfo Gilly, *The Mexican Revolution* (New York: The New Press, 2006).

18 Trotsky, *History of the Russian Revolution*, 351.

the masses into the realm of rulership over their own destiny.'[19] The
sudden synchronization between the cumulative changes that take
place over the decades along with the reawakening of the collective
consciousness produce a cataclysm that changes the course of history.
Trotsky devotes many pages to analysing the crisis of the Tsarist
regime, the contradictions that inhabited the provisional government
born of the February uprising, the ideological and political conflicts
that separated Mensheviks from Bolsheviks and which divided the
latter again on the eve of the insurrection.

The central subjects of his narrative, however, are the revolutionary
masses. They have nothing in common with the submissive, manipu-
lated, disciplined, controlled, disempowered crowds of the fascist and
Nazi rallies. They are not the 'ornamental' masses that fill the scenario
of modern totalitarianism. Trotsky devoted other works to the roots
of fascism. The revolutionary masses which he describes in his book
are conscious actors of history. They are the subaltern classes who, in
extraordinary historical circumstances, overthrow a power no longer
overwhelming and impregnable, and take their destiny into their own
hands, thus rebuilding society on new foundations. Revolution is a
collective act through which human beings liberate themselves from
centuries of oppression and domination. It is probably after reading
Trotsky's book – 'I think it has been years since I have consumed
anything with such breathless excitement', he wrote in a letter[20] – that
Walter Benjamin compared revolutions with nuclear fission, a blast
capable of releasing and multiplying the energies contained in the
past.[21] Trotsky's view of the masses is not at all mystical – Deutscher
distinguishes it from that of Thomas Carlyle and, one might add,
of Jules Michelet – since 'whereas Carlyle's crowds are driven only
by emotion, Trotsky's think and reflect.'[22] They belong to a Marxist
vision of history as an 'objectively conditioned process' in which

---

19   Ibid., xv.

20   Walter Benjamin, *Correspondence 1910–1940*, eds Theodor W. Adorno and
Gershom Scholem (Chicago: University of Chicago Press, 1994), 393.

21   Walter Benjamin, *The Arcades Project* (Cambridge, MA: Harvard University Press, 1999), 463.

22   Isaac Deutscher, *The Prophet Outcast: Leon Trotsky 1929–1940* (London,
New York: Verso, 2003 [1963]), 189.

human beings act based on their own choices, their objectives and their passions, but within a given framework, neither immutable nor elusive. Clairvoyant or short-sighted, resolute or ominous, the actions of individuals appear in Trotsky's book as superficial agitations that rest on the far more solid and profound layer of mass movement. In some circumstances, they can play a crucial role – think of the chapter on Lenin – but even then they are assumed to be completely in tune with the common mood. Revolution is an earthquake that human beings live and embody collectively, that individual personalities can, to a greater or lesser extent, influence and direct; but which they can neither create nor impede.

According to Trotsky, revolutions have their own 'laws' that regulate their development, and to which mass action conforms. The 'laws of history' are one of the obsessions of the late nineteenth century, the age of triumphant positivism, within which Russian Marxism was born and developed. For Trotsky, grasping these laws meant penetrating the secrets of history and controlling its movement. As a result, the task of the Marxist historian was to pursue 'the scientific discovery of these laws'.[23] From this point of view, a separation no longer exists between the historian and the Bolshevik leader, since both bring to light, in action as well as in the reconstruction of the past, an objective process that has its own internal logic. One of these 'laws', perhaps the most important, defined history as a long, progressive road along which Russia would advance from backwardness to development, from East to West, from Asia to Europe. As a Russian Jew who was born in a Ukrainian town and lived for many years as an exile in London, Paris, Vienna and New York, Trotsky – like many Russian intellectuals of his time, including Lenin – was a radical Westernizer. His vision for the modernization of the Tsarist empire, however, resonated with that of Marx, still unknown to him.[24] Far from being linear, the road leading Russia from East to West was tortuous and contradictory, shaped by the 'uneven and combined development' of global capitalism: the

---

23   Trotsky, *History of the Russian Revolution*, xv.

24   See the correspondence between Marx and the Russian Populists in Teodor Shanin (ed.), *Late Marx and the Russian Road: Marx and the 'Peripheries of Capitalism'* (London: Routledge, 1983).

most advanced ideas and the most modern social forms mingled with
a centuries-old primitiveness and profound obscurantism. Russia
was not an island, but the link in a chain that inscribed its destiny in
the future of Europe and the world. As a result, socialism in Russia
could jump with powerful momentum over the stages of industrial
capitalism that spread through Western Europe across four centuries.
This view of Russian history as part of a 'dialectical' totality – Trotsky
had formulated its principles in *Results and Prospects* (1906)[25] – was
not so far from Marx's own, as we will see further on; Trotsky simply
emphasized the 'difference in rhythms' without calling into question
the general direction of the historical process.

There is something paradoxical in a historiographical monument
such as *History of the Russian Revolution*. As he pointed out in his
introduction, Trotsky wrote his masterpiece as a historian, not as a
witness, and he carefully checked all the facts and dates of his reconstitution, but the spirit of this historical event runs through the pages
of his book. Only a witness – who was moreover, one of the main
actors – of this experience could have captured its epic dimension, the
imposing strength of a collective action that changes history. He wrote
his book in Turkey, where he lived outcast and vanquished, but his
gaze remained that of a victor. He described a successful revolution
with the undamaged enthusiasm of its actors and the self-confidence
of a champion who contemptuously threw his adversaries – including
former friends and comrades, like Julius Martov – into 'the dust-bin
of history'.[26] Stalin had come to power and Trotsky was in exile, but
the revolutionary process was not exhausted. Revolution was passing
through its Thermidorian and Bonapartist stages, but was not defeated
yet. He believed in the 'laws of history' because October 1917 had
been their testing ground. This unique combination of personal and
historical elements made his book a singular accomplishment.

Today, depicting revolution as an epic narrative whose mood has
been transmitted but not directly lived is a tour de force which only
a few masterful writers are capable of. This was the case, in recent

---

25   Leon Trotsky, *Results and Prospects* (New York: Pathfinder Press, 1969);
see also *History of the Russian Revolution*, 5–7.

26   Ibid., 845.

times, of two remarkable books on the French and the Russian Revolutions, by Eric Hazan and China Miéville respectively,[27] but these works do not set out to describe the 'laws of history'. Nor does a historiographical masterpiece like Arno J. Mayer's *The Furies* (2000), certainly the most important book on revolution published in the last five decades, whose analytical scrutiny is much more critical than apologetic.[28] Above all, these works do not inscribe revolutions into a historical progression: France in 1789, Haiti in 1804, continental Europe in 1848, Paris in 1871, Russia in 1917, Germany and Hungary in 1919, Barcelona in 1936, China in 1949, Cuba in 1959, Vietnam in 1975, and Nicaragua in 1979, just to mention the most relevant or known events. This impressive succession of upheavals and popular insurgencies does not constitute an irresistible ascension corresponding to causal necessity: all revolutions transcend their own causes and follow their own dynamic that changes the 'natural' course of things. They are human *inventions*, which do not reveal any ineluctable occurrence but rather build collective memory as the landmarks of a meaningful constellation. The belief that they belong to the regular and cumulative time of historical progression was one of the biggest misapprehensions of twentieth-century left-wing culture, too often burdened with the legacy of evolutionism and the idea of Progress.

Today, a widespread tendency — including amongst left-wing scholars — simply reverses the arrow of the old 'laws of history' to depict the defeat of revolutions as their inevitable outcome. The bitter and resigned verdict of Eric Hobsbawm, who posthumously paid homage to Plekhanov and other enemies of Bolshevism, is charged with a strong flavour of historical necessity: 'The tragedy of the October revolution was precisely that it could only produce this kind of ruthless, brutal, command socialism.'[29] I think rather, with China Miéville, that 'October is still ground zero for arguments about

27 Eric Hazan, *A People's History of the French Revolution* (London, New York: Verso, 2017); China Miéville, *October: The Story of the Russian Revolution* (London, New York: Verso, 2017).

28 Arno J. Mayer, *The Furies: Violence and Terror in the French and Russian Revolutions* (Princeton: Princeton University Press, 2000).

29 Eric Hobsbawm, *The Age of Extremes: A History of the World, 1914–1991* (New York: Vintage Books, 1994), 498.

fundamental, radical social change. Its degradation was not a given, was not written in any stars.'[30] And I also think with him that a different path was neither written in advance nor would be evident for us, one century after this great attempt at storming the heavens: 'That story, and above all the questions arising from it – the urgencies of change, of how change is possible, of the dangers that will beset it – stretch vastly beyond us.'[31]

Revolutions are history breathing in and out. Rehabilitating revolutions as landmarks of modernity and quintessential moments of historical change does not mean romanticizing them. Their susceptibility to lyrical recollection and iconic representation does not impede a critical gaze from grasping not only their liberating features but also their hesitations, ambiguities, misleading paths and withdrawals, all belonging to their multiple and contradictory potentialities, all included in their ontological intensity. The canonical classification of revolutions according to their social forces and political goals – religious, bourgeois, proletarian, peasant, democratic, socialist, anticolonial, anti-imperialist, national, and even fascist revolutions – does not really help historians who wish to apprehend their emotional dimension, which often crosses both chronological and political boundaries. As dramatic – mostly violent – breaks in the continuum of history, revolutions are intensely lived. In making them, human beings display a quantity of energies, passions, affects and feelings much higher than the spiritual standard of ordinary life. This is one of the reasons why most revolutions contain or engender aesthetic turns. The October Revolution produced an extraordinary effervescence and transformation in the realm of art, with the blossoming of avant-garde currents like futurism, suprematism and constructivism. In 1918–19, the fall of the German Empire and the Spartacist uprising in Berlin coincided with dadaism and, in the early 1920s, surrealism proclaimed the imperative of combining the overthrow of the established order with a spiritual liberation of the forces of the unconscious and of dreams. To miss the stormy and feverish charge of revolutions

---

30   Miéville, *October*, 307.
31   Ibid.

is simply to misunderstand them, but, at the same time, to reduce them to outbursts of passions and hates would be equally fallacious. Such a misinterpretation was committed at an exhibition, *Soulèvements*, which, although remarkable in many respects, privileged the aesthetic aspects of uprisings to the point of blurring their political nature. Catching the elegance of a gesture that reproduces the beauty of an athletic performance does not cast light on its political meaning. The cover illustration of the catalogue shows an adolescent throwing a stone. He is captured at the precise instant of launch, his body outstretched by this effort. A sense of lightness merging with corporeal harmony pervades this image by the photographer Gilles Caron.[32] If we look at uprisings through a purely aesthetic lens, the fact that this young man is a Unionist participating in an anti-Catholic riot in Londonderry in 1969 – as the caption explains – becomes a negligible detail. This is why, in highlighting the emotional power of revolutions, this book never forgets that they are essentially social and political events in which affect is always intermingled with other constitutive elements.

Shifting from aesthetics to history, other approaches are equally dubious, such as the widespread concept of 'fascist revolution'. George L. Mosse is right in stressing that fascism was projected towards the future and possessed a coherent worldview, as an alternative to both classical liberalism and communism. It certainly advanced an ensemble of myths, symbols and values that gave it a 'revolutionary' character and allowed it to mobilize the masses by 'nationalizing' them.[33] And fascism abused revolutionary rhetoric: one only need think of the pompous celebrations of the tenth anniversary of the 'fascist revolution' that took place in Italy in 1932, ten years after the 'March on Rome'.[34] Nonetheless, fascism never led any authentic revolution. Both Italian fascism and German National Socialism abolished the rule of law, destroyed democracy and established a completely new –

32   Gilles Caron, 'Manifestations anticatholiques à Londonderry' (1969), in Georges Didi-Huberman (ed.), *Soulèvements* (Paris: Gallimard/Jeu de Paume, 2016), 138.

33   George L. Mosse, *The Fascist Revolution: Toward a General Theory of Fascism* (New York: Howard Fertig, 1999).

34   See Maddalena Carli, *Vedere il fascismo. Arte e politica nelle esposizioni del regime 1928–1942* (Roma: Carocci, 2021).

totalitarian – political regime, but they came to power legally: Mussolini was appointed prime minister by the Italian king Vittorio Emanuele
III, and Hitler was chosen as German Chancellor by Paul von Hinden-
burg, the president of the Weimar Republic. Their 'synchronization'
(*Gleichschaltung*) of politics and society came later. In Spain, Franco
took power after three years of a bloody civil war, but he, also, did not
lead a revolution; a Spanish revolution arose from spontaneous mass
mobilization against his putsch. Despite its revolutionary rhetoric,
fascism clearly displayed a counterrevolutionary character.

Franco's coup was depicted by its actors as an 'uprising' –
levantamiento – a circumstance that points out the ambiguity of this
word and distinguishes it from a true revolution. Emphasizing the
conceptual discrepancy that separates revolt or rebellion from revolution, Arno J. Mayer opposes them as almost antipodal occurrences.
Revolts, he explains, have their roots in 'tradition, despair, and disillusionment'. They designate concrete and tangible enemies who
they transform into scapegoats. The aim of revolt is not to put down
a political regime; it is rather to change its representatives; usually,
their targets are individuals, not classes or institutions, nor power
itself. This is why they have a limited horizon and a short duration:
they can be endemic, Mayer observes, but are always territorially
circumscribed. Revolutions, on the contrary, raise hopes supported
by ideologies and utopian projections; they are frequently carried
out by forces that embody political projects, like the Jacobins or the
Bolsheviks. They consciously wish to change the social and political
order.[35] In short, they express great, sometimes universal ambitions,
as proven by both the Declaration of the Rights of Man and of the
Citizen of 1789 and the October Revolution, which aspired to extend
its influence on an international scale, beyond the Russian and European borders. Created in 1919, the Communist International was the
instrument of this universal intention.

While there will always be debate over where precisely to draw the
line between rebellion and revolution, it is still a useful distinction
to make. Celebrating rebellions means hypostatizing their lyrical
moment, when people stand up and act; interpreting revolutions

---

35   Mayer, *The Furies*, 30.

means inscribing their disruptive emergence into a process of creative destruction, when an order is destroyed and a new one is built. Like rebellions, however, revolutions are not always joyful or exciting. Many actors depict them as wonderful moments of weightlessness, when human beings are suddenly inhabited by the feeling of overcoming the law of gravity and, discarding all inherited forms of submission and obedience, become masters of their destiny. But revolutions can also draw their strength from despair or remain mired in their own contradictions. They can turn tragic, or unveil their dark sides early on. Jules Michelet describes the major steps of the French Revolution as eruptions of violence that, like a wave, liberated frustrations and anger repressed for too long. In the twentieth century, photographs recorded the emotional charge of collective actions, thus revealing both their ecstatic, euphoric spirit and the depth of their despair. The smiling faces of the insurrectionists of Paris and Milan, in August 1944 and April 1945, or of Havana in December 1958, contrast with the grave countenances of Berlin's insurgent workers in January 1919. The uprising of the Warsaw Ghetto, in April 1943, certainly gave its fighters a feeling of self-confidence and pride – they resisted for a month against a powerful army – but could not produce hope or collective radiance. The only images we have of this event were made by their executioners and show young women and men ready to die after being captured.[36] At the beginning of 1943, the members of the Jewish Combat Organization diffused a flyer that announced their action: 'All are ready to die as human beings.'[37] Forty years after the uprising, Marek Edelman, one of the leaders, recalled it as follows:

> The majority of us favored an uprising. After all, humanity had agreed that dying with arms was more beautiful than without arms. Therefore, we followed this consensus. In the Jewish Combat Organization there were only two hundred twenty of us left. Can

36   See Sybil Milton (ed.), *The Stroop Report: The Jewish Quarter of Warsaw Is No More!*, Introduction by Andrzej Wirth (New York: Pantheon Books, 1979); the report was originally written in 1943.

37   Quoted by Yisrael Gutman, *The Jews of Warsaw 1939–1943: Ghetto, Underground, Revolt* (Bloomington: Indiana University Press, 1989), 305.

you even call that an uprising? All it was about, finally, was that we not just let them slaughter us when our turn came. It was only a choice as to the manner of dying.[38]

Revolutions can also be surrounded by a tragic aura for less noble reasons. The entry of the Khmer Rouge forces in Phnom Penh, in April 1975, was undoubtedly a revolution: a neocolonial regime was overthrown by a nationalist guerrilla movement, a new power was installed, and the society was to be radically transformed. It was also the beginning of four years of terror and death: the city was immediately evacuated. It was not a festival of the oppressed, it was day one of a nightmare. And it was the extreme, paroxysmal epilogue of a militarized paradigm of revolution that had blurred the boundaries between resistance and oppression, liberating struggle and pitiless civil war. The horror of Khmer Rouge Cambodia was assuredly a mirror of the monstrous symbiosis of nationalism and Stalinism, but it was also the outcome of a long history of domination and more than a decade of intensive bombardment. Phnom Penh was occupied by an army of very young combatants coming from the jungle, where they had known nothing but the atrocities of war. According to Ben Kiernan, its most reputed historian, Pol Pot's regime arose from an indigenous revolution that took place in an explosive context: it 'would not have won power without US economic and military destabilization of Cambodia, which began in 1966'.[39] But the Cambodian case – a revolution resulting in totalitarianism and a genocide from the start – was paroxysmal rather than paradigmatic.

Rebellions can turn into revolutions, going from indignation to conscious transformation of the state of things, but revolutions can equally destroy – in Antonio Negri's words – the 'ontological power' of uprisings.[40] People stand up, Judith Butler points out, with shared

---

38   Marek Edelman's testimony in Hanna Kral, *Shielding the Flame: An Intimate Conversation with Dr. Marek Edelman, the Last Surviving Leader of the Warsaw Ghetto Uprising*, trans. Joanna Stasinka and Lawrence Wechsler (New York: Henry Holt, 1986), 10.

39   Ben Kiernan, *The Pol Pot Regime: Race, Power, and Genocide in Cambodia Under the Khmer Rouge 1975–79* (New Haven: Yale University Press, 1996), 16.

40   Antonio Negri, 'L'évènement soulèvement', *Soulèvements*, 43.

energy, strength and intentions.[41] Revolutions are revolts consciously oriented towards a radical change. As we will see in a chapter of this book, their bodies differ significantly. Revolts, like riots and upheavals, stem from *crowds*: transitional and mostly ephemeral concentrations of people who – as Elias Canetti has meticulously observed[42] – act spasmodically up to a final explosion that, like a discharge, precedes their disaggregation. Revolutions are usually conscious accomplishments by collective subjects.

The object of this book is revolution for better or worse. It does not select the good revolutions over the bad ones, a distinction that is often tricky or sterile, since revolutions are not fixed, univocal events ready to be either iconized or demonized; they are living experiences that change in the making, and, in most cases, they do not know their outcomes simply because their dynamic is unpredictable. Rather than moral judgement, naïve idealization or intransigent condemnation, they deserve critical understanding. This is the best way of grasping their historical meaning and transmitting their legacy. In a famous sentence, Marx wrote that modern revolutions cannot draw their 'poetry from the past', whereas Benjamin detected their hidden motor in a desire for redemption of the vanquished, the 'secret agreement between past generations and the present one'.[43] It is probably the case that revolutions waver on a knife's edge between both temporalities: they rescue the past by inventing the future.

Unlike most studies on revolutions, this essay does not devote a specific chapter to the controversial question of violence. There are multiple reasons for this absence, which does not result from any strategy of avoidance. The most important is that revolutionary violence runs across its pages as an overwhelming presence, whether explicit or subterranean. With few exceptions, revolutions are violent eruptions. Violence is inscribed into their genes and built into their ontological

---

41   Judith Butler, 'Soulèvement', ibid., 25.

42   Elias Canetti, *Crowds and Power*, trans. Carol Stewart (New York: Continuum, 1978 [1960]), 17–19.

43   Karl Marx, 'The Eighteenth Brumaire of Louis Bonaparte' (1852), *MECW*, vol. 11, 106; Benjamin, 'On the Concept of History', 390.

structure. Peaceful revolutions are exceptions, not the rule, and in many cases are only the harbingers of postponed blasts. In 1974, the Portuguese 'carnation revolution' was peaceful because it was triggered by a section of the army itself, and fifteen years later the so-called 'velvet revolutions' of Central Europe took place without bloodshed because the repressive forces had already been neutralized in the USSR. In 2011, the Egyptian insurgent youth peacefully overthrew Mubarak's dictatorship, but their inability to dismantle the repressive state apparatus ultimately led to the restoration of a military regime. In other Arab countries, from Libya to Yemen and Syria, revolutions quickly turned into civil wars.

A second reason for the absence of a chapter on violence is more directly historiographic. Conservative historians write as prosecutors who stigmatize revolutions as one – or even, more frequently, *the* – source of modern totalitarianism. They are usually divided into two categories: the undeclared apologists of fascism and the bearers of a political wisdom strongly attached to the postulates of classical liberalism. The covert apologists of fascism – think of scholars like Ernst Nolte in Germany, Stéphane Courtois in France, or Pio Moa in Spain – depict revolution as the origin of evil. The Jacobins invented a project of political extermination (Courtois)[44] and Lenin specialized in 'gassing the people' (Hélène Carrère d'Encausse);[45] the Bolsheviks practiced a class genocide that was later copied by the Nazis (Nolte, Courtois);[46] and Franco saved Spain from communism, which used the Popular Front as its Trojan Horse (Moa).[47] For conservative scholars

---

44   Stéphane Courtois, 'Introduction: The Crimes of Communism', in Courtois (ed.), *The Black Book of Communism: Crimes, Terror, Repression* (Cambridge, MA: Harvard University Press, 1999), 9.

45   Hélène Carrère d'Encausse, *Lenin* (New York: Holmes & Meier, 2001), 289.

46   Ernst Nolte, 'The Past that Will Not Pass' (1986), in James Knowlton (ed.), *Forever in the Shadow of Hitler? Original Documents of the Historikerstreit, the Controversy Concerning the Singularity of the Holocaust* (Atlantic Highlands, NJ: Humanities Press, 1993), 21–2; Courtois, 'Introduction', 15.

47   Pio Moa, *Los Mitos de la Guerra Civil* (Madrid: Esfera, 2003). In the 'Spanish Historikerstreit' raised by Pio Moa, his positions have been strongly supported by Stanley G. Payne, 'Mitos y tópicos de la Guerra Civil', *Revista de Libros*, 79/80 (2003): 3–5.

like François Furet, on the other hand, the French Revolution was the outburst of an insane political passion and the October Revolution a historical accident that obstructed the natural evolution of Western societies towards market economy and liberal democracy. Beginning by condemning Terror as a 'skidding off course' (*dérapage*), Furet would ultimately conclude that the French Revolution itself was a mistake, because the advent of modern liberalism did not need this outburst of violence.[48] All of them tend to depict revolutionary violence as the result of an ideological imperative or a political prescription. According to Martin Malia and Richard Pipes, the Russian Civil War resulted from Lenin's and Trotsky's ideological fanaticism and totalitarian will; the aristocratic reaction and the international anti-Bolshevik military coalition play a negligible role in their explanation of the endemic violence that devastated revolutionary Russia between 1918 and 1921.[49] All of them consider Terror as the most genuine expression of Jacobin and Bolshevik 'ideocracy'.

Excess, fervour and fanaticism all belong to revolution – a fact that nobody would seriously deny – but as its products, not its causes. It is revolution itself that engenders them, simply because revolutions cannot be decreed. Of course, fanaticism and ideology can be performative and unfailingly play a role in revolutions, but they cannot fabricate them. It goes without saying that revolutions require free and critical spirits prepared to denounce their excesses, authoritarianism or dead ends, but even the most enlightened advisors cannot prevent coercion and violence. And revolutionary fury is usually the belated outcome of decades or centuries of oppression, exploitation, humiliation and frustration: the sudden explosion of a powder accumulated

---

48   François Furet, *Interpreting the French Revolution* (New York: Cambridge University Press, 1981), and François Furet, *The Passing of an Illusion: The Idea of Communism in the Twentieth Century* (Chicago: University of Chicago Press, 1999). For a critical reassessment of the historiographical debate around Furet's interpretations, see Enzo Traverso, 'Révolutions: 1789 et 1917 après 1989. Sur François Furet et Arno J. Mayer', in *L'Histoire comme champ de bataille. Interpréter les violences du XXe siècle* (Paris: La Découverte, 2010), 61–90.

49   Martin Malia, *The Soviet Tragedy: A History of Socialism in Russia 1917–1991* (New York: Free Press, 1990); Richard Pipes, *The Russian Revolution* (New York: Knopf, 1990).

over time. Moreover, what enemies depict as fanaticism is frequently a set of coercive policies that channel and control this spontaneous violence, instead of allowing it to manifest without limits until its own exhaustion. In most cases, conservative criticism of revolutionary violence consciously ignores the explosive potential incubated over time. As for libertarian criticism, it seldom explains how revolutions could avoid coercion or preserve complete freedom without being destroyed.

Fanaticism plays a role in revolutionary politics when violence becomes a form of government, turns uncontrollable, and repression starts working as an engine unto itself. This happened with the French and the Russian Revolutions, during the Terrors of 1793–94 and 1918–21, but in these cases the politics of Terror radicalized a violence that was already inscribed in their respective historical contexts. Thus, condemning the excesses and criminal deviations of revolutionary Terror is as obvious and necessary – albeit easier retrospectively than during a civil war – as exorcizing violence is useless and misleading, insofar as it does not produce any critical understanding. This explains both Marx's famous remark on violence as 'the midwife of history' and Fanon's conception of revolutionary biopolitics as a 'counter-violence' that acts as a 'cleansing force' (*la violence désintoxique*).[50] A psychiatrist, the author of *The Wretched of the Earth* (1961) compared colonial oppression to a condition of permanent muscular atrophy or contraction, whose pent-up aggressiveness inevitably exploded in liberating violence. If 'colonialism is not a thinking machine, nor a body endowed with reasoning faculties', but rather 'violence in its natural state', it comes as no surprise that 'it will only yield when confronted with greater violence.'[51] Thereafter, Fanon emphasizes, 'the colonized man finds his freedom in and through violence.'[52] These assessments regarding violence displayed by colonized subjects could be extended – as Fanon himself suggests – to many other oppressed peoples, from European peasants under the Old Regime to Jews in

---

50   Frantz Fanon, *The Wretched of the Earth*, preface by Jean-Paul Sartre, trans. Constance Farrington (New York: Grove Press, 1963), 94.

51   Ibid., 61.

52   Ibid., 86.

the Nazi ghettos, whose 'thanato-ethics'[53] – dying fully armed – also expressed a peculiar form of bodily emancipation through struggle.

In 1919, writing in his diary in Petrograd while the Soviet power seemed on the verge of collapse in the face of the White Guard offensive and the international coalition, Victor Serge depicted a dramatic situation in which arms were the only audible voice:

> If Red Commissars, militants or commandants are taken by surprise they are invariably shot. For our part we don't spare former officers, or non-commissioned officers of any sort. War to the death with no humanitarian hypocrisy; there is no Red Cross and stretcher-bearers are not allowed. Primitive warfare, war of extermination, civil war.[54]

This is an eloquent description of violence as part of the ontological structure of revolution: an irreducible conflict, one might say in Schmittian terms, between friend and enemy. Revolutions are historical eruptions. In revolutionary times, the theory of norms, the rule of law, constitutional liberties, pluralism, ethics of discussion, and philosophies of human rights are abandoned, ignored and buried as useless vestiges of a previous age. This is certainly not a virtue, but it is a fact, and this goes also for revolutions that claim freedom and restore or establish democracy. The tragedy of revolutions lies in the fatal metamorphosis that drives them from liberation to the struggle for survival, and finally to the edification of a new oppressive rule; from emancipating violence to coercive violence. The key to durably preserving their liberating potential has not yet been found, but this is not a good reason to condemn liberation itself. In any case, revolutions do not care about law, and this is both for the best and for the worst. One need not share Walter Benjamin's messianism or Georges Sorel's theory of myth to understand revolution as the expression of a 'law-destroying' violence, which is the premise for the emergence of a new sovereignty.[55]

---

53   On this concept see Elsa Dorlin, *Se défendre. Une philosophie de la violence* (Paris: La Découverte, 2017), 68.

54   Victor Serge, 'The Endangered City', in *Revolution in Danger* (Chicago: Haymarket, 2011), 22.

55   See Walter Benjamin, 'Critique of Violence' (1921), *WBSW*, vol. 1, 249.

This book does not describe revolutions by following a chronological line, even if their periodization and historical interpretation are repeatedly mentioned and critically discussed. Its methodology lies in the concept of 'dialectical image', which grasps at the same time a historical source and its interpretation. Walter Benjamin elaborated this concept in *The Arcades Project*, his unfinished book started in 1927, but it has some affinities with the theory of images of both Aby Warburg and Siegfried Kracauer.[56] Without entirely sharing Benjamin's fascination with ruins, I have found in his critical observations many useful suggestions for interpreting the defeated revolutions. This implies a vanquished gaze that explains both my sympathy for Leon Trotsky as a historical figure and my critical distance – critical but imbued with admiration – with respect to his *History of the Russian Revolution*.

Understanding history, Benjamin argued, means looking at the past through its 'graphicness' (*Anschaulichkeit*) and fixing it 'perceptually'.[57] Since revolutions are 'dialectical leaps' that explode the 'continuum of history', writing their history supposes capturing their significance through images that condense them: the past 'crystallized as a monad'.[58] The dialectical images emerge from the combination of two essential procedures of historical investigation: collection and montage. This means, in Benjamin's terms, 'to assemble large-scale constructions out of the smallest and most precisely cut components. Indeed, to discover in the analysis of the small individual moment the crystal of the total event.'[59] The convolute N of *The Arcades Project*, devoted to the theory of knowledge, includes a quotation from André Monglond's study

---

56   See Beatrice Hanssen, 'Portrait of Melancholy: Benjamin, Warburg, Panofsky', *MLN*, 114, 5 (1999): 991–1013. Siegfried Kracauer's concept of silent movies as 'visible hieroglyphs' of the 'unseen dynamic of social relations' or buildings as 'hieroglyphs' that express 'the structure of the soul in terms of space' is quite close to Benjamin's 'dialectical image'. See Siegfried Kracauer, *From Caligari to Hitler: A Psychological History of the German Film* (Princeton: Princeton University Press, 1966 [1947]), 7, 75. See also Gerhard Richter, *Thought-Images: Frankfurt School Writers' Reflections from Damaged Life* (Stanford: Stanford University Press, 2007).

57   Benjamin, *Arcades Project*, 461.

58   Benjamin, 'On the Concept of History', 396.

59   Benjamin, *Arcades Project*, 461.

on Romanticism (1930): 'The past has left images of itself in literary texts, images comparable to those which are imprinted by light on a photosensitive plate. The future alone possesses developers active enough to scan such surfaces perfectly.'[60] This is the procedure we follow, interpreting the nineteenth and twentieth-century revolutions by assembling dialectical images. It may turn out that today, in the twenty-first century, we possess these powerful developers: this is our epistemological advantage. Dialectical images are not mirror images; they are not the reflected pictures of bygone events; they are lamps that cast a light over the past.[61] This book approaches the images of revolutions as Marx scrutinized the economic forms of capitalism: not as objects carefully observed through the lens of a microscope, but rather, as he explained in his preface to *Capital* (1867), as a whole of social relations to be caught by abstractions.[62]

This book, then, gathers the intellectual and material elements of a scattered and often forgotten revolutionary past in order to rearticulate them into a meaningful composition made of dialectical images: locomotives, bodies, statues, columns, barricades, flags, sites, paintings, posters, dates, singular lives, etc. To a certain extent, concepts themselves are treated as dialectical images, insofar as they emerge in their peculiar contexts as intellectual crystallizations of political needs and collective consciousness (or unconscious). That is why, instead of playing a purely decorative role, the numerous images that illustrate the book provide essential evidence of its demonstration. Reassessing the status of the concept of revolution in both political theory and intellectual history, this work investigates it through an entanglement with images, memories and hopes. Hence it perpetually connects ideas and representations, attributing equal importance to theoretical, historiographic and iconographic sources. This approach unveils and emphasizes the relevance of the past for left-wing radicalism, far beyond the legacy of exhausted political models (parties, strategies) that deserve to be historicized and critically understood

---

60 Ibid., 482.

61 See M. H. Abrams, *The Mirror and the Lamp: Romantic Theory and the Critical Tradition* (New York: Oxford University Press, 1971 [1953]).

62 *MECW*, vol. 35, 8.

rather than renewed or restored. This also explains the structure of the book: a montage of dialectical images, instead of a conventional procedure of linear reconstitutions. Because of the wide scope of its sources, it does not escape a certain degree of – consciously assumed – eclecticism that highlights the diversity of its objects. This is the price to pay when historians turn 'ragpickers'.[63] They can arrange and classify the objects that clutter their workshop, but they know that this operation of montage is not a definitive order; the proper place of many things does not depend on their own choices, which are simply a wager on the future.

During the twentieth century, we became accustomed to victories and defeats as military clashes: revolutions conquered power with weapons, defeats took the form of military coups and fascist dictatorships. The defeat we suffered at the turn of the twenty-first century, however, must be measured by different criteria. Capitalism has won because it has succeeded in shaping our lives and our mental habitus, because it has succeeded in imposing itself as an anthropological model, a 'way of life.' The most powerful armies are not invincible. The peasants of Vietnam, one of the poorest countries in the world a century ago, succeeded, through a struggle that can justly be defined as heroic, in defeating, first, Japanese and French colonialism, and then, despite the napalm attacks, American imperialism. What we have not managed to stop, however, is the ongoing process of universal commodity reifica-tion that, like an octopus, is enveloping the entire planet. Capitalism took its revenge through the current Vietnamese economic boom.

This is one of the reasons why the social and political movements of the last decade have placed the critique of capitalism at the centre of their action. Occupy Wall Street in the United States, the 15-M move-ment in Spain, *Nuit debout* in France, Gezi Park in Istanbul, the *gilets jaunes* again in France, the insurgent movement of the youth in Chile, and more recently the global antiracist wave started by Black Lives Matter in the United States, as well as similar movements on a global scale, from Hong Kong to Minsk – none of these have shown great

---

63   Walter Benjamin, 'An Outsider Makes His Marks', *WBSW*, vol. 2.2, 310.

interest in the strategic discussions of the past. They have invented new organizational forms and alliances, and sometimes created new leaderships, but they are mostly self-organized. They seek to experiment with new forms of life based on the reappropriation of public space, participation, collective deliberation, inventory of needs, and critique of the commodification of social relationships. They do not like political mediations.

The Left seems, instead, to have completely deserted the terrain on which it had, over the last century, accumulated considerable experience and recorded numerous successes: the armed revolution. This field is now entirely occupied by Islamic fundamentalism, which, through an impressive historical regression, has substituted Sharia for anticolonialism and national liberation. The experience of twentieth-century communism in its different dimensions – revolution, regime, anticolonialism, reformism – has been exhausted. The new anti-capitalist movements of recent years do not resonate with any of the left traditions of the past. They lack a genealogy. They reveal greater affinities – not so much doctrinal but rather cultural and symbolic – with anarchism: they are egalitarian, anti-authoritarian, anticolonial, and mostly indifferent to a teleological view of history. And yet they are not a backlash against the twentieth century, they embody something new. Being orphans, they must reinvent themselves.

This is simultaneously their strength, because they are not prisoners of models inherited from the past, and their weakness, because they are bereft of memory. They were born as a *tabula rasa* and did not work through the past. They are creative, but also fragile, for they do not possess the strength of the movements that, conscious of having a history and committed to inscribing their action in a powerful historical tendency, embodied a political tradition. The members of the communist parties fooled themselves into acting out the 'will' of history, but knew they belonged to a movement that transcended any individual destiny. This helped them fight (and sometimes win) in the most tragic moments. The new movements have a different relationship with politics, which could be defined to a large extent as instrumental, although not cynical: they 'use' it, without deluding themselves. They know that democracy must be reinvented and do not sacralise its hollowed institutions. Perhaps the organizational form that best suits these new movements is the federalism of the First International, at the antipodes of the Bolsheviks' hierarchical centralism. The International Workingmen's Association gathered different ideological currents, from the Marxists to the anarchists, in which parties, trade-unions, national liberation movements and circles of various kinds coexisted. Today, we need to federate and bring different experiences into dialogue, without hierarchies, in an 'intersectional' way, rather than circumscribing them on ideological bases. Perhaps for this reason, the Paris Commune has lately been rediscovered as an extraordinary experience of self-government and commonality rather than a prefiguration of the October Revolution.[64] Its actors did not resemble the twentieth-century industrial working class: they were artisans, precarious workers, young intellectuals and artists, women without a profession; the heterogenous and insecure social fabric of their lives recalls that of today's youth and other new marginals.

It is certainly exciting to rediscover the Paris Commune through a new lens, outside the communist canon that had made it a monument and embalmed it. But we must not forget either that it ended in massacre and that the Russian Revolution was also, among other things, an effort to overcome its shortcomings. Twenty years ago, one of the most interesting interpreters of the Mexican neo-Zapatista experience, John Holloway, wrote a book suggesting the possibility of changing the world without taking power.[65] During the Arab Revolutions, however, the question of power proved to be inescapable.[66] For the

---

64   See Kristin Ross, *Communal Luxury: The Political Imaginary of the Paris Commune* (London, New York: Verso, 2016). For an anarchist and ecologist reinterpretation of the Paris Commune, see Murray Bookchin, 'The Communalist Project' (2002), in M. Bookchin and Blair Taylor (ed.), *The Next Revolution: Popular Assemblies and the Promise of Direct Democracy* (London, New York: Verso, 2015), 17–38.

65   John Holloway, *Change the World Without Taking Power* (London: Pluto Press, 2019 [2002]). See a discussion on Holloway's thesis, with critical contributions by Holloway himself, Daniel Bensaïd and Michael Löwy, in Phil Hearse (ed.), *Take Power to Change the World* (London: IMG Publications, 2007).

66   See Gilbert Achcar, *Morbid Symptoms: Relapse in the Arab Uprising* (Stanford: Stanford University Press, 2016).

Rojava Kurds, too, the question of armed struggle is not a twentieth-century archaism.

This book wishes to avoid the symmetrical (though antipodal) traps into which so many historical interpretations of revolutions have fallen: either conservative stigmatization or blind apology, either counterrevolutionary exorcism or desperate idealization. We need a different approach to this revolutionary past made of both exciting insurgencies and tragic setbacks. The purpose of this book is by no means the definition or transmission of a revolutionary model, but rather the critical *elaboration* of the past. In short, this book aims at building neither a posthumous tribunal nor a museum, and even less an anachronic set of 'instructions for an armed uprising', in a neo-Blanquist style. Its ambition, however modest, is to 'work through' the past, just to preserve the meaning of a historical experience: if the revolutions of our time must invent their own models, they cannot do so on a *tabula rasa*, or without embodying a memory of bygone struggles, both their conquests and also, more frequently, their defeats. Of course, this is a work of mourning, but also a training for new battles.[67] Working through the past is unavoidable, not only because there are so many skeletons in the closet, but also because we cannot ignore the claim that the past has on us. Blasting the continuum of history, revolutions rescue the past. They will contain in themselves – whether they will be aware of it or not – the experiences of their ancestors. That is another reason why we need to meditate upon their history.

---

67   From this point of view, this book continues a reflection started with *Left-Wing Melancholia: Marxism, History, and Memory* (New York: Columbia University Press, 2017).

Chapter 1

The Locomotives of History

The nineteenth century, when it takes its place with the other centuries in the chronological charts of the future, will, if it needs a symbol, almost inevitably have as the symbol a steam engine running upon a railway.

H. G. Wells, *Anticipations of the Reaction of Mechanical and Scientific Progress upon Human Life and Thought* (1902)

The revolution of 1917 is a revolution of trains. History proceeding in screams of cold metal. The tsar's wheeled palace, shunted into sidings forever; Lenin's sealed stateless carriage ... Trotsky's armoured train, the Red Army's propaganda trains, the troop carriers of the Civil War. Looming trains, trains hurtling through trees, out of the dark.

Revolutions, Marx said, are the locomotives of history. 'Put the locomotive into top gear', Lenin exhorted himself in a private note, scant weeks after October, 'and keep it on the rails.'

China Miéville, *October: The Story of the Russian Revolution* (2017)

The Railway Age

One of Karl Marx's most famous sentences, appearing in *The Class Struggles in France* (1850), asserts that 'revolutions are the locomotives of history.'[1] For a century and a half, innumerable critics and exegetes have ritualistically repeated this powerful definition as a colourful but (in the last analysis) incidental metaphor, without trying to interpret its multiple meanings. In fact, this reference to the revolutions of 1848 as an extraordinary moment of acceleration in historical and political change is much more than a literary trope: it unveils Marx's culture and, beyond him, the nineteenth-century imagination. Far from being chosen by accident, the object of this metaphor points to a deep, substantial affinity between revolutions and trains that deserves to be carefully investigated. Moreover, this passage is no anomaly in writings that, from *The Communist Manifesto* (1848) to *Capital* (1867), contain recurrent allusions to trains and railroads.

Marx lived in the railway age, whose advent and diffusion he observed from London, its crucial starting point. The triad of iron, steam, and telegraph, which so profoundly shaped the nineteenth-century take-off of industrial capitalism, framed his way of thinking and his vision of historical change. When he wrote this passage in *The Class Struggles in France*, the first, 'heroic' period of railways had just finished and locomotives had become both a privileged topic of discussion in the public sphere and a common figure of speech in British and European literature. Following the opening of the first line between Liverpool and Manchester in 1830, railroads saw astonishing development, with a strong impact on England's economy and society. In twenty years they increased from under 100 miles to 6,000 miles, most of them built between 1846 and 1850. Passenger traffic grew simultaneously, far beyond the expectations of the earliest promoters who had conceived this means of transportation primarily for goods and minerals. In 1851, the Great London Exhibition attracted more than 6 million visitors, many of them arriving in the capital by train from the most remote corners of the country. The railway boom

---

1   Karl Marx, 'The Class Struggle in France', *MECW*, vol. 10, 122.

engendered strong economic growth by stimulating the production
of iron, which increased from 1.4 million tons in 1844 to 2 million tons
in 1850.[2] Railways necessitated the construction of lines, stations and
bridges, requiring the labour of hundreds of thousands of workers.
Trains broke the erstwhile quietness of the country with the passage of
smoking, shrieking machines. They transformed the urban landscape
as well, soon dominated by imposing stations that attracted tens of
thousands of travellers daily and became convergence points for road
networks and telegraph lines. Smoky clouds cloaking buildings and
people in cities and leaving streaks in the country sky regularly appear
in nineteenth-century paintings, from J. M. W. Turner's *Rain, Steam
and Speed* (1844) to Edouard Manet's *The Railway* (1873) to Claude
Monet's *The Gare Saint-Laʒare* (1877). Railways quickly became a
very profitable business that, monopolized by a small number of
companies, attained a prominent role in the national economy. Attracting the investment of many rich landowners, they were the site of a
new symbiosis between the old aristocracy and the newly ascendant
bourgeois classes. The Victorians who created this industry, Michael
Robbins writes in *The Railway Age*, looked like 'a race imbued with
some daemonic energy'[3] which did not falter in the following decades,
exerting a contagious effect on the global scale. In continental Europe,
the rail network increased enormously between 1840 and 1880: by the
end of the nineteenth century, a passenger could travel by train from
Lisbon to Moscow and beyond.[4] A similar growth took place in the
United States, where, at the end of the Civil War, railways became the
symbol of the transformation of the country into a world industrial
power. In the thirty years between the opening of the first track in 1838
and the completion of an integrated network joining the North and
the South with the West in 1869, they increased from 2,765 to 56,213
miles while gross investment in this economic sector grew from $927
million in 1850 to $2 billion in 1870, reaching $15 billion at the end

---

2   See Michael Robbins, *The Railway Age* (London: Routledge and Kegan
Paul, 1962).

3   Ibid., 37.

4   Eric Hobsbawm, *The Age of Capital 1848–1875* (New York: Vintage Books), 40.

of the century.[5] Thanks to the railroad, the inexhaustible lands of the Far West were expropriated and American capitalism took off. The myth of railways joined that of the Frontier, with analogous providential narratives of its ethical mission to unify a gigantic country into a single community blessed by God and racing towards progress. John Ford would celebrate this new mythology in *The Iron Horse* (1924), a movie that describes the building of the transcontinental railroad between 1862 and 1869.

This spirit was the subtext of Marx and Engels's famous passages in *The Communist Manifesto* where they celebrated the 'revolutionary role' played by the bourgeoisie in history. Modern industry, they wrote, had established the world market, which had given

> an immense development to commerce, to navigation, to communication by land. This development has, in its turn, reacted on the extension of industry; and in proportion as industry, commerce, navigation, railways extended, in the same proportion the bourgeoisie developed, increased its capital, and pushed into the background every class handed down from the Middle Ages.[6]

Like a train disrupting a peaceful rural landscape, capitalism had destroyed 'the most slothful indolence' inherited from the Middle Ages and, by creating the world market, had 'given a cosmopolitan character to production and consumption in every country'.[7] The bourgeoisie, they added,

> has subjected the country to the rule of the towns. It has created enormous cities, has greatly increased the urban population as compared with the rural, and has thus rescued a considerable part of the population from the idiocy of rural life. Just as it has made the country dependent on the towns, so it has made barbarian and

---

5   See Richard White, *Railroaded: The Transcontinentals and the Making of Modern America* (New York: Norton, 2011).

6   *MECW*, vol. 6, 486.

7   Ibid., 488.

semi-barbarian countries dependent on the civilized ones, nations
of peasants on nations of bourgeois, the East on the West.[8]

As a self-expanding economic system based on a continuous process of
accumulation – the transmutation money-commodity-money – capitalism does not know objective 'limits' (*Schränke*) but only 'barriers'
(*Grenze*) to breach and overcome. 'Commodities as such', Marx writes
in the *Grundrisse* (1857–58), 'are indifferent to all religious, political,
national and linguistic barriers. Their universal language is price and
their common bond is money.'[9] For the capitalist, 'the world market
is the sublime idea in which the whole world merges.' In this way it
builds a peculiar form of cosmopolitanism, 'a cult of practical reason'
which progressively destroys 'the traditional religious, national and
other prejudices which impede the metabolic process of mankind'.
Therefore capitalism 'feels itself to be free, unconfined, i.e. limited
only by itself, only by its own conditions of life'.[10]

When Marx and Engels wrote in *The Communist Manifesto* that the
bourgeoisie had 'accomplished wonders far surpassing Egyptian pyramids, Roman aqueducts, and Gothic cathedrals',[11] one may suppose
they were thinking of the spectacular railway bridges which so powerfully struck the Victorian imagination and filled the illustrations of
popular magazines, as well as of the majestic stations that appeared
in the big cities and which their architects conceived of as modern
Gothic cathedrals. In the age of steel and steam, the ruling classes did
not wish to break their link with the past; station halls and platforms

---

8   Ibid.

9   Karl Marx, 'Economic Manuscripts' (1857), *MECW*, vol. 29, 39.

10   Ibid., 384. On this idea of capitalism as a limitless economic system, see
John Bellamy Foster, Brett Clark and Richard York, *The Ecological Rift: Capi-
talism's War on the Earth* (New York: Monthly Review Press, 2010), 39–40, and
John Bellamy Foster, 'Marx's *Grundrisse* and the Ecological Contradictions of
Capitalism', in Renato Musto (ed.), *Karl Marx's Grundrisse: Foundations of the
Critique of Political Economy 150 Years Later* (London: Routledge, 2008), 100–1.
Marx borrowed this definition of 'limits' from Hegel, *The Science of Logic*, ed.
George di Giovanni (New York: Cambridge University Press, 2010), 98–101, 153.

11   *MECW*, vol. 6, 487. On the classicist diversity of nineteenth-century railway
stations, see Jürgen Osterhammel, *The Transformation of the World* (Princeton:
Princeton University Press, 2014), 300–2.

Railways in the Thirties: Sankey Valley Viaduct,
Lancashire, England. Postcard.

St Pancras Station, London, in the Nineteenth Century. Postcard.

were spacious and functional, but the façades displayed columns, rose windows, arcades, domes and towers. They were the visual evidence of what Arno J. Mayer has called 'the persistence of the old regime', the hybrid social form of a century that merged tradition and modernity, in which aristocratic institutions, customs, style and mentalities extended to the new ascending financial and industrial elites.[12]

A few years after *The Communist Manifesto*, Michel Chevalier, a disciple of Saint-Simon who became an advisor to Napoleon III, published an essay on railways that srikingly echoed the prose of Marx and Engels. He compared 'the zeal and the ardour displayed by the civilized nations of today in their establishment of railroads with that which, several centuries ago, went into the building of cathedrals'.[13] For the Saint-Simonians, railways possessed a mystical character as connectors of nations, to the point of creating a universal community based on cooperation and industrialism. If 'it is true', he wrote, 'that the word "religion" comes from *religare*, to "bind" ... then the railroads have more to do with the religious spirit than one might suppose. There has never existed a more powerful instrument for ... rallying the scattered populations.'[14] Marx avoided the mystical tones of the Saint-Simonians and other adepts of industrialism, but he shared their belief in the cosmopolitan mission of railroads, the symbol of the new industrial age.

No obstacle could resist the inexorable advance of capitalism, which brought modernity and destroyed the vestiges of feudalism like a running train eclipsing the pitiful, derisory slowness of horse-drawn carriages. Marx's words in *The Communist Manifesto* can be read as the analytical equivalent of a contemporary imagination that found in Dickens its most brilliant literary interpreter. The train, we read in *Dombey and Son* (1846), was 'defiant of all paths and roads, piercing through the heart of every obstacle ... through the fields, through

---

12   Arno J. Mayer, *The Persistence of the Old Regime: Europe to the Great War* (New York: Pantheon Books, 1981), Chapter 4.

13   Michel Chevalier, 'Chemins de fer', *Dictionnaire de l'économie politique* (Paris, 1852), 20; quoted in Walter Benjamin, *The Arcades Project*, trans. Howard Eiland, Kevin McLaughlin (Cambridge, MA: Harvard University Press, 1999), 598.

14   Ibid.

the woods, through the corn, through the hay, through the chalk, through the mould, through the clay, through the rock'; 'breasting the wind and light, the shower and sunshine', flying in and out of fields, bridges and tunnels.[15]

In the second half of the nineteenth century, railway fever had infected Russia, Asia, Latin America and the Middle East. In India, the first lines connecting Bombay, Calcutta and Madras opened in the early 1850s. Ten years later, the sub-continent had a railway network of 2,500 miles, nearly 4,800 in the 1870s, and 16,000 miles in 1890. For Marx, the development of Indian railways was a powerful illustration of his vision of traditional and archaic social forms shattered by the advent of modern, conquering industries. 'Indian society', he wrote in 1853 in the *New York Daily Tribune*, 'has no history at all, at least no known history.'[16] Its providential destiny was to be ruled and, from this point of view, the British Empire, as violent and brutal as it was, would undoubtedly have more fruitful consequences than its competitors, the Russian and the Ottoman empires. In India the British colonizers had two missions, 'one destructive, the other regenerating: the annihilation of old Asiatic society, and the laying the material foundations of Western society in Asia.'[17] Steam had severed the sub-continent from 'the prime law of its stagnation' by connecting it with the advanced world. Very soon, he predicted, this joining with the West through 'a combination of railways and steam-vessels' would demolish the bases of Oriental despotism.[18] Railroads were destroying the archaic social system of the country, which was grounded on the 'self-sufficient inertia of the villages'. The article's conclusion swept away any doubts: 'The railway-system will therefore become, in India, truly the forerunner of modern industry.'[19]

---

15   Charles Dickens, *Dombey and Son* (Oxford: Penguin, 1982), 236; see also Michael Freeman, *Railways and the Victorian Imagination* (New Haven: Yale University Press, 1999), 45–6.

16   Karl Marx, 'The Future Results of British Rule in India', *MECW*, vol. 12, 217.

17   Ibid., 217–18.

18   Ibid., 218.

19   Ibid., 220. It is true that Marx nuanced his position at the end of his life, writing in his notes that 'the suppression of communal landownership out there

It is known that, at the end of his life, in his correspondence with his Russian translator, Nikolai Danielson, and particularly with the famous populist leader Vera Zasulich, Marx had contemplated the possibility of a transition from the Russian agrarian commune (*obschina*) to modern socialism without passing through the 'Caudine Forks' of the capitalist system; but the realization of this hypothesis needed a socialist revolution.[20] Since the abolition of serfdom in 1861, Tsarist Russia had gradually taken the path of capitalism and the social premises of this synthesis between ancient and modern, pre-capitalist and post-capitalist collectivism, had begun to disappear. In 1894, ten years after Marx's death, Engels cited the development of Russian railways as proof that the romantic possibility his friend had envisaged had finally vanished. After the Crimean War, only one road was open to the Russian empire: the transition from a backward economy to capitalist industry. This conflict had dramatically exposed the weakness of the Tsarist army, which only a significant development of the railways could overcome. But creating an extended and solid railway system in such an immense country required rails, locomotives, rolling stocks, etc., and this meant developing a domestic industry. In a short while, Engels concluded, all the foundations of the capitalist mode of production were laid in Russia, with their inevitable consequences: 'the transformation of the country into a capitalist industrial nation, the proletarianization of a large portion of the peasantry and the decay of the old rural commune.'[21]

Creating the world market, modern capitalism connected cities and nations into a single gigantic network, comparable to the map of a continental railway. Because of its division of labour and its standardized

---

was nothing but an act of English vandalism, pushing the native people not forwards but backwards. Primitive communities are not all cast from.' (Draft of the Letter to Vera Zasulich, *MECW*, vol. 24, 365). On this reassessment and the anti-Eurocentric dimension of Marx's writings, see Kevin B. Anderson, *Marx at the Margins: On Nationalism, Ethnicity, and Non-Western Societies* (Chicago: University of Chicago Press, 2010).

20   Karl Marx, [Drafts of the Letter to Vera Zasulich], *MECW*, vol. 24, 353.

21   Friedrich Engels, 'Afterword to "On Social Relations in Russia"' (1894), *MECW*, vol. 27, 433. On the debate between Marx, Engels and the Russian populists, see Shanin (ed.), *Late Marx and the Russian Road*.

and synchronized production, modern industry undoubtedly needed railways for transporting raw materials and commodities. In fact, it found in railways both a vector and a mirror of its own productive rationality. Over the course of the nineteenth century, the rise of industrial capitalism required a homogeneous, global time, and railroads gave a powerful impetus to the regulation of time, first of all by stimulating the improvement of clock technology. In 1800, time was locally or regionally synchronized – but trains could not run without a national schedule, which implied the elimination of any time variation between different cities. At the end of the century, measurements of time had been coordinated and finally regulated on the international scale. In 1855, 98 per cent of public clocks in the UK were set to Greenwich Mean Time, which – after two conferences on 'world time', in Washington (1884) and Paris (1912) – became the official time of the planet. In parallel, the number of pocket watches increased from some 350–400,000 at the end of the eighteenth century to more than 2.5 million in 1875.[22] The age of capital corresponded with the age of railways; both triggered a process of economic, social and cultural rationalization. It is the cultural atmosphere depicted by Joseph Conrad in *The Secret Agent* (1907), a fascinating little novel about an anarchist plot to bomb the Greenwich Observatory and thus to 'explode time'.[23]

Secularization and Temporalization

As Michael Löwy has convincingly proved, there is a 'romantic' dimension to Marx's critique of capitalism. In *The Communist Manifesto*, he and Engels emphasized that, because of mechanical production, 'the work of the proletarians has lost all individual character, and, consequently, all charm.'[24] Workers no longer felt

---

22   Osterhammel, *Transformation of the World*, 69–76; Tom Kern, *The Culture of Time and Space 1880–1918* (New York: Harvard University Press, 1984), 11–15; and Eviatar Zerubavel, 'The Standardization of Time: A Sociohistorical Perspective', *American Journal of Sociology*, 88/1 (1982): 1–23.

23   Joseph Conrad, *The Secret Agent* (New York: Penguin, 2007).

24   *MECW*, vol. 6, 490.

themselves to be creators, insofar as they had become simple 'append-
ages of the machine', and their input was reduced to 'the simplest,
most monotonous, and most easily acquired knack'. In a passage that
almost prefigures the description of a Fordist factory, he and Engels
stressed that industrial capitalism had created a 'mass of labourers'
who, submitted to a military hierarchy, simply executed mechanical
tasks, mostly 'repulsive', 'like soldiers'.[25] But this lucid recognition
of the exploitation and alienation of wage labour does not inscribe
Marx within the not inconsiderable circle of romantic disparagers of
railways. He never wrote anything like the violent and contemptuous
words of those contemporary British novelists and poets, most of
them of aristocratic descent, like Wordsworth and Ruskin, for whom
railways fatally disfigured the rural landscape; or Thomas Carlyle,
who compared the steam railway with a 'devil's mantle'; or even Lord
Shaftesbury, for whom 'the devil, if he travelled, would have gone by
train.'[26] The advent of railways put an end to the eighteenth-century
literary tradition of travel stories, by removing the intensity of the
relationship between traveller and landscape and reducing space to
a simple geographic measurement. The Goethean days of journey
as a moment of fusion with nature and contemplation of the 'aura'
of a panorama were over.[27] Instead of contemplating the spectacle
of nature, passengers experienced the hectic rhythm of modernity.
Marx did not deplore the end of the 'aura' of the agrarian landscape,
whose static, slumbrous beauty had been shattered by the spasmodic
movement of the locomotives, those 'iron monsters' of modern times.
It is true that, besides scarring the quiet traditional landscape, railroads deeply impinged upon old landed property and the symbolic

---

25   Ibid., 490–1. See also Michael Löwy, 'Marxism and Romanticism', in
*On Changing the World: Essays in Political Philosophy, from Karl Marx to Walter
Benjamin* (Atlantic Highlands, NJ: Humanities Press, 1993), 1–15.

26   See Freeman, *Railways and the Victorian Imagination*, 13, 44–5; and Robbins,
The Railway Age, 62–3.

27   On the loss of landscape's 'aura' produced by the standardization of train
travels, analogous to the loss of the uniqueness of the work of art in the age of its
mechanical reproduction as analysed by Benjamin, see Wolfgang Schivelbusch,
*The Railway Journey: The Industrialization of Time and Space in the Nineteenth
Century* (Berkeley: University of California Press, 1986), 41–2.

power of aristocracy, but this simply meant the end of 'all feudal, patriarchal, idyllic relations'.[28]

Several references to railroads are included in *Capital*, where Marx defined them as an infrastructure that, together with ocean steamers and the telegraph, transformed communications and enabled the development of industrial capitalism. He quoted historical studies on the transportation system, as well as specialized books and articles on the evolution of their technology. In particular, he extensively mentioned the bulletins of the Royal Commission on Railways published in London in the 1860s. The first volume of *Capital* denounces, along with the accidents of circulation, the high number of casualties related to the exploitation of railway workers. Like locomotives, industrial machines too were depicted as 'mechanical monsters' possessed of a 'demon power'.[29] Once their 'giant limbs' were set in motion, their activity became frenetic and finally erupted into 'the fast and furious whirl of their countless working organs'.[30] The map of railway lines, which framed the territories of nations and continents with their intersections and bifurcations, gave a concrete, allegorical form to Marx's concept of capital as a 'social hieroglyph'.[31]

Modernity means mobility and railways established a new relationship between space and time: distances seemed dramatically reduced and time compressed by this intense process of acceleration. Jürgen Osterhammel has dubbed the nineteenth century 'the age of speed revolution'.[32] Since the 1840s, the topic of the 'annihilation' of space and time, appearing for the first time in a poem by Alexander Pope in 1751 and subsequently evoked by several writers, from Goethe to Balzac, became a common figure of speech to depict the advent of railways.[33] In 1842, Sydney Smith celebrated the way that 'man is become a bird.' Thanks to the locomotives, he wrote, 'everything is near, everything

---

28   Karl Marx, Friedrich Engels, 'Communist Manifesto', *MECW*, vol. 6, 486.

29   Karl Marx, 'Capital, Volume I', *MECW*, vol. 35, 385.

30   Ibid.

31   Ibid., 85.

32   Osterhammel, *Transformation of the World*, 74.

33   See David Harvey, *Paris, Capital of Modernity* (London: Routledge, 2003), 48.

is immediate: time, distance, and delay are abolished.'[34] In the *Grundrisse* (1857–58), his preparatory notes for *Capital*, Marx embraced this formula. Capitalism, an economic system that 'by nature drives beyond every spatial barrier', needed railways, the modern means of communication that, by conquering 'the entire earth' and transforming it into a gigantic market, produced the 'annihilation of space through time' (*den Raum zu vernichten durh die Zeit*).[35]

Railways also offered a metaphor for both the circulation of capital and its cyclical crises. As Wolfgang Schivelbusch has brilliantly shown, the concept of circulation, previously related to the lexicon of biology and physiology, in the nineteenth century enlarged its scope and was quickly metaphorized to express systems of communication and the unification of the social body. Circulation meant a healthy body, whereas any static element appeared as an obstacle or a symptom of disease. Cities, territories and nations began to be viewed as living bodies, the objects of what Foucault would later call modern biopolitics. Schivelbusch quotes a popular book by Maxime Du Camp, published at the time of Haussmann's reshaping of the French capital under the Second Empire, which was significantly titled *Paris, ses organes, ses fonctions, sa vie*. The wide boulevards that replaced the old labyrinth of small streets and redesigned the structure of the city along modern, rational lines, meant 'a double system of circulation and respiration'.[36] The social concept of 'traffic' (*Verkehr*) joined the physiological concept of 'circulation' (*Zirkulation*).[37] According to Marx, circulation is, alongside production, a crucial moment of capital's life, and the link between them is time. The three volumes of *Capital* depict a conceptual totality: the linear, homogeneous time of production in the first volume; the cyclical time of circulation in the second, where Marx analyses the process of rotation and enlarged reproduction of capital; and the organic time of capital in the third, where he reconstitutes the entire process as a unity of the time of

---

34   Quoted by Robbins, *The Railway Age*, 45.

35   Karl Marx, 'Economic Manuscripts' (1857), *MECW*, vol. 29, 10; original Marx, Engels, *Werke* (Berlin: Dietz Verlag, 1983), vol. 42, 445.

36   Schivelbusch, *The Railway Journey*, 195.

37   Ibid., 193–5.

production and the time of circulation.[38] He explains the cyclical crises of capitalist economy through 'overproduction': the creation of a mass of commodities that become superfluous for the valorization of capital (which he carefully distinguishes from the satisfaction of social needs). But these periodic crises take the form of a gap, a sudden, traumatic interruption of the permanent movement of capital circulation. Of course, Marx insisted that, far from being 'accidental', the periodic crises of capitalism were an intrinsic part of its nature. But even the lethal accidents which so frequently occurred in the 'railway age' and so deeply affected the nineteenth-century imagination were not the product of external interference; they appeared as an inevitable effect of the functioning of this new means of locomotion itself, both admirable and frightening. In the *Grundrisse*, Marx depicts the cyclical crises of capitalism as 'recurring catastrophes', as 'explosions, cataclysms' that destroy a section of capital itself to permit the restarting of the process of accumulation, that is, the valorization of capital or its capacity to make profits.[39] These cataclysms break the movement of capital whose circulation is permanent and cannot be stopped without paralyzing the system as a whole. Therefore, the crises of capitalism are reminiscent of both the heart attacks related to blood circulation in a living body and the train accidents that paralyze the railway networks.

All these metaphoric references to the railroads outline a general picture of a nineteenth-century perception of time. According to Reinhart Koselleck, locomotives embodied a new concept of secularization as the synthesis of a process of acceleration and time-shrinking. Initially, secularization was a canonical-juridical category that designated the transition from a clerical to a civil status; then, during the French Revolution, it became a juridical-political category that described the shift of sovereignty from a king ruling 'by the grace of God' to the people, and in parallel the state confiscation of Church property; finally, it turned into a philosophical-political category which indicated the meaning of history itself: 'salvation is no longer sought

38   See Stavros Tombazos, *Time in Marx: The Categories of Time in Marx's Capital* (Chicago: Haymarket Books, 2015).

39   *MECW*, vol. 29, 134.

at the end of history, but rather in the development and accomplishment of history itself.'[40] He quotes the article on railways published in 1838 by the German encyclopaedia *Brockhaus*, which attributed to them a 'salvific mission'. Locomotives were accomplishing God's purpose of establishing universal peace, an ethical goal to which Kant had already referred as 'perpetual peace', to be realized through cosmopolitan law. In 1871, the Lutheran theologian and promoter of foreign missions Carl Heinrich Christian Plath hailed the railway line connecting the Atlantic and Pacific coasts of the United States as a sacred mission: the unification of the planet by the railways would bring human beings together and accelerate the advent of the kingdom of God.[41] For enlightened thinkers, secularization meant the acceleration of time and the advent of Progress. Railways possessed social and ethical virtues.

Conceptualizing Revolution

Marx would have probably laughed at this naïve assessment, but his vision of revolutions as 'locomotives of history' belonged nonetheless to the same *zeitgeist*. This definition supposes a teleological vision of history, which runs on fixed rails along a path whose direction has been previously determined and whose destination is known. Revolution is a rush towards progress. Socialism inherited from 1789 a radically new vision of revolution as a historical break, a social and political rupture, the overthrow of the old regime and the instauration of a new power, and the transformation of the people into a sovereign subject. The concept of revolution comes from the Latin words *revolutio, revolvere*: returning to the origins. It means a kind of rotation by which something goes back to its starting point. In the seventeenth century, it became an astronomical concept that defined the rotation of planets around the sun. The modern concept of revolution appeared during the eighteenth century, but it was the French Revolution that codified it into a new paradigm. Revolution had become a projection of society into

---

40   Reinhart Koselleck, 'Zeitverkürzung und Beschleunigung: Eine Studie zur Säcularisation', *Zeitschichten: Studien zur Historik* (Frankfurt: Suhrkamp, 2002), 182.
41   Ibid., 193–5.

the future, an extraordinary acceleration of history. Koselleck defines it as an 'unconscious secularization of eschatological expectations':[42] socialist utopia was temporalized and projected into the future. The subject of this process of historical change had shifted from God to the proletariat, from a religious to a profane entity (secularization), and its movement had experienced a sudden acceleration (the revolutionary break). Justice and redemption did not belong to the religious sphere, to the kingdom of God; human beings did not have to wait until death and the end of time to reach paradise and happiness. They could struggle for a terrestrial redemption: the kingdom of God had to be conquered on earth; it had become a profane place. This also sheds light on a famous Homeric metaphor that Marx, in a letter to Ludwig Kugelmann, referred to the Paris Commune as an attempt at 'storming heaven' (*Himmel zu stürmen*). Like Titans who assaulted the Olympus, the French workers had overthrown their own rulers.[43]

The rationalized and standardized time of capital accumulation does not correspond with revolutionary time. The discrepancy that separates them is as deep as the opposition between the two antipodal 'revolutionary roles' played respectively by the bourgeoisie in building the world market and the proletariat in struggling for a community of free and equal human beings. Capital's temporality possesses the strength of an objective, economic process – the abstract time of market economy and commodity circulation – whereas the temporality of proletarian revolution is subjective, discontinuous; the first is quantitative and cumulative, the second is qualitative and unforeseeable, enigmatic, shaped by sudden accelerations and periods of apparent stagnation. In *The Eighteenth Brumaire of Louis Bonaparte* (1852), Marx distinguished between the 'bourgeois revolutions' of the eighteenth century, which 'stormed swiftly from success to success' by establishing a new economic and political rule, and the proletarian

---

42   Reinhart Koselleck, 'Historical Criteria of the Modern Concept of Revolution', in *Futures Past: On the Semantics of Historical Time*, trans. Keith Tribe (New York: Columbia University Press, 2004), 50. On the history of the concept of revolution, see Mayer, *The Furies*, Chapter 1.

43   Karl Marx, 'Letter to Ludwig Kugelmann' (12 April 1871), *MECW*, vol. 44, 132.

revolutions of the nineteenth century, which 'criticize themselves constantly, interrupt themselves continually in their own course, return to the apparently accomplished, in order to begin it afresh'.[44] In other words, socialist revolutions have their own, interior rhythm, and their conscious synchronization coincides with the desynchronization of capital accumulation. Walter Benjamin will describe revolutionary action as the irruption of a qualitative time that 'explodes the continuum of history'. It is the temporality of calendars, of landmarks of the past built as 'monuments of historical consciousness', which 'do not measure time the way clocks do'. The most evocative 'image of thought' of revolutionary tempo as a conscious break with the disciplinary, productive, and instrumental reason of capital time, is a famous episode from the July Revolution of 1830: 'On the first evening of fighting, it so happened that the dials of the clock towers were being fired at simultaneously and independently from several locations in Paris.'[45]

Thus, the definition of revolutions as locomotives of history is grounded in a conception of historical time in which they appear as irruptions into the time of capital. In Marx's view, time has distinct dimensions.[46] On the one hand, it means a philosophy of history inherited from Hegel and defined as a teleological arrow: the historical movement, the succession of modes of production and social formations, the search for human emancipation, and the transition from class societies to communism (the end of the 'prehistory' of humankind).[47] On the other hand, it means the time of capital accumulation depicted by political economy. In *The German Ideology* (1846), Marx and Engels unveiled the expansion of capitalism behind the movement of Hegel's 'world spirit'.[48] They retained a teleological vision insofar

---

44   Marx, 'The Eighteenth Brumaire', 106.

45   Benjamin, 'On the Concept of History', 395. See also Bjorn Schiermer, 'The (In)Actuality of Walter Benjamin: On the Relation Between the Temporal and the Social in Benjamin's Work', *Time and Society*, 25/1 (2016): 3–23.

46   Heinz D. Kittsteiner, 'Reflections on the Construction of Historical Time in Karl Marx', *History and Memory*, 3/2 (1991): 45–86.

47   Karl Marx, 'A Contribution to the Critique of Political Economy' (1859), *MECW*, vol. 29, 264.

48   *MECW*, vol. 5, 51.

as this expansion implied a universal development of productive forces, which was the premise for socialism. But socialism was a product of human agency. It could not be defined as the outcome of a 'natural' (*naturwürsicht*) process, according to the axioms with which political economy and classical liberalism observed capitalism; socialism meant that history had to be consciously constructed and oriented in line with political and strategic choices. In other words, the relationship between the subject and object of historical movement had to be reversed. This conception of the dialectic of history posited revolution as the outcome of the conflict between productive forces and property relations: when the existent relations of property no longer allowed the development of the forces of production, these relations needed to be changed.[49] But whereas in previous ages this transition appeared as a natural transformation of socio-economic structures themselves, the passage from capitalism to socialism could not take a spontaneous, ineluctable form. It supposed an act of human self-emancipation grounded in a project of social and political change; it stemmed from conscious revolutionary action. This introduced a third dimension of time, different from both the long view of history (in a Hegelian sense) and the abstract time of capital (defined by political economy): the concrete, *kairotic*, and disruptive time of revolution. Exceeding large historical cycles and exploding the spasmodic movement of capital, revolution possessed its own autonomy, a self-regulated time of human emancipation and agency.

Therein lies the ambiguity of Marx's metaphor of locomotives: the mechanical instruments of the international expansion of capitalism possess their own, intrinsic and irresistible dynamic of development; they destroy all social, economic, and cultural obstacles, and they overcome all national borders. Revolutions, however, lack such a semi-automatic dynamic; their universalism is a conscious construction. It is true that 1848 was a year of synchronous European revolutionary upheaval, just as 1789 had been the climax of a wave of Atlantic revolutions that swept from America to Haiti, passing through Paris, where it found its epicentre. But all these revolutions experienced ups

---

49   This concept is developed in Marx's famous introduction of 1859 to 'A Contribution to the Critique of Political Economy', *MECW*, vol. 29, 261–5.

and downs, throughout a discontinuous process that often resulted in defeats and restorations. The metaphor of locomotives seems to suggest an idea of permanent revolution, in Trotsky's sense: because of the globalization of productive forces, revolutions tend to transcend their original locus and internationalize themselves. 'A national revolution', the Bolshevik leader explained, 'is not a self-contained whole; it is only a link in the international chain.' Internationalism, he added, 'is no abstract principle but a theoretical and political reflection of the character of world economy, of the world development of productive forces and the world scale of the class struggle'.[50] Revolutionary locomotives thus embody a kind of alternative globalization, in that the expansion of socialism on a world scale follows the building of the world market and the laws of revolution correspond with those of capitalism. But the metaphor attributes to this process a character both teleological (rails and known destinations) and mechanical (the speed and power of an engine) that hurts Marx's vision of politics. Moreover, *The Communist Manifesto* devotes many pages to criticizing the illusions of utopian socialism whose eschatological expectations were rooted in a naïve faith in the emancipatory potentialities of modern industry and technology. In short, a discrepancy remains between Marx's vision of history and his approach to politics.

Energy and Labour Power

In the nineteenth century, locomotives offered a visual perception of the force and dynamism of an industrial civilization based on steam-machines: they exhibited the inexhaustible power of mechanical energy. From this point of view, Marx's conception of the development of productive forces has to be inscribed in the age of modern physics and thermodynamics, epitomized by Helmholtz's principle of energy conservation.[51] A large part of the first volume of *Capital* is devoted to

---

50   Leon Trotsky, *The Permanent Revolution* (Seattle: Red Letter Press, 2010 [1929]), 146. On Trotsky's theory, see Michael Löwy, *The Politics of Uneven and Combined Development: The Theory of Permanent Revolution* (Chicago: Haymarket Books, 2010 [1981]).

51   On 'the marriage of Marx and Helmholtz', see Anson Rabinbach, *The Human Motor: Energy, Fatigue, and the Origins of Modernity* (Berkeley: University

the analysis of the advent of modern industry, with the transition from manufacture to industry and the creation of new powerful machines. The concept of work inevitably changed. In the nineteenth century, the human body began to be observed as a *human motor*, whose physical and mental performance was carefully studied and measured. Society needed a science of labour aimed at improving productivity and reducing fatigue as much as possible. It was Hermann Helmholtz who, in 1847, reformulated this new vision of energy (*Kraft*) as a metaphor of industrial society and paved the way for conceiving of labour as a restraint on freedom rather than a means of self-fulfilment.[52] And it was Marx who elaborated a new concept of 'labour power' (*Arbeitskraft*) as a premise for socialism. In fact, *Capital* opens with a classical (Hegelian) definition of 'labour' (*Arbeit*) as a metabolic process between man and nature, an exchange that human beings can control and regulate by engaging both their intellectual and physical capacities. It is a corporal relationship that means appropriation, transformation, eventually domination, but also *belonging*, insofar as it implies a vision of human beings as part of nature.[53] Then, notably in the fourth section of *Capital*, labour becomes 'labour power', a new concept which takes a double meaning: it is labour transformed into commodity – the secret of the production of economic surplus – and, at the same time, a human activity emancipated from nature and applied to mechanical production. 'In its machinery system,' Marx writes, 'modern industry has a productive organism that is purely

---

of California Press, 1990), 72–4; see also Osterhammel, *Transformation of the World*, 651–2. According to Amy E. Wendling, Marx's critique of political economy 'superimposed a thermodynamic model of labour over the ontological model of labour he inherited from Hegel', *Karl Marx on Technology and Alienation* (New York: Palgrave Macmillan, 2009), 59. See also John Bellamy Foster and Paul Burkett, 'Classical Marxism and the Second Law of Thermodynamics', *Organization & Environment*, 21/1 (2008): 3–37.

52   Hermann Helmholtz, Über die Erhaltung der Kraft (1847); see Fabio Bevilacque, 'Helmholtz's *Ueber die Erhaltung der Kraft*: The Emergence of a Theoretical Physicist', in David Cahan (ed.), *Hermann von Helmholtz and the Foundations of Nineteenth-Century Science* (Berkeley: University of California Press, 1993), 291–333.

53   *MECW*, vol. 35, 187–8; original Karl Marx, *Das Kapital* (Berlin: Dietz Verlag, 1975), vol. I, 192–3.

objective, in which the labourer becomes a mere appendage to an already existing material condition of production.'[54] Insofar as they 'dispense with muscular power', machines could reduce fatigue and physical consumption. Under the capitalist factory system, however, they led to calamities such as the extreme extension of the working day, the introduction of hierarchical and oppressive forms of discipline, and even child labour (a tragedy which Marx strongly denounced as evidence of the immoral bases of capitalism). In some passages of his economic manuscripts of 1861–63, he explicitly related the advent of steam engines with labour control and discipline, by stigmatizing 'the introduction of steam as an antagonist to human power'.[55] Under socialism, however, machines would allow a dramatic reduction of necessary labour thanks to the development of productive labour power. This is why 'in a communist society there would be a very different scope for the employment of machinery than there can be in a bourgeois society.'[56] Capitalism, Walter Benjamin will write many decades later in reformulating this idea of Marx, turns technology into a 'fetish of doom' instead of making it a 'key to happiness'.[57]

Machines are motors that replace the muscular energy of workers and animals (locomotives were called 'iron horses'). Unlike living bodies, they do not grow tired and function relentlessly. Since the natural and moral limits of human beings are unknown to them, steam machines multiply energy and annihilate fatigue. They radically modify the old metabolic relationship between human beings and nature. In other words, they introduce an anthropological break between 'labour' and 'labour power' which Agnes Heller has depicted as the transition from a 'paradigm of work' to a 'paradigm of production'.[58] Now, socialism meant liberation *from* labour rather than *through* labour; liberation from compulsory work, finally executed by proper

---

54   Ibid., 389; *Das Kapital*, 407.

55   *MECW*, vol. 33, 340–1.

56   *MECW*, vol. 35, 396; *Das Kapital*, 414.

57   Walter Benjamin, 'Theories of German Fascism' (1930), *WBSW*, vol. 2/1, 321.

58   See Agnes Heller, 'Paradigm of Production: Paradigm of Work', *Dialectical Anthropology*, 6 (1981): 71–9. On this 'anthropological break' in Marx's thought, see also Massimo Tomba, 'Accumulation and Time: Marx's Historiography', *Capital and Class*, 37/3 (2013): 356.

machines, rather than a redemptive activity of self-fulfilment. Intellectual and physical faculties could be devoted to the accomplishment of creative tasks rather than to the satisfaction of primary needs. 'The song of emancipated labour', Anson Rabinbach writes in *The Human Motor*, the best study on this topic, 'can still be heard sotto voce in Marx's *Capital*, but it is drowned out by the roar of expanding productive forces driving the teleological motor of historical progress.'[59]

This conception contains the premises of a socialist utopia grounded on an idea of total freedom and human liberation from any material constraint and, at the same time, a dangerous idealization of technology that announces the controversial relationship between socialism and ecology in the twentieth century. In fact, Marx's entire oeuvre is shaped by an unresolved tension between two contradictory tendencies. On the one hand, a positivist attempt – so typical of the time – to discover the 'laws of motion' of the capitalist mode of production and, beyond capitalism, of history, which resulted in the evolutionary scheme of the succession of social formations described in his introduction to *Contribution to the Critique of Political Economy*. On the other hand, a dialectical vision of history as an open process, made of unpredictable turns and bifurcations, without a predetermined direction and whose final result depends on human agency.[60] In this second conception, the development of productive forces – science, technology, motors, machines, etc. – was a premise for both socialism and a negative dialectic that reinforced exploitation and destroyed nature itself. This tension between a 'determinist' and a 'constructivist' Marx,[61] that never found a satisfactory resolution in his work, makes sterile the antipodal portraits of him as either a 'Promethean' advocate of productivism, or the forerunner of modern political ecology.[62] According to Rabinbach, it was Engels who would overcome the ambiguities of his friend by

59   Rabinbach, *The Human Motor*, 81–2.

60   See Daniel Bensaïd, *Marx for Our Times: Adventures and Misadventures of a Critique* (London: Verso, 2009), 277–80.

61   Andreas Malm, *Fossil Capital: The Rise of Steam Power and the Roots of Global Warming* (London: Verso, 2016), 276. Unlike Malm, who distinguishes between an 'early' deterministic and a 'late' constructivist Marx, I argue that these tendencies always coexisted in Marx.

62   See respectively Ted Benton, 'Marxism and Natural Limits: An Ecological Critique and Reconstruction', in Benton (ed.), *The Greening of Marxism* (New

celebrating 'the marriage of Marx and Helmholtz'. In *Anti-Dühring* (1878), he fetishized technology by putting Marxism 'on the pedestal of energy and transcendental materialism'.[63]

It is no surprise that Marx, viewing modern technology and industrial machinery as the indispensable premises for a liberated society, expressed strong scepticism towards Luddism, the movement of machine breakers that spread significantly in the early nineteenth century, first in England – notably Lancashire and Wiltshire – and then in several continental countries affected by the industrial revolution. He observed its impressive propagation with both sympathy and condescension, recognizing its moral legitimacy but pointing out its political impotence and anachronistic character. Likewise, he emphasized the good reasons behind the revolt of colonized Indians against the British, but in his eyes it was historically doomed. In 1853 he ascribed colonial exploitation and oppression to the inevitable consequences of the march of progress, 'that hideous, pagan idol, who would not drink the nectar but from the skulls of the slain'.[64] Thus, the Luddites who smashed the weaving machines were simply expressing an immature form of struggle, which he stigmatized in *Capital* with the following words: 'It took both time and experience before the workpeople learnt to distinguish between machinery and its employment by capital, and to direct their attacks, not against the material instruments of production, but against the mode in which they are used.'[65]

The results of this naïve rebellion were counterproductive, insofar as it gave the 'anti-Jacobin power' a good pretext for responding with 'the most reactionary and forcible measures'.[66] It is true that capitalists used technology to impose brutal conditions of discipline and hierarchical submission upon labourers, transforming factories into hells

---

York: The Guilford Press, 1996), 157–86 and Paul Burkett, *Marx and Nature: A Red and Green Perspective* (Chicago: Haymarket Books, 2014).

63   Rabinbach, *The Human Motor*, 81. See Friedrich Engels, 'Anti-Dühring', *MECW*, vol. 25, Chapter 6.

64   Karl Marx, 'The Future Results of British Rule in India', *MECW*, vol. 12, 222.

65   *MECW*, vol. 35, 432.

66   Ibid., 426–8.

where the workers were treated like 'private soldiers and sergeants of an industrial army.' Machines, he added in a passage that almost prefigured the assembly line of a Fordist factory, trained workers 'to renounce their desultory habits of work, and to identify themselves with the unvarying regularity of the complex automaton.' Factory work, Marx wrote, 'exhausts the nervous system to the uttermost, it does away with the many-sided play of the muscles, and confiscates every atom of freedom, both in bodily and intellectual activity.'[67] But the enemy was a social system of exploitation, not its means. Alienation and bodily pain were not intrinsically related to industrial machinery. It was capitalism that turned machines against men; socialism would instead celebrate their alliance by 'liberating' the productive forces strangled by bourgeois property relations. In this Hegelian view, historical dialectics kept its positive outcome. 'Labour power' had to be delivered from its abstract character (its commodity form) and rescued by socialism as a concrete, creative process of building humanity's material environment: use values versus exchange values.[68]

This dialectic of technology, which simultaneously works towards the arrival of a liberated society and the reification of social relationships and human beings, did not spare the railways. Their extension in the nineteenth century produced the shift towards a new biopower and the advent of an ordered society. It is not by chance that the word 'class' entered the lexicon of ordinary people with the diffusion of train journeys. In fact, the annihilation of space and time through the railways was a process of both compressing time and regulating space. According to Mark Simpson, trains produced a 'disciplinary space' by making 'the bodies in motion the objects, not subjects of their velocity'.[69] As Michel de Certeau observed in *The Practice of*

---

67   Ibid., 425–6.

68   On the distinction between abstract and concrete labour in Marx, see Moishe Postone, *Time, Labour, and Social Domination: A Reinterpretation of Marx's Critical Theory* (New York: Cambridge University Press, 1996).

69   Mark Simpson, *Trafficking Subjects: The Politics of Mobility in Nineteenth-Century America* (Minneapolis: University of Minnesota Press, 2004), 93. Simpson applies to the railways the analysis of the modern prison elaborated by Michel Foucault in *Discipline and Punish*, trans. Alan Sheridan (New York: Vintage Books, 1977).

Everyday Life (1980), the train journey was a form of 'incarceration', in which passengers were 'pigeonholed, numbered, and regulated'.[70] They could not travel without buying a ticket, which was checked, and assigned them a fixed place; the time and destination of their journey were scheduled, and bodily functions (available space, dining cars, etc.) were indulged according to coach class. They were passive watchers of a landscape disappearing before their eyes by virtue of an overwhelming velocity that, in Marx's words, did not depend on them but was instead a 'purely objective' result of the steam machines.

Marxists abandoned the idea of the 'neutrality' of science and technology only after the Great War. A Heideggerian Marxist, Herbert Marcuse, codified this theoretical change by writing that 'technology as such cannot be isolated from the use to which it is put', and depicting a negative dialectic in which, rather than an emancipatory outcome, the conflict between forces of production and property relations could result in a reinforcement of domination.[71] But when he wrote these lines, in 1964, the railway age was over: technology had already produced total wars, industrial massacres and atomic bombs. In Marx's time, anti-technological criticism was the preserve of conservative thought. If romantic anti-capitalism sometimes surfaces in his writings, it never pervades the general orientation of his work. Of course, Marx did not join the reactionary discourse so widespread in his time that stigmatized the Luddites' 'barbarism', and which resulted in a law aimed at their repression in 1812, but he saw these wreckers as representatives of the past, not the future.

The legacy of the Luddites would be redeemed one century later by a new current of labour historians. In 1952, Eric Hobsbawm devoted to them a pioneering essay in which he defined their methods of struggle as a form of 'collective bargaining by riot'.[72] Later, E. P. Thompson

---

70   Michel de Certeau, *The Practice of Everyday Life*, trans. Steven Rendall (Berkeley: University of California Press, 2011), 111.

71   Herbert Marcuse, *One-Dimensional Man: Studies in the Ideology of Advanced Industrial Society* (Boston: Beacon Press, 1964), xvi.

72   Eric Hobsbawm, 'The Machine Breakers', in *Labouring Men: Studies in the History of Labour* (London: Weidenfeld & Nicolson, 1964), 60. For a good reconstitution of the historiographical debate on Luddism, see Philippe Minard, 'Le retour de Ned Ludd. Le Luddisme et ses interprétations', *Revue d'Histoire Moderne*

The Leader of the Luddites (1812). British Museum, London.

reinterpreted the movement of the machine breakers as an expression of the 'moral economy of the crowd'.[73] In his eyes, a large part of the eighteenth and nineteenth centuries saw the violent conflict between the market economy of rising capitalism and the 'moral economy' of the English plebs, deeply attached to their customs and the egalitarian tradition of their communities. In *The Making of the English Working Class* (1963), Thompson depicted the Luddites as an 'army of redressers'. According to him, Luddism was neither a 'blind protest' nor a 'primitive' form of trade-unionism. Its representatives were well organized and sometimes cultivated. Their opposition to the advent of industry and market capitalism was certainly 'romantic', insofar as they wished to preserve their traditional, communitarian customs, but

---

et Contemporaine, 54/1 (2007): 242–57. On the Luddite texts, see Kevin Binfield (ed.), *Writings of the Luddites* (Baltimore: Johns Hopkins University Press, 2004).

73   E. P. Thompson, 'The Moral Economy of the English Crowd in the Eighteenth Century', in *Customs in Common* (New York: The New Press, 1993), 185–257.

it looked towards the future, as attested by their introduction of the 10 Hour Movement.[74] In fact, the Luddites' rage against the machine did not express an anti-technological prejudice. They accepted the introduction of modern machines wherever this meant the improvement of their working conditions by reducing physical effort, fatigue and submission. They broke the machines that had only been installed in the factories in order to compress their salaries and transform labour into a form of slavery.

Railways epitomize this plural, complex, and sometimes ambiguous relationship of workers with the machines, as well as the multiple meanings of their sabotage. In fact, sabotage is not necessarily incompatible with a rhetorical discourse on the development of productive forces. Think of the European Resistance during the Second World War, in which railway workers played a prominent role. In René Clément's movie *The Battle of the Rails* (1946), sabotage is accomplished by skilled workers, technicians and railway managers who are proud of their machines. The sabotage itself does not imply any hostility towards locomotives but rather a complete mastering of their anatomy and operation. The purpose of sabotage was the preservation of a national technology and national system of transportation that had been confiscated by the Nazi occupiers. The French railway company supported the movie, which was recognized at the Cannes Film Festival as a paradigm of patriotic resistance.[75]

A different example of an anti-capitalist use of railways is offered by the 'boxcar politics' of the hobos, itinerant workers who stole rides on trains between the 1870s and the Great War. Contrary to commonplaces depicting them either as selfish, individualistic travellers, refractory to any form of collective action, or as romantic figures attached to the culture of the American Frontier, these were migrant

---

74   E. P. Thompson, *The Making of the English Working Class* (Harmondsworth: Penguin, 1968), Chapter 14, notably 593–604.

75   See Sylvie Lindeperg, 'L'opération cinématographique. Équivoques idéologiques et ambivalences narratives dans *La Bataille du Rail*', *Annales: Histoire, Sciences sociales*, 51/4 (1996): 759–79; and Christian Chevandier, 'La Résistance des cheminots: le primat de la fonctionnalité plus qu'une réelle spécificité', *Le Mouvement social*, 180 (1997): 147–58.

workers who felt a sense of belonging to the American working class of their time.[76] Their wandering was the hidden dimension of the expansion of capitalism, the standardization of time and the regulation of space in a unified country. They were 'lumpen-proletarians', the poorest and most unprotected layers of the working class, but in contrast to the *Lumpen* contemptuously depicted by Marx in *The Eighteenth Brumaire of Louis Bonaparte* (1851), they did not participate in counterrevolution; they were rather the vanguard of the working class in industrializing America. They were migrant workers whose living conditions were shaped by precarity (homelessness) and mobility (seasonal labourers whose movements followed the dynamic of the labour market). As unticketed travellers in boxcars, they were lawless bodies that did not submit to the instrumental rationality of the railways. Their hopping skill in 'riding the rods' implied a form of domestication of the machines, as well as a permanent game of cat-and-mouse with the railway guards. They had their own union within the Industrial Workers of the World (IWW), and their organizers travelled illegally to cities where strikes broke out. 'By hopping trains,' John Lennon emphasizes, 'hobos, both symbolically and practically, offered their bodies as resistance to the progress of an expanding capitalist society that the transcontinental railroad promised in its billowing smoke and roaring wheels.'[77]

Since Marx's death, his nineteenth-century optimism about technology and embrace of the railways as civilizing machines began to be considered more critically by some of his disciples. Without rehabilitating the memory of the English Luddites, Rosa Luxemburg nevertheless interpreted the process of economic globalization engendered by the creation of a world market as a human and social regression. Writing sixty years after the authors of *The Communist Manifesto*, she no longer considered revolutions as the 'locomotives of history.' Almost two chapters of *The Accumulation of Capital* (1913) are devoted to the

---

76 See the classic study by Nels Anderson, *The Hobo: The Sociology of the Homeless Man* (Chicago: University of Chicago Press, 2014 [1923]). 'In spite of all that has been said to the contrary, the hobo is a worker', 91.

77 John Lennon, *Boxcar Politics: The Hobo in US Culture and Literature 1869–1956* (Boston: University of Massachusetts Press, 2014), 4.

systematic destruction of peasant economies that followed the process of industrialization in Europe and the US, as well as the building of railroads in the European colonies. 'With the railways in the van, and ruin in the rear – capital leads the way, its passage is marked with universal destruction.'[78] Instead of rescuing entire continents from barbarism, archaism, and economic stagnation, the new means of communication introduced imperial rule and a sharpened form of exploitation. In the United States, railways followed the conquest of the West, and the Frontier meant the extermination of Native Americans. In South Africa, the British 'built railroads, put down the Kaffirs, organized revolts of the *uitlanders* and finally provoked the Boer War. The bell had tolled for peasant economy.'[79] This was the accomplishment of Cecil Rhodes's 'imperialist programme'. Far from being exceptions, these events expressed a general tendency in the colonial world. 'The triumphant march of commodity economy', she wrote, 'thus begins in most cases with magnificent constructions of modern transport, such as railways lines which cross primeval forests and tunnel through the mountains, telegraph wires which bridge the desert, and ocean liners which call at the most outlying ports. But it is a mere illusion that these are peaceful changes.'[80] In fact, these transformations brought 'periodical massacres' of a 'completely helpless and peaceful agrarian population.'[81] Mike Davis establishes an organic connection between the building of Indian railways and 'late Victorian holocausts'. During the 1870s, railroads absorbed thirteen times as much investment as all hydraulic works. British promoters invested in railways rather than in irrigation, canals and drainage, and this resulted in drought, scarcity, and finally famine in 1876. Peasants starved beside the new, shining locomotives that crossed the country.[82] The optimism expressed by Marx in 1853 had been tragically contradicted.

---

78   Rosa Luxemburg, *The Accumulation of Capital* (London: Routledge & Kegan Paul, 2003), 391.

79   Ibid., 396.

80   Ibid., 366–7.

81   Ibid., 367.

82   See the testimony of Lord Salisbury in Mike Davis, *Late Victorian Holocausts: El Niño Famines and the Making of the Third World* (London: Verso, 2001), 332.

'Máquinas Locas'

Railways played a significant role in the Mexican Revolution, once more putting into question the historical relationship between machines and human agency, between capitalist economic rationality and moral economy. During the nineteenth century they appeared as a symbol of progress and modernization, incessantly celebrated by the ruling elites. The project to connect the Pacific and Atlantic coasts of the country by train had been conceived in the 1830s, and the first railway line between Mexico City and Veracruz was inaugurated in 1873. Under the Porfiriato, the presidency of General Porfirio Díaz between 1876 and 1911, Mexico experienced a true railway boom, with an extension of its line network from 398 to more than 15,000 miles. On the eve of the revolution, the building of a national network was accomplished.[83] Railways were supposed to lift the country out of poverty and backwardness, bringing modernity and economic development. As in many other Latin American nations, liberalism viewed railways as the embodiment of the famous positivist motto: 'Order and Progress'.[84] Promoted by foreign investors, mostly British and American, railways opened the country to the world market and stimulated the beginning of modern industrialization. They also fuelled the concentration of landed property, with the extension of the *hacendado* (agrarian monopolies) and the reinforcement of a landlord aristocracy. In other words, what urban elites celebrated as the advent of progress was experienced by indigenous communities as a massive process of expropriation. Wherever the railroad appeared, traditional peasant communities were destroyed. The decades of the Porfiriato were dogged by campesino rebellions against the construction of railroads, which engendered a contradictory cultural landscape: on the one hand, progress idealized and defended as a positivist belief, codified by the official discourse and spread by the newspapers as a truism in public opinion; on the

---

83   See Teresa Van Hoy, *A Social History of Mexico's Railroads: Peons, Prisoners, and Priests* (Lanham: Rowman and Littlefield Publishers, 2008).

84   See Michael Matthews, *The Civilizing Machine: A Cultural History of Mexican Railroads 1876–1910* (Lincoln: University of Nebraska Press, 2013), 253. The author quotes a tasty poem by Miguel Bolaños Cacho that juxtaposes Marx and Comte as harbingers of Progress, 85.

other hand, a popular culture made of songs and oral storytelling that unveiled the reality of uprooted communities.[85] Mexico had become a paradigm for the antipodal diagnostics of modernity we mentioned above, a duality which existed within revolutionary culture itself. For the advocates of progress, its railway network illustrated what Marx and Engels called, in *The Communist Manifesto*, the 'civilizing' mission of capital.[86] Viewed from a different perspective, Mexico showed eloquently what Rosa Luxemburg called the 'universal destruction' brought by capitalism as a global economic system. These tensions exploded during the Mexican Revolution.

Between 1911 and 1917, railroads were constantly used by both government troops and rebellious forces. The former moved and joined the front lines almost exclusively by train; the latter preferred horses – the Mexican Revolution has entered our collective memory through the image of Villa and Zapata's cavalries, with riders wearing wide sombreros and bandoliers across their chests – but soon learned to make the most of railways, which broke their isolation and transformed a mass of sedentary peasants into an army of nomadic fighters. Trains transported troops, arms, food, fuel, and families, as well as doctors, nurses and wounded soldiers. They displaced the front lines, accelerated the movement of the belligerent forces and abruptly changed the power balance between them. Once a territory had been conquered, trains became caserns with offices, kitchens and hospitals. In *Insurgent Mexico* (1914), John Reed gives an admiring – and no doubt idealized – description of Villa's trains:

But Villa, although he had never heard of the Rules of War, carried with his army the only field hospital of any effectiveness that any Mexican army has ever carried. It consisted of forty box-cars enameled inside, fitted with operating tables and all the latest appliances of surgery, and manned by more than sixty doctors and nurses. Every day during the battle shuttle trains full of the desperately wounded ran from the front to the base hospitals at Parral, Jiménez and

---

85   See John Coatsworth, 'Railroads, Landholding, and Agrarian Protest in the Early Porfiriato', *Hispanic American Historical Review*, 54/1 (1974): 48–71.

86   *MECW*, vol. 6, 488.

Zapatista Train, Cuernavaca (1911).

Chihuahua. He took care of the Federal wounded just as carefully as of his own men. Ahead of his own supply train went another train, carrying two thousand sacks of flour, and also coffee, corn, sugar, and cigarettes to feed the entire starving population of the country around Durango City and Torreón.[87]

In a very short time, rebels learned to use trains proficiently and effectively, but their relationship with these modern means of transportation was purely instrumental: trains allowed them to win strategic battles or, pursuing a long tradition of peasant insurgency, to sabotage enemy citadels. In 1914, Pancho Villa's División del Norte conquered Torreón by mobilizing fifteen trains that transported troops, supplies, and even, as mentioned above, a military hospital equipped for surgery. Three years earlier, however, he had led a successful offensive on Ciudad Juárez with his soldiers hidden inside a freight train transformed into a Trojan horse, then protected this military bastion by cutting the railway lines. On many occasions, locomotives became bombs thrown against the enemy: the 'crazy machines' (*máquinas locas*) which so

87 John Reed, *Insurgent Mexico* (New York: D. Appleton, 1914), 144.

deeply penetrated the popular imagination. Sabotage was so frequent that in 1914 the railway lines were completely militarized.

For conservative propaganda, the cutting of railway lines and use of locomotives as instruments of sabotage were incontestable evidence of revolutionary barbarism. No doubt, the insurgent peasants were Mexican Luddites. This vision found a literary form in Mariano Azuela's *The Underdogs* (1915), one of the most important novels of the Revolution. It describes rebels invading a luxury bourgeois residence and destroying its precious furniture. Their vandalism does not spare the library, and particularly a rare edition of Dante's *Divine Comedy*, whose value is obviously unknown to them.[88] The Mexican Revolution was an act of barbarism against civilization. This is exactly the vision which one of the characters of Rafael Muñoz's *Vámonos con Pancho Villa* (1931) expresses in apodictic terms: 'a decivilizing wave' (*una ola decivilizatoria*).[89] A highly picturesque and enjoyable description of the Mexican revolutionary train is given by another great writer, Martín Luis Guzmán, in his novel *The Eagle and the Serpent* (1928), which explores the subversion of 'order and progress' implicit in the rebellious use of modern machines. The ordinary rationality of railway transportation – precise timetables and itineraries, the distinction between freight and passenger trains, ticket controls and the separation of passengers into classes – had been completely jettisoned. Trains had become sites of chaos and disorder, where rebels felt perfectly at home. Guzmán writes:

> The state of things was eloquently reflected in the passengers. To the destruction – or great deterioration – of the material instruments and mechanisms had followed a corresponding descent and deterioration in the spiritual make-up of those who still employed the damaged instruments. At every point life on the train showed

---

88   Mariano Azuela, *The Underdogs: A Novel of the Mexican Revolution*, trans. Ilan Stavans and Anna More (New York: Norton, 2015), 183. On railroads and the 'novelists of Revolution', see the excellent study by Jorge Raffinelli, 'Trenes revolucionarios: La mitología del tren en el imaginario de la Revolución', *Revista Mexicana de Sociología*, 51/2 (1989): 296.

89   Ibid., 298.

clearly a return to the primitive. The structured complexity of civilization was only partial effective. The distinction between freight and passenger cars had disappeared; coaches and boxcars were used interchangeably for the same purposes. As a result, the difference between people and bundles had disappeared; in certain places men, women and children were piled up like bundles; in other places suitcases and trunks were riding in the seats. But, even more, all the distinctions that link one's idea of bodily decorum to such things as chairs, tables and beds were gone. The passengers seemed nowhere so much at ease as in the freight cars, where they stretched out or sat up on the floor as they pleased. And there, as in the aisles and on the platforms of the coaches, a new pleasure, long forgotten, was rediscovered: that of eating on the floor, amidst all the dirt and the rubbish. At first, a few passengers, not caught up as yet in the rising tide of barbarism, attempted to stem the disorderliness a little; but they soon desisted. The tendency was like a snow-slide; only violent measures could have held it back.[90]

Thus, Villa's and Zapata's fighters learned to appreciate the benefits of modern technology – Zapata travelled between Cuernavaca and Mexico City by train, keeping his horse in a wagon – without abandoning the spirit of their Luddite ancestors, the English machine breakers. Trains connected the country with the cities and integrated the rural communities into the national market, but this was not the revolutionaries' goal. As Adolfo Gilly has magisterially explained, the Commune of Morelos was a form of rural communism grounded in the peasant tradition of collective land ownership. The Zapatistas were not interested in building the future as a modern, technological society. The development of productive forces was not their principal concern. Their utopia lay in the past, not the future.[91] When Villa and Zapata met in Mexico City on 6 December 1914, merging their armies, they felt uncomfortable. Their democracy was the emptiness of power: a

---

90   Martín Luis Guzmán, *The Eagle and the Serpent*, trans. Harriet de Onís (Gloucester, MA: Peter Smith, 1969), 126.

91   Adolfo Gilly, *The Mexican Revolution* (London: New Left Books, 1983), Chapter 8.

body neither represented nor incorporated into a central institution.[92] They wished to establish a decentralized system of egalitarian peasant collectivities, not to control a central power. Their upheaval reminds us of Marx's interest in the Russian *obschina* during his correspondence with Vera Zasulich, rather than his enthusiasm for modern railways.

Armoured Trains

Even more than in Mexico, railways played a strategic role in the Russian Revolution – particularly during its bloody civil war, from 1918 to 1921. But the multiple, interwoven dimensions they evinced in Marx's nineteenth-century narrative had now dramatically collapsed. After Plekhanov and Lenin's vigorous intellectual battle against Populism in the 1890s, Marxism entered Russia as a discourse of radical modernization.[93] All its interpreters, regardless of their political allegiance, were disparagers of Tsarist obscurantism and Russian backwardness, as well as partisans of progress and industrialization. Most of them had received a cosmopolitan education in exile that made them convinced Westernizers. They disagreed on the character of the Russian revolution, variously attributing to it 'bourgeois', 'democratic' or immediately 'socialist' goals, and had different appreciations of the relations between forces and the degree of Russian insertion into the global world. The Mensheviks foresaw a period of capitalist development which would lay the groundwork for socialism, whereas Trotsky, joined by Lenin and the Bolsheviks in 1917, viewed the construction of socialism as a global process, which could be set in motion by a socialist revolution in backward Russia before being fulfilled by the proletarian forces of advanced Western countries. All of them identified socialism with the development of productive forces, the condition for extracting Russia from feudalism

---

92   This conception of democracy is reminiscent of that developed in Claude Lefort, *Democracy and Political Theory* (Cambridge: Polity Press, 1991).

93   See Leopold Haimson, *The Russian Marxists and the Origins of Bolshevism* (Cambridge, MA: Harvard University Press, 1955); Andrzej Walicki, *The Controversy over Capitalism: Studies in the Social Philosophy of the Russian Populists* (Oxford: Clarendon, 1969).

and its 'Asiatic' indolence. In his preface to the French and German editions of *Imperialism* (1920), Lenin stressed the role of railroads as paradigms of modernization: 'a summation and the most striking index of the development of world trade and bourgeois-democratic civilization'.[94] In a famous formula, he defined socialism as 'government by the Soviets plus electrification'.[95] This cyclopean project of transforming the Soviet Union into a modern, industrial colossus would be fulfilled by Stalinism from the end of the 1920s onwards.[96] During the civil war, however, the Russian economy collapsed, its infrastructure was deeply damaged by military conflict, production fell far below pre-war levels, and famine arose. The Bolsheviks struggled for survival and, in such dramatic circumstances, they decided to militarize the railways. 'Without railways,' Lenin lucidly recognized in April 1918, 'not only will there be no socialism, but everyone will starve to death like dogs.'[97]

In the springtime of 1918, the Russian territory controlled by the Bolsheviks corresponded to the size of the old Moscow principality, and they possessed only one third of a railroad network of 35,000 lines, largely destroyed or disorganized. Seventy per cent of the locomotives were unfit for use. It was by mobilizing the inexhaustible energies of despair, as Victor Serge stressed in his autobiography, that they built the Red Army, repelled counter-revolutionary attacks, forced back the international military intervention, gained the support of the peasantry, and finally won the civil war.[98] In the months that followed the treaty of Brest-Litovsk, Soviet power was on the brink of collapsing: German troops occupied Poland, the Baltic countries, Belorussia and Ukraine, with the support of Denikin's White Army;

94 Vladimir I. Lenin, 'Imperialism: The Highest Stage of Capitalism', *LCW*, vol. 31, 190.

95 Vladimir I. Lenin, 'Our Foreign and Domestic Position and Party Tasks' (1920), ibid., 408–26.

96 See Stephen Kotkin, *Magnetic Mountain: Stalinism as Civilization* (Berkeley: University of California Press, 1997).

97 Vladimir I. Lenin, 'Session of the All Russia C.E.C.' (April 29, 1918), *LCW*, vol. 27, 309.

98 Victor Serge, *Memoirs of a Revolutionary*, trans. Peter Sedgwick (New York: New York Review of Books, 2012), Chapters 3 and 4.

a Czechoslovakian contingent had taken the Trans-Siberian railway line; British troops occupied the Caucasus and the northern territories of Archangel and Murmansk, while the White Guards of Kolchak advanced in Siberia and the Urals. Three years later, the Soviet regime had reconquered most of the territories of the former Tsarist empire. In this time span, the Soviet military forces grew spectacularly. In October 1917, the Red Guards had 4,000 men in Petrograd and 3,000 in Moscow; three years later the Red Army numbered more than 5 million.[99] The architect of this spectacular reconstruction was Leon Trotsky, an intellectual and a revolutionary leader with no military training, who had lived in exile until May 1917. According to several military historians, this reconquest took place along the railway lines, whose role was decisive (much more so than in the American Civil War, fifty years earlier).[100] In 1920, the Red Army possessed 103 armoured trains. It is true that mounted troops – immortalized by Isaac Babel in *Red Cavalry* in the 1920s – won strategic battles, but the war logistics, that is, the transportation of arms, troops and supplies, in the last instance depended on the railroads.

In his autobiography, written in 1929 from his Turkish exile, Trotsky devotes an entire chapter to the armoured train in which he had established his headquarters. 'During the most strenuous years of the revolution', he writes, 'my own personal life was bound up inseparably with the life of that train. The train, on the other hand, was inseparably bound up with the life of the Red Army. The train linked the front with the base, solved urgent problems on the spot, educated, appealed, supplied, rewarded, and punished.'[101] He gives a detailed description of this vehicle that functioned as 'a flying apparatus of administration'.[102] It included several offices which hosted secretaries,

99   Eric Wollenberg, *The Red Army* (London: New Park Publications, 1978 [1938]), 43; Isaac Deutscher, *The Prophet Armed: Trotsky 1879–1921* (London: Verso, 2004 [1954]), 405.

100   G. Balfour, *The Armoured Train: Its Development and Usage* (London: B.T. Batsford Ltd, 1981), quoted in Nicholas Bujalski, *Trotsky's Train and the Production of Soviet Space* (Ithaca: Cornell University working paper, 2013), 17. This seminar paper is the best study of the topic.

101   Leon Trotsky, *My Life* (New York: Charles Scribner's Sons, 1930), 323.

102   Ibid., 325.

stenographers, and advisors, as well as a telegraph, a radio station, a generator, a small printing shop, a kitchen, dining rooms, dormitories and bathrooms. It had a wagon with two cars, which allowed Trotsky to travel inland after arriving at a railway station. The chief of the Red Army had his own library, where he studied, wrote articles and even books, in particular *Terrorism and Communism* (1920), an ardent defence of Bolshevik terror against Karl Kautsky.[103] The train published a newspaper with a 'beatnik' title, *On the Road* (*V Puti*), which had a print run of 4,500 copies. It was propelled by two locomotives and, of course, it was equipped with artillery engines and machine guns. According to several scholars, Trotsky covered more than 100,000 km on this train.[104]

Chugging incessantly between front lines, sometimes the train was attacked or involved in military operations. Trotsky describes it as a 'staff headquarters on wheels' and a fighting instrument. He stresses that 'all the crew could handle arms. They all wore leather uniforms, which always make men look heavily imposing. On the left arm, just below the shoulder, each wore a large metal badge, carefully cast at the mint, which had acquired great popularity in the army. The cars were connected by telephone and by a system of signals.'[105] In two and a half years, this train provided accommodation for 405 people, and several of its soldiers were lost in battle.

During the civil war, Trotsky's train fulfilled both a strategic and a symbolic function.[106] It was the mobile war room of the Red Army, and also the messenger of the Bolshevik word. It connected all units with the army as a whole and relieved the isolation of its most remote sections along a front that stretched for 8,000 kilometres. Frequently, Trotsky spoke to the soldiers from the train. Very quickly,

---

103 Leon Trotsky, *Terrorism and Communism: A Reply to Karl Kautsky* (London: Verso, 2007 [1921]).

104 Robert Argenbright, 'Documents from Trotsky's Train in the Russian State Military Archive: A Comment', *Journal of Trotsky Studies*, 4 (1996): 9; N. S. Tarkhova, 'Trotsky's Train: An Unknown Page in the History of the Civil War', in Terry Brotherstone and Paul Duke (eds), *The Trotsky Reappraisal* (Edinburgh: Edinburgh University Press, 1992), 27.

105 Trotsky, *My Life*, 329.

106 See Bujalski, *Trotsky's Train*.

Red Armoured Train (1919).

Trotsky leaving his Armoured Train (1920).

this armoured train achieved an almost mythical dimension. In a tragic context of penury and economic disorganization, it did not epitomize the expansion of productive forces, but rather the conquering advance of world revolution. After the fall of the Central powers in November 1918 and the outbreak of revolutions in Germany and Hungary, Trotsky's armoured train materialized the promise of a connection between Soviet Russia and an imminent socialist upheaval in the West. On 8 November 1918, the day of the fall of the Hohenzollern empire in Germany, in a speech given at the military academy, the chief of the Red Army affirmed: 'Karl Marx says that revolution is the locomotive of history. And that is true.'[107] Disconnected from the cosmopolitan dynamic of world capitalism – an economic system whose general and irreversible crisis the Bolsheviks had diagnosed in the first four congresses of the Third International, between 1919 and 1922 – revolution appeared as a locomotive of history in the literal meaning of the word. It was driving Europe into socialism. Soviet Russia was running towards the future through an incredible acceleration of history: time seemed compressed and socialist utopia was temporalized by the building of a new society.

In 1920, the Bolsheviks dreamed of organizing the next congress of the Communist International in Berlin. The same year, the Congress of the Peoples of the East took place in Baku, Azerbaijan. Giving the closing speech, Zinoviev announced that the twentieth century would be a time of the liberation of colonial world, a gigantic wave of global emancipation as powerful as it was irresistible. And the ruling classes of the entire continent felt seriously threatened by this prospect. The *cordon sanitaire* which the Western powers assembled at Versailles in 1919 decided to build around Soviet Russia was both military and diplomatic: it was an international coalition comparable to the aristocratic alliance that marched against the French Revolution in 1792, and a political wall that tried to circumscribe and stop a contagion which, born in Petrograd and Moscow, threatened to spread to the whole planet. In 1921, at the apogee of the railway age, the 'world spirit' (*Weltgeist*) no longer travelled on a white horse: the portrait of Napoleon that, according to legend, Hegel depicted in Jena in 1806, had become obsolete. Now, the world spirit ran on an armoured train. The Great War had transformed the socialist revolution into a military action, which the Bolsheviks codified as a strategic paradigm: the locomotive of history could not but be armoured.

In the age of the crisis of capitalism, both classical liberalism and social democracy had exhausted their historical role. Capitalism had

---

107   Leon Trotsky, *How the Revolution Armed: The Military Writing and Speeches of Leon Trotsky*, trans. Brian Pearce (London: New Park Publications, 1979–81), vol. 1, 206.

paused its expansion, the world market had become the locus of a world economic depression and the bourgeoisie had turned counter-revolutionary, like its aristocratic ancestors in 1789. As for socialism, it could no longer cherish the illusion that triumph would automatically follow its electoral advances, as irresistible as the exponential rise of coal, steel and railroads. The age of progress and peaceful economic development was over. Revolution could no longer be thought of as the result of an organic process of social evolution; like in 1792, it became a military art, a question of tactics and strategy. The locomotives of history ceased to be symbols of technological acceleration and turned into purely political motors. Trotsky resolved the ambiguities of Marx's metaphor, which now expressed the 'autonomy of the political'.

The End of a Myth

Trotsky's armoured train epitomizes at once the apogee and the end of a revolutionary imagination founded on the metaphor of locomotives. From the end of the 1920s, trains abandoned the allegorical realm of revolution to symbolize instead Soviet society's surge towards modernity, industrialism and technological progress. A propaganda poster

Yury Pimenov, *Against Religion, For Industrial and Financial Plan, Complete Five-Year Plan in Four Years* (1930). Soviet Poster.

Soviet Poster (1939).

from 1930 depicts a high-speed iron horse launched on the road to the
future, against a background of factories and chimneys, framed by a
slogan announcing the first five-year plan fulfilled in four years, and
sweeping away everything in its path, notably religious prejudice and
other bourgeois calamities such as selfishness, drunkenness, laziness,
and patriarchy, embodied by different representatives of the old order.
After the end of the 1920s, trains became a predilect symbol of Soviet
propaganda celebrating the dreams and achievements of a new civilization: cosmopolitanism; industrial development; modernization of
backward regions; socialism as the fraternal fusion of European and
Asian peoples; and female emancipation (as travellers and railroaders,
they acquire independence and rush towards modernity).

In a broader historical perspective, it is the Great War that exhausted
the railway age. At the end of the nineteenth century, the second
industrial revolution transformed the energy sources of capitalist
development: coal and steam were replaced by oil and electricity.
Speed and strength took on a new dimension, related to dynamo

and combustion engines. Aircraft became the new symbol of the annihilation of space and time.[108] In 1909, Louis Blériot performed the first flight across the English Channel, showing to the world the accomplishments of 'French scientific genius combined with French élan and sang-froid'.[109] His flight opened the century of aviation, just as the first train link between Manchester and Liverpool in 1830 had inaugurated the century of railways. But aviation developed even faster than transport on rails. In 1927, Charles Lindbergh performed the first transatlantic solo flight from New York to Paris. Alongside airplanes, automobiles also appeared. Just before the outbreak of war, the Ford auto plants of Detroit began to produce vehicles through assembly lines. Cars shortly became the new symbols of mass transportation. Of course, trains were not abandoned, but their sovereign position in mass culture had been dethroned. Locomotives no longer materialized the utopian vision of a world hurtling towards the future. During the three decades of the European civil war, however, no comparable icons did appear. Immediately identified with war and destruction, aircraft were almost naturally incorporated first into nationalist, then into fascist imaginaries.[110] Hermann Goering, who had been a pilot during the First World War, was appointed to head the German Luftwaffe in 1935. In the same year, Leni Riefenstahl shot *Triumph of the Will*, a propaganda movie that opened with Hitler flying and landing in Nuremberg, like a Teutonic god, to attend the congress of the Nazi party. Mussolini was proud of his (limited) talents as an aircraft pilot and liked to be portrayed in the air (as in many futurist *aeroritratti*). Marinetti, the founder of futurism who joined the fascists in the 1920s, hailed the beauty of air warfare with its 'geometrical formation flights' and the 'smoking spirals from burning villages', while, in 1931, fascism celebrated the transatlantic flight to Rio de Janeiro

---

108   See Robert Wohl, *A Passion for Wings: Aviation and the Western Imagination 1908–1918* (New Haven: Yale University Press, 1994). On the advent of a new culture of speed, see Philipp Blom, *The Vertigo Years: Europe 1900–1914* (New York: Basic Books, 2008).

109   Quoted in Wohl, *A Passion for Wings*, 66.

110   On the relationship between flying and fascism, see Robert Wohl, *The Spectacle of Flight: Aviation and the Western Imagination 1920–1950* (New Haven: Yale University Press, 2005), especially Chapter 2.

by Italo Balbo, chief of the Italian Air Force and governor-general of Libya. In popular culture and political propaganda, pilots were iconic figures of virility, misogyny, and national strength. Aircraft as a means of mass destruction – which H. G. Wells had early foreseen in his *War in the Air* (1908)[111] – had been trialled to a limited extent during the First World War, then on a larger scale during the Ethiopian Wars and the Spanish Civil War, and finally hugely employed between 1939 and 1945 to annihilate entire cities. After Guernica and Hiroshima, airplanes could not easily become metaphors of revolutionary imagination.

In the century of mass culture and the assembly line, however, the end of railway mythology did not extinguish the allegorical function of locomotives. The discrepancy between a 'determinist' and a 'constructivist' Marx, or the conflict opposing the advocates of human emancipation *through* labour and those of liberation *from* labour seemed eclipsed, at the time of the European crisis, by a titanic clash between revolution and counterrevolution, communism and fascism, finally transformed into mechanical Molochs. The symbiotic relationship between human beings and machines acquired a new dimension. Liberation from work became a utopian option promulgated by marginal and heretical left-wing currents, whereas a redemptive vision of work (in collaboration with powerful machines) thoroughly permeated the hegemonic tendencies of socialist culture. In the eleventh of his theses on the concept of history, written in the first months of 1940, Walter Benjamin observed that the Protestant work ethic had been 'resurrected' by German social democracy 'in secularized form'. This 'vulgar-Marxist' conception of work as 'the source of all wealth and culture' – already codified by the Gotha Programme in 1875 – identified socialism with the development of the forces of production, with the result of recognizing 'only the progress in the mastery of nature, not in the retrogression of society'. And this fetishism of technique reminded him of 'the technocratic features which later emerged in fascism'.[112] This observation curiously avoids any reference to the most evident expression of this 'redemptive' concept, which at the

---

111   H. G. Wells, *The War in the Air* (London: Penguin, 2011).
112   Benjamin, 'On the Concept of History', *WBSW*, vol. 4, 393.

height of triumphant Stalinism was the myth of Stakhanov, the 'hero of socialist labour'. In 1935, Aleksei G. Stakhanov, a miner from the Donbass, had embodied the 'new man' of Soviet society by breaking all previous records for productivity. Heroic labourers and five-year plans merged in a vision of socialism as a Promethean building of a modern, industrialized world. In the same years, the nationalist German writer Ernst Jünger announced the advent of the Age of the Worker (*der Arbeiter*), the worker-soldier forged in the trenches of the Great War.[113] This fusion of nihilism and technology appeared to Hans Kohn as 'the apotheosis of a thoroughly mechanized and militarized worker, a modern machine-man'.[114] The military competition between Bolshevism and fascism had become a clash between two totalitarian machines. To reference Hannah Arendt, the triumph of *homo faber* had turned to madness.[115]

Thus, in the years between the two world wars, Marx's metaphor for revolutions as the 'locomotives of history' began to raise doubts, to the point where it was radically put into question. Romantic anticapitalism broke the boundaries of 'scientific' socialism and outlined a new profile of critical thought. Progress appeared as a dangerous illusion, a synonym of catastrophe, and fascism began to be perceived as a product of modernity, a barbarism engendered by the march of civilization itself. It was Walter Benjamin, a heterodox Marxist, who turned Marx's metaphor upside-down. He proposed a radically antipositivistic historical materialism that would have 'annihilated in itself the idea of progress'.[116] The paralipomena to his (now) famous theses

---

113   Ernst Jünger, *The Worker: Dominion and Form*, ed. Laurence Paul Hemming (Chicago: Northwestern University Press, 2017 [1932]).

114   Hans Kohn, 'The Totalitarian Philosophy of War', *Proceedings of the American Philosophical Society*, 82/1 (1939): 62.

115   On the distinction between labour (*animal laborans*), work (*homo faber*), and action (*vita activa*), see Hannah Arendt, *The Human Condition*, ed. Margaret Canovan (Chicago: University of Chicago Press, 1998 [1958]). On the 'madness' of *homo faber*, see Marco Revelli, *Oltre il Novecento: La politica, le ideologie e le insidie del lavoro* (Turin: Einaudi, 2001), 41–8. On the Bolshevism and fascism conflict between the two world wars, see Enzo Traverso, *Fire and Blood: The European Civil War 1914–1945* (London: Verso, 2016).

116   Benjamin, *Arcades Project*, 460.

The Ramp of Auschwitz.

on the concept of history contain the following sentence: 'Marx says that revolutions are the locomotives of history. But perhaps it is quite otherwise. Perhaps revolutions are an attempt by the passengers on this train – namely, the human race – to activate the emergency brake.'[117]

Putting it otherwise, history is running towards catastrophe. This is its secret telos. Revolution is not a roaring locomotive pulling civilization forwards; it is rather a conscious action to stop the tragic race of this train before it attains its destination. Instead of accelerating time and accomplishing its internal logic, revolution should break this linear historical time and open a new (messianic) time. Benjamin's definition of revolution mirrors the most dramatic moment of the twentieth century: its taste is as apocalyptic as Marx's fascination for locomotives was optimistic. Marx celebrated the 'demonic energy' of industrial capitalism and the rising workers' movement. Benjamin wrote in 1940, when it was 'midnight in the century'. Today, railways evoke Auschwitz sooner than glorious revolutions.

117   Walter Benjamin, 'Paralipomena to "On the Concept of History"', *WBSW*, vol. 4, 402.

Chapter 2

Revolutionary Bodies

Hegel, who stands everything on its head, turns the executive power into the representative, into the emanation, of the monarch. Since in speaking of the idea the existence of which is supposed to be the monarch, he has in mind not the real idea of the executive authority, not the executive authority as idea, but the subject of the absolute idea which exists *bodily* in the monarch, the executive authority becomes a *mystical extension of the soul which exists in* his body, *the body of the monarch.*

> Karl Marx, *Contribution to the Critique of Hegel's Philosophy of Law* (1843)

The woman in communist society no longer depends upon her husband but on her work ... Marriage will lose all the elements of material calculation which cripple family life. Marriage will be a union of two persons who love and trust each other. Such a union promises to the working men and women who understand themselves and the world around them the most complete happiness and the maximum satisfaction.

> Alexandra Kollontai, *Communism and the Family* (1920)

Marc Chagall, *Forward, Forward!* (1918). Gouache.
Musée National d'Art Moderne, Paris.

Insurgent Bodies

At the end of 1918, when he was Commissar for the Arts in Vitebsk, Marc Chagall painted *Forward, Forward!*, a canvas which he described as a study for the anniversary of the October Revolution. In this picture, revolution is evoked as a strip that, like a rainbow, rises through the blue sky while a young figure wearing traditional Russian clothes leaps forward over a village at the bottom. Revolution is a jump toward the future. In his autobiography, Chagall tells us that Lenin had turned Russia upside-down, just as he had flipped his pictures.[1] Many of the masterpieces he painted between 1918 and 1922, the time in which he led the People's School of Art in Vitebsk, are dominated by free-floating figures – peasants, rabbis, young lovers – reminiscent of the Jewish *luftmenshn*, aerial human beings. Still twenty years later, he realized *Revolution* (1937), a work in which Lenin appears as a kind of acrobat, upside-down with his arm stretched over a table, in front of a reluctant rabbi, in a landscape of civil war and red flags.

---

1 Marc Chagall, *My Life* (New York: Orion Press, 1960), 137. On Chagall's paintings of that time, see Angela Lampe (ed.), *Chagall, Lissitzky, Malevich: The Russian Avant-Garde in Vitebsk, 1918–1922* (London: Prestel, 2018).

Forward, Forward! tellingly portrays the revolution as it was perceived by its actors: a jump toward the future and a feeling of weightlessness. This feeling can very well coexist with the worst material conditions – the ravages of war, food shortages, penury – and arises from the deep conviction that everything is changing, that the old world is finishing and a new one is coming, brought about by a transformation from below. Building a new society is a difficult task, a titanic ambition that requires enormous sacrifices and whose outcome still remains uncertain, but the present is shaped by this exciting sensation of possessing wings and overcoming the law of gravity, a sensation that affects bodies like an electric pulse and energizes them. Revolution is also a corporeal experience.

Both actors and witnesses of revolutions have been astonished by the unexpected and extraordinary spectacle of the strength of human beings who suddenly merged and acted as a single body. When the vitality and intelligence of the multitude converge in conscious unity – the opposite of a heterogeneous mass or an urban crowd gathered from atomized elements – everything becomes possible. There is no need to invoke Hegel's well-used dialectical law of the transformation of quantity into quality in order to explain a phenomenon illustrated by many historical events. 'Storming the heavens': this image already quoted in the previous chapter captures the substance of this revolutionary mood.

Let me start from the witnesses, and not even the sympathetic ones. In his *Recollections* (1850), devoted to the French revolution of 1848, Tocqueville gives a remarkable description of the spectacle of Paris conquered by the labouring classes during the February uprising:

I spent the whole afternoon in walking about Paris. Two things in particular struck me: the first was, I will not say the mainly, but the unique and exclusively popular character of the revolution that had just taken place; the omnipotence it had given to the people properly so-called – that is to say, the classes who work with their hands – over all others. The second was the comparative absence of malignant passion, or, as a matter of fact, of any keen passion

– an absence that at once made it clear that the lower orders had suddenly become masters of Paris.[2]

In the French Revolution, the public scene had been dominated by men of letters coming from the bourgeois elite whereas the working class, despite their massive mobilization, 'had never been the sole leaders and masters of the state, either *de facto* or *de jure*.'[3] In 1848, on the contrary, Tocqueville observed with astonishment, revolution 'seemed to be made entirely outside the bourgeoisie and against it'. This was something new and frightening for the ruling classes. 'Nothing more novel', he added, 'had been known in our annals.' During the February insurrection, all representatives of the institutions of the July Monarchy as well as its repressive organs, from the army and the police up to the National Guard, had disappeared. The result was the complete overthrow of the 'natural' order of things. What appeared even more surprising in Tocqueville's eyes was the fact that, instead of spreading chaos, this meant the creation of a new order:

> The people alone bore arms, guarded the public buildings, watched, gave orders, punished; it was an extraordinary and terrible thing to see in the sole hands of those who possessed nothing all this immense town, so full of riches, or rather this immense nation: for, thanks to centralization, he who reigns in Paris governs France. Hence the affright of all the other classes was extreme; I doubt whether at any period of the Revolution it had been so great, and I would say that it was only to be compared to that which the civilized cities of the Roman Empire must have experienced when they suddenly found themselves in the power of the Goths and Vandals.[4]

In the following pages, Tocqueville takes off the mantle of the frightened observer and adopts an empathic style by describing the emotion he felt when, during the repression of the June uprising, he was once again surrounded by his aristocratic and bourgeois fellows. He was

2 Alexis de Tocqueville, *Recollections* (New York: McMillan, 1896), 92.

3 Ibid., 93.

4 Ibid., 94.

touched at recognizing among them 'many landlords, lawyers, doctors and farmers who were [his] friends and neighbours', and he felt relief after the massacre that followed the insurrection. In his words, counter-revolution had 'delivered the nation from the tyranny of the Paris workingmen and restored it to possession of itself'.[5]

The events of June 1848 revealed the birth of a new political body: the constitution of the oppressed and the labouring classes into a historical subject. In his recollections Tocqueville mentions some individual figures, and even describes the barricades, but it is only when speaking of his own class that he distinguishes its members ('landlords, lawyers, doctors'). Describing the popular classes of Paris, he paints them as a single body that acts by moving its different organs. He does not mention craftsmen, cobblers, carpenters, millers, carters, blacksmiths, bricklayers, washerwomen, tailors, basket makers, etc. He mentions exclusively the 'workingmen' and 'the people'. This people acted as a conscious body, what Marx, in the same years, called a 'class for itself'.[6]

It is interesting to juxtapose Tocqueville's recollections with those of an actor in another revolution. In *My Life* (1929), Leon Trotsky devotes similarly striking pages to portraying the effervescence of Petrograd in 1917 and the awakening of its proletarian classes. He did not write as an external observer but as a leader of the revolution, and so it was from inside the people itself that he experienced the molecular process through which it moved to the centre of the political stage. This meant, in his words, 'the inspired frenzy of history.'[7]

This frenzied inspiration was eminently creative. Describing the transformation of the people into a political subject, Trotsky explained the way in which he himself, a leader, had been absorbed by a people who 'suggested' the words of his speeches to him and transformed them into the wilful expression of an unconscious collective process:

I usually spoke in the Circus in the evening, sometimes quite late at night. My audience was composed of workers, soldiers, hard-working mothers, street urchins – the oppressed underdogs of the

5   Ibid., 230–1.
6   Karl Marx, 'The Poverty of Philosophy' (1847), *MECW*, vol. 6, 211.
7   Trotsky, *My Life*, 334.

capital. Every square inch was filled, every human body compressed to its limit. Young boys sat on their fathers' shoulders; infants were at their mothers' breasts. No one smoked. The balconies threatened to fall under the excessive weight of human bodies. I made my way to the platform through a narrow human trench, sometimes I was borne overhead. The air, intense with breathing and waiting, fairly exploded with shouts and with the passionate yell peculiar to the Modern Circus. Above and around me was a press of elbows, chests, and heads. I spoke from out of a warm cavern of human bodies; whenever I stretched out my hands I would touch someone, and a grateful movement in response would give me to understand that I was not to worry about it, not to break off my speech, but keep on. No speaker, no matter how exhausted, could resist the electric tension of that impassioned human throng. They wanted to know, to understand, to find their way. At times it seemed as if I felt, with my lips, the stern inquisitiveness of this crowd that had become merged into a single whole. Then all the arguments and words thought out in advance would break and recede under the imperative pressure of sympathy, and other words, other arguments, utterly unexpected by the orator but needed by these people, would emerge in full array from my subconsciousness. On such occasions I felt as if I were listening to the speaker from the outside, trying to keep pace with his ideas, afraid that, like a somnambulist, he might fall off the edge of the roof at the sound of my conscious reasoning.[8]

Instead of a charismatic leader who manipulates the masses by seducing and subjugating them with arguments, images and myths – according to a model well described by Gustave Le Bon or Mussolini – Trotsky had the impression of having become a kind of somnambulist or ventriloquist who expressed, like a medium, the voice of the mass itself, a crowd that had metamorphosed into 'a single whole'.[9]

What Trotsky described was a revolutionary body, not a crowd. The portrait of the spontaneous birth of a multitude and its transformation into an acting body has been magisterially sketched by Elias Canetti in

8   Ibid., 294.
9   Ibid., 295.

The Torch in My Ear (1981), where he narrates his participation in the Vienna riots of 15 July 1927.[10] A verdict that acquitted the policemen accused of killing workers during a demonstration had provoked an indignant reaction. The Palace of Justice immediately became the target of collective anger: flocking from the popular neighbourhoods, Viennese workers poured into the heart of the city and burned it. Canetti perfectly captured the dynamic mobilization of the popular classes of the Austrian capital. He described the irresistible physical attraction that this crowd exerted around itself and on him: 'its excitement, its advancing, and the fluency of its movement'; its swaying through the streets like a dance rhythmed by an internal, 'evil music'; its egalitarian character and the incredible strength that allowed it to overcome all fear and to reaggregate after police gunshots littered the ground with corpses; the species of fire that animated it from within, as well as the 'throbbing' in his head. He did not describe a mob with the scornful eye of Le Bon or Gabriel Tarde, who certainly recognized the contagious power and creative imagination of modern crowds but ultimately likened them to 'beasts', 'inferior races' and 'savages'.[11] Canetti was literally fascinated by the mass he had discovered that 15 July. Upon evoking that 'brightly illuminated, dreadful day', fifty-three years later, he still felt the surging of the crowd in his bones. 'It was the closest thing to a revolution that I have physically experienced', he wrote.[12] However, Canetti was not interested in revolutions. The crowd that he 'fully dissolved in', as described in his powerful recollections, was the protagonist of a dramatic but ephemeral outburst. It burned the Palace of Justice, but did not overthrow the government. Tocqueville and Trotsky, on the contrary, depicted a people constituted as a unique collective body and acting consciously to change history. Revolution, one could summarize with the words

10   Elias Canetti, *The Torch in My Ear* (New York: Farrar, Straus and Giroux, 1982), 244–52.

11   Gabriel Tarde, 'Les crimes des foules', *Archives d'anthropologie criminelle*, 7 (1892): 358; on Tarde and Le Bon, see also Susan Barrow, *Distorting Mirrors: Visions of the Crowd in Late Nineteenth-Century France* (New Haven: Yale University Press, 1981) and Robert A. Nye, *The Origins of Crowd Psychology: Gustave Le Bon and the Crisis of Mass Democracy in the Third Republic* (London: Sage Publications, 1975).

12   Canetti, *The Torch in My Ear*, 245.

of Martin Breaugh, is the plebeian experience that transforms the *animal laborans* into *ʒoon politikon*.[13]

Collective action, however, does not exhaust the diversity of revolution's fleshly experiences. The latter deal with both abstract, symbolic or metaphoric bodies – like the organs of sovereignty – and physical bodies, which, in their turn, are both people in movement and biopolitical objects. Bodies are, simultaneously, subjects and objects of revolutions: subjects of their events and objects of their consequences; subjects of their dramas and objects of their representations. Considered as historical processes, revolutions appear – and are felt by their actors – as significant moments of corporeal liberation and regeneration as well as the premises of new policies aimed at caring for and disciplining bodies. Since all these dimensions merge in the revolutionary maelstrom by creating kaleidoscopic configurations, conceptualizing this bodily experience is not an easy task. This chapter tries to explore and analyse these different dimensions in their reciprocal connections.

Animalized Bodies

Emancipatory violence never happens in isolation. The social and political break with the old regime requires a dramatic performance and a symbolic expression that affects the entire social body. There is an anthropological dimension to revolution which, at least for a while, appears as transgression. Its manifestation is usually ephemeral, but its impact on the collective imagination is durable and powerful. When Lenin defined revolutions as 'the festival of the oppressed and the exploited',[14] he suggested a metaphor that could be interpreted almost literally. Revolutions display excesses as well as a spectacularized and often ritualized violence – both symbolic and real – that is reminiscent of the bacchanals of a carnival and the authorized infringements of a festival. Many observations that Roger Caillois developed in comparing

---

13 Martin Breaugh, *The Plebeian Experience: A Discontinuous History of Political Freedom* (New York: Columbia University Press, 2013), xv.

14 Lenin, 'Two Tactics of Social-Democracy in the Democratic Revolution' (1905), *LCW*, 9: 113.

festivals and wars could be extended to revolutions. The overthrow of the old order produces a temporal interruption, a vacuum that is filled by a new social effervescence and the violation of all accepted conventions.[15]

Insurrections are usually outbursts of joyful passion, with people pouring into the streets, hugging each other, tasting the pleasure of gathering and feeling united into a warm community. There is a sensuality in this eruption of rejoicing that suddenly dissolves inhibitions and customary forms of politeness and decency, so that kissing strangers in the midst of an unknown crowd becomes a natural and delightful thing. There is an ecstasy of liberation. This explains the tendency – typical of so many revolutions – to transform a liberated square into a theatre where the historical events that have just occurred are replayed and fixed by the cameras, with men brandishing their weapons and girls carrying flags aloft like Delacroix's Marianne. Many testimonies have described the wild euphoria of those moments. But liberation may also show a different face, equally transgressive and 'sacred' but much less pleasant. Extravagance, sarcasm, offence, fury, outrage, scandal, farce, mockery and humiliation – up to and including killing – take on a 'religious resonance' that relates them to the most ancient ceremonies of human sacrifice and inscribes them into popular memory as rituals instead of reprehensible acts, murders or crimes. The more widespread and deep the social effervescence surrounding the revolution, the more impressive, if the old power shuts down, are these carnival transgressions. The enemy's body – an enemy as real as it is symbolic – is their prime target.

This carnival of corporeal atrocities usually occurs in the intense short time of the suspension of law, when the power shift is still in the making, or during the transitional moments of the revolutionary process. The paradigm of this uncontrolled, extreme, spectacularized and savage cruelty are the massacres of September 1792 – a historiographic topos of the French Revolution – perpetrated by the Parisian sans-culottes after the proclamation of the Commune and

---

15   Roger Caillois, *Man and the Sacred* (New York: Free Press, 1959), 163–80; Mikhail Bakhtin, *Rabelais and His World* (Bloomington: Indiana University Press, 1984 [1965]).

the imprisonment of the king. As several authors observed, it was an outrageous sacrificial ceremony in which blood expiated the sins of the *ancien régime*, with corpses mutilated and exhibited, then paraded through the streets like trophies. The public executions by the guillotine were not enough to satisfy the 'Dionysian impulsions' of the avenging crowds; they had to be involved in the accomplishment of justice.[16] Jules Michelet described with striking words the 'magnetic maelstrom' that swept up the spectators of these spontaneous lynchings and pushed them to participate in the atrocities: captured by dizziness, they followed the general movement and became actors of this 'awful sabbath'.[17] Revolutions are jumps into the future where, as Walter Benjamin suggested, the past is reactivated: in a flash, it irrupts into the present as an image and, as an ancestral drive, suddenly calls many conventions into question.[18]

The revolutionary carnival of 1792 reappeared in the twentieth century, with and without its paroxysmal forms of violence. Many historians of the Russian Revolution note the looting that took place in the Winter Palace after the October insurrection, when the soldiers of the Petrograd Soviet discovered, in the middle of a world war that had caused years of material privation, the tokens of aristocratic luxury: silver cutlery sets, crystal glasses, porcelain dishes and reserves of French wines. But the seizure of the Winter Palace was no 14 July; it was an action planned and managed by the Military Revolutionary Committee of the Petrograd Soviet, and the pillage was quickly stopped.[19]

Murderous carnivals took place also during the Spanish Civil War, particularly after Franco's putsch in the summer of 1936, when the Republican authorities had not yet established their own military control in the cities conquered by popular insurrections. In this time

---

16   Alain Corbin, *The Village of Cannibals: Rage and Murder in France, 1870*, trans. Arthur Goldhammer (Cambridge, MA: Harvard University Press, 1993), 87–116.

17   Jules Michelet, *Histoire de la Révolution française* (Paris: Gallimard, 1952), vol. 1.2, 1064.

18   Benjamin, 'On the Concept of History', 394.

19   John Reed, *Ten Days that Shook the World* (New York: Boni and Liveright, 1919), 336–7.

of chaos, fear and enormous social ebullience, the vacuum of central power was confirmed by the emotional and uncontrolled popular upsurge that combined joyful and awful moments. It was the time of mass execution of landowners, monks and priests by improvised anarchist squads. In Catalonia, according to the reports of foreign correspondents, insurgent forces burned and sacked practically every church and convent: 'The mob, drunk with victory, afterwards paraded the streets of Barcelona attired in the robes of ecclesiastical authorities.' Some priests had 'their heads and arms hacked off after death as a final vindictive act.'[20] The *paseos* stopped when the republican government re-established its own order.

At the end of the Second World War, popular uprisings organized by the Resistance added further episodes to this gallery of atrocities. The most notorious is probably the exhibition of Mussolini's and his mistress Claretta Petacci's corpses, on 29 April 1945, in Piazzale Loreto in Milan, hung by their feet after being booed and trampled. The myth of Il Duce's virility and overbearing sexuality turned against him.[21] In many Italian and French cities, the Liberation days saw, at the margins of joyful parades, flags and dances, the 'hideous carnival' of shaven-headed women accused of 'horizontal collaboration'.[22] The women were put up on a stage, often in the central square of a provincial town, and completely shaven: a spectacle of public humiliation amongst the insults and jeers of the audience. A newspaper from Lozère, in central

---

20   *Daily Express*, 27 July 1936, quoted in Paul Preston, *The Spanish Holocaust: Inquisition and Extermination in Twentieth-Century Spain* (New York: Norton, 2012), 224. On the Republican violence of the summer of 1936, see in particular José Luis Ledesma, *Los días de llamas de la revolución. Violencia y política en la retaguardia republicana de Zaragoza durante la guerra civil* (Zaragoza: Institución Fernando el Católico, 2003). Similar forms of anticlericalism had already taken place during the Paris Commune, with parodic ceremonies and the transformation of several churches into clubs. See Jacqueline Lalouette, 'L'anticléricalisme sous la Commune', in Michel Cordillot (ed.), *La Commune de Paris 1871: les acteurs, l'événement, les lieux* (Paris: Éditions de l'Atelier, 2020), 682–4.

21   Claudio Pavone, *A Civil War: A History of Italian Resistance* (London: Verso, 2014), 610–13.

22   See Alain Brossat, *Les Tondues: Un carnaval moche* (Paris: Manya, 1992), and Fabrice Virgili, *La France 'virile': des femmes tondues à la Libération* (Paris: Payot, 2000).

France, commented on this unpleasant show: 'The crowd is sheeplike; it can be childish and cruel. And yet it is the same crowd that, on the same morning, followed with dignity the coffins of our martyrs.'[23]

In all these episodes, the lightness and sensuality of the liberated bodies coexisted with the humiliation and offense of the injured ones in a single process which the uprising unfolded. These moments of uncontrolled violence originated from the vacuum of power, when 'the throne was empty' and all usual rules had been broken. During the French Revolution, Terror channelled and legalized violence by replacing anarchic crowd initiatives and, according to Robespierre and Danton, subjecting it to 'the sword of the law'.[24] In the Spanish Civil War, the *paseos* finished with the structuring of popular militias and the creation of a republican army. In many European countries, the establishment of new governments at the end of the Second World War put an end to extralegal executions.

These revolutionary carnivals powerfully affected collective imaginations. Between 1789 and 1794, the traumatism of the aristocracy was so profound and durable that it fed into the ideological and aesthetic representations of counterrevolution for more than a century. The lexicon of legitimism and reaction became zoological: revolutionaries were depicted as wild beasts and their bodies regularly animalized, in both propaganda pamphlets and scholarly works. According to Hippolyte Taine, author of *The Origins of Contemporary France* (1878), the Revolution had been the outburst of 'the animal instinct of revolt'. Portraying the ideal-type of its actors, he described a savage driven by his desire to destroy civilization: 'a barbarian or, worse still, a primitive animal, a grimacing, bloodthirsty and lascivious monkey that kills with sneering laughter and cavorts over the destruction that it has produced.'[25] In October 1871, the novelist Théophile Gauthier compared the Paris Commune to a city suddenly conquered by wild animals escaped from a zoo:

---

23   *La Lozère libre*, 15 October 1944, quoted in Alain Brossat, *La Libération, fête folle* (Paris: Éditions Autrement, 1994), 215.

24   Cited in Mayer, *The Furies*, 17.

25   Hippolyte Taine, *Les origines de la France contemporaine* (Paris: Laffont, 1972), 192.

In all major towns there are lion-pits, heavily barred caverns, designed to contain wild beasts, stinking animals, venomous creatures, all the refractory perversities that civilization has been unable to tame, those who love blood, those who are as amused by arson as by fireworks, those for whom theft is a delight, those for whom rape represents love, all those with the hearts of monsters, all those with deformed souls; a disgusting population, unknown in the light of day, pullulating in sinister fashion in the depths of subterranean darkness. One day it happens that a careless jailer leaves his keys in the doors of this menagerie, and the wild beasts rampage with savage roars through the horrified town. Out of the open cages leap the hyenas of '93 and the gorillas of the Commune.[26]

For the playwright Ernest Feydeau, the Commune meant the triumph of 'pure bestiality', while Maxime Du Camp described it as a peculiar case of 'ferocious lycanthropy'.[27] The women of the Paris Commune became the *pétroleuses* (fire-starters), prostitutes and criminals, bodies that had forgotten their sex and participated in riots excited by the spectacle of wildfire.[28] According to Gauthier, most Commune women 'had an air of striges and lamias' or looked like 'the moustachioed harpies of Shakespeare, by forming a hideous variety of hermaphrodites made with the ugliness of both sexes'.[29] At the end of the century, the influence of positivism pushed a naturalist novelist like Émile Zola to narrate the Commune as an example of pathology in the social body: its actors were people wasted by alcoholism and syphilis. In *Criminal Man* (1876), Cesare Lombroso, the founder of criminal anthropology,

---

26 Théophile Gauthier, *Tableau de siège: Paris, 1870–1871* (Paris: Charpentier et Cie., 1871), 373. See also Paul Lidsky, *Les écrivains contre la Commune* (Paris: La Découverte, 1999), 46.

27 Ernest Feydeau, *Consolation* (Paris: Amyot, 1872), 192; and Maxime Du Camp, *Les convulsions de Paris* (Paris: Hachette, 1880), 342; see also Lidsky, *Les écrivains contre la Commune*, 49, 60.

28 See Carolyn J. Eichner, *Surmounting the Barricades: Women in the Paris Commune* (Bloomington: Indiana University Press, 2004); Gay L. Gullickson, *Unruly Women of Paris: Images of the Commune* (Ithaca, NY: Cornell University Press, 1996).

29 Gauthier, *Tableau de siège*, 243.

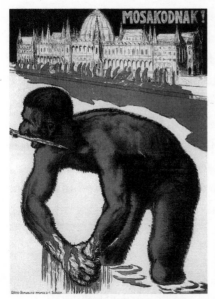

Anti-Bolshevik Propaganda Poster, Budapest, 1920 (left).
Bolshevism Brings War, Unemployment, and Starvation (1920). Poster
of the League for the Struggle Against Bolshevism, Berlin (right).

elaborated a prototype of the 'born criminal', identified by a certain
morphology – flat skull, hooked nose, protruding ears, heavy jaw,
prominent cheekbones, 'shifty' air – and assimilated to a savage, that
is, an intermediate species between ape and human. In Lombroso's
view, this type of 'born criminal' was particularly frequent amongst
regicides, terrorists, Communards and anarchists.[30]

The animalization of revolutionary bodies reached its peak in the
early 1920s, when the threat of an expansion of Bolshevism in Central
Europe became concrete with the Spartacist uprising in Berlin, the
council republics in Bavaria and Hungary, and the civil war in the Baltic
countries. At that time, nationalist posters depicted Bolshevism as a
monster whose blood was trickling into the waters of the Danube or
as a gorilla threatening the viewer with his dagger. In 1920, Winston
Churchill wrote a violent screed against the October Revolution,

---

30   Cesare Lombroso, Roberto Laschi, *Il delitto politico e le rivoluzioni* (Turin:
Bocca, 1890), 35, and Cesare Lombroso, *Criminal Man* (Durham: Duke University
Press, 2006 [1876]). On Lombroso's theory of 'criminal man', see Robert A. Nye,
*Crime, Madness, and Politics in Modern France: The Medical Concept of National
Decline* (Princeton: Princeton University Press, 1984), 97–131.

denouncing it as a catastrophic event that had thrown Russia into the hands of the 'enemies of the human race' by installing in power an 'animal form of barbarism', embodied by 'swarms of typhus-bearing vermin or troops of ferocious baboons amid the ruins of cities and corpses of their victims'. Their leader, Lenin, was a rampant monster atop a 'pile of skulls'.[31] In 1918, before the foundation of the fascist movement, Mussolini presented Bolshevism in his newspaper, *Il Popolo d'Italia*, as 'an outburst of zoological instincts'.[32] It was later, with the rise of National Socialism, that counterrevolution would replace animal metaphors with a biological racist discourse made of cancers, virus, diseases, cholera bacilli, etc.

The People's Two Bodies

The body politics of revolutions also possesses a theological dimension whose understanding requires a historical excursus. If fleshly metaphors have characterized the political lexicon since Antiquity, it was only in the sixteenth century that the analogy between natural body and political body was systematized and became a literary topos. The age of the great discoveries, which allowed the elaboration of world maps and the birth of modern cartography, was also that of a dramatic development in human anatomy. Both space and the body were carefully depicted in their components: space created by oceans, lands and rivers, and body constituted as a structure of flesh, bones, nerves and blood. One century after *De humani corporis fabrica* (1543) – Andreas Vesalius's anatomy treatise that offered the first complete representation of the human body as a complex structure of internal, hidden and interconnected organs – it became common to compare the state with a *corpus naturalis*, both of which were likened to Cartesian machines. It was Hobbes who, in the wake of John of Salisbury, Jean Bodin and Machiavelli, supplied the archetypal definition of sovereignty as a human body.[33] This metaphor opens the introduction to

31   Quoted in Sebastian Haffner, *Churchill* (London: Haus Publisher, 2005), 67.
32   Quoted in Emilio Gentile, *Mussolini contro Lenin* (Roma: Laterza, 2017), 138.
33   See Gianluca Bonaiuti, 'Di alcune metamorfosi della metafora del "corpo

Cover illustration of the original edition of Thomas Hobbes,
Leviathan (1651). Division of Rare and Manuscript
Collections, Cornell University Library.

Leviathan (1651), where the English thinker established a set of analogies between the body and the state: sovereignty as soul, prosperity as strength, laws as reason, administration as limbs, punishments as nerves, sedition as sickness, and civil war as death. Finding visual expression in his book's famous frontispiece – a Leviathan formed from the concentrated human bodies of the state's subjects – the sovereign was presented by Hobbes as an artificial person that represents, through his own body, the state's strength and virtue, and possesses a power like the head over each member of the body.[34] Abandoning the

politico" nella semantica europea', *Corpo sovrano: Studi sul concetto di popolo* (Roma: Meltemi, 2006), 15–48.

34   Thomas Hobbes, *Leviathan*, ed. C. B. Macpherson (London: Penguin Classics, 1985), 227–28.

old medieval doctrine of the divine right of kings, Hobbes defined the state as the result of a mutual contract by which everyone willingly alienated himself to a superior authority. The 'mortal God' embodying sovereignty emanated from the people, which was transcended by absolute power. Thus, the Hobbesian anthropomorphic metaphor of power lay in a new definition of the source of sovereignty, lying not with God but with the people, the 'great multitude' of the subjects. It merged a mythical representation – the biblical image of Leviathan – with a juridical construction that related the legitimacy of power to the consent of human beings.

If Hobbes's *Leviathan* epitomizes the transition from medieval political theology to the modern theory of sovereignty, its powerful visual representation is still based upon a conceptual dualism between the people as the new source of power's legitimacy, and the sovereign as a 'mortal God'. From this point of view, it does not call into question the doctrine of the 'king's two bodies' which, as Ernst Kantorowicz pointed out in the introduction to his eponymous book, '*mutatis mutandis* was to remain valid until the twentieth century.'[35] According to this medieval principle, there is a *corpus politicus*, immortal and emanating from God, which acts within a *corpus naturalis*, the physical and mortal body of the king, as a sort of *deus absconditus*.[36] The king's death did not dissolve the kingdom; it merely announced the 'migration of the "soul", the immortal part of kingship, from one incarnation to another', thus reaffirming its perennial character. From this point of view, the anthropomorphic representation of the Leviathan simply reformulated the theological idea of *corpus mysticum*, the ensemble of Christian community coalesced into an 'organic' body with head and limbs.[37]

The doctrine of the king's two bodies, Kantorowicz argues, found a dramatic and meaningful illustration in the liturgy of royal funerals, which he carefully depicts with reference to several medieval and early modern authors. The burials of French kings in the Abbey of

---

35　Ernst Kantorowicz, *The King's Two Bodies: A Study in Medieval Political Theology* (Princeton: Princeton University Press, 1997 [1957]), xviii.

36　Ibid., 12.

37　Ibid., 15.

Saint-Denis followed a rigorous ritual: when the coffin slipped into the vault, accompanied by the audience's lament of *Le roi est mort!* ('The king is dead!'), the royal banner was pulled down for a brief moment and immediately raised again, to cries of *Vive le roi!* ('Long live the king!').[38]

It is interesting to observe that the actors of the two greatest revolutions of modern times performed similar rituals. In the case of the French Revolution, the comparison does not deal, of course, with the burial of Louis XVI but rather with his execution at the Place de la Révolution on 21 January 1793. Decided by the National Con-

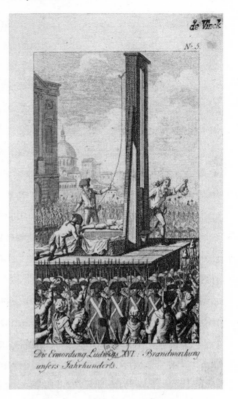

Execution of Louis XVI, Paris, January 1793 (Engraving).

vention and accomplished by the guillotine, this execution revealed a paradoxical contradiction in the revolutionary process. On the one hand – this was its symbolic dimension – it was supposed to fulfil the secularization of political power and society, up to the procedures of capital punishment. There was no royal exception: the execution of Louis XVI, Louis Capet, did not differ from that of ordinary enemies of Revolution. The guillotine – a mechanical, impersonal, silent and extremely rapid killing apparatus – both sacralized and democratized the ritual of capital punishment.[39] On the other hand, the royal execution assumed the character of a sacred act, of a foundational sacrifice on the part of the nascent republican power. The scaffold was surrounded by a rapturous crowd, the execution was announced by the beating

38 Ibid., 410.
39 Cited in Daniel Arasse, *The Guillotine and the Terror* (New York: Viking, 1990), 157.

of drums and, in a sort of parody of the medieval kings' burials, the stewards shouted *Vive la République!* when the executioner exhibited the severed head of the king.[40] Many excited onlookers jumped onto the scaffold to touch the royal blood and soldiers dipped their swords in it. 'The square became a theatre', writes Michelet, describing the public executions of the Terror years.[41] The solemnity of this execution was implicitly recognized by Robespierre himself, who depicted it as the accomplishment of natural right's 'sacred duty'. According to Camille Desmoulins, the king's blood 'sealed the decree that declared the French Republic'.[42] Instead of acclaiming the permanence of the monarchy, the execution of the king established the immortality of the Republic by celebrating the advent of people's sovereignty, the new *corpus politicus*.

The execution of the last tsar, Nicholas II, with his entire family took place under different circumstances, completely devoid of solemn ceremony. The Bolsheviks had envisaged a public trial like that of Louis XVI, but the deepening of the civil war, in the summer of 1918, did not allow them the time to prepare a spectacular legal action. Trotsky recalls learning of the tsar's execution from Yakov Sverdlov, the USSR head of state, coming back to Moscow after the fall of Yekaterinburg. The survival of the Soviet government was at stake and the Bolsheviks could not gift a 'live banner' to their enemies. The execution of the tsar, he explained in his *Diary in Exile* (1935), aimed at depriving the Whites of any hope of an eventual restoration: the historical break of the October Revolution was as radical as it was irreversible; the Bolsheviks would not accept any retreat or compromise. The imperial family, he concluded, had been the victim of the monarchic principle of dynastic succession.[43]

Relieving Soviet power of a burden, the execution of Nicholas II was not performed as a public spectacle. It was accomplished without solemnity, exactly like the proclamation of the new Soviet government

40 Ibid., 90.

41 Michelet, *Histoire de la Révolution française*, vol. 2.1, 782.

42 Cited in Arasse, *The Guillotine and the Terror*, 52–4, 90.

43 Leon Trotsky, *Diary in Exile* (Cambridge, MA: Harvard University Press, 1976), 80–2.

a few months earlier. The time to impose communist liturgies had not yet come. Emerging from two decades of underground struggle and a precarious life in exile, the Russian revolutionaries were still utter foreigners to any institutional rituals. The celebration of the immortality of socialism took place later, reaching its peak with Lenin's death. I will return later to the decision to embalm his corpse and exhibit it in a mausoleum, in the heart of Moscow. Here, it is worth merely emphasizing that his funeral was attended by huge crowds and that people did not stop visiting the coffin for weeks, thus pushing the Soviet leadership to transform the temporary tomb into a permanent and

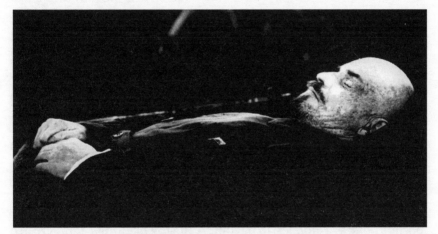

Lenin's Embalmed Body, Moscow (1924).

Lenin's Wooden Mausoleum, Moscow (1924).

more majestic wooden mausoleum. The announcement of the death
of the revolutionary leader marked the beginning of a vast campaign
focusing on the immortality of his ideas and lessons. On 27 January,
when the funeral started on Red Square, the radio widely disseminated
the message that dominated the entire ceremony: 'Lenin has died, but
Leninism lives!'[44] The following day, this slogan resonated across the
country through the Soviet newspapers. The headline in *Izvestiia*
clearly evoked the medieval doctrine of the king's two bodies: 'That
which was mortal in Lenin has died, but his cause and his legacy will
abide forever.'[45] *Pravda*'s editorial distinguished between Ilich, who
was no more, and Lenin, who remained an immortal presence amidst
the Russian people and communists all over the world. Vladimir May-
akovski devoted a poem to the immortality of Lenin that was reprinted
many times: 'Lenin and Death – these words are enemies / Lenin and
Life – are comrades / Lenin lived / Lenin lives / Lenin will live.'[46]

Already begun in previous years and de facto institutionalized
in 1923, the cult of the Bolshevik leader found its most significant
expression in a rich iconography that combined many variations on
the same basic elements: Lenin with outstretched arm pointing his
finger towards the future, surrounded by parading people, Red Army
soldiers, peasants ploughing fields, workers in their factories, etc. Some
posters possess a Hobbesian flavour. A Rostov placard of 1927, created
for the tenth anniversary of the October Revolution, portrays Lenin
as a statesman, within an oval frame, toward whom exulting masses
of workers and peasants converge from both sides of the picture. In
the background, the rising sun illuminates an idyllic rural landscape
juxtaposed with city buildings and factory chimneys. Less gigantic
than in most other images of the 1920s, this poster represents Lenin,
nevertheless, as a kind of Soviet Leviathan, a sovereign unifying in
himself a multitude of bodies.[47]

---

44   Cited in Nina Tumarkin, *Lenin Lives! The Lenin Cult in Soviet Russia*
(Cambridge, MA: Harvard University Press, 1983), 162.
45   Ibid., 165.
46   Ibid., 168.
47   Victoria E. Bonnell, *Iconography of Power: Soviet Political Posters Under
Lenin and Stalin* (Berkeley: University of California Press, 1997), 151.

'Celebration of October', Soviet Poster by F. Chernosenko, Rostov (1927).

These analogies between the practices of modern revolutions and the rituals of the king's two bodies cast a new powerful light on the process of secularization. The traumatic shift of sovereignty from kingship to the people that took place during the French Revolution should not be interpreted exclusively as the destruction of a social and political order and the abandonment of previous beliefs and values. Of course, the struggle against religion radically put into question its institutions and, with the decline of traditional representations, engendered a general disenchantment of the world; but this dramatic change produced neither the extinction of sacredness nor its retreat from society and power. The shift of sovereignty meant rather a transfer of sacredness from religion and tradition to secular values: from the worship of God, the saints, the Church and the king – with their laws, institutions and symbols – to the worship of secular values such as freedom, equality, humanity, nation and reason, embodied by their own institutions. This 'transfer of sacredness', according to Mona

Ozouf, resulted in the invention of new symbols and rituals, from the revolutionary calendar to the republican festivals that celebrated the advent of a regenerated nation and humanity.[48] In the last analysis, this is the true meaning of the iconoclastic waves that shape most revolutionary changes: the 'de-Christianization' of France under the First Republic, when Robespierre introduced the cult of the Supreme Being; the closing of Orthodox churches in Russia after the October Revolution; and finally, the anarchistic explosion of anticlerical violence during the Spanish Civil War. Burning churches, destroying icons, vandalizing relics, firing at Christian crosses, and killing priests announced the coming of freedom as a new sacred value. Thus, the new rituals of Jacobin France and Bolshevik Russia seem to confirm the famous assessment of Carl Schmitt in his *Political Theology* (1922) that 'all significant concepts of the modern theory of the state are secularized theological concepts.'[49] Adopting this interpretive key, both the execution of Louis XVI and the funeral of Lenin appear, despite their ostensibly dissimilar meanings (an execution and a burial), as secularized versions of the principle of the king's two bodies: the *people*'s two bodies.[50] The execution of the king celebrated the birth of the people's sovereign body, a new *corpus politicus* that could not exist without suppressing the *corpus naturalis* of the old monarch; the burial of Lenin already instituted the dualism of the people's body by distinguishing between the transient corporeal person of the leader and the immortality of socialism. The mummy of Lenin and the symbols

---

48   Mona Ozouf, *Festivals and the French Revolution* (Cambridge, MA: Harvard University Press, 1988), 267, 282.

49   Carl Schmitt, *Political Theology: Four Chapters on the Concept of Sovereignty* (Chicago: University of Chicago Press, 2005), 36.

50   On the concept of the 'people's two bodies', see Eric L. Santner, *The Royal Remains: The People's Two Bodies and the Endgames of Sovereignty* (Chicago: University of Chicago Press, 2011); Pasquale Pasquino, 'Constitution et pouvoir constituant: le double corps du peuple', in Jean Salem, Vincent Denis and Pierre-Yves Quiviger (eds), *Figures de Sieyès* (Paris: Éditions de la Sorbonne, 2008); and Jason Frank, 'The Living Image of the People', in Zvi Ben-Dor Benite, Stefanos Gerulanos and Nicole Jeer (eds), *The Scaffolding of Sovereignty: Global and Aesthetic Perspectives on the History of a Concept* (New York: Columbia University Press, 2017), 124–56.

of Leninism, however, could only play the role of a substitute for the impossible representation of the people, the new bearer of sovereign will. As we will see, the secularization of the political theology of royal sovereignty finally resulted in the installation of the people as a biopolitical object moulded and built by the new power.

The people's sovereign body is both an aporetic concept and an almost non-representable metaphor.[51] On the one hand, the real people – a multitude of bodies – that finds its unity in revolutionary action does not need any fictional representation: it exists by fighting against the state and its victory means the death of both the old regime and its representatives. The revolutionary crowds have their own symbols – think of Delacroix's *Liberty Leading the People* (1830) or Eisenstein's *October* (1927) – but do not act on behalf of an established power, simply because they are establishing it. On the other hand, the emergence of the symbols and institutions of a new sovereignty fatally corresponds with the retreat and invisibility of the multitude, the *corpus politicus* they supposedly represent. The sovereign body is a mythical and omnipotent entity – *Non est potestas super terram quae comparetur ei*, one could say, repeating the biblical quotation of *Leviathan*'s frontispiece – which exists exclusively by virtue of a constitutional charter or a fictive convention. Popular sovereignty is an oxymoron: sovereignty only exists as a power *over* the people. Following the art historian T. J. Clark, Eric Santner suggests that this impossible incarnation was magisterially expressed by David in his famous painting *Death of Marat* (1793). In this canvas, the spectral dead body of the French revolutionary – depicted lying in the bath, in a manner that breaks with all contemporary canons of the figuration of death – is overshadowed by the intense brown of the wall behind him, which fills most of the painting. According to Santner, the contrast between Marat's body and this empty yet overwhelming wall would perfectly illustrate the 'representational deadlock situated at the transition from royal to popular sovereignty'.[52]

---

51 See Frank, 'The Living Image of the People', 124, 142.

52 Eric L. Santner, *The Royal Remains*, 95. He refers to T. J. Clark, *Farewell to an Idea: Episodes from a History of Modernism* (New Haven: Yale University Press, 1999), 15–53.

Sovereign Body

According to Claude Lefort, democracy is the locus in which power becomes an 'empty place', a place that the people, its legitimate source and supposed holder, cannot occupy, and therefore a place that 'those who exercise public authority can never claim to appropriate'.[53] In this sense, democracy is the opposite of Absolutism, a representable power whose place is 'occupied', a power that builds society as a homogeneous body and creates an otherwise inexistent political community. This is why Lefort grasps the main features of democracy in 'disincorporation', by emphasizing the 'emptiness' and 'un-representability' of power.[54] Thinkers of juridical positivism such as Hans Kelsen have pointed out that democracy based on representative institutions always supposes a silent and anonymous people that does not participate in the elaboration of law: 'there can be no doubt', he wrote, 'that none of the existing democracies called "representative" are really representative.'[55] In other words, the installation of the people as a sovereign body – the Declaration of the Rights of Man and of the Citizen posits that 'the source of all sovereignty' lies in the people – is a fiction that implies its dissolution as a concrete physical ensemble. Since the first years of the French Revolution, the idea of popular sovereignty appeared suspect not only to aristocratic conservatism but also, for very different reasons, to some enlightened observers. According to Gaspar Melchor de Jovellanos, a Spanish admirer of the Jacobins, to speak of 'national sovereignty' was simply meaningless. As he argued, sovereignty always implies the distinction between

53   Claude Lefort, *The Political Forms of Modern Society* (Cambridge, MA: MIT Press, 1986), 279.

54   Claude Lefort, 'The Question of Democracy', *Democracy and Political Theory* (Cambridge: Polity Press, 1991), 27. See also Philippe Lacoue-Labarthe and Jean-Luc Nancy who, following Lefort, describe 'the desubstantialization of the body politics' as one of the main features of political modernity: *Retreating the Political*, ed. Simon Sparks (London: Routledge, 1997), 127. Criticizing Lefort's theory, Mark Neocleous defines democracy as the advent of a new form of 'incorporation' of sovereignty through the 'social body' of the people: 'The Fate of the Body Politics', *Radical Philosophy*, 108 (2001): 29–38.

55   Hans Kelsen, *General Theory of Law and State* (Cambridge, MA: Harvard University Press, 1945 [1925]), 289.

the ruler and the subjects and the people cannot be 'sovereign of itself'.[56] Carl Schmitt, a political thinker who certainly did not like revolutions, stressed the ambiguity of the concept of 'the people' in modern constitutional theory: whereas the sovereign people 'officially organized', that is, formed and defined by the law, was a fiction that existed exclusively through statesmen who acted on its behalf, the real people – the people ignored by the law, but the substance of common language – consisted precisely of those who do not rule, those who are excluded from power and 'can only say yes or no' or 'acclaim'.[57]

Notoriously, Sieyès tried to find a solution to this contradiction first by assimilating the people to the nation – 'the great body of citizens' as opposed to the aristocracy, an 'awful sickness' that 'devoured the living flesh' of France[58] – and then by reducing the nation to the Third Estate. Based on criteria of property and education, his distinction between 'active' and 'passive' citizenship excluded from political representation all manual workers, whom he elegantly called 'labouring machines' and 'human instruments of production'.[59] Thus he introduced a discriminating political principle that would become

56 Gaspar Melchor de Jovellanos, 'Notas a los Apéndices a la Memoria en defensa de la Junta central' (1810), *Escritos políticos y filosóficos* (Barcelona: Folio, 1999), 210. See Elias Palti, *An Archeology of the Political: Regimes of Power from the Seventeenth Century to the Present* (New York: Columbia University Press, 2017), 90–1.

57 Carl Schmitt, *Constitutional Theory*, Foreword by Ellen Kennedy (Durham: Duke University Press, 2008 [1928]), 302, 338, but also 131, 242. See also Giorgio Agamben, 'What Is a People?' in *Means Without End: Notes on Politics* (Minneapolis: University of Minnesota Press, 2000), 29–36.

58 Emmanuel-Joseph Sieyès, *Qu'est-ce que le Tiers État?* (Paris: Flammarion, 1988), 37, 164, 172–3; English trans. 'What is the Third Estate?' in E.-J. Sieyès, *Political Writings*, ed. Michael Sonenscher (Indianapolis/Cambridge, MA: Hackett, 2003).

59 E.-J. Sieyès, 'Dire de l'Abbé Sieyès sur la question du Veto royal à la séance du 7 septembre 1789', 'Esclaves', and 'La Nation', *Écrits politiques* (Paris: Éditions des Archives contemporaines, 1985), 75, 89, 236. On Sieyès's distinction between 'active' and 'passive' citizenship, see Nadia Urbinati, *Representative Democracy: Principles and Genealogy* (Chicago: University of Chicago Press, 2006), 138–61, also 167, 207; and Luca Scuccimarra, 'Généalogie de la Nation: Sieyès comme fondateur de la communauté politique', *Revue française d'histoire des idées politiques*, 33 (2011): 27–45.

David, *The Tennis Court Oath* (1791). Canvas. Musée Carnavalet, Paris.

a topos of classical liberalism, from Benjamin Constant to John Stuart Mill, across the entire nineteenth century. And even further: François Furet considered the opposition of Robespierre to representative institutions based on property and tax qualification as the source of an idealization of the people that led to the Terror.[60]

It is significant that one of the rare attempts to give a visual representation to the people's sovereign will – once again a painting by David, his sumptuous *Tennis Court Oath* (1791) – is a corporeal metaphor excluding the people. The canvas shows an excited and enthusiastic crowd, the members of a collective body gathered around Bailly, the Assembly President, as he reads out the establishment of the Constitution. Bailly, the body's head, dominates the scene, and three religious men are recognizable beneath him – Dom Gerle, Abbé Grégoire, and Rabaut Saint-Étienne, respectively a monk, a priest, and a Protestant father – who symbolize the new spirit of tolerance and the heart of the nation. This collective body, however, is composed of the third estate,

---

60   Maximilien Robespierre, 'Contre le régime censitaire' (1789), *Pour le bonheur et la liberté: discours* (Paris: Éditions La fabrique, 2000), 24–7; François Furet, *Interpreting the French Revolution* (New York: Cambridge University Press, 1981), 60.

the members of the Constituent Assembly: prosperous, respectable, well-dressed men whose gestures convey dignity and self-confidence despite the confused and excited general atmosphere. Recognizable on the top sides of the painting, ordinary people – including several women – are confined to two very high tribunes, far from the stage, and passively attend the historic ceremony.[61]

The ambiguities of the concepts of people and sovereignty largely explain their absence from the lexicon of Marx and Marxism, not to mention of Bakunin and the anarchist tradition. Whereas anarchism wished to abolish the state, Marxism posited the proletarian conquest of power as the premise of human self-emancipation that would make the state useless, putting it, according to Friedrich Engels, 'into the *museum* of antiquity, by the side of the spinning-wheel and the bronze axe'.[62] Both anarchism and Marxism aimed to destroy sovereignties.

In Marx's writings, corporeal metaphors are primarily used to describe the state, and at other times for the working class. 'This appalling parasitic body', he wrote in *The Eighteenth Brumaire* (1852), 'enmeshes the body of French society and chokes all its pores.' It is by demolishing this gigantic bureaucratic and military machine that the proletariat could restore to the 'social body' the forces and functions previously absorbed by this parasitic growth.[63] The measures adopted by the Paris Commune, he pointed out in *The Civil War in France* (1871), simply made the concept of sovereignty superfluous: universal suffrage, the revocability of the deputies, the abolition of the police, and public education were the first steps towards a stateless society, a political community in which the separation between rulers and subjects – the substance of sovereignty – no longer existed. As a 'working, not a parliamentary body, executive and legislative at the same time',[64] the Commune was not a controlled or ruled body, it was

---

61 For a different interpretation of this painting, which points out its visualization of sovereignty but does not pay attention to the exclusion of the people, see Antoine de Baecque, *The Body Politic: Corporeal Metaphor in Revolutionary France 1770–1800* (Stanford: Stanford University Press, 1997), 192–3.

62 Friedrich Engels, 'The Origin of the Family, Private Property and the State. In the Light of the Researches by Lewis H. Morgan' (1884), *MECW*, vol. 26, 272.

63 Marx, 'The Eighteenth Brumaire', 185.

64 Karl Marx, 'The Civil War in France' (1871), *MECW*, vol. 22, 331.

a self-managed body that could be established only by destroying the state's repressive apparatus. Marx defined revolution by two corporeal metaphors: a 'parasitic excrescence' was 'amputated'.[65] The goal of Guizot in 1848 as well as of Thiers in 1871 was to restore order by smashing this emancipatory potential of 'the proletarian body'. Marx's organic metaphors dealt with political action and collective imagination rather than with juridical forms of power. The Commune had been a living experience beyond any institutional dimension and its legacy was a realm of memory, a concept that he expressed again through a corporeal metaphor: 'its martyrs', he wrote, 'are enshrined in the *great heart of the working class*.'[66]

Of course, there is a continuity in Marx's political writings between 1848 and 1871. They similarly define the state as a repressive apparatus and a 'parasitic excrescence' that revolution tried to overthrow, in order to both constitute the proletariat as a new ruling class and transform the economic bases of the country by socializing the means of production. It was only after the experience of the Paris Commune, however, that Marx completely abandoned the model of the 'people's two bodies' by elaborating a new conception of direct democracy – which he presented as synonymous with proletarian dictatorship – opposed to representative institutions and popular sovereignty. In *Eighteenth Brumaire*, he vigorously denounced the suppression of universal suffrage by the Second Republic in May 1850 by means of a corporeal metaphor. By this measure, he wrote, the French bourgeoisie had 'cut in two the muscles which connected the parliamentary head with the body of the nation' and had transformed itself 'from the freely elected representatives of the people into the usurping parliament of a class'.[67] This dualism no longer existed with the Commune.

In *State and Revolution*, the essay he wrote in the summer of 1917, Lenin tried to systematize Marx's ideas on the Paris Commune and the proletarian dictatorship. The purpose of his essay was to 're-establish what Marx really taught on the subject of the state'.[68] At

---

65 Ibid., 332.
66 Ibid., 355.
67 *MECW*, vol. 11, 178.
68 Lenin, 'State and Revolution', *LCW*, vol. 25, 391.

that moment, Lenin's intellectual disposition was anti-authoritarian. His text dealt with Marx's writings on the revolutions of 1848 and the Paris Commune, but he reinterpreted them through the prism of the Russian Revolution, precisely when the Soviets were turning from organs of struggle to organs of power. In his view, the result of this transition was a new power acting from the beginning for its own extinction, a new ruling entity in which the 'people's two bodies' – the cleavage between its concrete *corpus naturalis* and its abstract *corpus politicus* – had become meaningless.

The state, he wrote, was a historically transitional institution. Since, in the past, many human communities had existed without a state, a stateless future was equally conceivable. According to Lenin, the state was a historical product of class society, and therefore a tool of the ruling class. This bourgeois state could not be transformed; it needed to be suppressed by a violent act. But this destruction was creative. The model of proletarian dictatorship was the Paris Commune, which had replaced the 'government of persons' with the 'administration of things'.[69] As a proletarian dictatorship, it was a state that created the premises of its own disappearance. In *Anti-Dühring* (1878), Engels mentioned the process of state extinction: 'The state is not "abolished": *it dies out*' (*stirbt ab*).[70] Differently from many forms of utopian socialism that prefigured an ideal society, Marx depicted communism as 'the real movement which abolishes the present state of things.' Antonio Negri has pertinently characterized this conception of revolution directed against sovereignty as 'an expansive constituent power', which is different from the idealization of insurgency as a purely 'destituent' power.[71]

This 'libertarian' moment of Lenin's theory is amazingly different from the authoritarianism he expressed after the conquest of power. Reading *State and Revolution* is both refreshing, in that it unveils a thinker far away from many stereotypical representations, and problematic. In his view, the organs of the proletarian dictatorship were

---

69   Ibid., 401; *MECW*, vol. 25, 268.

70   Ibid.

71   Antonio Negri, *Insurgencies: Constituent Power and the Modern State* (Minneapolis: University of Minnesota Press, 1999), 229.

both legislative and executive, with elected delegates assuring the 'administration of things' in a system without hierarchies. But how would democratic deliberation function and who would make decisions? In his essay, Lenin avoided any reflection on the centralization of power (an issue which he did not ignore in practice as a political leader amidst the Russian crisis). He completely neglected to consider the legal framework of the revolutionary state.[72] Did it need the law? Should it have a Constitution? Would it assure political pluralism? Would it preserve the conquest of individual and public liberties? What place was there for dissent within its institutions? Would it establish any form of censorship? The Bolsheviks would face these questions empirically and the Soviet Constitution of 1918 was not the product of a Constituent Assembly, which they had dissolved in December 1917. A proletarian dictatorship, which cannot be the state of exception of an existing regime but rather a constituent power, had to suspend and abolish laws with the purpose of creating a new order. In a vacuum, everything became possible. If Giorgio Agamben is right in defining 'constituent' as 'that figure of power in which a destituent potential is captured and neutralized',[73] the lack of a concept of sovereignty in revolutionary theory does not favour the preservation of an insurgent spirit; it instead creates the premises for an uncontrolled and extremely authoritarian constituent power.

Leon Trotsky also carefully avoided the concept of sovereignty in its conventional juridical meaning. His *History of the Russian Revolution* (1930–32) devoted an impressive chapter to the question of the twofold power that, since the collapse of the Tsarist regime, had shaped the Russian crisis by opposing the Soviets to the provisional government. Twofold power, he observed, was a sort of 'regulative principle' of all revolutions, as both the English and the French Revolutions had eloquently shown. The confrontation between the Presbyterian parliament of the English nascent bourgeoisie and Cromwell's plebeian

---

72   This was the conclusion of Norberto Bobbio, for whom Marxist political theory lacks any 'doctrine of the exercise of power'; see *Né con Marx né contro Marx* (Roma: Editori Riuniti, 1997), 49.

73   Giorgio Agamben, *The Use of Bodies* (Stanford: Stanford University Press, 2016), 267.

New Model Army, as well as the opposition between the monarchy and the National Convention in France, had found their equivalent in Russia in 1917. In all these revolutionary experiences, he explained, 'civil war gave to this double sovereignty its most visible, because territorial, expression.'[74] Both revolution and counterrevolution struggled to impose a unique authority.

It is interesting to observe that the term 'dual power' (*dvoevlastie*), which was originally used by Lenin in April 1917, comes from the Russian for 'power', *vlast*, an ancient Slavic word meaning authority, rule, control, and force. With a few exceptions, neither Lenin nor Trotsky used the modern Russian term 'sovereignty' (*suverenitet*), probably derived from the German or the French, which designates power in the juridical sense.[75] It appeared a too legalistic concept to revolutionary thinkers who wished to destroy the state as a juridical and political superstructure and to break up the entire architecture of international relations through a world revolution. After seizing power, the Bolsheviks announced their intention to publish all secret agreements established by Tsarism with the Western great powers. In March 1918, at Brest Litovsk, where the new Soviet government negotiated a separated peace with the central empires, the German and Austrian diplomats could not believe their eyes when Trotsky and Joffe, alighting from their train, started distributing leaflets to the enemies' soldiers agitating for mutiny and revolution. Sovereignty came back later, at the beginning of the 1920s, when Georgy Chicherin, the People's Commissar for Foreign Affairs, went to the Genoa conference of 1922 to negotiate the recognition of the USSR by the great powers.

In fact, this intellectual debate on revolution, twofold power, and the extinction of the state completely disappeared in just a few months with the outbreak of the Russian Civil War. Whereas in October 1917 the dualism of power affected the relationship between the provisional government and the Soviet congress, in December it had shifted – albeit for an ephemeral moment – to the opposition between the newly

---

74   Leon Trotsky, *History of the Russian Revolution*, trans. Max Eastman (Chicago: Haymarket Books, 2008), 150.

75   I am grateful to Nicholas Bujalski for this semantic explanation.

elected Constituent Assembly, dominated by the right wing of the Socialist Revolutionary Party, and the Soviet government controlled by the Bolsheviks, in coalition initially with the Left SRs. With the Civil War, however, the Soviets became an empty shell: the economy collapsed, industrial production fell dramatically and many factory workers, the social base of the Bolsheviks, joined the Red Army. With the organization of the counterrevolution and the birth of an international coalition against Soviet power, the latter reacted by setting in motion a quick and intense process of militarization. The people's two bodies reappeared as a proletarian dictatorship incarnated by the Bolshevik government: the immortal body of socialism had become a fiction and the physical body of the king corresponded now with a militarized party. In *State and Revolution*, after explaining that the proletariat needed 'state power, a centralized organization of force and an organization of violence' in order 'to crush the resistance of the exploiters', Lenin pointed out the hegemonic role of the communist party in terms that already announced a party dictatorship:

> By educating the workers' party, Marxism educates the vanguard of the proletariat, capable of assuming power and leading the whole people to socialism, of directing and organizing the new system, of being the teacher, the guide, the leader of all the working and exploited people in organizing their social life without the bourgeoisie and against the bourgeoisie.[76]

In a letter to Nikolai Bukharin of October 1920, Lenin expressed this view through a very simple syllogism: 'the proletarian class = Russian communist party = Soviet power'.[77] From the armoured train that he transformed into the general staff of the Russian Revolution, Trotsky wrote *Terrorism and Communism* (1920), an incendiary essay where he asserted and theorized the dictatorship of the Bolshevik party:

> We have more than once been accused of having substituted for the dictatorship of the Soviets the dictatorship of our party. Yet it can be

---

76 *LCW*, vol. 25, 409.
77 *LCW*, vol. 44, 445.

said with complete justice that the dictatorship of the Soviets became possible only by means of the dictatorship of the party. It is thanks to the clarity of its theoretical vision and its strong revolutionary organization that the party has afforded to the Soviets the possibility of becoming transformed from shapeless parliaments of labour into the apparatus of the supremacy of labour. In this 'substitution' of the power of the party for the power of the working class there is nothing accidental, and in reality, there is no substitution at all. The communists express the fundamental interests of the working class. It is quite natural that, in the period in which history brings up those interests, in all their magnitude, on to the order of the day, the communists have become the recognized representatives of the working class as a whole.[78]

In the following pages, the chief of the Red Army emphasizes the advent of revolutionary Terror against the counterrevolution as a kind of 'historical law'. Claiming the virtues of the Bolshevik party dictatorship, he justifies the suppression of political pluralism (all anti-Bolshevik parties outlawed), censorship, the creation of the Cheka (the organ of extralegal repression), the militarization of work and the trade-unions, and even the introduction of forced labour: 'obligation, and, consequently, compulsion, are essential conditions in order to bind down the bourgeois anarchy, to secure socialization of the means of production and labour.'[79] With similar arguments, one year later he would defend the forced Sovietization of Georgia – national self-determination sacrificed in defence of the Soviet regime – and the repression of the Kronstadt rebellion. In his eyes, revolutionary Terror was teleologically inscribed into history. It was the Terror of an ascending class, that embodied Progress and the future, against a declining class that represented the past and did not wish to relinquish its power. The Bolsheviks simply accelerated the 'march of History'. To the Menshevik leader Raphael Abramovich, who asked what the difference was between this kind of socialism and Egyptian slavery,

---

78   Leon Trotsky, *Terrorism and Communism: A Reply to Karl Kautsky* (London, New York: Verso, 2017), 104.

79   Ibid., 132.

Trotsky gave a scornful answer. Abramovich had forgotten that 'in Egypt there were Pharaohs, there were slave-owners and slaves. It was not the Egyptian peasants who decided through their Soviets to build the pyramids.' The Soviet compulsion, on the contrary, was 'applied by a workers' and peasants' government, in the name of the interests of the labouring masses'.[80] Reversing the criticism that twenty years earlier, at the second congress of the Russian social democracy, he had directed against Lenin's 'substitutionism',[81] Trotsky depicted the Soviet dictatorship as a kind of Hobbesian absolutism in which the people consented to complete submission to the sovereign in the name of a superior 'law of nature', *a lex naturalis* replacing freedom with constriction or, in the terms of the English philosopher, 'liberty' with 'obligation'. Translated into the theological political doctrine of the king's two bodies, this view corresponded with the medieval motto *rex vicarious Dei*: God (the people) was completely subsumed by the king (the party).[82]

Immortality

This brings us back to Lenin's body. The option of exhibiting it in a mausoleum began to be discussed by the Soviet government in the autumn of 1923, a few months before the death of the Bolshevik leader, when his health had dramatically worsened.[83] In an unofficial meeting of the Politburo attended by Kalinin, Bukharin, Trotsky, Kamenev and Rykov, the new party secretary, Stalin, suggested the organization of an imposing funeral. Arguing that incineration – the choice of Engels twenty-five years earlier – did not belong in Russian tradition, he mentioned that several members of the party had suggested embalming the leader, at least for a short period, in order to accustom the population to such an incommensurable loss. This proposal horrified Trotsky and Bukharin, who objected to transforming Lenin's remains into a

---

80   Ibid., 159.

81   Leon Trotsky, *Our Political Tasks* (London: New Park Publications, 1983 [1904]).

82   Kantorowicz, *The King's Two Bodies*, 89.

83   This discussion is well summarized by Tumarkin, *Lenin Lives!*, 175–82.

relic, like an Orthodox saint. As a Marxist and committed atheist, he himself never would have sanctioned such a step. In the following days, Nadezhda Krupskaya, Lenin's wife, joined her voice to their protest. This disagreement did not prevent the government from approving the principle of exhibiting Lenin's body during his funerals (Grigory Zinoviev, the secretary of the Communist International, supported this proposal in *Pravda*, the party newspaper, by emphasizing that Lenin's body belonged to the world revolution). Therefore, despite the public dissent of Krupskaya, Lenin's corpse was put on public view.

The interminable queues of ordinary people that continued after the funeral pushed the party to preserve the body indefinitely. This required a permanent crypt, and a competition was held to design it. Meanwhile, as Lenin's body began to show signs of decay, a team of doctors, anatomists and biochemists was urgently convened. The decision was taken to preserve the Bolshevik leader's body by injecting a special embalming liquid, abandoning the initial project of refrigeration. The result was a strange hybrid: not a relic made with biological remains but rather, according to the striking definition suggested by Alexei Yurchak, a 'sculpted portrait': a physical body made from 23 per cent of Lenin's corpse.[84] In August, the crypt on Red Square was replaced by a wooden mausoleum created by the modernist architect Konstantin Melnikov, and five years later the sarcophagus found its final resting place in a granite mausoleum realized by Alexei Shchusev. This austere building had been preferred over more avant-garde projects like that presented by the constructivist artist Vladimir Tatlin, creator of the *Monument to the Third International* (1919).

It is almost impossible to clearly indicate the inventor of the Lenin Mausoleum, which arose from a cumulative process of provisional decisions taken with contradictory motivations and purposes. The various steps of the process can be retrospectively enumerated, but this does not mean that they had been carefully planned. Considering a posteriori the chain of events, this paradoxical object undoubtedly crossed a threshold in building the aesthetic and liturgical features of a modern political religion: Lenin became an icon of worship. It

84 Alexei Yurchak, 'Bodies of Lenin: The Hidden Science of Communist Sovereignty', *Representations*, 129 (2015): 116–57.

signified a return, under the mantle of Leninism, to the Christian cult of saintly relics. Lenin's funeral was a religious ceremony, as the startling speech pronounced by Stalin on that occasion clearly implied. Enchaining the prescriptions of the dead leader – 'Departing from us, comrade Lenin enjoined us to hold high and guard the purity of the great title of member of the party ... to remain faithful to the principle of the proletarian dictatorship ... to guard the unity of the party as the apple of our eye', etc. – he concluded each sentence with the same invocation: 'We vow to you, comrade Lenin, that this behest too, we shall fulfil with honor.'[85]

The Lenin mausoleum, however, was more than the symbol of a new secular religion. Its walls echoed and merged with other, very different meanings: the utopian dreams of a revolution that sought to conquer the future. Rooted in an ancient belief of Christian eschatology, its quest for immortality was offered to the collective imagination as a myth translated into the language of modern science and technology. The decisive impulse to preserve Lenin's body indefinitely came from Leonid Krasin, the People's Commissar for Foreign Trade, who was appointed on 29 January to chair the funeral committee, subsequently transformed into the commission for the immortalization of Lenin's memory. An old Bolshevik, Krasin joined the 'god-building' movement created by Alexander Bogdanov and Anatoli Lunacharsky after the defeat of the first Russian revolution of 1905. Deeply convinced that human beings needed a faith and a spiritual message in order to fulfil their potential, the 'god-builders' regarded Marxism as a new humanist religion founded on the principles of historical materialism and the Promethean promises of modern science. According to Lunacharsky, scientific socialism was 'the most religious of all religions'. The 'god-builders' believed in immortality, which they portrayed as the final accomplishment of human liberation in a socialist future. Creating a synthesis between Marx's historical materialism, Darwin's evolutionism, Mach's 'empirio-criticism', and Fedorov's Christian philosophy, they interpreted socialism as a sort of deification of Man. In 1921,

---

85   Josef Stalin, 'On the Death of Lenin', *Collected Works* (Moscow: Foreign Languages Publishing House, 1953), vol. 6, 47–53.

Krasin explicitly defended his belief in immortality in a speech at the funeral of the Russian physicist Lev Karpov:

> I am certain that the time will come when science will become all-powerful, that it will be able to recreate a deceased organism. I am certain that the time will come when one will be able to use the elements of a person's life to recreate the physical person. And I am certain that when that time will come, when the liberation of mankind, using all the might of science and technology, the strength and capacity of which we cannot now imagine, will be able to resurrect great historical figures – and I am certain that when that time will come, among the great figures will be our comrade, Lev Iakovlevich.[86]

Given the circumstances, Krasin accepted the embalming of Lenin's body through the injection of liquids that preserved its exterior shape and allowed its exhibition in a sarcophagus, but he would have preferred to freeze it. Iced over and thus conserved in a state close to 'anabiosis' – neither life nor complete death – Lenin's body would await his eventual resurrection. And Krasin was not isolated in his belief. In the early USSR, many advocates of immortality were neither Lenin worshippers nor former 'god-builders'. They included radical atheists such as Alexander Agienko, founder of the 'League of Militant Godless', or the group of 'biocosmists' for whom death was 'logically absurd, ethically incomprehensible, and aesthetically ugly'.[87] If revolution aimed to create a new world, this meant not only new forms of production and social life, a new art and a new culture; it meant a new life whose inexhaustible potentialities could be accomplished through immortality. The tired and disenchanted gaze of Ahasuerus, the Wandering Jew condemned to ceaselessly travel through ages and continents, was unknown to a society suddenly infused with messianic, futuristic and Promethean expectations.

---

86 Cited in Tumarkin, *Lenin Lives!*, 181.

87 Cited in Nikolai Krementsov, *Revolutionary Experiments: The Quest for Immortality in Bolshevik Science and Fiction* (New York: Oxford University Press, 2014), 29.

Regeneration

Without becoming part of the ideological canon of Leninism, the quest for immortality was a widely discussed topic in the USSR of the 1920s, where it existed, despite its extravagant – not to say delirious – aspects, as one among many other utopian tendencies. In fact, this belief in resurrection was the paroxysmal expression of a project of human, social, and political regeneration that shaped most revolutionary experiences.

Regeneration was a keyword of the French Revolution. 1789 saw the blossoming of innumerable reform projects – state, administration, education, etc. – that quickly merged into a single process encapsulated by the noun *regeneration*. According to Mona Ozouf, regeneration meant 'a limitless programme, at the same time physical, political, moral and social, which claimed nothing less than the creation of a new people.'[88] Like other words of our political lexicon, regeneration achieved a new meaning. Antoine de Baecque points out that, until the middle of the eighteenth century, the use of this concept was mostly confined to the realms of morality (regeneration from vice), religion (regeneration from sins), and medicine (the regenerative faculties of surgery and other medical treatments that assisted bodily recovery). With the Revolution, regeneration became a therapy for both society and humanity.[89] As the linguist André-Pierre Reinhardt observed in 1796, 'the Jacobins claimed to be the regenerators of the human race.' They proposed 'regenerative laws', and their final goal was 'a regenerative Republic of the Universe'.[90] As for the Abbé Grégoire, in a famous essay published in 1788 he explained the advantages of the 'physical, moral, and political regeneration of the Jews' for French society as a whole. After tearing down the walls of the ghettos and breaking from isolation, the Jews would lose their prejudices and become 'useful' (*utiles*) for society.[91] With respect to Sieyès, he viewed

---

88   Mona Ozouf, 'Régénération', in François Furet and Mona Ozouf (eds), *Dictionnaire critique de la Révolution française. Tome 4. Idées* (Paris: Flammarion, 1992), 373.

89   De Baecque, *The Body Politic*, 131–56.

90   Ibid., 134.

91   Ibid., 136.

Chasse patriotique à la grosse bête (The Aristocratic
Hydra). Engraving. Musée Carnavalet, Paris.

the elections as a procedure to periodically 'regenerate' the body of
the nation's representatives. Revolutionary iconography depicted
the 'degenerated' bodies of the aristocracy and clergy through the
images of parasitic, fat, sometimes animal-like monsters: hydras and
harpies. In his newspaper *L'Ami du peuple*, Marat portrayed the aris-
tocrat as 'the man who has fattened himself by starving the people'.[92]
In 1791, after his unsuccessful flight to Varennes, Louis XVI began to
be caricatured as the 'pig-king' or the 'swine-king'.[93] This gallery of
animalized bodies faced the colossi of a regenerated nation engaged in
a 'patriotic hunt'. During the Terror, when the Committee of Public
Safety set the goal of regenerating the nation, its task was fulfilled by
the guillotine. Both its language and its images were pervaded with
body metaphors, as this statement of 1794 eloquently illustrates:

---

92 Ibid., 240.
93 Ibid., 68.

The French People will take up Hercules' posture. It was waiting for this robust government to strengthen all its parts, spread revolutionary vitality through its veins, immerse it in energy and complete its strength by the lightning of action. Laws, which are the soul of the national body, are immediately transmitted, and travel through it, circulating swiftly through all its veins, reaching from the heart to the extremities in an instant.[94]

The image of revolution as a surgical operation, however, preceded the Terror. In his above-mentioned programmatic essay, *What Is the Third Estate?* (1791), Sieyès developed the metaphor of surgically cutting off a limb, comparing the regenerative task of revolution to an 'excision of the oppressors from the body, a most desirable amputation'. Nobility was a morbid excrescence that threatened the health of the nation and needed to be removed:

> It is impossible to say what place the privileged body should occupy in the social order: that is to ask what place we want to assign in the body of an invalid to the malignant humour that eats it away and torments it. It must be *neutralized*; the health and interplay of all the organs must be re-established so thoroughly that the body no longer forms these morbid processes that are capable of polluting the most essential principles of vitality.[95]

The Russian Revolution produced a very similar corporeal symbolism, expressed through the codes of modern propaganda. In Soviet posters, the Tsarist aristocracy, White Guards, bourgeois classes, and leaders of the great powers were systematically represented as deformed, swollen, monstrous bodies, either ridiculous or frightening, and possessed by egoism and hatred. The placards of Viktor Deni, one of the most skilful and popular graphic artists of the USSR in the 1920s, were particularly effective in translating Bolshevik ideas into images and promoting mass mobilization against the enemies of the

---

94   Ibid., 310–11.
95   Sieyès, *Qu'est-ce que le Tiers État?* 172–3.

Soviets.[96] 'Capital' (1919) appears today as a satirical prefiguration of the cartoons of Scrooge McDuck: it shows an obese bourgeois, smirking with satisfaction, immersed in a pool of coins; his watch fob is a gold heart, suggesting that for him love means the transformation of time into money; in the background, his factories are enveloped by a spiderweb. The picture had an exceptional print run of 100,000. In the same year, as the civil war reached its climax, Deni realized 'Entente', where the three White generals, Denikin, Kolchak and Iudenich, were presented as rabid dogs kept on a leash by the agents of US, British and French imperialism. In 'Capital and Co.' (1920), strikingly symmetrical in its satirical composition to the contemporary representations of the Communist International, Nikolai Kochergin portrayed capitalism, imperialism, militarism, aristocracy and the Church as a fraternal community gathered under the gigantic body of a naked monster that protected them with its ermine cape. Flanked by Clemenceau and Lloyd George, Wilson dominated the company, as the true leader of a motley gang including White generals, landowners, speculators, pogromists, and representatives of all the traditional religions.

The hyenas, hydras and dogs of the French Revolution reappeared in Russia, during the 1920s, as hideous beasts against which the trenchant, liberating actions of the people were to be directed. They enriched the revolutionary iconographic canon of the interwar years in the anti-fascist photomontages of John Heartfield, as rabid dogs and menacing orcs. In step with these counterrevolutionary monsters, the Herculean colossi also returned, ready to decapitate them. Like Lenin stretching his arm towards the future, insurgent workers were mostly depicted as imposing figures. In *Bolshevik* (1920), a famous painting by Boris Kustodiev, a proletarian giant bestrides a throng across the streets of a Russian city and his red banner flows out of sight behind him. The posters of the Communist International showed energetic workers who either destroyed capitalist snakes and octopuses or liberated the world by breaking the chains that imprisoned it. Originating in the French Revolution, this image passed through

96 For a detailed description of these posters, see Bonnell, *Iconography of Power*, 202, 196–7.

Viktor Deni, *Capital*, Soviet Poster (1920).

Viktor Deni, *The dogs of the Entente: Denikin,
Kolchak, Yudenich*, Soviet Poster (1919).

Nikolai Mikhailovich Kochergin,
Capital and Co., Soviet Poster (1920).

Boris Mikhailovich Kustodiev, *Bolshevik* (1920).
The Tretyakov Gallery, Moscow.

The Communist International (1919).

many variations in the USSR and finally entered the Spanish Civil
War, where it inspired anarchist posters. Despite a clear propensity
to allegorize revolutionary struggle through highly gendered images
– naked bodies of male workers whose muscles were strengthened
by their moral virtues and political ideals – these liberating Hercules
could also take a more affable form. One of the most popular early
Soviet posters, Mikhail Cheremnykh's and Viktor Deni's 'Comrade
Lenin Cleanses the Earth of Scum', shows the Bolshevik leader up
on a globe sweeping away bankers, kings and popes. These textual
and visual metaphors of cleansing and amputation clearly expressed,
in Jacobin France and Bolshevik Russia alike, the idea that the social
body could be regenerated by violence. In times of civil war, violence
was no longer a choice but rather an inescapable necessity: it was the
premise for displaying the revitalizing work of revolution.

Just as the idea of regeneration in 1789 had been prepared by a
century of Enlightenment, in the early USSR it was pervaded by the

Mikhail Cheremnykh and Viktor Deni, *Comrade Lenin
Cleanses the Earth of Scum* (1920). Soviet Poster.

promises of modern science. The turn of the twentieth century saw
the birth of new disciplines such as endocrinology, genetics, haema-
tology, immunology, biochemistry and eugenics. Blood transfusion
was significantly developed and the improvement of surgery allowed
the first successful organ transplants. This is the context in which
Alexander Bogdanov, a former Bolshevik leader opposed to Lenin
after the 1905 revolution, reinterpreted the concept of regeneration
by shifting it from the social and political to the biological realm. In
his view, regeneration meant more than equality, social justice, new
institutions, new educational policies, new forms of production and
a new public sphere; regeneration meant the 'rejuvenation' of living
bodies through blood transfusion.[97]

---

97   For an intellectual portrait of Bogdanov, see James White, *Red Hamlet:
The Life and Ideas of Alexander Bogdanov* (Leiden: Brill, 2018); on his theories of
blood transfusion, see Nikolai Krementsov, *A Martian Stranded on Earth: Alexander*

Lenin playing chess with Alexander Bogdanov
during a visit to Maxim Gorky in Capri, 1908.

Bogdanov was an original although eclectic thinker who had studied
medicine, natural sciences and philosophy. His theory of organization, which he called *Tektology* (1913), was a synthesis of Spencer's
positivism, Haeckel's monism, Darwin's evolutionism, and Marx's
historical materialism: it set out to offer a coherent project for organizing a socialist society grounded in science and technology. One
of the founders of the 'god-building' movement, with Krasin and
Lunacharsky, Bogdanov merged religious eschatological expectations
with utopian plans that found a literary dimension in his science-fiction
novels, particularly *Red Star* (1908), in which he imagined a communist
society on Mars, a planet whose inhabitants had achieved the condition
of permanent youth thanks to regular blood transfusions. Distanced
from the Bolshevik leadership in the 1920s, Bogdanov supported Proletkult, a literary and aesthetic movement that found in him one of its
intellectual inspirations. Proletkult's claim of a new culture, based on
a *tabula rasa* of all previous traditions, corresponded with his radical
idea of futurity. Impelled by the achievements of medical science and
the development of transplants, he became the Russian harbinger of the

Bogdanov, Blood Transfusions, and Proletarian Science (Chicago: The University
of Chicago Press, 2011).

rejuvenation movement. Bogdanov's efforts were rewarded in 1926, when the People's Commissariat of Health Protection (*Narkomzdav*) announced the creation of an Institute of Blood Transfusion under his direction. Two years later, he died during a blood transfusion with a student suffering from a passive form of tuberculosis. The student survived; Bogdanov was afflicted by extensive haemolysis and passed away. The Soviet government organized state funerals and *Pravda* published an obituary written by his friend Lunacharsky. Many medical scholars were sceptical about Bogdanov's theories; some, alarmed by his resurrectionist ideas, accused him of obscurantism and irrationalism. Bogdanov, they wrote, wished to 'bring us back to ancient and medieval times'.[98] His utopianism, however, was at home in the spirit and imagination of the early USSR. He could create his institute of blood transfusion thanks to the support he received from the Soviet government, notably from Lunacharsky and Krasin, despite the reticence or open opposition of most medical scholars and institutions. In the 1920s, Soviet newspapers and magazines frequently published articles on rejuvenation.[99]

Leon Trotsky never wrote about rejuvenation and was a severe critic of Proletkult. In *Literature and Revolution* (1924), he radically rejected the idea of a proletarian culture, which he considered both simplistic and unrealistic. Faithful to a certain Marxist prescription, he thought that socialism could not be built on a *tabula rasa*: just as a socialist economy could exist only on the ground of the productive forces developed by capitalism, a socialist culture could not appear without thoroughly assimilating the cultural achievements of previous ages. Socialism did not mean just a negation but rather a dialectical 'sublation' of capitalism and its civilization. Trotsky's conception of literature and art was cumulative, not iconoclastic. Despite their radicalism, the Russian futurists appeared to him as a mirror of the rebellious naïvety and immaturity of the circles of Russian bohemia. His interpretation of Marxism therefore differed considerably from that of Bogdanov, the 'god-builders' and other 'biocosmists.' Nevertheless,

---

98   Cited in Krementsov, *A Martian Stranded on Earth*, 96.

99   See Mark D. Steinberg, *Proletarian Imagination: Self, Modernity, and the Sacred in Russia, 1910–1925* (Ithaca: Cornell University Press, 2002).

they shared a common vision of socialism as the edification of a new world and, in the last analysis, a Promethean spirit based on a symbiosis of science and utopia.

Some pages of *Literature and Revolution* sketch an impressive image of a future nature completely reshaped by technology and leading to a redefinition of human life itself. Socialism, Trotsky wrote, will realize 'titanic constructions'. In a socialist future, men 'will be accustomed to look at the world as submissive clay for sculpting the most perfect forms of life'. The boundaries that separate art and industry will be broken down, as well as the current cleavage between art and nature. According to the principles of functionalism, art will be 'formative' rather than 'ornamental' and will achieve a new harmonic relationship with nature, not in a Rousseauean sense – a romantic return to a primal and idyllic 'state of nature' – but rather through the complete submission of the planet to the needs of a superior civilization. This would bring significant changes in distribution of mountains and rivers, forests and seashores. Thanks to the conquests of technology, human beings would be able to 'move mountains' and transform 'the map of nature'. In the end, he predicted, men 'will have rebuilt the earth'. In his anthropocentric view, the relationship between human beings and nature had to be hierarchical: 'Through the machine, man in socialist society will command nature in its entirety.' Endorsing a kind of technological utopianism not so distant from Bogdanov's *Tektology*, Trotsky affirmed his conviction that 'the machine is the instrument of modern man in every field of life.'[100]

After reshaping nature, socialism would reshape human life itself by accomplishing a biopolitical plan that would ultimately take a eugenic form:

Man at last will begin to harmonize himself in earnest. He will make it his business to achieve beauty by giving the movement of his own limbs the utmost precision, purposefulness and economy in his work, his walk and his play. He will try to master first the semiconscious and then the subconscious processes in his own

---

100   Leon Trotsky, *Literature and Revolution* (Chicago: Haymarket, 2005), 205.

organism, such as breathing, the circulation of the blood, digestion, reproduction, and, within necessary limits, he will try to subordinate them to the control of reason and will. Even purely physiologic life will become subject to collective experiments. The human species, the coagulated *Homo sapiens*, will once more enter into a state of radical transformation, and, in his own hands, will become an object of the most complicated methods of artificial selection and psycho-physical training.[101]

The emancipated humanity of a socialist society would definitively supersede 'the dark laws of heredity and a blind sexual selection'. It would be able to overcome its 'morbid and hysterical fear of death' and put an end to the 'extreme anatomical and physiological disharmony' in a class society. In other words, socialism would create 'a higher social biologic type, or, if you please, a superman'.[102] The features of such a superior being would merge 'the heights of an Aristotle, a Goethe, or a Marx'. He would be 'immeasurably stronger, wiser, and subtler', and his body would become 'more harmonized, his movements more rhythmic, his voice more musical'.[103]

Trotsky was not alone in his eugenic and anti-ecological fantasies. In the same years, the filmmaker Dziga Vertov hailed the potential of cinema, an aesthetic creation based on the principles of montage, to prefigure the New Man of the future. In his essay 'Kino-Eye: A Revolution' (1923), he saw its role in this way:

I am the Cine-Eye. I create a man more perfected than Adam was created. … I take the strongest and most agile hands from one man, the fastest and best proportioned legs from another, the most handsome and expressive head from a third and through montage I create a new, perfect man.[104]

---

101   Ibid., 206.

102   Ibid., 207.

103   Ibid.

104   Dziga Vertov, 'Kino-Eye', *Kino-Eye: The Writings of Dziga Vertov*, eds Annette Michelson and Kevin O'Brien (Berkeley: California University Press, 1984), 17.

Although frightening, Trotsky's and Vertov's Übermensch was not altogether Nietzschean, insofar as he was not selected through the social inequalities of a class society and his superiority was to be measured with respect to the backwardness of his ancestors, not to the supposed inferiority of his contemporaries. More than to the Nazi 'New Man' whose triumph was planned in a world of slaves, this socialist superman should be compared to other utopian fantasies, like Fourier's phalansteries; Esperanto, a new artificial universal language; or Marx and Engels's glimpse, in the 1840s, of an impending obsolescence of nations in a world transformed by cosmopolitanism. It is true, however, that this vision of a technological and eugenic socialist future echoes some of the totalitarian temptations of the interwar years and could easily be inscribed into the colourful but ominous ideas that Ernst Bloch dubbed the 'cold streams' of utopian thought.[105]

Liberated Bodies

The 'regenerating' policies and myths of revolutions should not be separated from their liberating dimensions. Revolutions destroy authorities and hierarchies, invent new social and political institutions, and create new forms of life. They condense historical changes in short, abrupt upheavals.

As many scholars have observed, the culture of Enlightenment elaborated a new idea of freedom and equality that took slavery as a symbol of oppression. This rhetorical topos, however, was radically divided from the historical experience to which it referred. Slaves were discursive figures located in an imaginary realm, seldom pictured as really existing people who lived and worked in the European colonies. Several of the thinkers of classical liberalism engaged in the struggle for constitutional rights and individual liberties against absolutism were themselves slave owners or involved in the slave trade. It was only in 1788 that the first societies for the abolition of slavery were created in France and the United Kingdom. The following year, a representative of the French pro-slavery lobby, requesting a bigger

---

105   Ernst Bloch, *The Principle of Hope* (London: Basil Blackwell, 1986), 205–18.

Antillean representation at the Constituent Assembly, was answered sarcastically by Mirabeau that in Metropolitan France horses and mules did not vote.[106] The contradiction between the universal character of the Declaration of the Rights of Man and the persistence of slavery in the colonies was usually ignored in the debates of the Constituent Assembly and the Convention: the vision of black slaves as the victims of a natural condition of racial inferiority remained a powerful mental habit. The abolition of slavery, decreed by the Convention in 1794 and inscribed in the Constitution the following year, was a product of the slave revolution of Saint-Domingue that led in 1804 to the independence of Haiti, the first republic of liberated black slaves. This change was so enormous that, for at least a century, European thought was unable to integrate it into its philosophical and political categories: the event was silenced.[107] Old representations, however, began to disappear. In the collective imagination, slavery ceased to mean an abstract, timeless oppression, and black bodies no longer appeared as ornamental figures of Orientalist paintings; they became a figure of rebellion. 'The transformation of slaves, trembling in hundreds before a single white man, into a people able to organize themselves and defeat the most powerful European nations of their day', C. L. R. James wrote in *The Black Jacobins* (1938), 'is one of the great epics of revolutionary struggle and achievement.'[108]

The Atlantic Revolutions of the end of the eighteenth century – the American, French and Haitian Revolutions – were an unequal and heterogeneous process. They brought the independence of Haiti and the abolition of slavery in France, but none of them liberated women. The French Revolution showed some isolated signs of future change by giving a political dimension to the Enlightenment debates on female emancipation. The most significant expressions of this new sensibility were two famous texts that developed a critical reflection

106   See Domenico Losurdo, *Liberalism: A Counter-History* (London: Verso, 2010), 141.

107   Michel-Rolph Trouillot, *Silencing the Past: Power and the Production of History* (Boston: Beacon Press, 1995), Chapter 3.

108   C. L. R. James, *The Black Jacobins: Toussaint L'Ouverture and the San Domingo Revolution* (New York: Vintage Books, 1989), ix. See also Robin Blackburn, *The Overthrow of Colonial Slavery: 1776–1848* (London, New York: Verso, 1988).

on the blind spots of the universal Declaration of the Rights of Man
and of the Citizen. Both grounded on the principles of natural law,
Condorcet's 'On the Admission of Women to the Rights of Citizenship' (1790) and Olympe de Gouges's 'Declaration of the Rights of
Woman and the Female Citizen' (1791) denounced the exclusion or
restriction of women from citizenship as a 'tyrannical act' and called
for the extension of suffrage. Marital despotism, they argued, was
the equivalent of aristocratic oppression in the realm of the family.[109]
But revolutionary equality still meant the hierarchical submission of
female bodies. Both Condorcet and de Gouges, who were close to
the Girondins (she had dedicated her declaration to the queen, Marie-
Antoinette) were executed under the Terror.

Enlightenment philosophers did not share the same views about the
oppression of women. Unlike Brissot, Condorcet, Diderot, Helvetius
and d'Holbach, who favored complete citizenship and the end of any
discrimination, Rousseau and Kant theorized the natural inferiority
of women.[110] As with racism and colonialism, the women question
revealed the aporias of Enlightenment (including radical Enlightenment). During the French Revolution, the highest conquest of women
was, at the beginning of the Convention, in September 1792, a divorce
law which established equal rights for husbands and wives. Claimed
by revolutionary women like Olympe de Gouges, Sophie Condorcet,
and Madame de Staël, female suffrage was never considered. In 1804,
with the proclamation of Empire, all the advances of the Convention
were dismantled by Napoleon, who regarded women as 'machines
for making babies'.[111]

---

109   See Condorcet, 'On the Emancipation of Women. On Giving Women
the Rights of Citizenship' (1790), *Political Writings*, eds Steven Lukes and Nadia
Urbinati (New York: Cambridge University Press, 2012), 156–62; Olympe de
Gouges, 'Déclaration des droits de la Femme, dédiée à la reine' (1791), *Œuvres*,
ed. Benoîte Groult (Paris: Mercure de France, 1986), 101–12.

110   On this debate, see Jonathan I. Israel, *The Enlightenment that Failed: Ideas,
Revolution, and Democratic Defeat, 1748–1830* (New York: Oxford University
Press, 2019), Chapter 11, and Florence Lotterie, *Le genre des Lumières. Femme et
philosophie au xviii* siècle (Paris: Classiques Garnier, 2013).

111   Quoted in Jonathan I. Israel, *The Enlightenment that Failed*, 351.

Most historians of the French Revolution point out the active involvement of women in all its significant events – many mention a women's cult of the guillotine – which resulted in the creation of a number of clubs like the Paris Society of Revolutionary Republican Women.[112] Particularly rooted in the urban popular classes – the *tricoteuses*, the female sans-culottes – they combined social and political demands without separating the struggle for bread from that for citizenship. If the people's sovereign body was a constitutional fiction, female bodies were legally excluded from it. Thus, the distinction between active and passive citizenship was deepened by an additional gender discrimination which revolutionary power simply codified. In the autumn of 1793, the Jacobin Convention outlawed all women's clubs, aiming to neutralize one of the main sources of social agitation. The final exclusion of women from the revolutionary process as autonomous actors took place with the violent repression of their Paris uprising of 1795, when they marched on the National Convention to demand food, as well as a return to the Constitution of 1793 and to the democratic institutions of the Commune. The Convention issued several decrees that banned women from the public sphere and any political activity.

Based as it was on the philosophy of natural right, the French Revolution posited a universal concept of humankind that was unable to include the diversity of human beings. The rights of man were, in fact, the rights of men as opposed to those of women. Mirroring a tendency that had emerged in the eighteenth century, the political discourse of Revolution biologized old inequalities and gender hierarchies by reformulating them in the language of anatomy and physiology. Medical scholars explained that the location of genital organs – inside in women, outside in men – predisposed the former to domesticity and the latter to public life.[113] Pierre-Gaspard Chaumette, the *enragé* president of the Commune and an ardent defender of the Terror, complained that women were 'abandoning the pious

---

112   See Dominique Godineau, *The Women of Paris and Their French Revolution* (Berkeley: University of California Press, 1998).

113   See Denise Riley, 'Does a Sex Have a History? "Women" and Feminism', *New Formations*, 1 (1987): 39–40.

cares of their households and the cribs of their children' in order to
'come to public places, to harangues in the galleries, and at the bar of
the senate.' He concluded by asking rhetorically if it was to men that
nature had entrusted domestic tasks: 'Has she given us breasts to feed
our children?' and denouncing the 'impudent women who wait to
become men'.[114] As Joan W. Scott points out, the French Revolution
did not question a set of binary oppositions that would shape the entire
nineteenth century: men were identified with active citizenship, liberty,
autonomy, public life and voice; women were relegated to passive citizenship, duty, dependency, domestic life, and silence.[115] In 1904, Scott
observes, Olympe de Gouges was still upheld by medical scholars as
a typical example of revolutionary hysteria, a mental pathology due
to abnormal sexuality (excessive menstrual flow), narcissism (daily
baths) and immoral behaviour (refusal to remarry).

It was the Russian Revolution that, one century later, achieved the
greatest progress for women. It not only abolished all discriminatory
laws by instituting complete equality of rights between men and women
and recognizing the right of divorce and abortion; it also tried to
abolish the legacy of patriarchy and create the premises of a social life
whose organization would no longer be built upon the nuclear family.
The Soviet family code of 1918 promoted the unlimited freedom of
women to study and work and enshrined their right to choose a way
of life and a profession in a completely independent way.[116] In the
public debate engendered by these emancipatory laws, the definition
of family as a 'burden' and a 'cross', on a par with oppressive institutions such as slavery and serfdom, was quite common. The family
had to be demolished for a new social order to be built. In 1919, the
Soviet regime adopted policies that favoured the collective education

---

114   Quoted in Joan W. Scott, *Only Paradoxes to Offer: French Feminists and
the Rights of Man* (Cambridge, MA: Harvard University Press, 1996), 48.

115   Ibid. See Chapter 2, devoted to the French Revolution, 19–55.

116   Wendy Z. Goldman, *Women, the State and Revolution: Soviet Family
Policy and Social Life 1917–1936* (Cambridge: Cambridge University Press, 1993),
Chapter 1. See also Anna Krylova, 'Bolshevik Feminism and Gender Agendas
of Communism', in Silvio Pons (ed.), *The Cambridge History of Communism: 1.
World Revolution and Socialism in One Country 1917–1941* (New York: Cambridge
University Press, 2017), 424–8.

of children and the socialization of domestic tasks. Designated as the fundamental sources of women's 'enslavement', family and marriage had to be progressively eradicated. In the Bolshevik view, women's liberation could not be dissociated from the struggle for socialism. Since capitalism had transformed women into an object of property and ownership codified by tyrannical laws, the liberated woman could only arise from the end of reified and alienated social relations.

In 1922, homosexuality was decriminalized by abolishing the laws that punished 'sodomy'. It was generally considered a 'pathology', but viewed neither as a perversion nor as an offence to public morality.[117] It was less discussed in the USSR than in Weimar Germany, where the struggle against the infamous paragraph 175 of the criminal code was spearheaded by the League for Sexual Reform. Its inspirer, the physician Magnus Hirschfeld, founder of the Institute of Sexual Science, was invited to lecture in Moscow, where he established official contacts with the People's Commissariat of Public Health (*Narkomzdrav*).[118]

This ebullient time of deep transformations in everyday life lasted for more than ten years. In the middle of the 1930s, the Stalinist 'sexual Thermidor' restored the primacy of the nuclear family and re-established the illegality of both abortion and homosexuality.[119] During a decade of sexual revolution, however, the USSR experienced 'red love'.[120] Alexandra Kollontai, the Bolshevik leader who coined this slogan, elaborated the most advanced ideas on the 'new woman', a topic to which she devoted a seminal essay in 1918. The emergence of a socially independent and emancipated woman, she pointed out, was a product of the Great War, which sent an entire generation of

---

117   See Dan Healey, *Homosexual Desire in Revolutionary Russia: The Regulation of Sexual and Gender Dissent* (Chicago: University of Chicago Press, 2001), 126; Francis Lee Bernstein, *The Dictatorship of Sex: Lifestyle Advice for the Soviet Masses* (Dekalb: Northern Illinois University Press, 2007), 63.

118   Healey, *Homosexual Desire in Revolutionary Russia*, 132–3.

119   The expression 'sexual Thermidor' is from Tariq Ali, *The Dilemmas of Lenin: Terrorism, War, Empire, Love, Revolution* (London: Verso, 2017), 271. Frances Lee Bernstein opposes the 'sexual revolution' of the 1920s to the 'Great Retreat' of the 1930s: *Dictatorship of Sex*, 5.

120   The title of a book published by Alexandra Kollontai in 1923, *Red Love* (New York: Seven Arts Publishing, 1927).

young males to the front lines. This rocked the traditional relegation
of women to domestic life and opened to them the doors of many
professions previously reserved for men. In the postwar years, women
became industrial workers, employees, clerks, technicians and managers; female artists, writers and creators ceased to be exceptional
figures. According to Kollontai, the birth of the new woman implied
a deep psychological transformation, a 'radical re-education of our
psyche': many traditional female 'virtues' such as passivity, devotion,
submissiveness and gentleness – an image of women imposed by patriarchal society – were replaced by activity, resistance, determination,
and toughness; 'self-discipline' instead of 'emotional rapture'.[121]

This metamorphosis also affected sexuality. The 'new woman' did
not hide her 'natural physical drives, which signified not only an act
of self-assertion as a personality, but also as a representative of her
sex. The "rebellion" of women against a one-sided, sexual morality',
Kollontai explained, 'is one of the most sharply delineated traits of
the new heroine.'[122] This permitted any kind of sexual relationships,
no matter how unusual, provided they were neither harmful to the
human race nor based on economic calculation. She did not reject the
ideal of 'great love', but this was rare and its quest should not exclude
other forms of erotic friendship. In sexual matters, socialist freedom
meant 'an understanding of the whole gamut of joyful love-experience
that enriches life and makes for greater happiness. The greater the
intellectual and emotional development of the individual, the less place
will there be in his or her relationship for the bare physiological side
of love, and the brighter will be the love experience.'[123] Considered
as a form of 'proprietary attitude', jealousy was not admitted by a

---

121   Alexandra Kollontai, 'The New Woman', *The Autobiography of a Sexually Emancipated Communist Woman* (New York: Herder and Herder, 1971), 94.
On Kollontai's conception of love, see Michael Hardt, 'Red Love', *South Atlantic
Quarterly*, 116/4 (2017): 781–96. See also Matthieu Renault, 'Alexandra Kollontai
et le dépérissement de la famille … ou les deux verres d'eau de Lénine', in Félix
Boggio and Éwanjé Épée (eds), *Pour un féminisme de la totalité* (Paris: Amsterdam,
2017), 63–87.

122   Ibid., 93.

123   Alexandra Kollontai, *Selected Writings*, ed. Alix Holt (London: Allison
& Busby, 1977), 34.

Alexandra Kollontai (ca. 1900).

communist morality that advocated 'a comradely understanding of the other and an acceptance of his or her freedom'.[124] Free love was exigent and demanded not only reciprocal sympathy and attraction but also mutual respect: the autonomy of any loved partner was paramount. The ideal was 'Winged Eros' based on a sexually and emotionally fulfilled encounter between loving partners and attracting bodies, but the harshness of life, Kollontai wrote in 1923 regarding the years of civil war, had to leave room for 'wingless Eros', a 'purely biological' although consensual sexual relationship.[125]

Kollontai's writings on sexuality never mention Freud, despite the fact that *The New Woman* (1918) extensively quotes Grete Meisel-Hess,

---

124   Alexandra Kollontai, 'Theses on Communist Morality in the Sphere of Marital Relations', ibid., 231. This assessment corresponded with that of young Karl Marx, for whom 'the jealous person is above all a private property owner.' Quoted in Sheila Rowbotham, *Women, Resistance and Revolution: A History of Women and Revolution in the Modern World* (London, New York: Verso, 2014 [1974]), 76.

125   Kollontai, 'Make Way for Winged Eros: A Letter to Working Youth', *Selected Writings*, 276–92.

who had been a disciple of Freud in Vienna and became an outstanding figure of German left-wing feminism at the end of the Great War.[126] In the 1920s, psychoanalysis was the object of sharp debates in Russia, where it was supported by the Soviet government. Trotsky had discovered psychoanalysis during his exile in Vienna, between 1907 and the First World War, where he established a fruitful relationship with Alfred Adler, the first Marxist psychoanalyst. Despite reservations about psychoanalysis as a political doctrine, the chief of the Red Army believed in its virtues as a clinical practice and emphasized its complementarity with Marxism for developing a materialist psychology.[127] Thus, he sponsored the State Psychoanalytic Institute based in Moscow, as well as other currents of Russian psychology such as psycho-technique (Isak Spielrein) and pedology (Aron Zalkind). In the second half of the 1920s Zalkind moved away from psychoanalysis, accusing it of 'biologism' and of overemphasizing the role of sexuality in human agency at the expense of class consciousness. Even without quoting Freud, Kollontai's acceptance of a substantial connection between sexual and social liberation in many respects anticipated the ideas of Wilhelm Reich, the thinker of Freudian Marxism. But they never met: she was the Soviet ambassador in Norway when Reich went to Moscow in 1929 to give a lecture on 'Psychoanalysis as a Natural Science'.[128] Since capitalism repressed sexual instincts and produced alienated social relations, Reich argued, the task of socialist revolution consisted in liberating the sexual energies which were suffocated by bourgeois morality; this was the premise for a socialist happiness maintained by fulfilling orgasms (what in Kollontai's terms could be called the climax of 'winged love').

'Winged Eros' certainly did not mean a normative separation between love and sex, but this new approach to sexuality disturbed

126   See Beatrice Farnsworth, *Alexandra Kollontai: Socialism, Feminism, and the Bolshevik Revolution* (Stanford: Stanford University Press, 1981), 167.

127   See Alexander Etkind, 'Trotsky's Offspring: Revolutionaries, Psychoanalysis, and the Birth of Freudo-Marxism', *Times Literary Supplement*, 9 August 2013, 14–15.

128   See Galina Hristeva and Philip W. Bennett, 'Wilhelm Reich in Soviet Russia: Psychoanalysis, Marxism, and the Stalinist Reaction', *International Forum of Psychoanalysis*, 27/1 (2018): 54–69.

the sensitivities of some more Victorian or ascetic spirits. Lenin, who did not hide his extramarital relationship with Inessa Armand, has often been classified in this category because of his rejection of the so-called glass of water theory. To suppose that in a communist society the satisfaction of sexual desires would be as simple and trivial as drinking a glass of water, he complained in 1920, was a complete misunderstanding. Far from being Marxist, this assumption appeared to him as 'purely bourgeois', practically 'an extension of bourgeois brothels', and he deplored its popularity among the youth: 'This glass of water theory has made our young people mad, quite mad.'[129] Clara Zetkin, who recalls this assessment in her recollections on Lenin, also quotes other, more nuanced passages. After rejecting any grief over 'monastic asceticism', he emphasized that 'communism ought to bring with it not asceticism but joy of life and good cheer called forth, among other things, by a life replete with love.'[130]

Sexual liberation had to be combined with health and production, whose relevance was dramatically emphasized with the outbreak of the Russian Civil War. Free love could not ignore the necessity of stopping the endemic growth of poverty, unemployment, prostitution, venereal disease, child abandonment and, in some cases, true famine. The fulfilment of sexual desire was not so easy in a state of malnutrition. Since its foundation in 1918, the People's Commissariat of Health had promoted a campaign for 'sexual enlightenment' (*polovoe prosveshenie*) that often conflicted with the socialist goal of dissolving the nuclear family.[131] Economic, social and cultural recovery passed through new life customs and new individual and collective hygienic practices. The struggle against alcoholism, tobacco and dirt demanded a regulated and healthy life; physical and intellectual activities had to be harmoniously combined in order to participate in the conscious

---

129 Clara Zetkin, *Reminiscences of Lenin* (London: International Publishers, 1934), 54.

130 Ibid., 65. On Lenin's views on sexuality, see Bernstein, *Dictatorship of Sex*, 34–8.

131 Bernstein, *Dictatorship of Sex*, 4. See also Tricia Starks, *The Body Soviet: Propaganda, Hygiene, and the Revolutionary State* (Madison: University of Wisconsin Press, 2008). The hygienist policies of the Soviet regime during the 1920s are deeply analysed in both these works.

work of building a new civilization. In this perspective, bodily practices had to be disciplined; sexual activities could become inimical
to both health and productivity. Sex outside of marriage began to
be discouraged and socialism started to be identified with virtuous,
productive, and healthy bodies. Bodies had to be as clean as the houses
they inhabited. Sexual abstinence and asceticism – moderation in food
and fun, rejection of alcohol and smoking – became the virtues of
these new men and women. Asceticism was opposed to the bourgeois
decadence that embraced vice, excess, parasitism, and degenerate
customs. In Soviet iconography, both kulaks and NEP beneficiaries
were depicted as fat, corrupt and despicable. Conscious Soviet citizens
should clean their houses just as Lenin cleansed the planet of capitalist
and imperialist scum. As Nikolai Semashko, director of *Narkomzdrav*,
explained, 'physical culture destroys the psychological bases for sexual
anomalies.'[132] One of the numerous educational pamphlets of his
Commissariat, *Workers Take Hold of Your Health* (1925), gave essential advice to Soviet citizens: 'Labour, correct leisure, adequate food
intake, normal sex life for adults, and sport for all ages: these are the
foundations of a healthy life.' Socialism meant hygiene: in the words
of Lenin himself, 'the fight for socialism is at the same time the fight
for health.'[133] As Tricia Starks suggests, following the NEP years a
new rhetoric based on antipodal bodily metaphors – pure/polluted,
healthy/diseased – overlapped with a traditional Bolshevik rhetoric
grounded on the dichotomy between socialism and capitalism as the
new world against the old regime.

   In short, sexual revolution and puritanical asceticism coexisted
during the 1920s. In 1926, the psychiatrist Aron Zalkind published
an astonishing essay that prescribed twelve 'sexual commandments',
the indispensable rules for a healthy and collectively beneficial communist life. They include monogamous love, 'sexual abstinence until
marriage', and sexual acts permitted only at the end of 'a chain of
profound and complex experiences uniting lovers' and 'not often
repeated'. Since 'sexuality must be subordinated to class interests',
'flirtation, courtship, coquetry, and other methods of specifically

---

132   Quoted in Starks, *The Body Soviet*, 198.
133   Ibid., 169–71.

Adolf Strakhov, *Emancipated Woman: Build Socialism!* (1926).

sexual conquest' should be rigorously banned.[134] In other words, socialism was a severe and monastic workhouse. In the late 1920s, however, Zalkind's essay was available in Soviet bookshops side by side with Alexandra Kollontai's books depicting socialism as an erotic accomplishment. Nikolai Bukharin, one of the defenders of the NEP before being defeated by Stalin in 1928, stigmatized Zalkind's views as 'nonsense and philistine scum', and Semashko criticized them as 'trashy literature' that wrapped itself in the mantle of enlightenment.[135] Fourier and Cabet had reappeared in Soviet Russia.[136]

Liberation and the regeneration of bodies were progressively replaced by corporeal discipline. In this way, socialism was redefined as a biopolitical power that, in Foucauldian terms, applied the

134 Cited in Bernstein, *Dictatorship of Sex*, 39–40.

135 Ibid., 29.

136 See Étienne Tassin, 'Le rêve, le désir et le réel. Marx ou Cabet', *Tumultes*, 47 (2016): 43–60.

tools of sovereignty to human life itself, by protecting, caring for, controlling, disciplining, and managing human beings considered not only as citizens but also as physical lives. The people's two bodies began to combine the purity of the political body – Leninism – and a biopolitical natural body, not immortal yet, but regenerated and rejuvenated as much as possible. Granted, from this point of view Stalin's 'sexual Thermidor' was prepared and heralded during the 1920s, but the utopian streams of revolution run through the entire decade in a permanent tension with the authoritarian tendencies related to the necessity of reorganizing the USSR in the middle of a military and economic catastrophe.

Productive Bodies

Lenin's writings are a meaningful mirror of this shift of the Russian Revolution towards a new form of biopower that coexisted with sexual liberation. During the years of the Russian Civil War, he discovered the virtues of Taylorism. In 1913, on the brink of the Great War, he published an article in *Pravda* titled 'A "Scientific" System of Sweating', in which he criticized Frederick W. Taylor's 'scientific management' as 'the latest method of exploiting the workers'. It was, the Bolshevik leader frowned, 'sweating in strict accordance with all the precepts of science'.[137] By March 1918, however, he had revised his judgement. In a programmatic intervention titled 'The Immediate Tasks of Soviet Government', he pointed out the twofold nature of Taylorism: under capitalism, it was 'the harshest form of enslavement', since its purpose was 'wringing out of the working people surplus amounts of labour, strength, blood and nerves;' under socialism, it would fulfil a different goal. As 'the last word in the scientific organization of production', it could be adopted in the USSR to obtain 'an immediate increase in the efficiency of human labour'.[138] He therefore recommended its introduction in Soviet industry. In conditions of civil war and an almost total collapse of the economy, when production had fallen to one third of its prewar levels, the most advanced 'art of the extortion of sweat'

137   Lenin, 'A "Scientific" System of Sweating', *LCW*, vol. 18, 594–5.
138   *LCW*, vol. 42, 79–80.

appeared to him extremely beneficial. In fact, Lenin suggested the adoption of an even more authoritarian form of Taylorism: unlike in the American factories of Henry Ford, where piecework linked wages to productivity, in the USSR it took the form of 'compulsory labour service' whose transgression had to be punished as a 'criminal offense'.[139] Here, the rationalization of production was not only a necessity due to the extreme disorganization of the economy; it was a promising way of transitioning from a backward, rural country to a modern society. Constrained by discipline and efficiency, the Russian workers would gradually abandon the laziness, tardiness, and unreliability inherited from their peasant ancestors.

Highly prized by Lenin, J. Ermanski's *The Taylor System* (1918) distinguished American scientific management, exclusively devoted to intensifying the process of labour, from a Soviet industrial rationalization that did not pursue purely quantitative goals by increasing workers' exploitation but sought to integrate the workers themselves into the management system.[140] At the end of the civil war, Trotsky organized a national conference on scientific management in which both partisans and opponents of Taylorism expressed their views. The question remained open. One decade later, the outcome of this debate was Stakhanovism. Alexey Stakhanov, the hero of labour and symbol of the Soviet New Man, was not simply a tireless, enthusiastic, Promethean worker who had mined a record 100-plus metric tons of coal in four hours and forty-five minutes. He was a producer who merged his incredible capacity for work with technical competence and a high level of professionalism. Stakhanovism integrated the workers into the management system as executors and planners as well.[141] It

---

139   Ibid., 80. Lenin referred to Frederik W. Taylor, *Shop Management* (New York: Harper & Brothers, 1911), which he had probably read in the German translation published in Berlin the following year. On Lenin's reception of Taylor, see James G. Scoville, 'The Taylorization of Vladimir Ilich Lenin', *Industrial Relations*, 40/4 (2001): 620–6, and Rainer Traub, 'Lenin and Taylor: The Fate of "Scientific Management" in the (Early) Soviet Union', *Telos*, 21 (1978): 82–92.

140   Ibid., 89.

141   This is the conclusion of Lewis H. Siegelbaum, *Stakhanovism and the Politics of Productivity in the USSR 1935–1941* (New York: Cambridge University Press, 1990), 295.

Futuristic drawing of Aleksei Gastev by Tolkachev (1924).

epitomized the fusion of physical strength with modern technology. Stakhanovist workers benefited from high salaries and a welfare system that included leisure, sport and cultural activities like concerts, lectures, museums and exhibition visits. In *The Revolution Betrayed* (1936), Trotsky's critique of Stakhanovism focused essentially on its abandonment of the principles of socialist egalitarianism: Stakhanovism should not be confused with forced labour – a practice reserved for the Gulag – but it did introduce a new, anti-socialist work ethic.[142]

In the 1920s, the harbinger of scientific management in the USSR was Alexey K. Gastev, the 'Russian Taylor'. An original figure – teacher, journalist, essayist, factory worker, poet, and autodidact engineer – Gastev belonged to the generation of the founders of Bolshevism, with whom he had shared the experience of revolution and exile. Before 1917 he had been a close friend of Bogdanov, and, at the beginning of the 1920s, he became one of the representatives of the Proletkult, a movement which he depicted as 'the essence of the philosophy of the industrial proletariat'.[143] In 1920, Gastev created in Moscow the Central Institute of Labour (CIT), which received

---

142   Leon Trotsky, *The Revolution Betrayed* (Chicago: Haymarket, 1973), 89–94.

143   Cited in Rolf Hellebust, 'Alexei Gastev and the Metallization of the Revolutionary Body', *Slavic Review*, 56/3 (1997): 500–18, notably 504.

support from the Soviet government and promoted the introduction of scientific management into Russian factories.

Expounding a messianic view of machines and theorizing the transformation of human bodies into mechanical entities, he celebrated the advent of socialism as the triumph of technology. Already before the Russian Revolution, he had filled his poems with iron metaphors that glorified industrial work. In 'We Grow Out of Iron' (1914), he announced the advent of a new age of producers pumped with 'iron blood' and boasting 'steel arms and shoulders', who finally coalesced into an 'iron form'.[144] In the 1920s, he described communism as the metamorphosis of flesh into metal: a new society based on iron discipline and iron will, made of iron nerves and iron faces. Claiming his filiation with the great utopian thinkers and writers of the nineteenth century, from Fourier to Jules Verne and H. G. Wells, Gastev imagined socialism as a world of self-regulated machines. 'The future society', he wrote, 'will be managed by "production complexes" wherein the will of the machines and the force of human consciousness will merge in an unbreakable world.'[145] Gradually, human choices and deliberations by voting would be replaced by self-managed machines. These innovations would create a new humankind adapted to the rule of technology, that is, reshaped by the standardization of its language, gestures and thought. Human beings, he wrote, will be 'soulless and devoid of personality, emotion, and lyricism.'[146] In short, they would become mechanical entities. From being 'objects of control', machines would become 'subjects'. Going beyond Bogdanov's 'tektology', this vision of an 'ideal' socialist world took the form of a negative ontology (human beings replaced by machines as the subjects of history) with a vaguely Heideggerian taste *avant la lettre*. It also prefigured the fascist idealization of the 'work-militiaman' (*der Arbeiter*) depicted by Ernst Jünger in his eponymous essay of 1932, where he announced the mechanization of work, the disappearance of all boundaries between

---

144   Ibid., 505.

145   Cited in Richard Stites, *Revolutionary Dreams: Utopian Vision and Experimental Life in the Russian Revolution* (New York: Oxford University Press, 1989), 151.

146   Ibid., 152.

art and technology (already exemplified by photography), and finally
the emergence of a new 'human type' with a metallic body.[147] Rather
than a creation of socialist revolution, Jünger's 'work-militiaman' was
a product of the Great War, the industrialized conflict that opened
the twentieth century, but his features scarcely differed from those of
Gastev's socialist ironmen. The analogies between 'We Grow Out of
Iron' and a nationalist pamphlet like *Battle as Inner Experience* (1922),
written respectively at the beginning and at the end of the Great War,
are astonishing. The poem by Gastev idealizes the workers forged by
the machines:

> They are impetuous, they are bold, they are strong. They demand
> even greater strength. I look at them and stand up straight. Into my
> veins flows new iron blood. I have grown still higher. I myself grow
> steel shoulders and arms immeasurably strong. I have merged with
> the building's iron. I have risen. My shoulders force out trusses,
> upper girders, roof. My feet are still on the earth, but my head is
> above the building. I still gasp for breath from these inhuman/
> superhuman [*nechelovecheskie*] efforts.[148]

Jünger, meanwhile, celebrates the new race born from the outbreak
of modern war, the industrial battle that 'springs from eternal nature
upon whose ground every civilization grows and into which it must
sink if it is not sufficiently hard before the iron ordeal.' The battle
was a cathartic moment that gave birth to a new elite of heroes: 'It
hammered, engraved, hardened us and transformed us into what we
are today ... we will remain warriors for the rest of our lives.'[149]

Gastev's ideas were highly influential in the Soviet aesthetic avant-
garde, where they were supported by the constructivist movement of
the New LEF (Left Front of the Arts). According to artists such as

---

147   Ernst Jünger, *The Worker: Dominion and Form* (Evanston: Northwestern
University Press, 2017).

148   Alexei Gastev, 'We Grow Out of Iron', quoted in Hellebust, 'Metallization
of the Revolutionary Body', 505.

149   Ernst Jünger, 'Der Kampf als innere Erlebnis', *Sämtliche Werke* (Stuttgart:
Klett-Cotta, 1980), vol. 7, 11. See also Thomas Nevin, *Ernst Jünger and Germany:
Into the Abyss, 1914–1945* (Durham: Duke University Press, 1996), 71–4.

Meyerhold, N=A1+A2 (Biomechanical Theatre).

the graphist and photographer Alexander Rodchenko, the playwright
Sergei Tretyakov, and the theatre director Vsevolod Meyerhold, the
October Revolution had to be extended to the domain of aesthetic
creation by overcoming any separation between art and production.
Meyerhold, in particular, tried to apply Taylorism to the stage by
inventing a new way of performing in which actors would control
all the expressive resources of their bodies. The correlation between
bodies, movements and time had to change. Whereas the traditional
theatre asked actors to display emotions, Meyerhold's pieces showed
the potentialities of biomechanics, a science based on the principle
that 'the body is a machine, and the person working is a machine-
operator.'[150] He formulated this rule through a mathematical formula:
$N=A1+A2$, in which N (the actor) resulted from the addition of A1
(the machine-conceptualizer) and A2 (the body who executes, or the
machine-operator).[151]

Rooted in a messianic view of the proletariat as the redeemer of
history – a proletariat redefined as an industrial working class at the
beginning of the Fordist age – this idea of revolutionary corporeal
discipline obviously transcended the Russian experience. In 1919–20,

150   Quoted in Jonathan Pitches, 'The Theatricality Reflex: The Place of
Pavlov and Taylor in Meyerhold's Biomechanics', *Science and the Stanislavsky
Tradition of Acting* (New York: Routledge, 2006), 49.

151   Marie-Christine Autant-Mathieu, 'De l'Octobre théatral au dressage des
arts', in Nicolas Liucci-Goutnikov (ed.), *Rouge: Art et utopie au pays des Soviets*
(Paris: Réunion des Musées Nationaux, 2019), 140.

the years of the occupation of the auto plants in Turin, Italy, Antonio Gramsci elaborated an impressive theory of socialism as redemption *of* (rather than liberation *from*) labour. His articles for *L'Ordine Nuovo*, the socialist newspaper of the Piedmont capital, significantly reso- nated with the Soviet debates, which the Italian Marxist thinker did not know yet. According to Gramsci, the factory councils created by the workers in the occupied Fiat plants were the potential organs of proletarian dictatorship: socialism expressed the intrinsic rationality of industrial production and should be organized as a factory system. Industrial labour had forged the peculiar psychology of the worker, a being who could not live without order, discipline, organization, and rationality. Shaped by his labour experience, this psychology was eminently collectivistic. As a producer, Gramsci wrote, the worker was 'the revolutionary force who embodied the mission of renewing [*rigen- erare*] human society' and was a 'founder of new states'.[152] Therefore, socialism meant the conquest of power by the producers who were to manage society along the lines of a factory model. Whereas the citizen was the abstract subject of sovereignty in the bourgeois state, socialism would replace him with the producer himself. The communist society would be structured 'on the model of a large engineering work' and its core would be the factory council, the organ of its worker brain. In Gramsci's terms, the factory was the realm in which the working class became a specific 'organic body' and its natural organization, the factory council, had to replace the representative institutions of ancient sovereignty. This was his own interpretation of Marx's theory of the 'dissolution' of the state. Extended to the ensemble of society, the factory was building the new proletarian state that would replace the old bourgeois state. Socialism was a community of producers organized into a gigantic factory. Furthermore, this model could be extended on a global scale. Gramsci imagined a kind of universal factory council that would manage 'the wealth of the whole world in the name of the whole of humanity'.[153]

---

152   Antonio Gramsci, 'The Factory Worker' (1920), *Pre-Prison Writings*, ed. Richard Bellamy (Cambridge: Cambridge University Press, 1994), 153.
153   Antonio Gramsci, 'The Factory Council' (1920), ibid., 167.

A fragment on Taylorism from Gramsci's *Prison Notebooks* (1934) echoes the Soviet debates of the 1920s by emphasizing both the necessity of overcoming the limits of capitalist 'labour management' and the incompatibility of free sexuality with the ethic of industrial work. Whereas Taylorism transformed workers into 'trained gorillas' by breaking the 'psycho-physical nexus of qualified professional work', socialism would re-establish such a nexus on a superior level, by creating a 'new type' of conscious worker, able to control and manage the labour process in which he was involved. This superior kind of producer and human being, Gramsci stressed, was the outcome of an almost eugenic plan: 'A forced selection will ineluctably take place; a part of the old working class will be pitilessly eliminated from the world of labour, and perhaps from the world *tout court*.'[154] This regenerated, 'superior' anthropological specimen would possess some corporeal features and ascetic habits forged by his role as producer. 'It is worth insisting on the fact that in the sexual field', he wrote, 'the most depraving and "regressive" ideological factor is the enlightened and libertarian conception proper to those classes which are not tightly bound to productive work.'[155] A proletarian elite should show to its class the most suitable style of life for a conscious producer. Proletarian power, he explained, meant 'self-coercion and self-discipline (like Alfieri tying himself to the chair).'[156]

This biopolitical reshaping of human beings as productive and disciplined bodies fetishized both the *homo faber* and the development of productive forces. The advent of the New Man as an ascetic producer was incompatible with the hedonism of the socialist 'winged Eros'.

---

154   Antonio Gramsci, 'Americanism and Fordism' (1934), *The Antonio Gramsci Reader: Selected Writings 1916–1935*, ed. David Forgacs (New York: Schocken Books, 1988), 290.
155   Ibid., 288.
156   Ibid., 289.

Chapter 3

Concepts, Symbols, Realms of Memory

In revolution, everything happens incredibly quickly, just like in dreams in which people seem to be freed from gravity. … During revolution, people are filled by spirit and differ completely from those without spirit. During revolution, everyone is filled with the spirit that is otherwise reserved for exemplary individuals; everyone is courageous, wild and fanatic, and caring and loving at the same time.

Gustav Landauer, Revolution (1907)

Fixing a Paradigm

Revolutions have changed the face of history but have rarely created 'realms of memory' shared on a global scale. Of course, some of their events have become universal metaphors – like the storming of the Bastille or the Winter Palace – but they remain projections of national events. The Atlantic Revolutions of the last quarter of the eighteenth century – a cycle of uprisings that swept from America to France to Saint-Domingue (Haiti), establishing the ideological and political bases of our modernity – are deposited in essentially national memories. They were obviously correlated in the consciousness of their actors, but their entanglement did not produce supranational memories: whereas the American and French revolutions are frequently opposed as two antipodal paradigms, the Black Jacobins have been silenced for a century and a half and therefore excluded from an essentially Western revolutionary canon. In 1848, the 'Springtime of Peoples' was a virtually synchronous wave stretching from Palermo to Paris, from Frankfurt to Vienna, but its traces are national. The 'Five Days of Milan' do not mean anything outside of Italy, nor does the Frankfurt National Assembly outside of Germany. The 1960s were street-fighting years from Prague to Mexico, from Berlin to Tokyo, but the catchword 'May '68' limits the event within national borders: the barricades of Paris's Latin Quarter. This seems to confirm Pierre Nora's observation that 'the only European incarnations are negative', like Verdun and Auschwitz: a battle of the Great War that involved French, British, and German armies, and a Nazi camp where Jews and Resistance fighters from a dozen European countries were deported and exterminated.[1] At once an omnipresent heritage and an ungraspable memorial object, revolutions have today again become, to use Edmund Burke's famous phrase exhumed by Marx and Engels, 'spectres haunting Europe'. They speak to us of the past, but perhaps they are still announcing the future.

Their universal legacy is, first of all, a concept. If the word 'revolution' is old, it is only after 1789 that it takes on, in all languages, its modern significance. Borrowed from astronomy, it was previously used to designate a 'rotation', meaning the re-establishment of stable institutions after a period of troubles. This is how the British defined their 'Glorious Revolution' of 1688, the peaceful restoration of monarchy on a constitutional basis, while the upheaval led by Cromwell in the 1640s was considered a 'Civil War'. And it was retrospectively, after 1789, that the French Revolution re-signified the birth of the United States. Relieved of an unjust and oppressive domination, the colonials wished to recover their legitimate rights, not to repeat Cromwell's gesture. Their rebellion was a 'War of Independence', and one would have to wait two decades for it to become the 'American Revolution'.[2] In 1789, history did not retrace its path, but made an

---

1 Pierre Nora, 'Y a-t-il des lieux de mémoire européens?', in *Présent, nation, mémoire* (Paris: Gallimard, 2011), 386.

2 Arno J. Mayer, *The Furies: Violence and Terror in the French and Russian Revolutions* (Princeton: Princeton University Press, 2000), 26.

enormous forward leap.[3] According to Marx, the Jacobins 'performed the task of their time – that of unchaining and establishing modern bourgeois society – in Roman costumes and with Roman phrases'.[4] They thought they were re-enacting an ancient piece, but they were inventing the future: revolution had become a political caesura that created new institutions by affirming the sovereignty of the people. On a terrain fertilized by the thinkers of the Enlightenment, the idea of progress was embodied by social forces that ensured its double consummation, at once material and moral. History had a *telos* and revolutions were the 'locomotives' that allowed human beings to reach it. They shattered the linearity of history, introducing a powerful acceleration that threw the world into a new and ascendant temporality, in which nothing remained in its place; where, by virtue of a secret emancipatory tropism, everything seemed to be turning towards a utopian horizon.[5]

Everyone, from its defenders to its detractors, agrees upon seeing revolution as a social and political *rupture*, even if their appreciations diverge radically. This is the meaning with which this concept was finally inscribed in our historical consciousness. From the beginning, a symbiotic link intermingled revolution and counterrevolution. Throughout the nineteenth century, revolution appeared to the eyes of its contemporaries as a singular amalgam of innovation and chaos, the upsurge of a new power and the fall of society into disorder and violence. This double perception fixed the political horizon of modernity. At once topological and ontological, the distinction between *left* and *right*,[6] determined during a fateful meeting of the National Assembly in August 1789, spread beyond French borders to redefine the political map, first of Europe and then of the world. From the

---

3   See Alain Guéry, 'Révolution: un concept et son destin', *Le Débat*, 57 (1989): 106–128.

4   Karl Marx, 'The Eighteenth Brumaire of Louis Bonaparte' (1852), *MECW*, vol. 11, 104.

5   Reinhart Koselleck, 'Historical Criteria of the Modern Concept of Revolution' (1969), in Keith Tribe (ed.), *Futures Past: On the Semantics of Historical Time* (Cambridge, MA: MIT Press, 1985), 43–57.

6   See Norberto Bobbio, *Left and Right: The Significance of a Political Distinction*, trans. Allan Cameron (Chicago: Chicago University Press, 1996).

1790s onwards, Jacobinism became a European insurgent movement against the Old Regime. Threatened from within by the Vendean War, and from without by an aristocratic coalition of monarchies, the French Revolution was exported, or, to use the words of Arno J. Mayer, *externalized*:[7] it disseminated its values and its social conquests (the civil code), becoming first a model to be followed (the Jacobin movements which emerged almost everywhere), and then a new despotism to be torn down (the awakening of national consciousnesses against Napoleonic rule).

Innovation and chaos, the promise of the future and barbarism: these are the poles between which the interpretations of the French Revolution oscillated for more than a century. Though Kant and Hegel condemned the Terror, they recognized in this event a great historical turning point. First of all, it was the *signum prognosticum* of an emancipated world regulated by reason, the premise of cosmopolitan law and the proof that humanity had finally reached adulthood. It remained therefore, despite its violence, a decisive step in moral progress that had given a juridical form to its general values. In *The Conflict of the Faculties* (1798), a work written at the end of his life, when many of the first enthusiastic supporters of Jacobinism in Germany had become disappointed and turned to romantic conservatism, Kant emphasizes the universal dimension of the French Revolution. 'Such a phenomenon in human history', he points out, '*is not to be forgotten*, because it has revealed a tendency and faculty in human nature for improvement' that nobody could ignore. That event 'is too important, too much interwoven with the interest of humanity, and its influence too widely propagated in all areas of the world', he adds, for its lessons not to be assimilated by 'the minds of all men'.[8]

Hegel, in his *Lectures on the Philosophy of History* (1822–30), defines the French Revolution as nothing less than the accomplishment of

---

7   Mayer, *The Furies*, 597–9.

8   Immanuel Kant, *The Conflict of the Faculties*, trans. Mary I. Gregor (Lincoln: University of Nebraska Press, 1992), 159. On Kant and the French Revolution, see André Tosel, *Kant révolutionnaire* (Paris: Presses universitaires de France, 1988), and Domenico Losurdo, *Autocensura e compromesso nel pensiero politico di Kant* (Naples: Bibliopolis, 1983).

philosophy: the passage from 'abstract thought' to its fulfilment in reality. This was a 'glorious mental dawn', he concludes, stressing the 'jubilation' and the 'spiritual enthusiasm' that 'thrilled through the world, as if the reconciliation between the Divine and the Secular was now first accomplished.'[9] In his *Jena Lectures* (1805–06), Hegel had already stressed his view of the French Revolution as a powerful step forward in the march of history, despite his criticism of the tyrannical features of the Jacobin dictatorship of Robespierre and Napoleon's Empire. He disliked them, nevertheless he regarded them as the expression of the dialectic of history and, therefore, as the embodiment of the absolute spirit.[10] Herbert Marcuse pertinently observed that Hegel idealized the Restoration state, but he looked upon it as embodying the lasting achievements of modernity, from the German Reformation to the French Revolution.[11]

In 1848, the year of the 'Springtime of Peoples', the emancipatory promise of the French Revolution became democratic, national, and, for some of its actors such as Marx and Blanqui, already *socialist*. Others, like the Italian patriot Giuseppe Mazzini, leader of the ephemeral Roman Republic, saw in the uprisings of 1848 the confirmation of a federalist European project whose lines they had drawn in the previous decade. For all these republican, democratic, and socialist revolutionaries, violence was an inevitable dimension of liberating action and the concept of dictatorship often featured in their political debates. It was in reassessing the wave of 1848 revolutions that Marx theorized the 'dictatorship of the proletariat', the political form of

9   G. W. F. Hegel, *Philosophy of History*, trans. J. Sibree (New York: Home Library Company, 1902), 556, 557–8. For a synthesis on this topic, see also Joachim Ritter, 'Hegel and the French Revolution' (1956), *Hegel and the French Revolution: Essays on the Philosophy of Right* (Cambridge, MA: MIT Press, 1982), 35–9, and, in a broader perspective, Ferenc Feher, *The French Revolution and the Birth of Modernity* (Berkeley: California University Press, 1992).

10   *Hegel and the Human Spirit: A Translation of the Jena Lectures on the Philosophy of Spirit (1805–6)*, ed. Leo Rauch (Detroit: Wayne State University Press, 1983), 157.

11   Herbert Marcuse, *Reason and Revolution: Hegel and the Rise of Social Theory* (London: Routledge, 1955 [1941]), 409. See also Georg Lukács, *The Young Hegel: Studies in the Relations Between Dialectics and Economics*, trans. Rodney Livingstone (London: Merlin Press, 1975 [1938]), 311.

the insurgent people capable of creating a new power and defending it against the threat of restoration by the old ruling classes. In 1848, revolution was no longer a *signum prognosticum* of the accomplishment of philosophy; it had become a political theory grounded in half a century of historical experience. Writing in 1850, Marx defined 'the class dictatorship of the proletariat' as the expression of the 'permanence of the revolution', acting as 'the necessary transition point to the abolition of class distinctions generally' and 'to the abolition of all the social relations of production on which they rest'.[12]

It was in the cataclysmic context of the European crisis at the end of the Great War, at the edge of the collapse of the dynastic empires and amid the Russian Revolution, that Lenin codified the theory of Marx in *State and Revolution* (1917). He wrote his text in the summer, during a moment of rest and recovery, and his purpose was eminently practical, since he wished to rearm the Bolshevik party and prepare it for insurrection. He aimed at 'reestablishing Marx's authentic doctrine of the state' by systematizing many ideas that the author of *The Communist Manifesto* had expounded in fragmentary form,[13] so revealing an irresistible temptation to build a Marxist *canon*. Now, Marx did not elaborate a complete theory of the state, even less a doctrine of proletarian dictatorship. His writings outline some general ideas and formulate some hypotheses based on the experience of the revolutions of the nineteenth century. He mentioned again the 'proletarian dictatorship' in a letter of 1852 to Joseph Weydemeyer (a German socialist who had emigrated to the United States), where he defined it as the political form of the transition to a 'classless society'.[14] The Paris

---

12   Karl Marx, 'The Class Struggle in France' (1850), *MECW*, vol. 10, 127. For a careful reconstitution of the concept of dictatorship in Marx as well as in the debates of the socialist movement in 1848, see Hal Draper, *Karl Marx's Theory of Revolution* (New York: Monthly Review Press, 1986), vol. 3, notably Chapter 4, 58–67. See also Frederic L. Bender, 'The Ambiguities of Marx's Concepts of Proletarian Dictatorship and Transition to Communism', *History of Political Thought*, 2/3 (1981): 525–55.

13   V. I. Lenin, 'State and Revolution' (1918), *LCW*, vol. 25, 390.

14   Letter to Joseph Weydemeyer of 5 March 1852, *MECW*, vol. 39, 62–5. On Weydemeyer's article on dictatorship and Marx's letter, see Draper, *Karl Marx's Theory of Revolution*, vol. 3, Chapter 15.

Commune, which he depicted as a workers' state – 'the political form at last discovered under which to work out the economic emancipation of labour'[15] – was rather for him a kind of anti-dictatorship: destruction of the centralized state apparatus; dismantlement of its repressive organs and creation of a popular militia; suppression of the state bureaucracy and replacement of parliamentarism by new legislative and executive elected organs; universal suffrage; imperative mandate of the elected, paid with workers' wages; and self-management of the producers themselves. It was Friedrich Engels who, in his preface to the second edition of Marx's *Civil War in France* (1891), defined the Paris Commune as the supreme example of proletarian dictatorship:

> Of late, the German philistine has once more been filled with wholesome terror at the words: Dictatorship of the Proletariat. Well and good, gentlemen, do you want to know what this dictatorship looks like? Look at the Paris Commune. That was the Dictatorship of the Proletariat.[16]

Marx's concept of dictatorship is not clearly codified and swings between a definition of the *social content* of a proletarian power and its *political form*, that is, an absolute power installing a new class rule which, according to the circumstances, can or cannot be framed by democratically elected institutions.[17] In his view, revolution was a product of the collision between the forces of production and the property relations of a given society, but neither did its outbreak depend exclusively on this conflict nor were its political forms pre-established. This is why *The Civil War in France* (1871) analysed the Paris Commune as a workers' state without characterizing it as a dictatorship (he probably thought that it had not been dictatorial enough). Marx's idea of revolution clearly implied the overthrow of capitalism, but he left its phases and modalities to the creative invention

---

15   Karl Marx, 'The Civil War in France' (1871), *MECW*, vol. 22, 334.

16   Friedrich Engels, 'Introduction to K. Marx's *The Civil War in France*' (1891), *MECW*, vol. 27, 191.

17   See Jacques Texier, *Révolution et démocratie chez Marx et Engels* (Paris: Presses Universitaires de France, 1998), 131–44.

of the insurgents themselves: this was a question of historical phenomenology rather than of political ontology. Neither the time nor
the form of revolutions can be foreseen; one might rather think that
they always surprise their actors. Furthermore, Marx's allusions to
proletarian dictatorship exclusively referred to continental Europe;
some interpreters suggest that he did not exclude the possibility of
a peaceful transition to socialism in both the United Kingdom and
the United States.[18] As for Friedrich Engels, at the end of his life he
openly dismissed any insurrectionary model of revolution. One of his
last texts, a new introduction to Marx's *The Class Struggles in France*
(1895), drew this balance sheet:

> The time of surprise attacks, of revolutions carried through by small
> conscious minorities at the head of masses lacking consciousness
> is past. Where it is a question of a complete transformation of the
> social organization, the masses themselves must also be in on it,
> must themselves already have grasped what is at stake, what they
> are fighting for, body and soul. The history of the last fifty years
> has taught us that.[19]

This was the time in which, despite the archaic and discriminatory
institutions of the Prussian empire, Engels interpreted the growth of
German social democracy as an almost 'natural process' that unfolded
'spontaneously', 'steadily', and 'irresistibly'.

By 1917, the Great War had swept away the optimistic prognostics
of the older Engels and revolutions had once again become military
uprisings. In the Russian turmoil of that crucial year, Lenin resolved
Marx's questions by extracting some ideas from his writings and fixing
them into a coherent doctrine based on four basic assumptions:

1. The state is a transitional institution. In the past, human communities could exist without a state and therefore we can imagine a

---

18   Ibid., 23. See also Karl Marx, 'On the Hague Congress' (1872), *MECW*,
vol. 23, 255.

19   Friedrich Engels, 'Introduction to Marx's *The Class Struggles in France*'
(1895), *MECW*, 27, 520. On this reassessment by the older Engels, see Texier,
Révolution et démocratie, 169–224.

future emancipated community without a state. The state is a historical product of the class society and results from the 'irreconcilability of class antagonisms'.[20] In a capitalist society, it is inevitably a bourgeois state, i.e., a tool conceived and used in order to defend the interests of the ruling class.

2. Revolution is a mass uprising of the oppressed that reverses the bourgeois state and establishes a revolutionary power. A bourgeois state cannot be transformed; it has to be destroyed by a violent action (Lenin quotes Marx's term: *Zerbrechung*). This confirms the role of violence as 'midwife [*Geburtshelferin*] of every old society pregnant with a new one', according to Marx and Engels's words.[21] At the end of the First World War, the idea of a peaceful transition to socialism struck Lenin as simply unrealistic and laughable.

3. Revolution is a creative destruction. Dismantling the old oppressive state, the proletarian classes establish a new power: a proletarian dictatorship. This new power is democratic – its organs are elected by universal suffrage – and repressive at the same time: it aims at consolidating proletarian rule against any attempt by the old ruling classes to restore their power. The model of proletarian dictatorship is the Paris Commune, which abolished the old army and police and replaced them with a workers' militia (*Garde nationale*). As a proletarian dictatorship, the Commune did not build representative but rather working institutions. It replaced the 'government of persons' with the 'administration of things'. The elected representatives of the Commune were executives; they were permanently replaceable and did not have any privileges.

4. Because of its own nature, structure and function, the proletarian dictatorship is doomed to disappear. It is a state that creates the premises of its own extinction. When society becomes able to conduct a complete form of self-management, the state will become useless,

---

20   Lenin, 'The State and Revolution', 392.

21   Ibid., 404. See Karl Marx, 'Capital' (1867), *MECW*, vol. 35, 739; and Friedrich Engels, 'Anti-Dühring: Herr Eugen Dühring's Revolution in Science' (1878), *MECW*, vol. 25, 171. For a critical reconstitution of the Marxist debate on revolutionary violence, see Étienne Balibar, 'Reflections on *Gewalt*', *Historical Materialism*, 17 (2009): 99–125; and Titus Engelschall, Elfriede Müller and Krunoslav Stojaković, *Revolutionäre Gewalt: Ein Dilemma* (Berlin: Mandelbaum, 2019).

superfluous and will start to vanish. According to Engels's formula, the state 'dies out of itself' (*der Staat stirbt ab*)[22] and its vestiges will be placed 'into the museum of antiquity, by the side of the spinning-wheel and the bronze axe'.[23]

Having established the principles of orthodox Marxism, Lenin emphasized the cleavage that separates them from both social-democratic reformism and anarchism. Whereas the former simply renounced destroying the state, as was proven in 1914 by their vote for war credits, the latter had not abandoned the illusion of 'abolishing' the state. The discrepancy between Marxism and anarchism does not concern the final goal: communism as a society without classes or state. Their divergence lay in the means for achieving this goal. In contrast to the anarchists who wished to 'abolish' the state and rejected the principle of the proletarian dictatorship in name of their 'anti-authoritarianism', Lenin considered revolution as an extremely 'authoritarian' act. However relevant their differences might be, Marxism and anarchism share the same final objective: a stateless society. This is why, considering this teleological homogeneity, an advocate of juridical positivism like Hans Kelsen held Marx for one of the greatest thinkers of anarchism.[24]

Writing in the middle of a revolution, Lenin did not depict the proletarian dictatorship as a coercive power acting during a civil war (the experiences of both the French Revolution and the Paris Commune) but rather identified it with Soviet democracy. Despite its utopian approach to the question of the state – positing its 'extinction' in a self-emancipated human community – Lenin's essay presents many aporetic aspects. Depicting the organs of proletarian dictatorship as purely executive – its elected representatives assure the 'administration of things' – it does not clearly explain how democratic deliberation would work and how its elected executive agents can be controlled. Lenin completely neglects the political-juridical dimension – the legal framework – of the revolutionary state and gives no clue regarding

---

22   Lenin, 'State and Revolution', 401. Engels, 'Anti-Dühring', 268.

23   Engels, 'Origin of the Family', 272.

24   Hans Kelsen, *The Political Theory of Bolshevism* (Berkeley: University of California Press, 1948), 10–13.

fundamental issues such as political pluralism, individual and public liberties, the place for dissidence, and censorship.[25] Classical dictatorship may suspend laws, but it is legally allowed to do so and it acts in order to re-establish them. In a vacuum, however, everything becomes possible. In its most naïve formulation, the Marxist depiction of a communist future simply confirms the most pessimistic Weberian assessments about the 'iron cage' of cold rationalization and bureaucratization as the ineluctable destiny of Western modernity. Think of Nikolai Bukharin's and Evgenii Preobrazhensky's words in *The ABC of Communism* (1919), where they anticipated the functioning of a classless and stateless society. In their views, the sceptics' objections – 'who is going to supervise the whole affair?' – did not deserve to be seriously considered: 'It is not difficult to answer these questions. The main direction will be entrusted to various kinds of book-keeping offices or statistical bureaus.'[26] Read today, such a naïve trust in 'governance by numbers' is quite baffling.

A few years later, Lenin defended the idea of a necessary *party* dictatorship during the civil war. In 1921, he not only claimed a party dictatorship but even called for the suppression of all tendencies within the Bolshevik party.[27] His views had changed empirically, during the civil war, when the Bolsheviks felt isolated and the soviets were virtually emptied because of the disorganization of the economy and the transformation of workers into soldiers.

There is a significant discrepancy between Lenin's theory of revolution and his empirical management of power, between his concept of proletarian dictatorship and the phenomenological form that it took under his rule, a gap which he never tried to fill. Nor was his attempt to codify Marx's ideas as a coherent doctrine situated in a political theory of dictatorship. For the classical tradition of political thought, dictatorship is a state of exception that, as Giorgio Agamben

---

25   Norberto Bobbio sketched these critical observations in *Which Socialism? Marxism, Socialism, and Democracy* (Cambridge: Polity Press, 1987).

26   Nikolai Bukharin and Evgenii A. Preobrazhensky, *The ABC of Communism* (London: Merlin Press, 2007), 91.

27   See Martin Malia, *The Soviet Tragedy: A History of Socialism in Russia 1917–1991* (New York: Free Press, 1994), 167–8.

has convincingly explained, is a state of 'indeterminacy' both external and internal to the domain of law.[28] Through this concept, law tries to include in itself its own suspension. In other words, the state of exception is the interruption of law permitted by the law itself. It separates the norm from its application and therefore introduces – and recognizes – a zone of anomy inside the law: a force of law without law. Roman Law, Agamben argues, distinguished between *auctoritas* and *potestas*: the first embodied by a personal, physical, one could say 'biopolitical' authority; the second by a juridical and representative body. The state of exception was the junction of *auctoritas* and *potestas*, 'two heterogeneous yet coordinated elements',[29] in the figure of the dictator.

This distinction is the source of two opposed currents in the history of juridical thought: on the one hand, the thinkers of political sovereignty and, on the other, those of juridical positivism: *decisionism* versus *normativism*, two traditions embodied in the twentieth century by Carl Schmitt and Hans Kelsen. Schmitt thinks of the state as forged and shaped by an existential and political will (*Nomos*); Kelsen, on the contrary, as a structure of formalized norms. The former posits the priority of power, the latter that of law. For decisionism, it is power that determines the norm, as the original source of any juridical system; for normativism, on the contrary, it is the law that determines power, which exists only thanks to a system of rules that structure it. In fact, power is usually the result of a combination of force and law. As Norberto Bobbio points out, power without law is blind, but law without power is meaningless and ineffective. In other words, power not framed by a system of juridical constraints becomes illegitimate; but norms without content are an empty shell. This is why Weber did not wish to dissociate force (*Macht*) and legitimacy (*Herrschaft*). For Schmitt, norms simply followed decisions; for Kelsen, norms fixed the meaning and content of power. Claiming the Hobbesian matrix of his political thought, Schmitt emphasized that authority makes the

---

28   Giorgio Agamben, *State of Exception* (Chicago: The University of Chicago Press, 2005), 3.
29   Ibid., 86.

law – *Auctoritas facit legem* – whereas Kelsen tended to replace the concept of sovereignty with that of 'fundamental norm'.[30]

When this precarious and delicate articulation between power and law, decision and norms, is broken, and power completely 'emancipates' itself from the constraint of norms, the state of exception becomes structural, permanent, and destroys the law itself. In this case, the state of exception can become the source of a totalitarian power. That is the experience of the twentieth century. In juridical terms, Hitler and Mussolini were charismatic leaders that embodied *auctoritas*, a total power, but they were not 'dictators'. Their power expressed a state of exception as *iustitium*, not as dictatorship (they embodied a limitless power rather than a conferred dictatorial power).[31] With them, the meaning of dictatorship changed. In the past, it was a form of power distinct from despotism or tyranny. Far from being antipodal to democracy, it was a form of democracy in exceptional historical circumstances. Its archetype was Cincinnatus who, called by the Roman senate to defend the republic in 458 and 439 BC, became a dictator for a temporary period and then, after liberating the city, went back to his farm.

Undoubtedly, a *normativist* conception of the state cannot be of great help in analysing the establishment of proletarian dictatorship. In *Dictatorship* (1922), Carl Schmitt distinguished between classical dictatorship – a state of exception that suspended law but was authorized by a legal power – which he called 'commissarial dictatorship', and 'sovereign dictatorship', which emanated from a revolutionary, constituent power. The Soviet government belonged to this second category, like the Jacobin power during the French Revolution and Cromwell's absolute power during the English Revolution. The source on which the Comité de salut public and the Cheka, the organs of Terror in the French and Russian Revolutions, ultimately depended were the National Convention in 1793 and the Soviet government between 1918 and 1921. 'From the perspective of a general theory of the state,' Schmitt stressed, 'the dictatorship of a proletariat identified

---

30   This debate is well summarized by Norberto Bobbio, *Teoria generale della politica* (Turin: Einaudi, 1999), 183–99.

31   Agamben, *State of Exception*, 41–5.

with the people at large, in transition to an economic situation in which the state is "withering away", presupposes the concept of a sovereign dictatorship, just in the form it stands at the root of the theory and practice of the National Convention.'[32]

In short, it was Schmitt, not Lenin or Trotsky, who inscribed the dictatorship of the proletariat within a general theory of dictatorship. The main reason for this doctrinal aporia lies in the Marxist conception of revolution as destruction of sovereignty, as democracy against the state. While it was initially depicted as a force of destitution – an authoritarian power acting to eliminate any form of authoritarianism – during the Russian Civil War the Bolsheviks reformulated the doctrine of proletarian dictatorship as a new theory of sovereignty. Revolutionary *Potentia* became the *Potestas* of a revolutionary state; revolutionary *Gewalt* was replaced by state *Macht*.

Counterrevolution

Like Kant and Hegel, the greatest thinkers of legitimism clearly recognized the historical and universal significance of the French Revolution. Counterrevolution does not exist without revolution, and the two are deeply entwined. Scholars are used to distinguishing between two main ideological currents of counterrevolution: reaction and conservatism. Reaction is a radical refusal of modernity and the values introduced by the Enlightenment – first among them the Rights of Man – in the name of an idealized past embodied by the Old Regime. This was the posture of Joseph de Maistre and Louis de Bonald. Conservatism is a defence of tradition and an attempt to adapt it to the historical circumstances created by the revolution itself. In 1814, Restoration did not mean a simple return to absolutism; it was rather the establishment of constitutional monarchies that found a compromise between a dynastic order and the transformations introduced by the French Revolution. The 'Indian summer' of aristocracy after 1814 accompanied the rise of industrial capitalism. In the nineteenth century, conservatism kept the balance between the gentry and the

---

32   Carl Schmitt, *Dictatorship: From the Origin of the Modern Concept of Sovereignty to Proletarian Class Struggle* (Cambridge: Polity Press, 2014), 179.

bourgeoisie, the former outdated but still hegemonic as a cultural model and ruling over the 'persistent' dynastic states; the latter controlling the financial and industrial elements of still largely agrarian economies but not yet equipped with a worldview, a style of life, and its own institutions. René de Chateaubriand and Edmund Burke were its main representatives in France and the United Kingdom. Burke's hatred for Jacobinism was as radical as his convinced endorsement of the market economy.

During the great upheavals, however, reaction and conservatism converged in counterrevolution. In the 1790s, Burke and Maistre inspired the international military coalition opposed to revolutionary France. A similar convergence took place again half a century later, when both an absolutist like Juan Donoso Cortés and a partisan of classical liberalism like Tocqueville could welcome the massacre of the Parisian workers in June 1848.

In the 1790s, the philosophical background of counterrevolution was irrationalism, which considered the idea of a world regulated by reason as downright nonsensical. Created by God, the world of Legitimism was organized by Providence, not reason. Rejecting the doctrine of natural law, Burke opposed the 'historic rights' of the British aristocracy to the 'rights of man and citizen' proclaimed by the French Revolution, which were in his eyes the expression of an abstract and artificial rationality.[33] Burke, however, represented the 'moderate' current of counterrevolution: he was attached to the juridical framework of the British monarchy, had approved of American independence and looked positively on the development of market society. In continental Europe, counterrevolution was far more radical and sometimes took on an almost apocalyptic flavour. Its thinkers considered social and political inequalities to be just as natural as the vocation of human beings to obey their superiors. Contemptible and despicable, mankind deserved only to be chastised. History was a torrent of blood, a perpetual massacre, a slaughter in which human beings were punished for their sins. Authority, hierarchy,

---

33 Edmund Burke, *Reflections on the Revolution in France*, ed. L.G. Mitchell (Oxford: Oxford University Press 1993 [1790]).

discipline, tradition, submission, and honour: these were the values of counterrevolution.

For Maistre, the reversal of Absolutism and the execution of Louis XVI were events as preposterous as 'the instantaneous fructification of a tree in the month of January'.[34] His providential vision of history drove him to even accept the Terror as a sort of divine punishment against a sinful humanity and as the annunciation of an apocalyptic vengeance: 'If the vilest instruments are employed, punishment is for the sake of regeneration', and consequently, 'each drop of Louis XVI's blood will cost France torrents.'[35]

The darkest and most colourful figure of counterrevolution, Maistre was depicted by Émile Faguet as 'a fierce absolutist, a furious theocrat, an intransigent legitimist, apostle of a monstrous trinity composed of Pope, King and Hangman'.[36] Maistre denounced the French Revolution as an attack on the metaphysical foundation of a divine political order. Unlike Burke, who considered counterrevolution as a social and political process whose climax was a necessary war against republican France, Maistre viewed it as the imponderable result of Providence itself. Whereas Burke developed a conservative criticism of Enlightenment, Maistre rejected it in the name of an apocalyptic form of irrationalism. Since the French Revolution was 'radically bad' and possessed a 'satanic character', counterrevolution was more than a political strategy accomplished by human actors; it was a divine, providential, and almost metaphysical accomplishment: 'the restoration of the monarchy ... will be not a contrary revolution, but the contrary of revolution.'[37]

According to Isaiah Berlin, Maistre's counterrevolution prefigured, behind this anachronistic and obscurantist façade, the modernity of fascism and totalitarianism: he postulated a political order based on

---

34   Joseph de Maistre, *Considerations on France* (1797), ed. Richard A. Lebrun, preface by Isaiah Berlin (Cambridge: Cambridge University Press, 1994), 4.

35   Ibid., 8, 13.

36   Quoted by Isaiah Berlin, 'Joseph de Maistre and the Origins of Fascism' (1990), *The Crooked Timber of Humanity*, ed. Henry Hardy (Princeton: Princeton University Press, 2013), 97.

37   Maistre, *Considerations on France*, 38, 41, 105.

terror and theologically conceived as total rule. Literally fascinated by violence, Maistre idealized the executioner, the sacred agent of this divine order. The violence that he administered possessed the seal of sacredness. In his *St Petersburg Dialogues* (1821), written during the years of Restoration, he depicted the hangman as the pillar of his own political theology. 'All greatness, all power, all subordination', he wrote, 'rests on the executioner', whom he presented as 'both the horror and the bond of human association. Remove this incomprehensible agent from the world, and in a moment, order gives way to chaos, thrones fall, and society disappears. God, who is the author of sovereignty, is therefore the author of punishment.'[38]

Donoso Cortés, whom Carl Schmitt considered one of his main inspirations, embodied the connection between classical counterrevolution and modern fascism. This Spanish philosopher, essayist and statesman, Schmitt pointed out, was 'one of the greatest political thinkers of the nineteenth century',[39] in whom he found a peculiar fusion between an 'eschatological prophet' and an 'ambitious professional diplomat'.[40] In the age of classical liberalism, Donoso Cortés had perfectly understood the dilemma of 1848 – a historical confrontation between Catholic absolutism and atheistic socialism – which prefigured the crucial alternative of the twentieth century: revolution or counterrevolution, Bolshevism or fascism, anarchism or authoritarianism. In the wake of Maistre, Donoso Cortés was 'the most radical of the counterrevolutionaries, an extreme reactionary and a conservative of almost medieval fanaticism',[41] but these were the features that so

---

38   Joseph de Maistre, *St Petersburg Dialogues: Or, Conversations on the Temporal Government of Providence*, ed. Richard A. Lebrun (Montreal: McGill-Queen's University Press, 1993), 20. See also Berlin, 'Joseph de Maistre and the Origins of Fascism', 119–120.

39   Carl Schmitt, 'The Unknown Donoso Cortés' (1929), *Telos*, 125 (2002): 85. See also Carl Schmitt, 'On the Counterrevolutionary Theory of the State (de Maistre, Bonald, Donoso Cortés)', Chapter 4 of his *Political Theology: Four Chapters on the Political Sovereignty*, ed. Georg Schwab (Chicago: University of Chicago Press, 2006) 53–65.

40   Schmitt, 'The Unknown Donoso Cortés', 83.

41   Carl Schmitt, 'A Pan-European Interpretation of Donoso Cortés' (1944), *Telos*, 125 (2002): 101.

irresistibly attracted Schmitt himself. Donoso's writings, notably his *Discourse on Catholicism, Liberalism, and Socialism* (1851), had helped his German admirer to build some of his own fundamental concepts – decision, sovereignty, and dictatorship – as secularized political theological concepts rather than abstract juridical norms. It is Donoso who, one century earlier, had stigmatized liberalism as the mirror of an impotent *clase discutidora* and asserted the legitimacy of a dictator against the impersonal rule of law. Like Hobbes, Donoso knew that law does not establish any political order, but can become effective only when based upon a concrete authority. Embodied by worshipping soldiers, Catholic absolutism was a spiritual power incomparably superior to liberalism, a legal and mechanical order based upon the market and rational law (what Hans Kelsen called *Gesetzmässigkeit*). In 1849, Donoso welcomed the repression of the aborted insurrection in Barcelona, Sevilla and Valencia with an energetic speech that clearly proposed a dictatorship against revolution: 'When legality is enough to save society, legality; when it does not suffice, dictatorship.' Under certain circumstances, he thought, 'dictatorship is a legitimate government.'[42] Two years later, he explained that revolutions were a 'sickness' of both rich and free countries, the opposite of a world full of slaves, where 'religion taught charity to the rich and patience to the poor; taught the poor to be resigned and the rich to be merciful.'[43] Schmitt was fascinated by Donoso Cortés's allegorical style, his descriptions of history as a gigantic labyrinth in which sinful human beings were lost or as a boat piloted by a crew of drunk sailors in the middle of a tempest. Schmitt also liked Donoso's aristocratic contempt for human beings, depicted as a rabble of corrupted sinners who only deserved to be crushed to death (Donoso's 'contempt for man knew no limits'[44]). He appreciated this forceful imagination and certainly agreed with Donoso's plea for an authoritarian leadership: human beings needed to be ruled, that was their destiny.

---

42   Donoso Cortés, 'Discurso sobre la dictadura' (1849), *Discursos políticos*, ed. Agapito Maestre (Madrid: Tecnos, 2002), 6–7.

43   Donoso Cortés, 'Discurso sobre la situación general de Europa' (1850), *Discursos políticos*, 38.

44   Schmitt, *Political Theology*, 58.

The clash between revolution and counterrevolution lasted until the Great War, reinforced and exacerbated by the traumatic experience of the Paris Commune. In the second book of *The Origins of Contemporary France* (1878), Hippolyte Taine analysed the French Revolution with the help of the sciences then in vogue, from zoology ('the animal instinct of preservation') to race theory (the revolutionary crowds compared to 'negroes in a slave-hold') to heredity (revolution as an atavistic regression of civilized society to an ancestral barbarism). The Jacobins were madmen, as were the Communards: at the origin of the uprisings of 1789 and 1791, there was 'a pathological seed which, penetrating the blood of a suffering and profoundly ill society, had caused the fever, the delirium, and the convulsions of revolution.'[45] Similarly, Cesare Lombroso, the famous Italian criminologist, distinguished between 'revolution' and 'revolt' as profoundly different social phenomena, the one 'physiological' and the other 'pathological'.[46] Despite its name, the French Revolution belonged to this second category, and offered an inexhaustible reservoir of objects of study for the criminal sciences.

1917 opened a new cycle in the history of revolutions. For millions of people across the world, the October Revolution constituted, like 1789, the *signum prognosticum* of the emancipated humanity of the future. The Bolsheviks recognized in the Jacobins their precursors, in the framework of a historical continuity which Albert Mathiez had pointed out in 1920.[47] Unlike its French ancestor, however, the Russian Revolution never succeeded in projecting itself across the continent. The attempts to follow its example failed everywhere, from Germany to Hungary, from the Baltic Countries to Italy, where the *Biennio Rosso* of 1919–20 just preceded Mussolini's rise to power. Instead of being externalized – a task for which the Bolsheviks had

---

45   Hippolyte Taine, *Les origines de la France contemporaine. La Révolution: I. L'anarchie* (Paris: Laffont, 1972 [1878]), 123.

46   Cesare Lombroso, 'Le rivoluzioni e il delitto', *Delitto, genio, follia. Scritti scelti* (Turin: Bollati Boringhieri, 1995), 648–59. See also Sergio Luzzatto, 'Visioni europee della Rivoluzione francese', *Ombre rosse. Il romanzo della Rivoluzione francese nell'Ottocento* (Bologna: Il Mulino, 2004), Chapter 1.

47   Albert Mathiez, *Le bolchevisme et le jacobinisme* (Paris: Librairie du Parti socialiste et de l'Humanité, 1920).

created the Communist International in 1919 – the Russian Revolution had to fall back and defend itself tooth and nail during a bloody civil war, against an international coalition entirely comparable to that of 1792. Stalinism resulted from this retreat, but the revolution's call was vigorous and ran throughout the twentieth century, an epoch during which, despite conflicts and ruptures, the words 'revolution' and 'communism' became near synonyms. In 1920, Bertrand Russell defined Bolshevism as a synthesis of the French Revolution and original Islam: the attraction of its messianism appeared as irresistible as that of Muhammad in the seventh-century Arab world.[48]

Like Legitimism after 1814, in the 1920s the profile of counter-revolution also changed. The collapse of the European dynastic order fixed by the Congress of Vienna – what Karl Polanyi defined as 'The Hundred Years' Peace' – had rendered obsolete that philosophy which, for a century, had inspired the partisans of order and found its pillars in Catholicism, anti-republicanism, and conservatism. As many historians have observed in the wake of Zeev Sternhell and George L. Mosse, from the end of the nineteenth century the right became 'revolutionary' and conquered a mass support that it did not have, except for very short periods of time, in the previous century.[49] With the Great War, the nationalization of the masses took a great step forward. Nationalism acquired symbols and rituals borrowed from a Jacobin model – the people in arms – previously abhorred. Its leaders, often of plebeian origin, had discovered politics in street fights and the revolutionary lexicon suited them better than parliamentary rhetoric. It was in Germany that, in the aftermath of the war, an ideological constellation called 'conservative revolution' took form, whose most popular figure was the writer Ernst Jünger, alongside respected essayists and scholars such as Oswald Spengler, Moeller van den Bruck and Werner Sombart.[50] They were no longer nostalgic for

48 Bertrand Russell, *The Practice and Theory of Bolshevism* (New York: Harcourt Brace and Howe, 1920), 3.

49 Zeev Sternhell, *La droite révolutionnaire 1885–1914. Les origines françaises du fascisme* (Paris: Folio-Gallimard, 1997); George L. Mosse, *The Fascist Revolution: Towards a General Theory of Fascism* (New York: Howard Fertig, 1999).

50 See Stefan Breuer, *Anatomie de la Révolution conservatrice* (Paris: Éditions de la Maison des Sciences de l'Homme, 1996), and also Jeffrey Herf, *Reactionary*

the Old Regime, and had ceased to vituperate modernity in the name of cultural pessimism. They wanted to find a synthesis between the inherited values of anti-Enlightenment and a technological modernity that fascinated them. Across the 1920s, the 'conservative revolutionaries' converged progressively towards fascism. They wanted to erect a new order, indeed a new civilization, opposed at once to liberalism – seen as a heritage of the nineteenth century – and to communism. This new order was resolutely modern, for the ambition of fascism was to create a 'New Man', representative of the new dominant race forged in the trenches. In 1932, Mussolini celebrated the tenth anniversary of the 'Fascist Revolution' which, in imitation of its French ancestor, invented its own secular liturgy. Through symbols, rites, images and slogans, it created its own cult of the 'supreme being', one now incarnated by a charismatic, living leader.[51] In the case of National Socialism, this revolutionary rhetoric was equally strong, whereas it was utterly absent from Francoism, which came to power by crushing the left during a civil war. In Spain, any fascist 'revolutionary' discourse belonged to the early Falangism, which nonetheless was quickly absorbed by National-Catholicism. All fascist movements or regimes transcended the legacy of Legitimism.

Katechon

As we saw above, Carl Schmitt was the first political thinker to accomplish the conceptual transition from classical counterrevolution to fascism. Fascism claimed its modernity, and Mussolini denied being a disciple of Joseph de Maistre in a famous article written in 1932 for the *Enciclopedia Italiana Treccani*. He did not look at the Old Regime, he looked to the future. 'Fascism has not chosen de Maistre for its

---

Modernism: Technology, Politics, and Culture in Weimar and the Third Reich (New York: Cambridge University Press, 1985).

51   See Emilio Gentile, *The Sacralization of Politics in Fascist Italy* (Cambridge: Harvard University Press, 1996); Simonetta Falasca-Zamponi, *Fascist Spectacle: The Aesthetics of Power in Mussolini's Italy* (Berkeley: University of California Press, 1997), and Maddalena Carli, 'Par la volonté du Duce et par l'œuvre du parti: le mythe du chef dans le guide historique de l'exposition de la révolution fasciste', *Les Cahiers du Centre de recherches historiques*, 31 (2003): 2–12.

prophet', he wrote, adding that 'monarchical absolutism is a thing of the past, and so is the worship of the church.'[52] Schmitt, however, did not suggest the restoration of the past: he looked at new forms of absolute power – the total state – which he considered to be secularized versions of classical Absolutism. As he explained in his *Political Theology* (1922), the entire lexicon of modern political theory was composed of secularized theological categories.[53]

This assessment brings us back to the relationship between Schmitt and Cortés. As Reinhard Mehring suggests, the German juridical thinker transformed the Spanish reactionary into a kind of 'autobiographical mask'.[54] This mimicry reveals an intellectual background that was unusual for the Weimar years, when the harbingers of the Conservative Revolution came either from *völkisch* nationalism or from a cultural pessimism alien to the Catholic tradition. The names of Paul de Lagarde, Julius Langbehn and Arthur Moeller van der Bruck are neglected in Schmitt's writings, whereas he was an ardent admirer of Joseph de Maistre, Charles Maurras, and Léon Bloy, the representatives of French legitimism and Catholic nationalism. And, despite its reactionary features, his radicalism exposed him to the influence of the aesthetic transgressions of dadaist writers like Theodor Däubler and Hugo Ball, a constellation that put him far beyond the *Zentrum*'s political conformism. Like Donoso Cortés, Schmitt always considered himself as a Catholic outsider.

According to Schmitt, Donoso Cortés's political theology had one fatal limitation: he did not know the *katechon*.[55] This concept, which he discovered in 1932 in Paul's second letter to the Thessalonians, became a pillar of Schmitt's own political theology insofar as it offered a spiritual foundation for his ideological choices. The idea of a restraining force (*Aufhalter*) that delays the advent of the Antichrist and prevents the world from falling into complete impiety was embodied

---

52   Benito Mussolini, *The Doctrine of Fascism* (Berkeley: The University of California Press, 2019), 14.

53   Schmitt, *Political Theology*, 36.

54   Reinhard Mehring, *Carl Schmitt: A Biography* (Cambridge: Polity Press, 2014), 198.

55   Carl Schmitt, *Glossarium: Aufzeichnungen der Jahre 1947–1951*, ed. Eberhard von Medem (Berlin: Duncker & Humblot, 1951), 63.

in the Middle Ages by the Christian emperors. Schmitt theorized this category for the first time in *The Nomos of the Earth* (1950), but he had used it in many letters and occasional texts since the beginning of the 1930s.[56] Fundamentally, he thought the *katechon* could also find a secularized form and the search for its modern equivalent became the secret tropism of his political commitment. In 1919, this overpowering religious force inspired the Bavarian Freikorps; after 1930, Schmitt claimed this role for the president, whom he suggested apply article 48 of the Constitution; and after 1933 he attributed the same role to Hitler, whom he saw as a national redeemer.

In 1944, in a lecture on Donoso Cortés he delivered at the University of Madrid, Schmitt implicitly compared the *katechontic* role of the German troops defending the Third Reich against the advance of the Red Army with the struggle the European counterrevolution waged in 1848 against atheistic socialism. In his eyes, the entire European civil war opened in 1914 became understandable through this 'great world-historical parallel'.[57] Any historical time, Schmitt argued in *Glossarium* (1951), had its own *katechon*. Once the era of Christian emperors was exhausted, new 'temporary, transient, splinter-like and fragmentary holders' appeared to fulfil their historical task. Sometimes, the secular aspect of this spiritual force was less than beautiful. From 1789 until the battle of Stalingrad, nevertheless, the *katechon* had recognizable enemies: atheism, socialism and Bolshevism. Whatever form it took, the *katechon* showed a heroic dimension and displayed Promethean strength.

Revolution and counterrevolution were radically opposed; they could neither converge nor find a compromise. They were neither similar nor equivalent, against a conventional wisdom that tends to place them in the same category of totalitarianism by focusing exclusively on their shared hostility (for opposite reasons) to classical

---

56   Carl Schmitt, 'The Christian Empire as a Restrainer of the Antichrist (*Katechon*)' in *The Nomos of the Earth in the International Law of the Jus Publicum Europeum*, ed. G. L. Ulmen (New York: Telos Press, 2003), 59–61. See Felix Grosseutschi, *Carl Schmitt und die Lehre vom Katechon* (Berlin: Duncker & Humblot, 1996). On the concept of *katechon*, see in particular Massimo Cacciari, *Il potere che frena: Saggio di teologia politica* (Milano: Adelphi, 2013).

57   Schmitt, 'A Pan-European Interpretation of Donoso Cortés', 105.

liberalism. They did not converge, but their trajectories revealed a striking symmetry. Socialist revolution and national or fascist revolution rejected the traditional ideas and practices of both reformism and parliamentarism, social democracy and liberalism. Bolshevism and fascism claimed a state of exception – proletarian dictatorship or fascist total state – able to adopt radical measures and change the established order. They radically disagreed on the means – mass mobilization from below or charismatic leadership – but neither saw any alternative to a violent break with the past. Both looked to the future by mobilizing a political imagination inhabited by utopias (classless society) or myths (a timeless racial order). The rare attempts at finding a synthesis between these antipodal options were ambiguous – think of the passion of the late Georges Sorel for both Mussolini and Lenin,[58] or the ephemeral experience of 'national Bolshevism' in Germany[59] – and invariably failed: overcoming the opposition between revolution and counterrevolution was simply inconceivable. Their symmetry deserves to be analysed, nonetheless.

An emblematic mirror of the impossibility of a 'dialogue' between Marxism and fascism is a letter sent by Walter Benjamin to Carl Schmitt in 1930, in which he stressed how much his book *The German Tragic Drama* (1928) owed to *Political Theology* and *Dictatorship*, two works that exposed Schmitt's theory of sovereignty. His own 'working methods as a philosopher of art', Benjamin wrote, significantly corresponded with the 'approach to the philosophy of the state' developed by the conservative juridical thinker.[60] Ten years later, Benjamin

---

58   The ambiguities of Sorel towards Lenin and Mussolini are emphasized by Isaiah Berlin, 'Georges Sorel', *Against the Current: Essays in the History of Ideas*, ed. Henry Hardy (New York: Viking Press, 1980), 296–332.

59   On the Bolshevik side, this option was – paradoxically – defended by the most internationalist of the Central European revolutionaries: Karl Radek. See Pierre Broué, *The German Revolution 1917–1923* (Chicago: Haymarket, 2006 [1971]), 889–98. On the nationalist side, see Otto Ernst Schüddekopf, *Like Leute von Rechts: Nationalbolshewismus in Deutschland von 1918 bis 1933* (Stuttgart: Kohlhammer, 1960). See also Michael Pittwald, *Ernst Niekisch: Völkischer Sozialismus, nationale Revolution, deutsches Endimperium* (Cologne: Papyrossa Verlag, 2002).

60   Walter Benjamin, *Gesammelte Briefe*, ed. Christoph Gödde and Henri Lonitz (Frankfurt/M: Suhrkamp, 1995–2000), vol. 3, 558. The letter is reproduced in Jacob Taubes, *To Carl Schmitt: Letters and Reflections*, ed. Keith Tribe,

mentioned again both the 'Antichrist' – fascism – and the 'state of exception' of the oppressed in his famous theses 'On the Concept of History' (1940), a powerful text that mingled Marxism and messianic hopes, secular and theological categories. The sixth thesis evokes the Messiah who 'comes not only as the redeemer' but also 'as the victor over the Antichrist', and the eighth thesis argues that, according to 'the tradition of the oppressed', 'the "state of emergency" [*Ausnahme-zustand*] in which we live is not the exception but the rule.'[61] In 1930, Schmitt did not answer Benjamin's letter, but he carefully read the book and, years later, noted in the margins of the second edition of *The German Tragic Drama* these significant words: 'an insuperable intensity of the arguments and an insurmountable distance from the interlocutor.'[62]

Impossible under the Weimar Republic – because of Benjamin's communism and Jewishness – this dialogue was reattempted, after the Second World War, by the Jewish anarchist and nihilist theologian Jacob Taubes. Banned from German universities, Schmitt had retired in Plettenberg and no longer played any public role in the Federal Republic or elsewhere. When he died, in 1985, Taubes wrote an obituary that was a remarkable tribute to him. Without trying to overcome the gap that separated the 'secularized messianic dart of Marxism' from the political thought of an 'apocalyptic prophet of the counterrevolution', he recognized that he himself was an 'apocalyptic spirit' who felt 'close' to the German thinker, despite their radical political antagonism.[63]

Introduction by Mike Grimshaw (New York: Columbia University Press, 2013), 16–17, 46–7. See also Howard Eiland and Michael W. Jennings, *Walter Benjamin: A Critical Life* (Cambridge, MA: The Belknap Press, 2014), 350.

61   Walter Benjamin, 'On the Concept of History' (1940), *WBSW*, vol. 4, 391–2.

62   Quoted by the editors of a letter sent by Jacob Taubes to Schmitt in July 1970. See Jacob Taubes and Carl Schmitt, *Briefwechsel*, eds Thorsten Palzhoff, Martin Treml, Herbert Kopp-Oberstrebink (Munich: Wilhelm Fink, 2012), 247, note 41.

63   Taubes, 'Carl Schmitt: Apocalyptic Prophet of the Counterrevolution' (1985), *To Carl Schmitt*, 8.

Remembering this shipwrecked dialogue which took place during the Weimar Republic points out the complexity of German political culture in the 1920s and the 'dangerous liaisons' between a Jewish-Marxist critic like Walter Benjamin and a Catholic conservative thinker like Carl Schmitt.[64] Transcending the boundaries of its original realm, it is also meaningful insofar as its proper realm – political theology – casts a light on a broader ensemble of *structural symmetries* between revolution and counterrevolution that could be summarized this way:

Walter Benjamin *Revolution*	*Carl Schmitt* *Counterrevolution*
Destruction of juridical and political order	Decisionism
Anarchy	Leviathan as total state
Proletariat	Dictator
Proletarian dictatorship	Fascism
Jewish Messianism	Catholic Theology
Antichrist = Fascism	Antichrist = Bolshevism
Messiah against Antichrist	Katechon against Antichrist
Communism as secularized Messianism	Fascism as secularized Absolutism
Vanquished	Sovereign
Remembrance	Tradition
Uprising from below	Decision from above
Revolutionary Left	Extreme Right

Iconoclasm

Revolutions wish to erect a new order and create their own system of values, but they always begin by destroying the symbols of prior domination. Iconoclasm is consubstantial with them, and it explains their antinomic relation with the materiality of the realms of memory.[65] To triumph, revolutions must destroy not only the established order

64   On this shipwrecked correspondence, see Susanne Heil, *Gefährliche Beziehungen: Walter Benjamin und Carl Schmitt* (Stuttgart: J. B. Metzler, 1996).

65   See Dario Gamboni, *The Destruction of Art: Iconoclasm and Vandalism since the French Revolution* (London: Reaktion Books, 2007). Considering the Paris Commune, this topic is well analyzed by Bertrand Tillier, *La Commune de Paris: Révolution sans images? Politique et représentations dans la France républicaine 1871–1914* (Paris: Champ Vallon, 2004).

with its institutions but also their symbols and emblems, sometimes their buildings and their sites. In most cases, their *pars construens* transcends and escapes this disruptive moment and does not belong to it even if this iconoclastic fury is one of its premises. The conventional assessment, that the French Revolution introduced irreversible transformations into European societies, is undoubtedly true, but this was the accomplishment of the revolutionary process, not the immediate result of the revolutionary uprising. In other words, without the French Revolution feudalism would not have been abolished in Central Europe and the civil code would not have been established – but this task fell to Napoleon. The Napoleonic Wars were of course inscribed in a mutation that began in 1789, but the Ninth of Thermidor had marked a break, and the Empire had turned the page on the First Republic. The Parisian Arc de Triomphe belongs to the history of the French Revolution in the same way that the Stalinist Constitution of 1936 belongs to that of the Russian Revolution; the two are inscribed in the *longue durée* of the revolutionary process, but they no longer belong to – they even contradict – the radiance of the Revolution as an event, as a break in the historical continuum, as a violent passage from one social and political order to another. They rather symbolize the transformation of revolution into a new despotic order. The revolutionary spirit cannot be bottled and displayed in museums. The Carnavalet Museum reifies the French Revolution as a historical object that finds its place in a national heritage, and inscribes it into the state annals rather than in a collective memory of emancipation. In a different register, the iconography showing the aligned profiles of Marx, Engels, Lenin and Stalin illustrates the history of the USSR rather than transmitting a revolutionary memory. It would no doubt be easier to find counterrevolutionary sites of memory, such as the Saint-Michel fountain, where the archangel killing the serpent symbolizes the repression of June 1848,[66] or the Basilica of Sacré-Cœur in Montmartre, erected to sanctify the destruction of the Paris Commune.[67] Unlike these monuments, revolutionary realms of memory

---

66 Dolf Oehler, *Le Spleen contre l'oubli. Juin 1848, Baudelaire, Flaubert, Heine, Herzen* (Paris: Payot, 1996), 22.

67 Cf. David Harvey, 'The Building of the Basilica of Sacré-Cœur', *Paris, Capital of Modernity* (London: Routledge, 2006), 311–40, and François Loyer, 'Le

possess an essentially symbolic and immaterial character; their deepest meaning lies in the *void* left by the destructive force of revolution itself.

Much evidence illustrates this simple fact. When in 1880 the Third Republic instituted July 14 as a national holiday[68] – today an occasion for military parades – the very nature of the revolutionary event that inspired this celebration was completely eclipsed. And similar considerations could be extended to other sites, symbols or cultural practices institutionalized by the Third Republic – think of the Pantheon or the Marseillaise – which transformed the memory of the French Revolution into a national patrimony not very different from the Palace of Versailles. Once domesticated, the revolutionary legacy could coexist with both the bourgeois order and the colonial empire.

For the rioters of the Faubourg Saint-Antoine, the taking of the Bastille was originally just a practical necessity – to obtain powder for their weapons – but it quickly turned into an act of symbolic destruction.[69] The fortress only held seven prisoners, but it had been a materialization of aristocratic rule since the Middle Ages. In his *History of the French Revolution* (1847), a historiographical monument that could also be read as a mirror of 1789 in the nineteenth-century French collective memory, Jules Michelet describes the magnitude of the task accomplished by the Parisian people:

> The Bastille, though an old fortress, was nevertheless impregnable, unless besieged for several days and with an abundance of artillery. The people had, in that crisis, neither the time nor the means to make a regular siege. Had they done so, the Bastille had no cause for fear, having enough provisions to wait for succor so near at hand, and an immense supply of ammunition. Its walls, ten feet thick at the top of the towers, and thirty or forty at the base, might long laugh at cannon-balls; and its batteries firing down upon Paris, could, in the meantime, demolish the whole of the Marais and the Faubourg

---

Sacré-Cœur de Montmartre', in Pierre Nora (ed.), *Les lieux de mémoire. Tome 3. De l'archive à l'emblème* (Paris: Gallimard, 1992), 450–73.

68   See Christian Amalvi, 'Bastille Day: From Dies Irae to Holiday', in Pierre Nora (ed.), *Realms of Memory: The Construction of the French Past* (New York: Columbia University Press, 1992), vol. 3, 117–59.

69   See Jean-Clément Martin, *Violence et révolution. Essai sur la naissance d'un mythe national* (Paris: Éditions du Seuil, 2006), 61.

Saint-Antoine. Its towers, pierced with windows and loop-holes, protected by double and triple gratings, enabled the garrison, in full security, to make a dreadful carnage of its assailants.[70]

Thus, Michelet concludes, the seizure of the Bastille was an act inspired and allowed by the irresistible strength of the insurgent people, not based on a calculated assessment of the balance of forces. Far from being reasonable, he emphasizes, 'it was an act of faith.'[71] How to explain this successful attack? The answer, Michelet suggests, lies in the symbolic dimension of this building: 'The Bastille was known and detested by the whole world. Bastille and tyranny were, in every language, synonymous terms.' Thus, 'the Bastille was not taken; it surrendered. Troubled by a bad conscience it went mad, and lost all presence of mind.'[72]

Commenced the day after its capture, its demolition would not be completed until 1806. The assault on the Bastille became an example that would largely be followed across the country, with innumerable destructions of churches and castles. As Hans-Jürgen Lüsebrink and Rolf Reichardt emphasize, the impact of this event pertained to its collective and anonymous character, tied to the action of crowds rather than to the charismatic influence of revolutionary leaders. The most significant features of the storming of the Bastille are its *iconicity* (its symbolic power), its *theatricality* (the staging of a public spectacle) and its *emotivity* (an action which affected the collective imagination and aroused a spontaneous identification) which made of it an example to be followed.[73]

The iconoclasm of the French Revolution – paradigmatic of all modern revolutions – would become the object of fierce controversies beginning in the 1790s, with the Republican tradition seeing in it the outlet of a popular anger at once legitimate and irrepressible,

---

70   Jules Michelet, *History of the French Revolution*, ed. Gordon Wright (Chicago: University of Chicago Press, 1967), 162.

71   Ibid.

72   Ibid., 176.

73   Hans-Jürgen Lüsebrink and Rolf Reichardt, *The Bastille: A History of a Symbol of Despotism and Freedom* (Durham: Duke University Press, 1997).

Jean Testard, *The Fall of the Bastille* (Between 1789
and 1794). Château de Versailles, France.

and conservative opinion stigmatizing it as the expression of *vandalism*. The destruction of ecclesiastical and noble property often took
on a ludic character, and played out like a people's festival in which,
according to popular recollection, social hierarchies were mocked and
overthrown. Trying to channel and contain this popular wave, on 14
August 1792 the National Assembly enacted a decree that prescribed
the systematic destruction of all monuments erected to 'prejudice',
to 'tyranny', and to 'feudality'. The Abbé Grégoire explicitly forged
the concept of 'revolutionary vandalism' in 1794, in the period of the
systematic destruction of the edifices of the Old Regime, by emphasizing its peculiar strength: its destructiveness was inseparable from
a 'regenerative' task.[74]

As well as scornfully belittling the manifestations of revolutionary
iconoclasm, the concept of 'vandalism' fails to grasp its methodical

---

74   See Bronislaw Baczo, 'Vandalism', in François Furet and Mona Ozouf
(eds), *Dictionnaire critique de la Révolution Française. Idées* (Paris: Flammarion,
1992), 507–22.

and conscious dimension. Unlike the 'ritual pillages' of premodern times – such as the traditional lootings that took place in Rome after the announcement of a pope's death[75] – the iconoclastic moments of modern insurrections not only carefully select their targets but also follow a rational procedure that cannot be reduced to a spontaneous outburst. Of course, they ritualize and give spectacular form to a powerful collective emotion that is released by the fall of a hated order. In February 1848, many portraits of Louis-Philippe were destroyed or disfigured, and processions headed by the bust of the overthrown king, with a rope around his neck, swept through several French cities in a sort of mimetic repetition of the ceremonies that had established his power. In most cases, however, revolutionary iconoclasm resulted from an ensemble of extremely precise and carefully planned initiatives that Emmanuel Fureix depicts as 'surgical gestures'.[76] In May 1871, the Paris Commune decided to demolish the private home of Adolphe Thiers, the chief of the Versailles government that was laying siege to the insurgent French capital. Located in the affluent area of Place Saint-Georges, it contained a collection of antique art pieces that were transferred to a museum while its furniture was donated to widows and orphans. Antoine-Matthieu Demay, the craftsman (member of the International Workingmen's Association) who directed the demolition, pointed out that this measure had nothing to do with vandalism. These art objects, he declared in a public meeting of the Commune, 'belong to the history of humankind and we wish to conserve the intelligence of the past in order to build the future. *We are not barbarians.*'[77]

The same division was inevitably reproduced when the Paris Commune, by a decree of 12 April 1871, decided to demolish the Vendôme Column. This Napoleonic memorial, the decree says, was 'a monument of barbarism, a symbol of brute force and of false glory, an affirmation of militarism, a negation of international law, a permanent

---

75   See Carlo Ginzburg, 'Saccheggi rituali: Premesse a una ricerca in corso', *Quaderni storici*, 65/2 (1987): 615–36.

76   Emmanuel Fureix, *L'œil blessé. Politiques de l'iconoclasme après la Révolution française* (Paris: Champ Vallon, 2019), 265.

77   *Journal des journaux de la Commune* (Paris: Garnier Frères, Libraires-Éditeurs 1872), vol. 2, 505. Quoted by Fureix, *L'œil blessé*, 263.

insult from the vanquishers to the vanquished, a perpetual attack on one of the three great principles of the French Republic, fraternity.' Prosper Olivier Lissagaray, the first historian of the Paris Commune, described the ceremonial demolition:

> On the 16 May, at two o'clock, an immense crowd thronged all the neighbouring streets, rather anxious as to the result of the opera-tion. ... A rope attached to the summit of the column was twisted round a capstan fixed at the entrance of the street. The Place was crowded with National Guards; the windows, the roofs were filled with curious spectators. ... The bands played the Marseillaise, the capstan turned about, the pulley broke and a man was wounded. Already rumours of treason circulated among the crowd, but a second pulley was soon supplied. ... At half past five the capstan again turned, and a few minutes after the extremity of the column slowly displaced itself; the shaft little by little gave way, then, sud-denly reeling to and fro, broke and fell with a low moan. The head of Bonaparte rolled on the ground, and his parricidal arm lay detached from the trunk. An immense acclamation, as that of a people freed from a yoke, burst forth. The ruins were climbed upon and saluted by enthusiastic cries, and the red flag floated from the purified ped-estal, which on that day had become the altar of the human race.[78]

After the military suppression of the Commune, the painter Gustave Courbet, president of its Fine Arts Commission, was considered responsible for this act of 'vandalism'. He was imprisoned for several months in Sainte-Pélagie and condemned to pay enormous reparations. In fact, Courbet had not determined the column's demolition. For all that he considered it 'an unhappily pretentious work of art which makes the foreigner laugh', 'a monument devoid of any artistic value, and one which perpetuates the ideals of war and conquest espoused by the imperial dynasty', he had suggested its relocation, notably by

---

78   Prosper Olivier Lissagaray, *History of the Commune of 1871*, trans. Eleanor Marx Aveling (London: Reeves and Turner, 1886 [1876]), 291. See also Michel Cordillot, 'La colonne Vendôme', in *La Commune de Paris 1871*, 731–3.

Bruno Braquehais, *The Vendôme Column
Demolished* (1871). Musée d'Orsay, Paris.

installing its bas-reliefs as a museum display at the Invalides.[79] In April,
however, as events unfolded, the Council of the Commune decided
to demolish the column in a public and spectacular ceremony, and
Courbet, as one of its members, endorsed this choice. During the
trial, he played the role of scapegoat in the symbolic war that opposed
the iconoclasm of revolution to the charge of vandalism made by the
restored moral and political order.

Erected in 1810 to commemorate the Napoleonic 'Grande Armée'
on a site that had hosted a statue of Louis XIV (destroyed in 1792),
the column was modified several times under the Restoration, the July
Monarchy and the Second Empire, topped first by an equestrian statue
of Henri IV, then by a new statue of Napoleon I dressed as a Roman
emperor, before being demolished under the Commune. It would be

---

79   Quoted in Alda Cannon and Frank Anderson Trapp, 'Castagnary's "A
Plea for a Dead Friend" (1882): Gustave Courbet and the Destruction of the
Vendôme Column', *Massachusetts Review*, 12/3 (1971): 502. On this episode,
see also Linda Nochlin, 'Courbet, the Commune, and the Visual Arts', *Courbet*
(New York: Thames & Hudson, 2007), 84–94, and Jonathan Beecher, 'Courbet,
Considérant et la Commune', in Noël Barbe and Hervé Touboul (eds), *Courbet,
peinture et politique* (Ornans: Les Éditions du Sekoya, 2013), 51–64.

St Petersburg, Peter and Paul Fortress. Nineteenth-
century anonymous photograph.

reconstructed at the beginning of the Third Republic, between 1873
and 1875. Once more, a monument became the target of the iconoclastic wave carried by a revolution that wanted to smash temporal
continuity and mark a rupture with the history of the victors. In May
1871, the demolition of the Vendôme Column fulfilled several purposes: it sought to mobilize the Parisians in defence of the Commune;
it sent a clear message to the government in Versailles, signalling
that the workers of Paris would not surrender without a fight; and
finally, it accompanied an appeal to the major French cities for help
(which the *Journal Officiel de la Commune* published the same day as
the destruction of the column).[80]

The Russian Revolution, during which the destruction of Orthodox churches and Tsarist palaces was just as systematic as in 1790s
France, worked out an interesting theoretical reflection on its own
iconoclasm. The occasion came in 1924, when the Soviet regime
decided to transform the Peter and Paul Fortress into a Museum of
the Revolution. Originally, this building had been the imperial family
tomb before becoming a Tsarist prison. After 1917, it was successively
a penitentiary for counterrevolutionary officers, a Bolshevik Party

---

80   See Fureix, *L'œil blessé*, 307.

office, and finally, during the civil war, the site of a military garrison. The transformation into a museum of so charged a site of memory strongly posed the question of the relationship of the revolution to Russia's past, at the moment when the former capital changed its name to become Leningrad; when the remains of the charismatic leader of October 1917, who had only just died, were to be embalmed in a mausoleum in Moscow; and when Trotsky, leader of the Red Army, was ousted from power.[81] It was the moment when a transition took place between the eruptive temporality of the revolutionary event – the caesura of October and of the Civil War – and the temporality of a consolidated Soviet regime that finally led to Stalinism. One could interpret such a transition, through Trotsky's lens, as a Soviet Thermidor. But this transition was not only political; it was also a shift towards a new regime of historicity. The passage from one temporality to the other was not ineluctable and implied a modification of the relationship between the revolution and the past. For the Russian avant-garde, notably for the supporters of futurism and suprematism, the revolutionary spirit was, by its own nature, incompatible with museums. The revolution should not create museums, it should destroy them. Museums conserve what is dead, whereas the revolution wanted to break with the past and project human beings toward the future; it must pursue its force, not take a step backwards by freezing itself as history.

The debate was vibrant and the transition was not without tensions. On the one hand, the premises of the Soviet regime had been posed by the revolution itself and, on the other hand, its spirit was perpetuated until the end of the 1920s. Petr Stolpianskij, the tour guide of the museum during this period, did not want to tell a linear history of the revolution, but rather to transmit its message by placing the visitors before a succession of 'dialectical images' articulated by Sergei Eisenstein's idea of montage.

---

81   On the metamorphoses of this historical building, see the indispensable PhD dissertation by Nicholas Bujalski, *Russia's Peter and Paul's Fortress: From Heart of Empire to Museum of Revolution 1825–1930* (Ithaca, NY: Cornell University, 2020).

Burned Church in Barcelona, 1936. Anonymous photograph.

Other revolutions deployed a similar iconoclastic fury. Arriving in Barcelona in December 1936, at the beginning of the civil war, when the city still displayed its revolutionary mettle, George Orwell observed that 'every church had been gutted and its images burnt.' In several places in the city, he saw churches 'being systematically demolished by gangs of workmen'.[82] In most regions seized by the anarchists, 'churches were wrecked and the priests driven out or killed.'[83] In what resembled spontaneous carnivals, militiamen damaged relics, dressed up in soutanes, pantomimed benedictions and fired on effigies of Christ. When republican troops occupied a village, churches were frequently used as latrines. Deeply impressed by this spectacle of impious savagery, Orwell interpreted it as the manifestation of an ersatz belief that conferred a sacred character to its own violence:

> Some of the foreign antifascist papers even descended to the pitiful lie of pretending that churches were only attacked when they were used as fascist fortresses. Actually, churches were pillaged everywhere and as a matter of course, because it was perfectly well understood that the Spanish Church was part of the capitalist racket. In six months

---

82   George Orwell, *Homage to Catalonia* (New York: Harcourt, 1952 (1938]), 4.
83   Ibid., 49.

in Spain I only saw two undamaged churches, and until about July
1937 no churches were allowed to reopen and hold services, except
for one or two Protestant churches in Madrid.[84]

In October 1956, the Hungarian insurgents destroyed the statue of
Stalin that stood in the city park of Budapest. Forty years later, it was
the Berlin Wall that was torn down. But the revolutions of 1989, as we
have seen, did not have the ambition of constructing a new order. In
Berlin, the former Palace of the Republic of the GDR, unanimously
judged to be atrocious, was demolished to reconstruct the former
Hohenzollern Castle: as for the Vendôme Column, history was turning
back to the past. Not far away, near Nikolaiviertel, there remained a
statue of Marx and Engels on whose pedestal someone had graffitied:
'We are not guilty' (*Wir sind Unschuldig*).

Symbols

For Ernst Bloch, the author of *The Principle of Hope* (1954–59), the
dreams of a better world arise from the tensions of a 'non-synchronic'
world, in which different and sometimes antipodal temporalities,
belonging to different eras, coexist in the same social space. In his
view, this heterogeneous structure of historical time – he called it
Ungleichzeitigkeit – is the source of utopian thinking and imagination,
in which the past and the future merge to invent new aesthetic and
intellectual configurations. Thus, his work consisted primarily in exca-
vating the past as an inexhaustible reservoir of experiences, ideas and
objects that bear witness to the search for a liberated future: imprints,
vestiges, traces (*Spuren*) of collective dreams, the images that portray
a desired community of free and equal human beings. *The Principle
of Hope*, a three-volume book like an impressive encyclopaedia of
utopias, from Antiquity to the twentieth century, is paradoxically
devoid of any prediction of a future world.[85] It is rather a historical
investigation of 'future pasts', a critical inventory of the innumerable

---

84   Ibid., 52.
85   Ernst Bloch, *The Principle of Hope*, trans. Neville Plaice, Stephen Plaice
and Paul Knight (Cambridge, MA: MIT Press, 1986), 3 vols.

ways in which people have imagined or 'anticipated' the future down the ages. This dialectical journey into the past looking for the future transforms Bloch into a kind of archaeologist who, with incredible erudition, patiently unearths and recomposes the 'daydreams' (*Tagträume*) of our ancestors: exhibitions, circuses, dancing, travel literature, novels, folklore, tales, poetry, paintings, operas, popular songs, movies and more. Bloch analyses utopias inscribed into the entire spectrum of human knowledge, from medicine to architecture, via aesthetics and technology.

However, this collector is far from being a naïve humanist. He neither believes in automatic progress nor idealizes the results of science. He does not simply classify utopias, distinguishing between technical, geographical, social, and political utopias, insofar as his historical reconstruction is as empathically selective as it is analytically critical. On the one hand, there is the 'cold stream' of utopias prefiguring a hierarchical, authoritarian, and oppressive order like Plato's *Republic*, Saint-Simon's *New Industrial Order*, and Étienne Cabet's *Icaria*, a frightening pre-totalitarian microcosm; on the other hand, the 'warm stream' of libertarian and communist utopias well represented by Thomas More, Charles Fourier, and Karl Marx: respectively, the most inspired Renaissance humanist, the inventor of the Phalansteries as realms of harmonious coexistence between nature and technology, and the thinker of human emancipation through class struggle. In the twentieth century, the apocalyptic age of wars and revolutions, utopias had become both concrete and possible, abandoning their previous character of abstract fantasy. By the end of the Great War, when Bloch wrote *The Spirit of Utopia* (1918), utopian hopes corresponded with political projects and were condensed into new revolutionary symbols.[86]

After 1917, among the most powerful symbols of revolution were certainly Sergei Eisenstein's movies. In 1927, the tenth anniversary of Soviet power, *October* created a synthesis between iconoclasm and memory of the revolution, between its signification of a historical *caesura* and its invention of a new *tradition*. The film opens with the

---

86   Ernst Bloch, *The Spirit of Utopia* (Stanford: Stanford University Press, 2000).

destruction of the statue of the tsar in February 1917 and concludes
with the taking of the Winter Palace in November. In both sequences,
the protagonist is the masses in movement. Eisenstein shot them in
a lyrical and heroic spirit that saw the events through a collective
rather than individual lens. In depositing themselves in the collective
unconscious of at least two generations, these scenes have forged and
canonized an image of revolution that transformed it into a symbol
and a realm of memory.

Born as a propaganda work commissioned by Sovkino, the Soviet
state film agency, and inspired by John Reed's chronicle *Ten Days that
Shook the World* (1919), Eisenstein's movie did not set out to depict
the fateful October days as a realistic historical reconstruction; its
goal was to represent their historical meaning, by showing through
imagery the Bolshevik conception of revolution: a mass insurrection
led by a vanguard party and taking the form of a military action. In
this spirit, he also planned to shoot a movie of Marx's *Capital*. As
he wrote in 1930, his cinema was a form of art that accomplished a
synthesis between experience, emotions and thought by giving it a
dynamic character:

> In the early times, the times of magic and religion, science was
> simultaneously an element of emotion and an element of collective
> knowledge. With the advent of dualism [from the Enlightenment
> onwards] things became separated and we have, on the one hand,
> speculative philosophy, and, on the other, the element of pure
> emotion. We must now go back, not to the primitive stage of the
> religious state but towards a similar synthesis of the emotional
> element and the intellectual element.[87]

Movies are privileged devices able to dynamize abstract ideas by
transforming and condensing thoughts into images. This corresponds
quite well to what Walter Benjamin called 'thought-images' or 'figures
of thought' (*Denkbilder*) – images that transcend words and condense

---

87   S. M. Eisenstein, 'The Principles of the New Russian Cinema' (1930),
Selected Works: I. Writings 1922–34, ed. Richard Taylor (Bloomington: Indiana
University Press, 1988), 199.

in themselves ideas, experiences and emotions.[88] This is why certain sequences of *October*, like the teeming masses in the Nevsky Prospect during the July insurrection or the storming of the Winter Palace, have achieved the iconic status of a metaphor and a symbol.[89] They catch the meaning of a historical event by showing its dynamism, its emotional dimension, and simultaneously fix a military paradigm of revolution as armed insurrection (the latter reinforced by the participation in the movie of Antonov Ovseyenko, the secretary of the Military committee of the Petrograd Soviet in 1917). We know that the Winter Palace was not 'stormed' by mass action – both chronicles and historical accounts, including those of the Bolsheviks, emphasize this point – but peacefully surrendered. Still, the revolution required its symbol, its own seizure of the Bastille. And this is also the reason why certain photograms from *October* have become a metaphor of revolution as a timeless event. According to Siegfried Kracauer, in *October* Eisenstein takes some incidents – the drawbridge episode, or the assault on the Winter Palace – 'out of the time of action and ... dilates them to magnify an emotion or drive home a thought'.[90] This is the secret of Eisenstein's *pathos* that grasps the climactic moment of revolution and turns it into a thoughtful and timeless constellation of images, a procedure that Benjamin called 'dialectics at a standstill'.[91] In his *History of the Russian Revolution* (1932), Trotsky captured this moment as the 'boiling point' of the dialectic of revolution: 'the critical point when accumulating quantity turns with an explosion

---

88   See Walter Benjamin, 'Thought Figures' (1933), *WBSW*, vol. 2, 722–7. See Gerhard Richter, *Thought-Images: Frankfurt School Writers' Reflections from Damaged Life* (Stanford: Stanford University Press, 2007).

89   According to Robert A. Rosenstone, '*October* tells us neither what happened nor what might have happened.' It rather 'creates a symbolic or metaphoric expression of what we call the Bolshevik Revolution', *History on Film/Film on History* (New York: Routledge, 2018), 60.

90   Siegfried Kracauer, *Theory of Film: The Redemption of Physical Reality* (Princeton: Princeton University Press, 1997 [1960]), 235.

91   Walter Benjamin, *The Arcades Project*, trans. Howard Eiland and Kevin McLaughlin (Cambridge, MA: The Belknap Press, 1999), 462. Georges Didi-Huberman has renamed this 'crystals of time': *Devant le temps. Histoire de l'art et anachronisme des images* (Paris: Éditions de Minuit, 2000), 218.

Sergei Eisenstein, The Storming of the Winter Palace, *October* (1927).

into quality.'[92] This symbol, metaphor, or *Denkbild* has nourished the revolutionary imagination of the 'short' twentieth century.

The transformation of an event into a symbol passes through multiple mediations which can modify its meaning. Despite their manifest universalism and global dimension, revolutions often end by inscribing themselves into a national heritage. If 14 July was originally a revolutionary event, today it has become above all else a French national holiday.

No similar metamorphosis has taken place in the case of the Paris Commune, which continues to symbolize revolution in the collective imaginary, well beyond French borders.[93] Its memory remains singularly refractory to all forms of institutionalization or semantic reinterpretation: it is hard to imagine a military parade in memory of the Paris Commune. There are practices and objects, ephemeral and transitory though they are, which commemorate revolution as a trans-historical and transnational experience, sometimes turning

---

92   Leon Trotsky, *History of the Russian Revolution* (Chicago: Haymarket, 2008 [1932]), 819.

93   Georges Haupt, 'La Commune comme symbole et comme exemple' (1972), *L'historien et le mouvement social* (Paris: François Maspero, 1980), 45–76.

into common objects, practices or rituals. Here, I will consider some symbols – the barricade, the red flag, and songs – before addressing visual traces.

The origins of the barricade are uncertain, but it had its first deployment in 1588, in Paris, in a France decimated by religious wars, when the population rose up against the entry of Henri III's troops. It reappeared during the Fronde, sixty years later, to then be eclipsed until the French Revolution, during which it resurfaced for a brief moment in May 1795 (Prairial Year III), during the riots against the Thermidorian Convention.[94] The barricade is made of heterogenous objects – overturned carts, furniture, barrels, paving stones – that the population piles up in the street to stop military forces that wish to take back control of the city. An invention of crowds, it dominated the revolutions of the nineteenth century: it reappeared in Paris in 1830, during the July Revolution, as well as in Belgium, then throughout Europe in 1848. It attained its apogee during the Paris Commune, before experiencing a progressive decline. But it manifested again in Russia in 1905 and 1917, in Berlin in 1919, in Barcelona in 1936 and 1937, in many European cities in 1944 and 1945, and back to Paris in May 1968, when its nature had changed and, largely deprived of its practical and military functions, it only preserved a symbolic dimension.

If the barricade has so profoundly impacted the spirit and is enduringly engraved in collective memory, this was always by virtue of its both anonymous and spectacular character. It has no leaders and is not determined from above. It is the spontaneous creation of crowds who draw, in emergency, on a capacity for self-organization unsuspected by observers who see in them only a naturally subjugated population. In his *Recollections* (written in 1850), Tocqueville describes the careful procedure of building a barricade in the streets of Paris adjacent to the Hôtel de Ville, during the days of June 1848. His social, psychological and existential distance from the insurgent workers gives his words the taste of an entomological account:

---

94 The best historical accounts are Mark Traugott, *The Insurgent Barricade* (Berkeley: University of California Press, 2010), and Eric Hazan, *A History of the Barricade* (London, New York: Verso, 2016).

I resolved to go and assure myself of the real state of things, and repaired to the neighbourhood of the Hôtel de Ville. In all the little streets surrounding that building, I found the people engaged in making barricades; they proceeded in their work with the cunning and regularity of an engineer, not unpaving more stones than were necessary to lay the foundations of a very thick, solid and even neatly-built wall, in which they generally left a small opening by the side of the houses to permit of ingress and egress.[95]

Another hostile observer, Gustave Flaubert, depicted the Paris barricades of February 1848 as follows in *Sentimental Education* (1869):

> The railings of the Convent of the Assumption had been torn away. A little further on he noticed three paving-stones in the middle of the street, the beginning of a barricade no doubt, then fragments of bottles and coils of wire, to obstruct the cavalry ... Men endowed with a kind of frenetic eloquence were haranguing the populace at the street corners; others were in the churches ringing the tocsin as loudly as ever they could; lead was being cast for bullets, cartridges were being rolled; the trees on the boulevards, urinals, benches, railings, gas-burners, everything was torn off and thrown down. Paris, that morning, was covered with barricades. The resistance which was offered was of short duration. The National Guard was everywhere – so that at eight o'clock the people, by voluntary surrender or by force, had got possession of five barracks, nearly all the town halls, the most favourable strategic points. Of its own accord, without any effort, the Monarchy was melting away in rapid dissolution.[96]

The barricade is spectacular, as it paralyzes the city and redraws its landscape. These are the subaltern classes that, with a sudden overthrow of social hierarchies, reorganize urban space. But the barricade transcends strictly sociological divisions and takes on an authentically

---

95   Alexis de Tocqueville, *Recollections* (New York: Macmillan, 1896), 191.

96   Gustave Flaubert, *Sentimental Education*, ed. Adrianne Tooke (London: Wordsworth, 2003), 303–4.

popular character. Alongside workers, it includes women and children as well as other social groups, from students to artists. Its function is double, both practical and symbolic. It gives a form to revolt in protecting insurgents, in controlling neighbourhoods, in neutralizing the intervention of repressive forces, in imposing relations of force, and it forges, in its welding, the revolutionary crowd. The barricade, writes Alain Corbin, is 'a machine to produce the people which, across the nineteenth century, never ceases to come upon insurrection.'[97] A site of action, it creates an emotionally intense sociability which is proper to it and which can shift, very quickly, from festival – order upended – to sacrifice, during combat: to perish on the barricade is thereby charged with a sacred aura, the revolutionary equivalent of dying on the field of honour for the patriotic narrative. This is why, notwithstanding or perhaps in virtue of its ontologically ephemeral character, it has engendered an enduring visual tradition, from painting to photography and cinema.

There are two daguerreotypes of the Paris barricades of June 1848 that depict the same street, rue Saint-Maur Popincourt, on 25 and 26 June, before and after the attack by the troops of general Lamoricière, one of the bloodiest days of the insurrection. Their author is an amateur photographer, M. Thibault, who took the scene from a distance, giving it a pictorial character. We know the date of these daguerreotypes because they were published in July by the magazine *L'Illustration* and later included in a special issue on the insurrection. They are regarded as the first examples of photographic illustration in the press,[98] and possess the aura of 'history phantoms:'[99] the trace of an inaugural wave of insurgent battles. In the history of art, the best-known barricade is Ernest Meissonier's canvas of the same name exhibited at the Salon of 1851, which depicts the victims of military repression on rue de la Mortellerie, near the Hôtel de Ville. The

---

97   Alain Corbin, 'Préface', in Corbin and Jean-Marie Mayeur (eds), *La Barricade* (Paris: Publications de la Sorbonne, 1997), 7–30.

98   See Thierry Gervais, *The Making of Visual News: A History of Photography in the Press* (London: Bloomsbury, 2017), 16–17.

99   Georges Didi-Huberman, *Désirer Désobéir. Ce qui nous soulève, 1* (Paris: Éditions de Minuit, 2019), 223–6.

Thibault, *Barricade of the rue Saint-Maur-
Popincourt before the army assault*, 25 June 1848.

Thibault, *Barricade of the rue Saint-Maur-
Popincourt after the army assault*, 26 June 1848.

Ernest Meissonier, *La Barricade* (1851).
Canvas. Musée du Louvre, Paris.

barricade has been destroyed and the dead bodies of young men are
sprawled over its scattered cobbles; their torn clothes evoke the colours
of the French flag. Meissonier was an artillery captain in the National
Guard who had participated in the massacre of the insurgents and had
been traumatized by the magnitude of the bloodshed:

> When the barricade of the rue de la Mortellerie was taken – he
> witnessed – I realized all the horror of such warfare. I saw the
> defenders shot down, hurled out of windows, the ground strewn
> with corpses, the earth red with the blood it had not yet drunk.[100]

Despite expressing his unease and even compassion for the victims,
his painting was conceived – T. J. Clark suggests – as a warning to
the labouring classes: revolutions will be pitilessly crushed. Lying on
the streets, the corpses are anonymous, faceless, and overwhelmed by
the halo of death that surrounds them. In this image where, according
to a Fourierist critic, 'the flesh and the clothes are confused with the

___

100   Quoted in T. J. Clark, *The Absolute Bourgeois: Artists and Politics in France
1848–1851* (London: Thames and Hudson, 1973), 27.

paving stones', the barricade has become an 'omelet of men' (*omelette d'hommes*).[101] For the conservative Augustin Thierry, Meissonier's canvas expressed a guilty ambiguity: unarmed, the corpses risked appearing as innocent victims. 'One does not counsel peace', he admonished, 'by insulting the victors and speaking in anger to the vanquished. One does not persuade men of the horror of civil war by calling vengeance.'[102] This episode proves that any conservative appropriation of the image of the barricade is almost impossible.

Pictures of the barricades would become current during the Paris Commune – the most famous are those of the Place de la Concorde[103] – particularly before the attack by the Versailles troops. They reappeared with the revolutions that followed the end of the Great War. In 1919, images of the Spartacist uprising in Berlin saw a wide diffusion in the form of postcards immortalizing the barricades.[104] After its national unification in 1871, Germany had become the European capital of publishers and the press, with dozens of newspapers and illustrated magazines. Each press agency possessed its own teams of photographers. During the January 1919 uprising, the armed workers came to the press district and occupied its heart, the Mosse building, where they used the imprint to publish the Spartakus League's newspaper, the *Rote Fahne*. With their cumbersome cameras standing at strategic points on streets and squares, photographers had become familiar to the insurgents and their presence lent solemnity to the events they shot. Sometimes, barricades were erected expressly for the cameras, with workers and soldiers repeating the gestures of the battle. This is the case for the many pictures of executions, which were staged after the event in order to show the courage of the insurrectionists and celebrate their sacrifice. What this proves is that the actors possessed

---

101   Ibid., 27–8.

102   Ibid., 27.

103   See Jean Baronnet and Xavier Canonne (eds), *Le Temps des cerises. La Commune de Paris en photographies* (Paris: Pandora Publishers/Éditions de l'Amateur/Musée de la Photographie, 2011).

104   Neue Gesellschaft für Bildende Kunst (ed.), *Revolution und Fotografie. Berlin 1918/19* (Berlin: Nishen Verlag), 1990. See also Enzo Traverso, 'The German Revolution', in Michael Löwy (ed.), *Revolutions* (Chicago: Haymarket, 2020), 209–61.

Willy Römer, Berlin, 11 January 1919 (*Freiheit-Postkarte*).

a clear awareness, not only of the historical dimension of the events in which they were involved, but also of their symbolism. In 1919, tens of thousands of 'freedom postcards' (*Freiheit-Postkarte*) were already circulating in Germany with the portraits of the martyrs of the Spartacist uprising and the Munich Soviet Republic.

The Berlin insurrection was doomed to failure. The social-democrats still controlled the majority of the labour movement and the insurgent workers were isolated. Born in the middle of this turmoil, the Spartakus League was far from being hegemonic. When Rosa Luxemburg's and Karl Liebknecht's attempt at stopping the insurrection failed, they took its leadership, willingly sacrificing themselves. In both Berlin and Munich, barricades did not prove very effective. The symbolic shift from the nineteenth-century barricades to the storming of the Winter Palace summarizes a significant change of paradigm in representing revolution: it is no longer the insurgent people but rather an organized army that seizes power. From this point of view, the Bolsheviks answered some questions put forward by Auguste Blanqui in his reflections on the defeat of June 1848. In his 'Instructions for an Armed Insurrection' (1868), he strongly emphasized the ineffectiveness of the barricades, even pointing at them as the main cause of the debacle. In July 1830 and February 1848, he stressed, the successful tactics of erecting barricades had been 'nothing but a stroke of luck.' In June, they proved to be useless, not to say calamitous. His charge was severe:

> As soon as the uprising broke out, barricades were erected here and there in the workers' districts, haphazardly, at many different locations. Five, ten, twenty, thirty, fifty men, assembled at random, the majority unarmed, started to overturn carriages, dig up paving stones and pile them up, sometimes in the middle of the street, more often at intersections, in order to block the roads. Many of these barriers would hardly present an obstacle to the cavalry. Sometimes, after making a rough start on the construction of their defenses, those building a barricade left it to set off in search of rifles and ammunition. In June there were more than six hundred barricades; thirty at most bore the brunt of the fighting. Of the others, at nineteen out of every twenty not a single shot was fired. Hence those glorious reports relating the sensational capture of fifty barricades where not a soul was to be found. While some dug up paving stones, others went in small groups to disarm the *corps de garde* or to seize gunpowder and weapons from the gunsmiths. All of this was done neither in unison nor under leadership but according to individual whim. Meanwhile, a certain number of barricades that were higher, stronger and better constructed gradually started to attract defenders, who gathered around them. The location of these principal fortifications was determined not by careful calculation but by chance. Only a few, as a result of rudimentary military inspiration, were designed to block the openings of important roads.[105]

The alternative to these mistakenly conceived and badly made barricades that wasted time, encumbered the streets, and blocked circulation, was the creation of a military organization made of experienced revolutionaries, both motivated and disciplined, able to act with the strength and effectiveness of a government army.[106] As a pure, ecstatic moment

---

105   Louis Auguste Blanqui, 'Instructions for an Armed Uprising' (1868), *The Blanqui Reader: Political Writings 1830–1880*, ed. Philippe Le Goff and Peter Hallward (London, New York: Verso, 2018), 203.

106   Ibid., 206.

of fraternity and collective action – the constitution of the people by erecting barricades – revolution was ineluctably defeated; it could not win except as an 'armed insurrection' (*prise d'armes*). According to Trotsky, this reflection was pertinent: Blanqui had misunderstood the social and political conditions for triggering insurrection, but his critical observations on the causes of the revolution's defeat in June 1848 were lucid and valuable.[107]

Since 1848, the barricade has been inseparable from the red flag. The latter had already been used, during the French Revolution, as a warning device by authorities against the troubles menacing public order, and had been the object of a dispute, beginning in 1791, between royalists and republicans. In the words of Jaurès, 'there was in the history of the red flag an ambiguous period in which its meaning oscillated between the past and the future.'[108] It seems that it takes its current significance from a sort of semiotic reversal: deployed by the royal authorities during the executions of sans-culottes, the latter appropriated it and began to make of it their emblem (this occurred with the insurrection of 10 August 1792, when the revolutionary crowds stormed the Tuileries Palace, put an end to the monarchy and established the National Convention, which proclaimed the Republic in September). It reappeared in 1830 and, like the barricade, became the symbol of the insurgents in all the revolutions of 1848. During the 'Springtime of Peoples', it was evidently not opposed to national flags, but it distinguished the socialist movements that fought, beyond liberal and democratic demands, for a 'social republic'. From 1848 to the Cold War, the red flag represented, for conservative forces, a symbol of blood and hate, brandished by Bolsheviks with a knife between their teeth; for left-wing movements, it was a symbol of the combat for an egalitarian society. According to Marc Angenot, in 1848 the red flag became the metaphor of a radical break with the ruling order that announced 'a counter-society with its own laws and rituals'.

---

107   Trotsky, *History of the Russian Revolution*, 742–3.

108   Jean Jaurès, 'Les Drapeaux' (1904), in Maurice Dommanget (ed.), *Histoire du drapeau rouge. Des origines à la guerre de 1939* (Paris: Éditions de la Librairie Étoile, 1967), 482.

On the barricades, it appeared as the sign of the 'metamorphosis of the ordinary world into a new, utopian reality'.[109]

From 1848 to the age of decolonization, red flags and national flags coexisted within a complex and often conflicting relationship: they mingled in national liberation struggles and clashed in imperial countries. The Russian Revolution proclaimed the right to self-determination for the nations of the Tsarist empire, but the outbreak of the civil war frequently produced a conflict between the defence of soviet power and the recognition of national independence. During the Second World War, the Red Army converged with the Resistance movements that, both in Europe and Asia, took a strong national character. In August 1944, tricolour flags decked the streets of Paris as a symbol of liberation; one year later, they had already become a symbol of colonial oppression in Algeria: after the bloody repression of the national movements in Sétif and Guelma, the population was forced to parade and bow in front of the French flag.[110]

This symbolic conflict between red and national flags was already apparent in 1848, even if it was clearly softened by the socialist support for national liberation. In France, this crucial year saw the defeat of the red republic by the tricolour republic in June. On 25 February, when the insurgent forces raised red flags over the main entrance of the Hôtel de Ville and nearby rooftops in Paris, anti-socialist republicans vehemently protested. Lamartine, their most charismatic representative, pronounced a passionate speech against 'the banner of terror' that we can see as summarizing the arguments of a coming century of Red Scare. Spurning 'this bloody flag' that had been dragged through the Terror of 1793, he defended the tricolour, 'the flag of Republic and Empire', which was 'known the world over as a symbol of France, of French glory, and of French liberty'.[111] He won, and it was from

---

109   Marc Angenot, 'Le drapeau rouge: Discours et rituels', in *L'esthétique de la rue. Colloque d'Amiens*, ed. Françoise Coblence, Sylvie Couderc, Boris Eizykman (Paris: L'Harmattan, 1999), 73–99.

110   See Yves Benot, *Massacres coloniaux. 1944–1950: la IV République et la mise au pas des colonies françaises* (Paris: La Découverte, 2001).

111   Quoted in Raoul Girardet, 'The Three Colours', in Nora (ed.), *Realms of Memory*, vol. 3, 17.

an Hôtel de Ville decorated with tricolours that he proclaimed the Second Republic. The following day, Auguste Blanqui retorted that the tricolour flag was no longer the flag of the Republic but rather 'that of Louis-Philippe and the monarchy'. It was the flag that had 'been bathed twenty times in the blood of the workers', whereas the red flag had 'received the double consecration of defeat and victory' and had become the symbol of the labouring classes. 'From this day forward', Blanqui explained, 'this banner is theirs'. Yes, it was 'the flag of blood', as Lamartine had claimed, but only because it was coloured with 'the blood of the martyrs who made it the standard of the Republic'. Its removal from the Hôtel de Ville was therefore 'an insult to the people, a profanation of its dead'.[112]

In 1871, however, there was no Lamartine to stand up for the tricolour when the Paris Commune raised the red flag again. On 4 May, the soldiers of the National Guard paraded at the Hôtel de Ville swearing an oath of loyalty to the red flag; they were ready 'to die by defending the red banner'.[113] *Le Père Duchesne* – a newspaper that borrowed its title from Jacques Hébert's homonymous journal during the French Revolution – explained in similarly passionate words why the tricolour and the red standard had become incompatible:

We want nothing more to do with the fraudulent flag of your shameful – allegedly moderate and respectable – Republics. We want nothing more to do with a flag under which Louis-Philippe's paunchy confederates gabbed and guzzled and under which December's soldiers feasted and massacred. ... When a nation's standard has been dragged through such shameful quagmires, its fabric has to be changed and so its colour. The red flag, which is red only because it is drenched in the blood of the people spilled by the forces of reaction, must replace the flag on which Hoche's blood has been covered up by the spattered brains of Le Creusot's miners ...[114]

---

112   Louis Auguste Blanqui, 'For the Red Flag!' (1848), *The Blanqui Reader*, 74.

113   *Journal Officiel de la Commune*, 5 May 1871, quoted in Fureix, *L'œil blessé*, 39.

114   Quoted in Girardet, 'The Three Colours', 17–18.

After the violent repression of June 1848 and the 'bloody week' that crushed the Paris Commune in May 1871, counterrevolution made the red colour an object of fetishistic demonization; nothing red could be tolerated, and burning red fabrics became a ritual of purification and a practice of public safety. In 1849, Léon Faucher, the state secretary of the first conservative republican government, issued a circular letter directed to the prefects that contained very precise instructions: 'The red flag is a plea for insurrection; the red cap recalls blood and mourning; bearing these sad marks means provoking disobedience.' Therefore the government ordered the immediate banishment of those 'seditious emblems'.[115] After the Paris Commune, a witness wrote in his memoirs that the city was seized by 'a crazy rage against all that was red: clothes, flags, ideas, and language itself ...' The colour red, he explained, had become 'a mortal disease' whose return should be avoided absolutely, as we do 'the plague and the cholera'.[116]

This symbolic war of colours restarted in 1917, when the Soviet Republic almost naturally adopted the red flag. During the Russian Civil War, the revolutionary terror became the 'Red Terror' and an anti-Bolshevik wave swept the world, from Europe to the United States, as a 'Red Scare'. The Soviet avant-garde took over the colour red as a revolutionary symbol and used it on a large scale in their aesthetic creations. In *Beat the Whites with the Red Wedge* (1919), a lithograph by the suprematist painter El Lissitzky, the clash between revolution and counterrevolution becomes a confrontation of abstract forms and colours: a red triangle breaks, arrowlike, into a white circle.

Revolutionary memory also possesses a sonic dimension. It is transmitted through songs which, created as incitation to struggle, subsequently become identity markers, and go on to change their meaning. The universally known example is that of the Marseillaise.[117] Composed

---

115   Quoted in Fureix, *L'œil blessé*, 295.

116   Louise Lacroix, *Les écharpes rouges: Souvenirs de la Commune* (Paris: Laporte, 1872), 8–9. Quoted in Fureix, *L'œil blessé*, 66.

117   See Michel Vovelle, 'La Marseillaise: War or Peace', in Nora (ed.), *Realms of Memory*, vol. 3, 29–74.

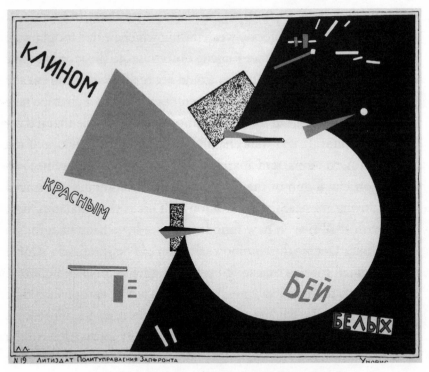

El Lissitzky, *Hit the Whites with the Red Wedge!*
(1919). Canvas. Tate Gallery, London.

by Joseph Rouget de L'Isle during the night of 25 April 1792, the day following the declaration of war, originally under the title *War Song for the Army of the Rhine*, this simultaneously revolutionary and patriotic marching song rapidly spread far and wide. It was prohibited under the Restoration and made its great return in 1848, and then under the Paris Commune. It was again the Marseillaise that would accompany the Russian Revolution of 1917 — even if, in the socialist version of Petr Lavrov, a Russian *narodnik* philosopher who had participated in the Paris Commune, the *patrie* has disappeared to be replaced by the 'labouring people' and the 'famished people'.[118]

When he returned to Russia from his Swiss exile in April 1917, Lenin was welcomed by an orchestra that played first the Marseillaise, then the Internationale. The two hymns coexisted during the revolution and the first years of Soviet power, which opted finally for the second at

---

118 Orlando Figes and Boris Kolonitskii, *Interpreting the Russian Revolution: The Language and Symbols of 1917* (New Haven: Yale University Press, 1999), 62.

the beginning of the 1920s. It was while hiding in Paris, in June 1871, in the aftermath of the bloody week during which he had fought with the Commune, that the poet Eugène Pottier wrote the words of this socialist anthem. But its diffusion would not really begin until twenty years later, when the Flemish composer Pierre Degeyter gave it a new musical score, charging it with a pathos that the words themselves could not attain. It was thus chanted during the conferences of the Socialist International and anarchist demonstrations, before becoming the official hymn of the Communist International.[119] Endowed with a strong messianic connotation – 'This is the final conflict', 'The earth shall rise on new foundations, we have been naught, we shall be all', 'Decree the common salvation', 'The International will be the human race' – this song exalts struggle as an emancipatory, indeed redemptive act, in a nearly religious sense, and gives lyrical form to the utopia that steeps the socialist culture of the nineteenth and twentieth centuries. Its ritualization in the demonstrations of the workers' movement – the singing of the Internationale remained an essential component of the communist liturgy, from the procession to the partisan congress – makes of it a realm of memory which, unlike other symbols, more successfully escapes the disenchanting forces of institutionalization and bureaucratization. During the 1960s and 70s, the notes of the Internationale resounded not only amid the austere décor of communist regimes, but also in the marches of youthful revolt in the Western world.

Whatever the prism through which we observe them – as a terrible rupture or as a process spread out across time – revolutions are not reducible to their intense and jubilant moments; they end, in most cases, in defeat. Their memory is steeped in mourning. The commemoration of fallen combatants and the sacralization of martyrs is what maintains the reminiscence of revolutions, the same as of wars. Unlike wars, however, for revolutions it is not always a matter of official memory, engraved in the stone of monuments. Far more

---

119   Maurice Dommanget, *Eugène Pottier. Membre de la Commune et chantre de l'Internationale* (Paris: EDI, 1971), Chapter 3.

often it takes the form of a 'Marrano' memory, hidden or forbidden, cultivated like a counter-memory held up against the narrative of power. The mausoleums of Lenin and Mao are, from this point of view, both macroscopic and misleading examples. Beside them, we should also pay attention to the underground memory of the subaltern classes, like that illustrated by Diego Rivera in his fresco 'The Blood of the Revolutionary Martyrs Fertilizing the Earth' (1927). Discreet, anonymous flowers are left at the foot of the Communards' Wall, in the Père Lachaise cemetery, every year since the massacre of May 1871. The first public commemoration took place in 1878, in the form of a fraternal banquet organized by *L'Égalité*, Jules Guesde's newspaper, before becoming a tradition following the amnesty of the Communards in 1880. Imposing marches took place in 1936, during the Popular Front. On that occasion, left-wing newspapers pointed out the meaning of such a ritual: 'There is in this cemetery a great joy which does not profane the dead, but defies death', wrote *L'Humanité*, while for *Le Populaire*, 'before death, life marched.'[120] However, the commemoration of Karl Liebknecht and Rosa Luxemburg in the cemetery of Friedrichsfelde in Berlin shows that the political signification of the ritual can vary. A privileged site for large communist meetings under the Weimar Republic, this Revolutionary Memorial (*Revolutionsdenkmal*) was created in 1926. Its designer, the architect Ludwig Mies van der Rohe, future director of the Bauhaus, had chosen a sober installation, modernist in its geometric lines devoid of any ornamental decoration.[121] This communist memorial featured a symbol – sickle and hammer inside a star – and an inscription of the forty-eight poet Ferdinand Freiligrath popularized by Rosa Luxemburg in the German workers' movement, which evoked the perennial character of the socialist ideal: 'I was, I am, I will be' (*Ich war, Ich bin, Ich werde sein!*).

---

120 Quoted in Franck Frégosi, 'La "Montée" au Mur des Fédérés du Père Lachaise. Pèlerinage laïque partisan', *Archives de Sciences Sociales des Religions*, 155 (2011): 170. Madelaine Rebérioux, 'Le mure des Fédérés: Rouge, sang craché', in Pierre Nora (ed.), *Les lieux de mémoire* (Paris: Gallimard, 1984), vol. 1, 619–49.

121 See Michael Chapman, 'Against the Wall: Ideology and Form in Mies van Der Rohe's Monument to Rosa Luxemburg and Karl Liebknecht', *Rethinking Marxism*, 29/1 (2017): 199–213.

It goes without saying that this monument was destroyed under the Nazi regime.[122] Luxemburg's death then was turned into a 'Marrano' memory that Paul Celan celebrated in a lyric poem where the legacy of the Spartacist insurrection becomes a meaningful silence: 'The Landwehr Canal makes no murmur. / Nothing stops.'[123] When it was rebuilt in the 1950s after the founding of the GDR, the profile of the memorial had changed. Much larger, monumental and imposing, it was now called the Memorial of the Socialists (*Gedenkstätte der Sozialisten*). Its name no longer evoked revolution and had taken on a purely commemorative connotation (*Gedenken*) and the Luxemburg's inscription had been replaced by a new aphorism: 'The dead exhort us' (*Die Toten mahnen uns*). The meetings of a subversive movement had given way to celebrations of a regime that enlisted ancestors to legitimize its authority.[124]

Thought-Images: 'Man at the Crossroads'

One of the most powerful 'thought-images' of the interwar years is undoubtedly Diego Rivera's mural titled 'Man, Controller of the Universe', installed in the Palace of Fine Arts of Mexico City in 1934. Impressive for its magnitude – 4.80 x 11.45 m – this extraordinary fresco illustrates in a single scene a Marxist conception of history, a vision of socialism and a revolutionary paradigm that merit careful

---

122   Ariane Jossin, 'Un siècle d'histoire politique allemande: commémorer Liebknecht et Luxemburg au Zentralfriedhof Friedrichsfelde de Berlin', and Élise Julien, Elsa Vonau, 'Le cimetière de Friedrichsfelde: construction d'un espace socialiste (des années 1880 aux années 1970)', *Le Mouvement social*, 237 (2011): 115–33, 91–113; Paul Stangl, 'Revolutionaries' Cemeteries in Berlin: Memory, History, Place and Space', *Urban History*, 43/3 (2007): 407–26. See also Matthew Fink, *Revolutionary Symbolism and History: The Revolutionsdenkmal, the Berlin-Friedrichsfelde Friedhof, and the Concept of Revolution*, Seminar Working Paper, Cornell University, 2020.

123   Paul Celan, 'Schneepart', *Gesammelte Werke*, ed. Beda Allemann and Stefan Reichert with Rolf Bücher (Frankfurt: Suhrkamp, 1983), vol. 2, 337. See also John Felstiner, *Paul Celan: Poet, Survivor, Jew* (New Haven: Yale University Press, 1995), 254.

124   Catherine Epstein, *The Last Revolutionaries: German Communists and Their Century* (Cambridge, MS: Harvard University Press, 2004), 190.

scrutiny. Conceived as a work of art for the masses, the purpose of this magnificent painting, according to Rivera, was to develop 'a language that could be understood by the workers and the peasants of all lands'.[125] It aimed at transmitting ideas and values through a unity of correlated images, exactly like the paintings that cover the walls of Medieval and Renaissance cathedrals, even if the Mexican muralist painted in the twentieth century and had thoroughly assimilated the lessons of cubism, expressionism, and the Russian avant-garde. Deeply convinced that in a troubled age of wars and revolutions, 'art and thought and feeling must be hostile to the bourgeoisie', he wished to 'use [his] art as a weapon'.[126] Mingling concepts, history and political messages, his images were a vigorous plea for socialist revolution.

Before attempting an analytical description of this fresco, a few words on its highly emblematic genesis are indispensable. In November 1932, Diego Rivera was commissioned to realize a gigantic mural that would decorate the lobby of the new Rockefeller Center in New York, in the heart of Manhattan. This skyscraper was meant to become a 'city in the city', hosting the offices of banks, companies, trade institutions from different countries, philanthropic associations, shopping malls, and multiple cultural activities, including the Radio Corporation of America. Frequented daily by tens of thousands of people, this 'Rockefeller City' was to celebrate both the accomplishments of its owners and those of their nation. According to Merle Crowell's guidelines, which explicitly referred to the myth of the American Frontier – celebrated by Frederick Jackson Turner's canonical work a few decades earlier[127] – the Rockefeller building's ambition was to be a symbol of American economic and social progress. Titled 'New Frontiers', this text mentioned the spirit of a 'new understanding' between the economic and social forces of American capitalism and the labour movement, a 'new understanding' that prefigured the New Deal. In

---

125   Diego Rivera, 'The Revolutionary Spirit in Modern Art', *The Modern Quarterly*, 6/3 (1932): 53.

126   Ibid., 57.

127   Frederick Jackson Turner, *The Frontier in American History* (New York: Holt and Company, 1920).

Diego Rivera, *Man, Controller of the Universe* (1934).
Mural. Palacio de Bellas Artes, Mexico City.

this spirit, John Rockefeller Jr. and his wife, Abby, a philanthropist
and patron of the arts, commissioned Diego Rivera to create a fresco
that, without illustrating events or portraying personalities, would
depict, the guidelines went on, 'man at the crossroads and looking
with uncertainty but with hope and high vision to the choosing of a
course leading to a new and better future.'[128]

What happened is well known. In November 1932, Rivera signed
a contract; in March 1933 he started working, and, with the support
of a team of expert assistants including artists Lucienne Bloch and

---

128   Quoted in Catha Paquette, *At the Crossroads: Diego Rivera and His Patrons
at MoMa, Rockefeller Center, and the Palace of Fine Arts* (Austin: University of
Texas Press, 2017), 93. Paquette's book is the most detailed and careful account
of the genesis of Rivera's mural. The painter's version of the story is in Diego
Rivera, with Gladys March, *My Art, My Life: An Autobiography* (New York:
Citadel Press, 1960), 204–8.

Ben Shahn, less than two months later two-thirds of the fresco was completed. On 24 April, the *World Telegraph* published an article announcing that John Rockefeller Jr. had financed a work of communist propaganda in his own building; on 1 May, a portrait of Lenin appeared in the mural. Nelson, John Rockefeller's son, wrote to Rivera complaining that this image would shock most of the American visitors and asking him to replace Lenin with 'some unknown man'. The artist refused, and suggested by way of compromise to include Abraham Lincoln – symbol of American unification and the abolition of slavery – as a kind of symmetrical counterpoint to the Bolshevik leader; but no agreement was found. Nine days later, Rivera was paid and fired, and the fresco was covered, waiting for an alternative solution. After the failure of the tentative plan by Nelson and Abby to transfer it to the Museum of Modern Art that had recently been opened in New York, John Rockefeller Jr., the legal owner of the mural, decided to have it destroyed. By 9 February 1934, Diego Rivera's fresco no longer existed. The news aroused a wave of protests among intellectuals and artists in the United States, who stigmatized a deplorable expression of bourgeois 'vandalism': could an American billionaire buy the Sistine Chapel and destroy it? Particularly vociferous were the artists who were then painting the walls of the Coit Tower in San Francisco, and included this episode in their murals (notably the sections titled 'The Library' by Bertrand Zakheim and 'Industries in California' by Ralph Stackpole).[129] With the money he had received, Rivera paid his assistants and realized two political murals – *Portrait of America* and *The Fourth International* – for two New York buildings belonging to communist dissident organizations. In June he signed a contract with the Mexican government to repaint the fresco just destroyed in New York, and by the end of the year 'Man, Controller of the Universe' (*El hombre controlador del universo*) was installed in the Palace of Fine Arts in Mexico City. Relieved from any constraint, Rivera radicalized his political positions. Despite its changed title, the fresco faithfully reproduced its original version, but several significant details had changed.

Of course, one could observe that this clash between a revolutionary artist like Rivera and the Rockefeller family was more than predictable. The Mexican painter had never concealed his political convictions. One year before the Rockefeller proposal, he had clearly expressed his relationship with entrepreneurial patronage by explaining in *The Modern Quarterly* that revolutionary artists had to 'use the most advanced technical achievements of the bourgeois art but must adapt them to the needs of the proletarian revolution', and that he considered himself a kind of 'guerrilla fighter' who took 'the munitions from the hands of the bourgeoisie'. The examples he gave were eloquent: 'The guerrilla fighter can sometimes derail a train, sometimes blow up a bridge, but sometimes he can only cut a few telegraph wires', repeating that it was 'in the quality of a guerrilla fighter' that he had come to the United States.[130] With such premises, it was perfectly obvious that his mural at the Rockefeller building would not be a celebration of capitalism

---

129   See Anthony W. Lee, *Painting on the Left: Diego Rivera, Radical Politics, and San Francisco's Public Murals* (Berkeley: University of California Press, 1999), 149–54.

130   Rivera, 'Revolutionary Spirit in Modern Art', 56.

and Wall Street philanthropy. Nonetheless, between November 1932, when he signed the contract, and the end of 1934, when the repainted mural was exhibited in Mexico City, several historical changes occurred that certainly contributed to the radicalization of his convictions and behaviour. A simple reminder of the most significant events of that crucial biennium will suffice as explanation.

At the end of January 1933, Hitler was appointed German chancellor; one month later, the Reichstag burned and the Nazi regime was installed; in May, the *Gleichschaltung* was achieved and the Weimar Republic had been destroyed. Fascism was spreading in Europe. From his Turkish exile, Leon Trotsky wrote that this meant a historical defeat for the German labour movement and proved the failure of Stalinism. As a consequence of this severe assessment, he launched an appeal for a new communist international, a Fourth International. As we will see, this political turn left some traces in Rivera's fresco. In the United States, Franklin Roosevelt embarked on his presidency at the darkest and most dramatic moment of the economic depression and took energetic, almost 'dictatorial' measures that announced the advent of the New Deal. In the springtime of 1934, the 'battle of Toledo' saw 10,000 striking workers of the Electric Auto-Lite opposed by the National Guard in Ohio, and a few weeks later a general strike took place in Minneapolis, both actions led by left-wing radical organizations; these strikes created the premises for the foundation of the CIO one year later. In February 1934, Vienna became the stage of a defeated workers' uprising led by the Schutzbund, the militia of the Austrian Socialist Party facing a fascist reaction. In France, on 6 February, a far-right demonstration that threatened to turn into a coup d'état resulted in fifteen killed and produced a spontaneous anti-fascist mass reaction: this was the beginning of the Popular Front that won the elections two years later. In Spain, a violent strike of Asturian miners broke out in October 1934. In China, Mao Zedong started on the Long March that lasted three years and moved the army of his China Soviet Republic from Jiangxi to Shaanxi. And finally, in Mexico, the left-wing nationalist leader Lázaro Cárdenas was elected president in 1934; he defended an almost socialist six-year plan – conceived along a Soviet model – that promoted the creation of peasant cooperatives against the latifundia, a national system of public education, and the nationalization of key industries. In short, these world events pushed Diego Rivera to give an even stronger revolutionary dimension to his ambitious mural. This is the explosive context in which he realized 'Man, Controller of the Universe'. In his autobiography, he describes that mural as a warning: 'If the United States wished to preserve its democratic forms, it would ally itself with Russia against fascism.'[131] This post-World War II interpretation is probably tinged with hindsight, but it is obvious that his fresco announced a tremendous clash between fascism and socialism.

The mural itself depicts a monumental landscape whose multiple components are symmetrically disposed. Epic scenes of mass action and conceptual representations combine in a complex but remarkably ordered ensemble by creating a sort of regulated dynamism.[132] The man at the crossroads stands in almost perfect equilibrium between the past and the future, evil and happiness, egoism and fraternity, disease and health, prejudice and enlightenment, obscurantism and progress, capitalism and socialism. He looks grave, conscious that the future depends on his choice. His central position as well as his jacket and gloves show him to be a skilled worker, a technician or a pilot, since he is located at the crux of a complex machine with two crossed ellipses, like the propellers of an aircraft ready to start. The piston engine and wheels that surround him are reminiscent of a factory – they irresistibly evoke the photographs of Lewis Hine's *Men at Work* (1932) and even the industrial work depicted by Rivera himself in Detroit during the previous years – which is organically connected with a natural foundation made of a variety of tropical shrubs and crops, located at the bottom of the fresco. These luxuriant plants seem doomed, rationally cultivated as though in a greenhouse, since they are related to the mechanical engine that absorbs their vital juices and distributes them through an elaborate system of measurements and clocks. According to Anita Brenner, the *New York Times* journalist

---

131   Rivera, *My Art, My Life*, 206.

132   Rivera was very attached to this aesthetic principle which he called 'dynamic symmetry.' See David Craven, *Diego Rivera as Epic Modernist* (New York: Simon & Schuster, 1997), 109.

who interviewed Rivera in April 1933, this natural foundation was 'a representation of the earth as an open book, with the chief elements of organic life in geological strata on its pages and plants sprouting on the soil surface'.[133]

The meaning of the ellipses is suggested by the painter himself in a 'detailed verbal description' carefully recorded by his friend Bertram Wolfe, the American Marxist historian who devoted a book to the Mexican artist in 1939. In the first project for the Rockefeller building, the telescope – located to the right of the man at the crossroads – brought to 'the vision and understanding of man the most distant celestial bodies', whereas the microscope – located to his left – made 'visible and comprehensible to man infinitesimal living organisms, connecting atoms and cells with the astral system'.[134] As for the two inferior ellipses, they illustrated how the machinery controlled by the 'Worker' – Wolfe reproduced Rivera's word in capitalized form – transformed the 'cosmic energy' captured by its antennae into a 'productive energy'.[135] In the final version of the fresco painted in 1934, however, the cosmic energy of natural life only appears in the two inferior ellipses. The telescope showing planets and stars is contained within the ellipse directed towards the revolutionary masses, whereas the microscope, which reveals cells and bacteria including diseased and cancer-causing cells, is located within the ellipse directed towards the forces of war. Illuminated by two gigantic lenses installed symmetrically on either side of the machinery, the ellipses bear the metaphorical embodiments of decadence and progress. On the left, just under the disease cells, a high society reception takes place, with elegant ladies and gentlemen dancing, smoking, playing cards and sipping cocktails (John Rockefeller Jr. is recognizable among them). Beside them, but outside of the machinery frame, a mass demonstration of workers is violently repressed by mounted policemen. Displayed as a horizontal row along the fresco, these images of street protests show readable signs: 'We want bread!' or 'We want jobs, not charity',

---

133   Quoted in Paquette, *At the Crossroads*, 154.

134   Bertram D. Wolfe, *Diego Rivera: His Life and Times* (New York: Knopf, 1939), 358.

135   Ibid.

a slogan that scornfully alludes to Rockefeller's philanthropy. On
the right, framed by the ellipses of stars and cosmic energies that,
irradiating the vital forces of nature, shift to a maternal image of
breast-feeding, is Lenin. In solemn posture, he grasps the hands of
a worker, a peasant and a soldier, thus sealing their alliance. Beyond
the iron wall of the machine, symmetrical with respect to the street
demonstration, young female athletes symbolize healthy life (probably
inspired by Dziga Vertov's *Man with a Movie Camera*).[136] According
to Rivera's 1932 indications, the peasant produces the fundamental
riches of mankind; the urban worker 'transforms and distributes the
raw materials given by the earth', and the soldier 'represents sacrifice'
in a world subordinated to the forces of religion and war.[137] Belonging
to different races – the worker is black – they also embody a universal
spirit of human fraternity. In 1934, their alliance is realized by Lenin,
the architect of the October Revolution who gave power to the soviets
of workers, peasants and soldiers.

The extreme poles of the fresco, in which an audience of students
(left) and workers (right) watch the lens screens, are equally charged
with symbolic value. On the left, a teacher explains Darwin's theory
of evolution as a plea for harmonious relationships between animals
and human beings, in front of a humanized monkey who, like a father,
looks at the screen and gives his hand to a child. Next to Darwin, an
electric plant and a radiograph illustrate the human capacity to domesticate nature through the instruments of science, while a multiracial
audience of students conscientiously attends the lesson. On the right,
a red flag appeals for a new communist movement: 'Workers of the
world unite in the Fourth International!' The flag is held by Leon
Trotsky, Friedrich Engels and Karl Marx. Behind Trotsky stands a
black worker and someone resembling Jay Lovestone, the American
dissident communist leader; behind Marx, with a teacher's bearing,
stands Wolfe, who was then the director of the New York Workers
School. This image, one may observe, expressed Rivera's augury:
Marx and Engels play the role of theoretical inspirers of Trotsky's
movement – Marx holds a scroll of his doctrine – but both Lovestone

---

136   See Craven, *Diego Rivera*, 126.
137   Ibid., 359.

and Wolfe belonged to Bukharin's communist dissident movement and criticized the creation of a new International. The two classical statues towering over the extreme poles of the fresco are distinctly allegorical figures. The one on the right, just behind Trotsky and Marx, represents a decapitated Caesar: his head has fallen on the ground where the spectating workers use it as a seat. His hand holds a bundle of sticks, a symbol of Italian fascism, onto which a Nazi swastika has been added. According to Rivera's explanation, this headless statue represents 'the liquidation of Tyranny'.[138] The statue on the left is a strange Zeus or Jupiter with a Christian cross around his neck, whose hands have been cut off by lightning, a natural force which human intelligence has transformed into useful electricity (analogous to science, which defeats religious beliefs).

The epic dimension of the fresco, which also unveils its historical context, spreads out from the upper layer: a threatening army of soldiers with guns, bayonets and gas masks, supported by flame-throwers, planes and tanks, faces the ordered parade of a proletarian movement bearing red flags. Behind this red sea, we catch a glimpse of the Kremlin towers and Lenin's mausoleum. Whereas the socialist revolution is symbolized by Trotsky and his appeals for a new International, the socialist stronghold still remains the USSR. In this titanic clash between revolution and counterrevolution, the soldiers who represent the latter are clearly evocative of the First World War. Their dehumanized bodies, hidden by helmets and gas masks, evoke the industrial massacre of total war, and their weapons reveal the transformation of science and technology into means of mass destruction. These figures were common in the 1920s and 1930s – think of many expressionist canvases – and Jupiter's statue, whose towering bust merges with them, probably represents the synthesis of mythology and technology that so deeply shaped many forms of reactionary modernism in those years.[139] From this point of view, the 'Worker' driving the machine at the core of the fresco inevitably smacks of Jünger – *Der Arbeiter* (1932) – and corresponds with the

---

138   Ibid., 358.
139   See Herf, *Reactionary Modernism*.

famous 'Moloch' scene in Fritz Lang's *Metropolis* (1927).[140] If inscribed
into the general worldview of the fresco, however, it appears as a
powerful illustration of the Marxist conception of technique. This
man 'at the crossroads' possesses the secret to 'control the universe'
and is facing a tremendous choice: in Walter Benjamin's words, he
can use technology as a 'key to happiness' or transform it into a 'fetish
of doom'.[141] In other words, the antagonistic forces of revolution and
counterrevolution, fascism and communism, are struggling to conquer
the machinery – modern technology – that will give them the capacity
to decide the future.[142]

Whereas images of men and women at work are recurrent in Rivera's
murals, the 'Worker' of the Museum of Fine Arts' fresco takes on a
much more profound metaphorical significance. The painter himself
described him as a kind of 'collective hero', a 'man-and-machine' who
would rule the society of the future, where he would be 'as important
as air, water, and the light of the sun'.[143] This Promethean figure that
merges humanity and technology can certainly scare us, but he does
not look like an anonymous Heideggerian *Gestell*. Rivera frequently
depicted capitalism as a source of oppression and alienation – think
of *Frozen Assets* (1931), where the skyscrapers of New York tower
over a subterranean guarded dormitory in which sleeping men lie
like corpses in ordered rows – but usually tended to celebrate both
technology and factory work as creative forces. As Terry Smith has
convincingly argued, in Rivera's paintings, and particularly in his
Detroit murals, workers never appear as robots or dehumanized
figures. Unlike in Fritz Lang's *Metropolis*, where they are modern
slaves, in Rivera's murals they maintain the air of peasants, while the

---

140   See Ernst Jünger, *The Worker: Dominion and Form* (Evanston: North-
western University Press, 2017 [1932]). On Fritz Lang's allegorical reference to
the Great War in *Metropolis*, see Anton Kaes, *Shell Shock Cinema: Weimar Culture
and the Wounds of War* (Princeton: Princeton University Press, 2009), 168–72.

141   Walter Benjamin, 'Theories of German Fascism' (1930), *WBSW*, vol.
2/1, 321.

142   From this point of view, Rivera's mural was the exact opposite of Fritz
Lang's *Metropolis*, which finished with the celebration of the alliance between
'brain' (the boss) and 'arm' (the workers) sealed through the 'heart'.

143   Rivera, *My Art, My Life*, 183. See also Craven, *Diego Rivera*, 144.

machines themselves often take an anthropomorphic dimension. In the mural cycle *Detroit Industry* (1932–33), the stamping presses of the Ford automotive plant almost become an Aztec goddess.[144] His factories are cubist and futurist, sometimes reminiscent of Vertov's cinema, but they do not appear as Fordist plants with assembly lines.

The vision of history suggested by Rivera's mural is undoubtedly evolutionistic – as evidenced by the portrait of Darwin at its left pole – but it does not lead to a linear historical time, nor does it join with the peaceful and cumulative idea of progress defended by social democracy. It rather results in a vision of historical discontinuities and political bifurcations: humankind is at the crossroads. Of course, the technique represented in this fresco is 'neutral' – it can be used indiscriminately by both fascism and communism – and Rivera's philosophical horizon is far from any kind of Heideggerian Marxism.[145] Only fascism will transform technology into an 'iron cage' of total rule; mastered by liberating, proletarian forces, it will neither alienate human beings nor destroy nature. Facing the alternative between romantic anti-capitalism and Promethean socialism, the Mexican painter did not hesitate to choose the latter. He had defended the former in many murals and canvases where he celebrated the harmonious and organic relationship of indigenous peasants with their earth/time mother, but the future at stake in the 1930s depends entirely on the mastering of technology. Like in Marx's *Grundrisse* and *Capital*, the development of the productive forces – including science

---

144   Terry Smith, *Making the Modern: Industry, Art and Design in America* (Chicago: University of Chicago Press, 1993), notably 'Rivera in Detroit', 199–246; the reference to the anthropomorphic machines, 223.

145   In 1941, Marcuse still argued that 'technics by itself can promote authoritarianism as well as liberty, scarcity as well as abundance, the extension as well as the abolition of toil.' See Herbert Marcuse, 'Some Social Implications of Modern Technology' (1941), *Technology, War and Fascism: Collected* Papers, ed. Douglas Kellner (New York: Routledge, 1998), 41. Twenty years later, he nuanced his thought: 'In the face of the totalitarian features of this society, the traditional notion of the "neutrality" of technology can no longer be maintained. Technology as such cannot be isolated from the use to which it is put; the technological society is a system of domination which operates already in the concept and construction of techniques.' See Herbert Marcuse, *One-Dimensional Man: Studies in the Ideology of Advanced Industrial Society* (Boston: Beacon Press, 1964), xvi.

and technology – was the premise for the passage from the realm of necessity to the realm of liberty.[146] Socialism as the accomplishment of the 'right to be lazy' (*droit à la paresse*), according to the striking formula of Paul Lafargue,[147] did not fit with this age of moderniza-tion, five-year plans and the battles of the Red Army in defence of socialism. Rivera recognized that fascism could be modern and based on technical and scientific foundations, but he did not abandon the idea of Progress, which he identified with technology and industrial civilization, a gigantic machine that socialism should domesticate according to its ethical and social purposes. This was probably the premise for the misunderstanding between the revolutionary painter and the Rockefellers: both believed in Progress, even if they radically disagreed over the means to achieve it. Rivera thought progress to be an egalitarian community of self-emancipated producers; the Rocke-fellers saw it as capitalism moderated by philanthropy.

In 'Man, Controller of the Universe', socialism appears as a gigantic machine, like in Alexei Gastev's futurism or Antonio Gramsci's *Prison Notebooks*. In this sense, Diego Rivera's imposing fresco magisterially illustrates a vision of history and socialism, as well as a model of com-munist revolution. Today, this powerful 'thought-image' has become a fascinating realm of memory of the twentieth century.

* * *

Reciprocally attracted and related to each other, concepts, experi-ences, symbols and memory constitute the multiple poles of a single revolutionary magnetic field. Revolutions give concepts a concrete dimension and their translation into reality transforms them into symbols and creates political paradigms that finally become realms of memory. Insofar as, unlike spontaneous rebellions, they consciously change the course of history, revolutions are concepts converted into

---

146   According to Marx, the development of the forces of production is the material condition for a free society, in which 'wealth is no longer measured by labour time but by available time.' See Karl Marx, 'Economic Manuscripts of 1857–58', in Karl Marx, Friedrich Engels, *MECW*, vol. 29, 94. See also Roman Rosdolsky, *The Making of Marx's 'Capital'* (London: Pluto Press, 1977), 426.

147   Paul Lafargue, *The Right to Be Lazy, and Other Studies* (Chicago: C.H. Kerr, 1907).

action, that is to say, performative concepts that possess an élan and a dynamic strength. They also create 'figures of thought': ideas that, more than merely being expressed in words, condense into images. Thus, the French Revolution became a revolutionary model in the nineteenth century and the October Revolution forged a new paradigm consciously assumed by most revolutions of the twentieth century. This paradigm was at once a theory – Lenin's *State and Revolution* – a narrative – Trotsky's *History of the Russian Revolution* – and a realm of collective imagination that crystalized into symbolic figures: the execution of the king; the Paris Commune; the storming of the Winter Palace; Emiliano Zapata on horseback with his sombrero, his gun, and his shoulder cartridges; Trotsky speaking from his armoured train; Mao Zedong proclaiming the People's Republic of China from Beijing's Tiananmen Square; Fidel Castro and Che Guevara entering Havana, and so on. The metamorphosis of ideas and events into symbols can be a contradictory process – we saw this with the Bastille and the Vendôme Column – since the iconoclastic fury of revolutions often removes the material basis of collective experience, which therefore becomes a purely virtual realm of memory. And the translation itself from concepts into actions and from experiences into images is ineluctably reshaped by the passage from the revolution as event to the revolution displayed as a historical sequence: the event is a disruptive and liberating moment, but its symbols belong to a collective remembrance, to a revolutionary *tradition* that, by iconizing the event, separates it from the present. In this way, ideas were incorporated into a scholastic canon – the doctrine of Marxism-Leninism – and symbols created a frozen archive ready to be exhibited in the rooms of a museum. We know Pierre Nora's apodictic assessment: 'there are sites, *lieux de mémoire*, in which a residual sense of continuity remains', only because 'there are no longer any *milieux de mémoire*, settings in which memory is a real part of everyday experience.'[148] This sentence is useful in grasping a general tendency, but needs to be qualified. Not only does it neglect what Walter Benjamin calls *Jetztzeit* – the instant in which 'memory flashes up', when the past is

---

148   Pierre Nora, 'General Introduction: Between Memory and History', *Realms of Memory: The Construction of the French Past*, vol. 1, 1.

reactivated and interacts with the present by forming with it a sort of constellation[149] – but also forsakes the performative character of the realms of memory themselves, even those most institutionalized, re-codified and deprived of their original meaning. Think of the celebration of the anniversary of the October Revolution in 1941, when the Red Army marched in Moscow, in front of Stalin, on its way to the front line. In the last analysis, the revolutionary tradition is the insoluble contradiction between an ecstatic moment of self-liberation and its inevitable transformation into organized action. Their intimately conflictual relationship corresponds with the passage, in the field of art history, from the avant-garde to classicism, from Bohemianism to academia. This transition has changed customs and minds; it has been experienced as an inner laceration for many existences and has damaged the lives of several generations of revolutionaries. We know that traditions can be 'invented',[150] can modify events themselves by surrounding them with a mythic halo and changing the perception of them; but the persistence of traditions proves that their objects have not died yet. During the nineteenth and twentieth centuries, revolutionary traditions proved that, for millions of people, changing the world was not a fantasy but rather an end inscribed within the horizon of their historical time: a possible and concrete utopia.

---

149   Benjamin, 'On the Concept of History', 391.

150   Eric Hobsbawm and Terence Ranger (eds), *The Invention of Tradition* (New York: Cambridge University Press, 2012).

Chapter 4

The Revolutionary Intellectual, 1848–1945

Thousands of educated young people, both workers and bourgeois, tremble beneath an abhorred yoke. To break it, do they think of drawing the sword? No! The pen, always the pen, nothing but the pen. Why not both, as befits the duty of a republican? In times of tyranny, to write is good, but when the enslaved pen becomes powerless then to fight is better. Ah, but no! They found a newspaper, they go to prison, and yet no-one thinks to open a book of manoeuvres, so as to learn in the space of twenty-four hours the profession that gives our oppressors all their force, and that would put our revenge and their punishment within our reach.

Auguste Blanqui, *Instructions for an Armed Uprising* (1868)

Historical Boundaries

The purpose of this chapter is to define the figure of the revolutionary intellectual as it appeared between 1848 and the Second World War, the century of the biggest upheavals of political modernity. Since the adjective 'revolutionary' is highly polysemic and frequently abused, it is worth clarifying the meaning with which it will be employed in the following pages. Its scope will be at the same time extremely wide, insofar as it includes a plurality of ideological and political currents, from anarchism to communism, and circumscribed, since it refers exclusively to those men and women of ideas who consciously acted against the ruling social and political order. Marx implicitly suggested this definition in 1843, when he wrote, in his famous eleven theses on Feuerbach, that the philosophers had interpreted the world but the time had come to change it. Considering this premise, revolutionary intellectuals are those who not only elaborated or defended innovative, rebellious and subversive theories but also chose a conduct of life and a political commitment that aimed at their accomplishment. Michael Bakunin, Karl Marx and Rosa Luxemburg, who wrote extensively on revolutions and led political movements, certainly were revolutionary intellectuals. The most popular revolutionary icon of the nineteenth century, Giuseppe Garibaldi, was not. He was a man of action, but he never fixed his ideas in a theory or an essay. Nor could Theodor W. Adorno be considered as a revolutionary intellectual: his criticism of domination was powerful and certainly inspired several radical movements – particularly in postwar Germany – but he carefully rejected any form of political engagement or allegiance, betraying a fearful and passive attitude, always respectful of authority. His thought possessed a sharp critical dimension but remained abstract and purely introspective. According to Lukács, this posture was unable to overcome the 'reified consciousness of the bourgeoisie', whereas a revolutionary commitment meant precisely a new relationship between theory and praxis.[1] In the eyes of this philosopher who, between publishing such books as *Theory of the Novel* (1916) and *History and Class Consciousness* (1923), had participated in the Soviet republic of Bela Kun and led the fifth division of the Hungarian Red Army, Max Horkheimer and Theodor W. Adorno were the managers of a luxury and elitist 'Grand Hotel Abyss' (*Grand Hotel Abgrund*), which was 'equipped with every comfort' but located 'on the edge of an abyss, of nothingness, of absurdity'.[2] Between those ideal-types, however, there were many intermediate forms of commitment. Halfway between Adorno and Lukács, for

1   Georg Lukács, *History and Class Consciousness: Studies in Marxist Dialectics*, trans. Rodney Livingstone (Cambridge, MA: MIT Press, 1971 [1923]), 317.

2   Georg Lukács, 'Preface' (1962), *The Theory of the Novel: A Historico-Philosophical Essay on the Forms of Great Epic Literature* (Cambridge, MA: MIT Press, 1971), 22. Lukács's ironical assessment (which alluded to Adorno's middle name: Wiesengrund) is the title of Stuart Jeffries, *Grand Hotel Abyss: The Lives of the Frankfurt School* (London, New York: Verso, 2016).

instance, there was Walter Benjamin, a 'homeless', non-party radical thinker with limited academic attachment.

Many thinkers whose names are historically related to some major cultural, scientific or technical revolution had mentalities, habits and tastes that were quite conformist or conservative. The invention of psychoanalysis was certainly an intellectual revolution, but Freud claimed bourgeois respectability and struggled his entire life to win legitimacy and public recognition for his movement. Einstein overthrew the traditional patterns of physics but his political commitment – noble as it was – was by no means subversive: as a convinced anti-fascist, he persuaded President Roosevelt to create an American atomic bomb. Discomposing forms in his cubist paintings, Picasso upended the inherited rules of artistic figuration, but he admitted himself that he was unfit for politics. *Guernica* was undoubtedly the highest point of aesthetic anti-fascism in the 1930s, but he remained in France under German occupation, protected by his international celebrity, and became a fairly passive fellow traveller of communism in the postwar years. In contrast to a revolutionary artist like John Heartfield, who did not distinguish between aesthetic creation and political action and devoted his entire life to inventing images able to spread political messages, Picasso lived for art, not politics. Therefore, the concept of revolutionary intellectual analysed in this chapter has nothing to do with the many 'revolutionary' innovations typically acclaimed by the media and transformed into widespread assumptions, not to say advertising trivialities. The twentieth century is the age of 'revolutionary' captains of industry who, from Henry Ford to Bill Gates, changed the means of production and consequently the way of life of millions of people. The former was a white supremacist: a few years after introducing the principles of 'scientific management' in the assembly lines of his Detroit auto plants, he published his famous anti-Semitic pamphlet *The International Jew*. The second has become a philanthropist, certainly not a supporter of guerrilla movements.

These examples are obvious enough, but they have to be mentioned to avoid misunderstanding. The typology of the revolutionary intellectual that will be examined in the following pages is far from exhaustive, but its premises explain why it omits certain towering figures of critical thought. They also help us to distinguish the heroes of this chapter from those of the postwar years, when many radical thinkers found a welcoming haven in academia: a significant sociological change that transformed the conditions of production of theory itself.[3] This meant the decline not only of revolutionary but also, more broadly speaking, of 'public' intellectuals, authors who write for a relatively large audience, put their knowledge in the service of a cause, take positions on social, political and ethical issues, and denounce the abuses of power and oppressive measures of the rulers; those who, one could say with Edward Said, belonged 'on the same side with the weak and unrepresented'.[4] In the West, the end of urban bohemia and the advent of the mass university, combined with a long period of peaceful and democratic political life, has favoured the retreat of most intellectuals into campuses: they rarely play a public role and tend to produce esoteric works usually consumed within their own social space. This retreat of critical thought into academia has corresponded with the reification of the public sphere, a fatal junction that significantly changed the status of 'revolutionary' intellectuals. Postwar intellectuals are 'dissenters' like Noam Chomsky, Edward Said or Jean-Paul Sartre, more rarely activists directly involved in revolutionary action. This latter mode was relatively common in the South – think of personalities like Amilcar Cabral, Frantz Fanon or Che Guevara – but quite exceptional in the West, except for the rebellious decades of the 1960s and the 1970s.

Given that its chronological boundaries vary from one continent to another, historicizing the age of revolutionary intellectuals is not an easy task. In Europe, it runs from the revolutions of 1848 to the Second World War. In the colonial world, despite a few exceptions, it starts later, after the Russian Revolution, and reaches a peak with the Cuban Revolution: two moments that announce respectively the beginning and the apogee of decolonization. Of course, revolutionary intellectuals existed both before 1848 and after 1958, but they were

---

3   On this transformation, see the famous essay by Russell Jacoby, *The Last Intellectuals: American Culture in the Age of Academe* (New York: Basic Books, 1987).

4   Edward Said, *Representations of the Intellectual: The 1993 Reith Lectures* (New York: Vintage, 1996), 22.

anomalies: before the 'Springtime of the Peoples' they emerged from a social structure inherited from the Old Regime, which forcefully limited their breeding ground; after 1945, they transmigrated to the colonial world.

The historical background of the revolutionary intellectual corresponds with the rise of aesthetic and literary modernism: the birth of mass society as the result of a broad process of urbanization and industrialization.[5] This means immigration, the boom in communications, the end of illiteracy, the rise of journalism, and the emergence of a modern public sphere. In the political field, this is the age of parliamentary debates and the organization of the labour movement as a new subject. The revolutionary intellectual appears in pre-democratic societies still shaped by the persistence of the Old Regime, in which most cultural institutions show their aristocratic origins and the habits of nobility still define the horizon of the ascending industrial and financial elites; in which the lower classes are stigmatized as 'dangerous' and the socialist left is excluded from political power. At that time, the academy was dominated either by conservatism, as in the United Kingdom, Germany, Austria and Italy, or national-republicanism, as in France. When European universities were a privileged realm of the romantic defence of *Kultur* against modern *Zivilisation* and played the role of ideological guardians of authority, the critique of exploitation, oppression and authoritarianism, as well as demands for freedom and democracy, were largely embodied in a declassed, fragile and economically precarious intelligentsia ready to jump onto the barricades. Whether anarchist or socialist, this revolutionary intelligentsia fighting for democracy and social justice inevitably 'conspired' against the established order. In the age of the first globalization – a transformation of the world that corresponded with the apogee of nationalism – revolutionary ideas circulated widely from one nation to another, from one continent to another, as did the men and women that embodied them. Revolutionary intellectuals were cosmopolitan actors in a time of virulent

---

5   David Cottington, *The Avant-Garde: A Very Short Introduction* (Oxford: Oxford University Press, 2013), and, from the same author, 'The Formation of the Avant-Garde in Paris and London 1880–1915', *Art History*, 35/3 (2012): 596–621.

nationalism. Their relationship with economic and political power was comparable to that of bohemianism and the aesthetic avant-garde with academism and its institutions: it was a radically antagonistic relationship. 'Heterodoxies overlapped', wrote Eric Hobsbawm, observing the 'existential connection' that united Marxists and anarchists with the artist and cultural avant-garde, both being 'opposed to and by bourgeois orthodoxy'.[6]

After the collapse of the European dynastic order in 1914 and the Russian upheaval of 1917, the revolutionary intellectual broke away from the margins and became a central actor of the new 'Thirty Years' War' that lasted until 1945 (or the early 1950s in Asia). The clash between revolution and counterrevolution, capitalism and socialism, fascism and anti-fascism, national liberation and imperialism, propelled the revolutionary intellectuals onto the stage of an international tragedy that they would play out – literally incarnating it in their flesh and soul – as both heroes and victims.

On closer examination, the organic relationship between theory and action at the heart of the revolutionary intelligentsia was a general feature of the age of mass culture and industrial capitalism, which the collapse of the old dynastic order in 1914 dramatically intensified. There is a significant parallelism, from this point of view, between left-wing thinkers and more conformist and conservative scholars, whose theories and programmes tended to become increasingly practical. At the turn of the twentieth century, Marxism focused on the economy and politics, producing a remarkable number of studies on the transformations of capitalism and the advent of imperialism, as well as a vigorous debate on organizational forms and the means of political action. Think of the works of Karl Kautsky on the agrarian question, of Rudolf Hilferding on the emergence of financial capital, and of Rosa Luxemburg, Bukharin and Lenin on imperialism. Think of the controversy between Lenin, Martov, Luxemburg and Trotsky on the political party. Think of the debate on reform and revolution that opposed 'orthodox' and 'revisionist' Marxists – Kautsky and

---

6   Eric Hobsbawm, 'Socialism and the Avant-Garde, 1880–1914' (1980), *Uncommon People: Resistance, Rebellion and Jazz* (London: Weidenfeld and Nicolson, 1998), 172.

Luxemburg against Eduard Bernstein – within the German social democracy. And think of Trotsky's theory of permanent revolution, that announced the historical turning point of October 1917.

All these disputes, even the most theoretical, had practical purposes. But this is also true for Frederick W. Taylor's theory of 'scientific management', Walther Rathenau's conception of the planned war economy, John Maynard Keynes's treatise on money, and, from different perspectives, the studies of both Hans Kelsen and Carl Schmitt on constitutionalism. Whereas Marxist thinkers discussed how to overthrow capitalism and the bourgeois state, their conservative counterparts studied how to rationalize and preserve capitalism and how to reinforce the state machine – the tool of sovereignty – against a revolutionary upheaval. During the interwar years, the strategic reflections of Antonio Gramsci and John Maynard Keynes are almost perfectly symmetrical: the former thought about the paths of a successful revolution in the West; the latter meditated on the ways to save capitalism from its historical crisis. Everywhere, theory experienced an empirical turn. Bolshevism and fascism were the most radical versions of this change of direction. In the age of the global crisis of capitalism and international civil war, the revolutionary intellectual could no longer remain an isolated figure like Marx in the nineteenth century, working daily at the British Library and exchanging letters with a network of correspondents all over the (Western) world. It is significant that even Gramsci, who was confined to a fascist prison where he could not exchange his political reflections with anyone, elaborated a conception of the revolutionary party as a 'collective' intellectual.

National Contexts

The emergence of the revolutionary intellectual was the result, then, of a process running all through the nineteenth century and coalescing, on the brink of the Great War, in a social group with a distinct ideological and political profile as well as a peculiar geographical distribution. Apprehending this new historical actor also requires one to distinguish between different cultural and semantic contexts in

which the words 'intellectual' and 'intelligentsia' take some nuances.[7]
Both terms have a long history, but their conceptualization followed
different paths.

In France and Western Europe, the word 'intellectual' is usually
related to the Dreyfus Affair, the political crisis that deeply shook
the Third Republic in *fin-de-siècle* France.[8] Before that, it already
existed and was used – infrequently – to designate certain new actors
of modernity: scholars, writers, journalists, clerks, lawyers, in short,
people living by the pen. The word often took a negative meaning.
Unlike 'intellect' – a noble human faculty – the 'intellectual' was cast
as a modern, 'cerebral' agent divorced from nature, condemned to
sterile and uncreative thinking, shut inside an artificial world made of
abstract values. The cleavages drawn by the Dreyfus Affair quickly
corresponded with the opposition between the Third Republic and its
enemies: on the one hand a political regime grounded in the culture
of the Rights of Man, on the other, the conservative culture of anti-
Enlightenment. Michel Winock summarizes this dichotomy as the
conflict between antipodal values: truth against authority, justice
against order, reason against instinct, universalism against nationalism,
progress against tradition, and individualism against holism.[9] The
defenders of Captain Dreyfus represented freedom and modernity;
his enemies, conservatism and anti-republicanism. Dreyfus was a Jew,
and anti-republicans were violently anti-Semitic. The paradigms of
this antagonism are respectively Émile Zola, the famous author of
J'accuse!, and Maurice Barrès, the inspirer of the Action Française.
In *Scènes et doctrines du nationalisme* (1902), the first manifesto of the
French conservative revolution, Barrès offered the following definition of the intellectual: 'an individual thinking that society should be
based on logic.'[10] Barrès's intellectual despises 'instinct' and has no

---

7   See Christophe Charle, *Les Intellectuels en Europe au XIXe siècle. Essai
d'histoire comparée* (Paris: Seuil, 1996).

8   See Christophe Charle, *Birth of the Intellectuals 1880–1900* (Cambridge:
Polity Press, 2015 [1990]).

9   Michel Winock, *Nationalism, Anti-Semitism, and Fascism in France* (Stanford: Stanford University Press, 1998), 117.

10   Maurice Barrès, *Scènes et doctrines du nationalisme* (Paris: Félix Juven
Éditeur, 1902), 45.

doubts about his superiority over ordinary people. He possesses a kind of dangerous Kantianism, holding that real human beings, with their peculiarities and cultures – 'our young inhabitants of Bretagne, Lorraine, Provence and Paris' – should be replaced by a 'universal man', an 'ideal, abstract man, always the same'. Horrified by such a view, Barrès thought that France needed 'men strongly rooted in our land, in our history, in our national consciousness'.[11]

In France, anti-intellectualism was rooted in the historical divide introduced by the Revolution between liberalism and the Old Regime. In the eyes of conservative thinkers, the intellectuals were the mirror of decadence, one of the great myths of European reaction at the turn of the twentieth century: cut off from nature, imprisoned in an artificial cage of abstract values, where all is quantified and measured, where their entire reality has become anonymous, impersonal, and mechanical – anti-poetic, in fact, as ugly as a metropolis – they embodied the most repellent features of modernity. Unable to understand the genius of a nation, which is rooted in a land, intellectuals were 'cosmopolitan'. Alien to concrete, *national* peculiarities transmitted from one generation to the next like family property, they championed universal and abstract values such as justice, equality and freedom. In the eyes of the proponents of conservatism, the Jews embodied the most accomplished form of intellectualism.

In Germany, the cleavage between tradition and modernity pervaded the entire culture as a radical clash opposing *Kultur* and *Zivilisation*, community (*Gemeinschaft*) and society (*Gesellschaft*), and, once again, Germanism and Judaism. Unlike in France, where intellectuals were well represented within the institutions of the Third Republic – above all the universities which, including the Sorbonne, were Dreyfusard bastions – in Germany the gulf between scholars (*Gelehrte*) and intellectuals (*Intellektuelle*) was almost insuperable and even deepened under the Weimar Republic. There, scholars belonged to state institutions, embodied science and order, and transformed the universities into strongholds of nationalism. Whereas academia educated the superior layers of state bureaucracy and selected the political elites,

11   Ibid., 56. On Barrès as harbinger of a French conservative revolution, see Zeev Sternhell, *Maurice Barrès et le nationalisme français* (Paris: Fayard, 2000 [1972]).

the realm of intellectuals was located in civil society, outside of the academy.[12] Temples of tradition, some of the best universities were located in small cities and rural regions. The intellectuals, on the contrary, were at home in the big cities, where they emerged with the rise of a powerful culture industry.

In both France and Germany – but this observation could easily be extended to many other countries – the representatives of conservative intelligentsia were legion. Nationalist writers and ideologists, thinkers of counter-Enlightenment, anti-Semitic propagandists, romantic traditionalists, and 'conservative revolutionaries' were frequently at home with newspapers and magazines, but they categorically refused to call themselves 'intellectuals'. They could use modern tools to fight against modernity, but this label exclusively designated their enemies. Unlike France, however, where the 'intellectuals' – both defined and self-defined as such – identified themselves with state institutions, in Germany this occurred only after the Great War. As for the revolutionary intelligentsia, a marginal layer composed of anarchist, socialist and rebellious writers, artists and thinkers clearly oriented against capitalism and the established order, they were inclined to support neither the Third Republic nor the Weimar Republic, two political regimes born from the bloody repression of the Paris Commune, the Spartacist uprising, and the Bavarian Soviet Republic. In 1900, at the end of the Dreyfus Affair, Paul Lafargue declared that the 'intellectuals' had always acted as servants of power. In contrast to Jean Jaurès, who advocated for the defence of Dreyfus as a struggle for justice and equality against militarism, authoritarianism, anti-republicanism and anti-Semitism, Karl Marx's son-in-law was clearly reluctant to plead the cause of a military officer. Most scholars, Lafargue argued, had 'sold science itself to the capitalist bourgeoisie', and those who

---

12   The classic study on the topic is Fritz Ringer, *The Decline of the German Mandarins: The German Academic Community 1890–1933* (Cambridge, MA: Harvard University Press, 1969). On the dichotomy between scholars and intellectuals in Germany, see Gangolf Hübinger, '"Jurnalist" und "Literat". Vom Bildungsbürger zum Intellektuellen', in Hübinger and Wolfgang J. Mommsen (eds), *Intellektuelle im Deutschen Kaiserreich* (Frankfurt: Fischer, 1993), 95–110. For a useful synthesis of the most important pieces of this debate, see *Deutsche Intellektuelle 1910–1933. Aufrufe, Pamphlete, Betrachtungen* (Heidelberg: Verlag Lambert Schneider, 1984).

extolled the abstract values of justice and freedom supported class injustice in practice. He despised scientists, economists, lawyers, members of Parliament and journalists: 'the higher they raise their heads, the lower they bow their knee.'[13] The intellectuals who joined socialism, he concluded, were debarred from any kind of privilege and remained external to any state institution. In short, his definition of the revolutionary intelligentsia did not differ very much from the portrait of Parisian bohemia depicted half a century earlier by Théophile Gautier: 'love of art and hatred of the bourgeois'.[14]

The intellectuals that stunningly entered the fray during the Dreyfus Affair – famous novelists like Zola, the future president Georges Clemenceau, many Sorbonne professors, the republican representatives of the cultivated bourgeoisie, well described by Proust in many pages of his *Recherche* – were no longer the bohemian artists and writers who had climbed the barricades in 1848 and led the Commune in 1871: professional conspirators like Auguste Blanqui, artists like Gustave Courbet, writers like Jules Vallès, and teachers like Louise Michel. Those who built a bridge between this revolutionary intelligentsia and the 'intellectuals' were relatively marginal actors, whose interventions could be effective but did not appear in the foreground. They were outsiders, like Bernard Lazare or Mécislas Golberg.

At the end of the nineteenth century, the word 'intelligentsia' arrived in the West from Russia, where it had become quite common in the

---

13   Paul Lafargue, 'Socialism and the Intellectuals' (1900), in *The Right to Be Lazy and Other Studies* (Chicago: Charles Kerr, 1907), 83, 81. Lafargue shared this hatred for scholars and academic intellectuals with Georges Sorel, with whom he had briefly led the socialist journal *Le Devenir social*. 'Can you conceive', asked Sorel in *Le Procès de Socrate* (1889), 'of anything more horrible than government by professors?' Quoted by Isaiah Berlin, 'Georges Sorel', *Against the Current: Essays in the History of Ideas*, ed. Henry Hardy (New York: Viking Press, 1980), 315.

14   Théophile Gautier, 'Compte rendu de *La vie de Bohème* de Murger et Barrière' (1849), in Jean-Didier Wagneur, Françoise Cestor (eds), *Les Bohèmes 1840–1870. Écrivains, journalistes, artistes* (Paris: Champ Vallon, 2012), 553. See also Jerrold Seigel, *Bohemian Paris: Culture, Politics, and the Boundaries of Bourgeois Life, 1830–1930* (New York: Viking Press, 1986) and Mary Gluck, *Popular Bohemia: Modernism and Urban Culture in Nineteenth-Century Paris* (Cambridge, MA: Harvard University Press, 2005).

1860s to describe men of letters who held political commitments. This semantic transfer shows a circular movement, since the word was a Russian adaptation of the German *Intelligenz* or the Polish *inteligencja*.[15] In Russia, however, this word possessed a peculiar meaning. Differently from Western intellectuals, Isaiah Berlin observes, the members of the Russian intelligentsia shared much more than some interests or a similar social position; they 'considered themselves as being a dedicated order, almost a secular priesthood, devoted to the spread of a specific attitude to life, something like a gospel'.[16] And who were the *intelligenty*, the members of the intelligentsia? They were a minority of outcasts, in a twofold sense: on the one hand, as a group of cultivated people in a nation of illiterate peasants and, on the other, as representatives of literature, journalism, and liberal arts in a society with a still embryonic and repressed public sphere. Their clash against absolutism pushed them towards political radicalism, and tsarist despotism had transformed them into rebels and conspirators. Since the mid-nineteenth century, many had been expelled from Russian universities and sometimes exiled. Whereas a small section of them came from the aristocracy (Herzen, Bakunin, Vera Figner and Kropotkin belonged to the landed gentry) and others from the clergy (Nikolay Chernyshevsky and Nikolay Dobrolyubov), the majority were born in a lower middle class of small landowners and provincial clerks (Sergei Nechaev, Dimitry Karakozov, Vera Zasulich, or Lenin's brother Alexander Ulyanov), and even, in some cases, from a Jewish milieu (Mark A. Natanson and Aaron I. Zundelevich). Regardless of origin, the members of the Russian intelligentsia formed a group

15   The German origins of the Russian word are stressed by Richard Pipes, '"Intelligentsia" from the German "Intelligenz"? A Note', *Slavic Review*, 30/3 (1971): 615–18; on the Polish origins of the concept see Andrzej Walicki, *A History of Russian Thought from the Enlightenment to Marxism* (Stanford: Stanford University Press, 1979), xv. Mentioned in passing by Walicki, this thesis is developed by Aleksander Gella, 'An Introduction to the Sociology of the Intelligentsia', in Gella, (ed.), *The Intelligentsia and the Intellectuals: Theory, Method, and Case Study* (London: Sage Publications, 1976), 12–13, and particularly by Nathaniel Knight, 'Was the Intelligentsia Part of the Nation? Visions of Society in Post-Emancipation Russia', *Kritika*, 7/4 (2006): 733–58.

16   Isaiah Berlin, 'The Birth of the Russian Intelligentsia', *Russian Thinkers* (London: Hogarth Press, 1978), 117.

of *déclassés* or *raznochintsy*, meaning 'people of no estate in particular', in a society that was experiencing a process of urbanization and industrialization within the structures of absolutism.[17]

Located at the heart of this violent clash between conservatism and modernization, the *intelligenty* were naturally attracted to the most radical political ideologies, from populism to nihilism, from anarchism to socialism. Historians commonly describe the rise of this revolutionary intelligentsia through the characters of a classic novel: Ivan Turgenev's *Fathers and Sons* (1862). Nikolai, the father, epitomizes the first generation of democratic liberalism, largely influenced by German idealism and keen on modernity, but finally impotent to change the state of things. The nihilism of the following generation is embodied by Bazarov, a friend of Nikolay's son, who has abandoned his medical studies and embraced a radical form of materialism by transforming science into a destructive tool: he repudiates 'everything'.[18] Whereas Nikolai represents the democratic and liberal generation of the 1840s, the generation of Herzen and Belinsky that followed the Decembrist Revolt, Bazarov epitomizes that of the early 1860s, that of Chernyshevsky, reflected in Nechaev's *Revolutionary Catechism*. In 1909, when he was exiled in Vienna, Leon Trotsky sketched a striking portrait of 'Bazarov's esthetic nihilism' and the spirit of the *raznochintsy*:

> The small number of intellectuals, their rootlessness, their lack of rights, and their poverty: all this pushed them to create a group, to build a 'community.' A sharp struggle for self-preservation gave them a state of mind of permanent moral élan and transformed them into an original messianic order. Their hostility toward everyday individualism was the other side of their miserable condition. They did not possess anything and lived by supporting each other:

---

17 Martin Malia, 'What Is the Intelligentsia?' in Richard Pipes (ed.), *The Russian Intelligentsia* (New York: Columbia University Press, 1961), 5. See also Gary Soul Morson, 'What is the Intelligentsia? Once More, an Old Russian Question', *Academic Questions*, 6 (1993): 20–38.

18 Ivan Turgenev, *Fathers and Sons*, trans. Richard Freeborn (Oxford: Oxford University Press, 1991), 50.

this is the old secret of the political economy of Russian radical intellectuals.[19]

But these features were transmitted to the following generation. According to Trotsky, this period lasted until the revolution of 1905, when revolutionary intellectuals broke their isolation and abandoned both their messianic and sectarian tendencies. Martin Malia suggests that the revolutionary intelligentsia reached its peak with the generation of Turgenev's 'grandsons', the populists and Marxists who arose in the 1890s, after the assassination of Alexander II.[20] Thus, it is the Russian intelligentsia as a whole that appeared as a revolutionary actor.

Physiognomies

In 1929, the Cologne photographer August Sander published *Face of Our Time* (*Antlitz der Zeit*), the first step of a very ambitious project which the advent of National Socialism would prevent him from completing.[21] This book, intended to offer a photographic portrait of German society, includes a picture titled 'Revolutionaries'. It shows three men sitting close together on the threshold of a brick house. In the middle, looking at the camera, is Erich Mühsam, flanked by Alois Lindner and Guido Kopp, who rests his hand on Erich's shoulder with a gesture of friendly intimacy. Erich Mühsam was an anarcho-communist essayist, poet and playwright who had been imprisoned twice: first for his anti-war propaganda, then for his participation in the Bavarian Revolution of spring 1919. Lindner and Kopp were communists who had followed a similar path. Mühsam died in the Oranienburg concentration camp in 1934; Kopp survived Buchenwald, and Lindner emigrated to the Soviet Union, where he was persecuted

19   Lev Trockij, 'Hanno sete di cultura' (1908), *Letteratura e rivoluzione*, trans. Vittorio Strada (Turin: Einaudi, 1973), 274.

20   Malia, 'What Is the Intelligentsia?', 2. See also Allen McConnell, 'The Origin of the Russian Intelligentsia', *Slavic and East European Journal* 8/1 (1964): 1–16.

21   August Sander, *Citizens of the Twentieth Century: Portrait Photographs 1892–1952* (Cambridge, MA: MIT Press, 1986).

August Sander, *Revolutionaries* (Alois Lindner, Eric
Mühsam, Guido Kopp). *Face of Our Time* (1929).

by Stalinism and disappeared in 1943. Both Kopp and Lindner produced autobiographical texts.[22]

Sander had met Mühsam through their mutual friend Paul Frölich, a
German communist who in 1916 had participated in the Zimmerwald
socialist conference against the First World War and became a KPD
deputy at the Reichstag in the 1920s, before being expelled and creating a dissident left-wing socialist party (SAP). A prolific essayist,
Frölich was imprisoned by the Nazi regime in 1933 and the following
year fled to the United States, where he wrote a biography of Rosa
Luxemburg. *Face of Our Time* also includes a portrait of Frölich
titled 'Communist Leader', which Sander placed in his overall project
amongst other pictures of politicians. The image of Lindner, Mühsam
and Kopp belongs to the second section – 'Working Types' – thus
emphasizing that, beyond being a political commitment, revolution
was actually their 'professional' activity. The same section contains

---

22   See Chris Hirte, *Erich Mühsam. Eine Biographie* (Freiburg: Ahriman Verlag,
2019), and Norman Dankerl, *Alois Lindner. Das Leben des bayerischen Abenteurers
und Revolutionärs* (Viechtach: Lichtung, 2007).

August Sander, *Communist Leader* (Paul Frölich). *Face of Our Time* (1929).

August Sander, *Proletarian Intellectuals*, (Else Lasker Schuler, Tristan Rémy, Franz Wilhelm Seiwert, Gerd Arntz). *Face of our Time* (1929).

another group portrait, 'Proletarian Intellectuals' (1925), that brings together the poet Else Lasker-Schüler, the French writer Tristan Rémy, the Dadaist painter Franz Wilhelm Seiwert, and the graphic artist and designer Gerd Arntz. The adjective of the title implicitly refers to the movement for a 'proletarian culture' that had been created in Russia and other countries after the October Revolution and to which all of them belonged at that time. In fact, their clothes look less proletarian than those of Lindner, Mühsam and Kopp – Lasker-Schüler is dressed in the Russian style – but they equally express a feeling of spiritual community.

August Sander's project was thoroughly unusual for his time. In one of the few texts he wrote on his work, 'Photography as Universal Language' (1930), he described his portraits as endeavouring to encapsulate the German society of his time by grasping the personality of its actors.[23] Alfred Döblin, who prefaced *Face of Our Time*, described Sander's work as 'writing sociology, not by writing, but by producing photographs'.[24] And Walter Benjamin complimented the book in his 'Little History of Photography' (1931), pointing out that it possessed at once a highly aesthetic and a 'scientific' dimension. Sander, Benjamin wrote, had 'compiled a series of faces that is in no way inferior to the tremendous physiognomic gallery mounted by an Eisenstein or a Pudovkin'.[25]

As for Sander himself, he defined his portfolio of portraits as a 'cartography of origins' (*Stammappe*).[26] Despite the ambiguity of this concept – *Stamm* means also stock or tribe, with a racial connotation – his approach had nothing to do with the racist theories or the nationalist currents of physiognomic thought of his time. Unlike Hans Günther or Ferdinand L. Clauss, who collected human portraits in order to detect a biological essence behind faces and expressions and then classified

---

23   August Sander, 'Photography as a Universal Language' (1931), *The Massachusetts Review*, 19/4 (1978): 674–9.

24   Alfred Döblin, 'Faces, Images, and Their Truth', in Sander, *Face of Our Time* (Munich: Schirmer/Mosel Verlag 1994), 13.

25   Walter Benjamin, 'Little History of Photography' (1931), *WBSW*, vol. 2/2, 520.

26   On Sander's approach to the photographical portrait and archive, see Andy Jones, 'Reading August Sander's Archive', *Oxford Art Journal*, 23/1 (2000): 3–21.

them in a racialized archive, Sander assembled a catalogue of social
types ordered according to their professions and economic activities.
Not only was his *Stammappe* not hierarchical – in his portfolio, the
Roma or the unemployed are as important as bankers and statesmen
– but he was careful to portray them as self-authoring subjects. Far
from being passive objects seized by the camera within a given spatial
continuum, they chose their own gestures, expressions, environment,
and costume – everyday dress, Sunday best, or overalls – as well as,
in many cases, the objects they wished to exhibit as symbols of their
profession. The photographer captured and recorded the image that
self-aware people wished to give of themselves. He did not grasp a
moment of their life; he fixed their identity.[27] Borrowing the phenomenological language of Jean-Paul Sartre, an author clearly indebted to
the German theory of Gestalt, Sander's portraits could be defined as
'inseparable ensembles' in which 'the physical, the social, the religious,
and the individual are closely mingled' until being condensed into
a 'living synthesis'.[28] In a famous essay on photography written just
before *Face of Our Time*, Siegfried Kracauer distinguished these kinds
of images from those that appeared as mere objective reproductions of
reality, by calling them 'monograms' or 'memory images' – meaningful
graphic figures that preserved the unforgettable and expressed in a
fragment a person's real history.[29] Sander's physiognomic portraits
caught both the subjectivity of individuals and the social features of
their historical time.

---

27   On the opposition between Sander's and Clauss's physiognomic conceptions, see Richard T. Gray, *About Face: German Physiognomic Thought from Lavater
to Auschwitz* (Detroit: Wayne State University Press, 2004), 369–80. Gray points
out that in 1936, the Nazis confiscated all copies of *Antlitz der Zeit* conserved in
Sander's studio and destroyed the printing plates of the book (ibid., 378). As for
the racist thinkers, see Hans F. Günther, *The Racial Elements of European History*
(London: Methuen, 1927), and particularly *Rassenkunde des Deutschen Volkes*
(Munich: Lehmann Verlag, 1937), and Ludwig Ferdinand Clauss, *Rasse und Seele:
Eine Einführung in den Sinn der Leiblichen Gestalt* (Munich: Lehmann Verlag, 1934).

28   Jean-Paul Sartre, *Anti-Semite and Jew: An Exploration of the Etiology of
Hate* (New York: Schocken Books, 1995 [1946]), 64.

29   Siegfried Kracauer, 'Photography' (1927), *The Mass Ornament: Weimar
Essays*, trans. Thomas Y. Levin (Cambridge, MA: Harvard University Press,
1995), 51.

'Revolutionaries' is a very interesting collective portrait, especially if compared with other images of Sander's archive, both those of craftsmen and manual workers and those of representatives of the German ruling class. The young farmers, the pastry cook, the master locksmith, the bricklayer and other workers may not have belonged to high society but their poses transmit a strong feeling of self-confidence. They completely identify with their work, even the humblest kind, for it gives them a sense of dignity and is, in many cases, a source of social pride. The physiognomy of established artists and members of academic institutions – pianists, composers, conductors, art scholars and philosophers – emphasizes their subjectivity, since they wish to appear as singular creators and thinkers rather than mere representatives of their professions. All of them, however, exhibit the external features of people who enjoy a successful activity, public recognition, and a solid inscription in a social world. The representatives of the ruling class – industrialists, businessmen, bankers, advertising managers – have no need to display the luxury of their existence or strike an arrogant pose: their power is etched into their composure, the sober elegance of their suits and the quiet gravity of their faces. The common thread of these portraits is an entanglement of morality, honourability and respectability – an ensemble of qualities condensed by the German word *Sittlichkeit* – that legitimates their authority.[30] They provide magisterial evidence of bourgeois self-awareness in 1929, at the apogee of the Weimar Republic, just before the Great Depression.

The contrast between these images and the group portrait of Müsham and his fellow revolutionaries is astonishing. Their shabby clothes testify to their economic precariousness, not to say poverty, which mirrors an interior spiritual disquiet. Instead of self-satisfaction, the gravity of their faces betrays fear and their closeness seems to express intimacy and solidarity as well as mutual support in the face of danger. Under dishevelled hair, Mühsam's gaze is at once sharp and uncanny. Their environment is neutral and does not contain anything

---

30   On the role played by the notion of *Sittlichkeit* in *fin-de-siècle* Germany, see George L. Mosse, 'Jewish Emancipation: Between *Bildung* and *Sittlichkeit*', *Confronting the Nation: Jewish and Western Nationalism* (Hanover-London: Brandeis University Press, 1993), 13–145.

with which they could show a harmonious or organic relationship. All of them wear glasses and this is the main mark of their status as intellectuals. They compose a trio of marginal and uprooted conspirators, a team of seditious bohemians.

In 1921 Mühsam published an article in the communist magazine *Die Aktion*, in which he pointed out that intellectuals did not naturally belong to the proletariat. Despite recognizing their capacities and education, workers expressed towards them both 'caution and suspicion'. In order to be accepted, they had to prove their political usefulness in the class struggle. Back in 1906, however, he had published an essay in *Die Fackel*, the Viennese journal of Karl Kraus, in which he did not hesitate to depict himself as a 'bohemian'. Bohemians, he contended, are 'the outcasts who fight outside of all organizations, together with criminals, vagabonds, whores, and artists'.[31] As social outcasts, bohemian artists do not conceive of their creations as a business, and as political activists they detest any kind of authoritarian and hierarchical organization. Bohemian intellectuals express a 'nihilistic temperament' made of 'radical scepticism' and 'the radical negation of all conventional values'. They defend the self against 'the instincts of mass society' and their role consists in winning the labouring classes to their own side. His conclusion was as joyful as it was apocalyptic: 'Criminals, vagabonds, whores, and artists: this is the bohemia that will clear the path for a new culture.'[32]

The bohemian lifestyle exactly reverses the bourgeois ethos of work, moderation, 'worldly asceticism', economic rationality, capital accumulation, and the search for respectability. Against these values, bohemians despised money, rejected bourgeois prejudices, defended an anti-productive ethics and free love, and opposed a gratuitous aesthetic creation to the market that turns art into a business. In their view, freedom meant not only anti-authoritarianism but also egalitarianism and the end of class divisions.[33]

---

31   Erich Mühsam, 'Bohemia' (1906), *Liberating Society from the State and Other Writings: A Political Reader*, ed. Gabriel Kuhn (Oakland: PM Press, 2011), 56.

32   Ibid., 58.

33   See the chapter on bohemianism in Enzo Traverso, *Left-Wing Melancholia: Marxism, History, and Memory* (New York: Columbia University Press, 2016), 120–50.

In 1929, when he posed before Sander's camera, Mühsam's bohemian anarchism had been tested by twenty years of struggles, wars, defeated revolutions and imprisonment; yet his gaze still revealed a *self* that could not be simply dissolved into a mass movement. His relationship with German communism was as solid as it was conflictual. In 1920 he had been a mass leader in Munich. After having miraculously survived the bloody repression of the Bavarian Soviet Republic, he suffered years of persecution and returned to his original status of intellectual outsider. His itinerary was certainly peculiar, but perhaps it reveals a general tendency.

Bohemians and Déclassés

In contrast to anarchism, which always welcomed bohemian artists and writers as its own natural representatives, Marxism looked at the intelligentsia with suspicion, never quite coming to terms with a strange actor that appeared simultaneously deeply attractive and highly repulsive. Insofar as Marxist thinkers were themselves intellectuals – sociologically speaking, at least – such paradoxical behaviour clearly revealed a crisis of identity and a reluctant self-definition. This uncanniness began with Marx and Engels, whose philosophical and political career started with sharp polemics within the small German circle of left-wing Hegelians. Essays and books like 'The Jewish Question' (1843), *The Holy Family* (1844), *The German Ideology* (1845) and *Poverty of Philosophy* (1847) were violent – often highly satirical – settlings of scores with Bruno Bauer, Ludwig Feuerbach, Moses Hess, Max Stirner, Pierre-Joseph Proudhon and other representatives of the young, quasi-bohemian anarchist and socialist intelligentsia of the 1840s.

A passage from *The Communist Manifesto* (1848) suggests the birth of the socialist intelligentsia as the result of a split within the ruling class through which, in a time of deep economic and social crisis, a section of the bourgeoisie renounces its origins and values in order to join the field of the subaltern classes. This separation is a consequence of class struggle and a token of the growing strength of the proletariat that breaches the united front of its enemies. On the eve

of the European revolutions of 1848, Marx and Engels advanced this
diagnostic:

> Finally, in times when the class struggle nears the decisive hour,
> the progress of dissolution going on within the ruling class, in
> fact within the whole range of old society, assumes such a violent,
> glaring character, that a small section of the ruling class cuts itself
> adrift, and joins the revolutionary class, the class that holds the
> future in its hands. Just as, therefore, at an earlier period, a section
> of the nobility went over to the bourgeoisie, so now a portion of
> the bourgeoisie goes over to the proletariat, and in particular, a
> portion of the bourgeois ideologists, who have raised themselves to
> the level of comprehending theoretically the historical movement
> as a whole.[34]

This definition of the revolutionary intellectual irresistibly resembles
a self-portrait, so it is interesting to observe that the authors of *The
Communist Manifesto* did not consider bohemian artists and writers as
potential allies of the insurgent proletariat. In *The Eighteenth Brumaire
of Louis Bonaparte* (1852), Marx disparaged them as a group of marginal types, 'decayed roués with dubious means of subsistence and of
dubious origin' that almost naturally supported a liar, authoritarian,
and demagogic aspiring dictator like Louis Bonaparte, 'the chief of the
lumpen-proletariat' of the French capital. Once in power, Napoleon
III had discarded them along with the newspapers that had supported
his political adventure. Marx mentioned the 'literati' among a variegated crowd composed of 'vagabonds, discharged soldiers, discharged
jailbirds, escaped galley slaves, swindlers, mountebanks, *lazzaroni*,
pickpockets, tricksters, gamblers, *maquereaux* [pimps], brothelkeep-
ers, porters, organ grinders, ragpickers, knife grinders, tinkers, and
beggars;' in short, he concluded, 'the whole indefinite, disintegrated
mass, thrown hither and thither, which the French call bohemia.'[35]

---

34   Karl Marx, Friedrich Engels, 'Manifesto of the Communist Party' (1848),
MECW, vol. 6, 494.
35   Karl Marx, 'The Eighteenth Brumaire of Louis Bonaparte' (1852),
MECW, vol. 11, 149. The best study on this topic is Hal Draper, 'The Concept of

Karl Marx (1861).

Bourgeois deserting their own class to join the proletarian field, or lumpen 'literati'? Marx's definition of the rebellious intellectuals of his time swung between these two poles without finding any synthesis. From a sociological point of view, his friend Friedrich Engels, a socialist thinker who managed his family's textile factories in Manchester, fits the first option quite well; as for Marx, a young German philosopher who settled in Paris, was then expelled from the French capital and fled to Brussels, went on to direct a democratic newspaper in Cologne in 1848 before emigrating to London, where he lived 'with dubious means of subsistence', probably fits the second definition much better, that of a lumpen intellectual. But this condition of social precarity and intellectual bohemianism certainly did not correspond with his self-identity. His entire life in London was a desperate effort to hide his poverty behind a bourgeois façade, and his ferocious anti-bohemianism revealed simultaneous awareness and horror of this reality. His journalistic work certainly did not allow him to live in a middle-class Soho house with his family and a servant. If he did live this way, it was only thanks to the generosity of his friend Engels. As Marx wrote to him in 1858, 'The show of respectability which has so

Lumpenproletariat in Marx and Engels', *Économies et sociétés*, 6/12 (1972): 2285–312. Draper points out the tendency of both men to metaphorize this concept, 2304.

far been kept up has been the only means of avoiding a collapse.'[36] In his private life, however, he indulged a few bohemian customs: he worked hard but irregularly, writing through the night and waking up at noon. What is sure is that his status as intellectual permanently interfered with both his political judgements and his public image. In the debates of the First International, he frequently accused Bakunin of being a bourgeois ideologist and doctrinaire severed from the authentic proletarian classes, whereas the anarchists (as Proudhon had done previously) denounced the authoritarianism of the Marxists, whose ideas of 'proletarian dictatorship' were nothing but a 'government by scientists (the most distressing, odious, and despicable type of government in the world)'.[37]

At the end of the nineteenth century, Karl Kautsky, the 'pope' of the Second International and the director of *Die Neue Zeit*, the theoretical journal of German Social Democracy, reformulated and nuanced Marx's assessment. Undoubtedly, a superior section of the intelligentsia – he spoke of German 'mandarins' – was organically linked with the ruling classes, but he preferred to define the intellectuals as an intermediate and relatively independent social stratum. Since their identity and social consciousness were grounded neither in land ownership nor in the property of the means of production, but rather in the role they played in cultural superstructures, intellectuals were susceptible of joining both antagonistic classes of capitalist society. In fact, they elaborated the ideas of both the bourgeoisie and the proletariat. They were certainly unable to build their own society, but without their support, the bourgeoisie could not manage its power nor could the proletariat imagine a socialist future. In short, the intelligentsia was a kind of new 'middle class' whose heterogeneous structure pushed its different components to join either the bourgeois or the proletarian classes, either capitalism or socialism.

---

36   Karl Marx to Friedrich Engels, July 15, 1858, *MECW*, vol. 40, 328–31. See also Gareth Stedman Jones, *Karl Marx: Greatness and Illusion* (Cambridge, MA: Belknap Press, 2016), 328.

37   Quoted by Lewis S. Feuer, *Marx and the Intellectuals: A Set of Postideological Essays* (New York: Anchor Books, 1969), 53–4. See also William Gleberzon, 'Marxist Conceptions of the Intellectuals', *Historical Reflections*, 5/1 (1978): 84.

Imbued with positivism and evolutionism, Kautsky's socialism meant the reorganization of human life according to the principles of economic, technical, and scientific progress that was embodied by a specific social layer:

> The vehicle of science is not the proletariat, but the *bourgeois intelligentsia*: it was in the minds of individual members of this stratum that modern socialism originated, and it was they who communicated it to the more intellectually developed proletarians who, in their turn, introduce it into the proletarian class struggle where conditions allow that to be done. Thus, socialist consciousness is something introduced into the proletarian class struggle from without [*von Aussen Hineingetragenes*] and not something that arose within it spontaneously [*urwüchsig*].[38]

In 1902, Lenin quoted this passage, emphasizing that, 'exclusively by its own effort', the working class was unable to elaborate a socialist programme since it could not overcome the primary stage of a purely trade-unionist consciousness. Learning from their own struggles, workers could claim better wages and implement their living conditions, but they could not put into question the entire structure of social relations that determined their exploitation. This is why socialism meant more than protective labour legislation. The theory of socialism, Lenin pointed out, 'grew out of the philosophic, historical, and economic theories elaborated by educated representatives of the propertied classes, by intellectuals'. And he recalled that 'by their social status the founders of modern scientific socialism, Marx and Engels, themselves belonged to the bourgeois intelligentsia.'[39]

In Russia, socialism came with populism and it was amongst the *Narodniki* that Marx found his first and most enthusiastic readers

---

38   Karl Kautsky, 'Das Programm der Sozialdemokratie in Österreich', *Die Neue Zeit*, 20/3 (1901–02), 79. Quoted by Lenin, 'What Is to be Done?' (1902), *LCW*, vol. 5, 384.

39   Ibid., 375. On this debate at the second congress of the Russian social-democracy, see Lars T. Lih, *Lenin Rediscovered: What Is to Be Done? In Context* (Chicago: Haymarket 2008), 529–38.

in the 1870s. Even if it was against them that Marxism emerged a decade later as both an independent current of thought and a political project, the legacy of populism remained extremely influential. Lenin's conception of a socialist idea brought to the labouring classes from outside – introduced within the proletariat by the intellectuals – clearly reproduces a populist model. Like the *Narodniki*, the Bolsheviks were enlighteners who embodied the mission of awakening consciousness and spreading a message of liberation. This vision was also instrumental in building a centralized and hierarchical organization of conspirators that Lenin maintained even after the revolution of 1905, when the soviets emerged as an alternative power created by the insurgent masses themselves. During the acrimonious debates that followed the split of the Russian social-democracy between Bolsheviks and Mensheviks in 1903, both tendencies accused each other of intellectualism: according to Lenin, the enemies of centralism were petty-bourgeois intellectuals affected by the virus of individualism and irreducibly refractory to proletarian discipline; according to Rosa Luxemburg and Leon Trotsky, Lenin sought to reproduce within a socialist party the hierarchical relations of a factory, where workers had to execute the tasks fixed by managers and technicians, a specific subset of the bourgeois intelligentsia.[40] Nonetheless, all currents of the Russian social-democracy admitted that a gap existed between the labouring class and the intellectuals. Leon Trotsky, president of the soviets of Saint-Petersburg in 1905 and one of the strongest critics of Lenin's centralism before the October Revolution, observed that differently from the worker, who came to socialism almost spontaneously, 'as part of a whole, along with his class', the intellectual could not come to socialism without 'breaking his class umbilical cord as an individual, as a personality'.[41]

In the early 1920s, Lukács suggested a dialectical synthesis – in the sense of a Hegelian *sublation* (*Aufhebung*) – of this opposition through

---

40   Rosa Luxemburg, 'Organizational Questions of the Russian Social Democracy' (1904), *The Rosa Luxemburg Reader*, eds Peter Hudis and Kevin B. Anderson (New York: Monthly Review Press, 2004), 248–65; Leon Trotsky, *Our Political Tasks* (London: New Park Publications, 1983 [1904]).

41   Leon Trotsky, *The Intelligentsia and Socialism* (London: New Park Publications, 1974).

his concept of 'class consciousness'. Intellectuals who break with their class bring knowledge 'from outside' to the proletarian class, but it is only when the latter appropriates it to the point of establishing a complete homogeneity between the subject and the object of knowledge that 'class consciousness' emerges. Thereafter, the intellectuals do not belong to the revolutionary movement as representatives of their own group but only as an expression of this class consciousness that condenses theory and practice, a worldview and a political project, a class and its historical mission.[42]

The terms of this theoretical debate could be summarized as follows: a) the intellectuals are a bourgeois layer; b) they can join the proletariat only by deserting their own class; c) the proletariat needs the intellectuals in order to build its socialist ideology; d) declassed intellectuals – lumpen or bohemians – are an unstable and unreliable social stratum that tends to join the political reaction, as in France in 1848. One of the most striking aspects of this debate lay in *self-negation*: nobody was ready to admit that the overwhelming majority of Marxist leaders, activists and thinkers were themselves declassed intellectuals. According to Freud, denial is a psychological defence mechanism that allows a subject to ignore or remove an uncomfortable reality. Wedded to a teleological vision of history that posited the transition from capitalism to socialism as an ineluctable process bringing the triumph of science, culture, technological progress, and a higher development of productive forces, Marxist thinkers could not imagine these colossal accomplishments being carried out by marginal actors. However skilled they were – many were talented men and women, some of them towering figures of their time – most of these revolutionary intellectuals lived as outcasts. Marx spent most of his life in exile as an uprooted intellectual. Kautsky, the most respected theoretician of *fin-de-siècle* Marxism and certainly the most 'established' among the socialist thinkers of his time, was a journalist who never remotely thought of becoming a university professor. All Russian Marxist thinkers, both Bolsheviks and Mensheviks, were cosmopolitan

---

42   Georg Lukács, 'Intellectual Workers and the Problem of Intellectual Leadership', *Tactics and Ethics 1919–1929: The Questions of Parliamentarism and Other Essays*, ed. Rodney Livingstone (London, New York: Verso, 2014), 12–18.

intellectuals who, when they were not hosted by Tsarist prisons, lived precariously in Western Europe where they animated the isolated circles of political emigration. This self-negation lasted until 1917, when the social-democratic conception of a molecular and cumulative process of social change was replaced by a vision of historical bifurcations, discontinuities and breaks. In 1914, the collapse of the European order opened a new historical landscape in which lucid and audacious minorities could suddenly take the helm of mass movements and revolutionary upheavals. Exiting from their marginality, socialist intellectuals could become decisive actors of their time.

Revolutionary outcasts had different social origins but shared a common condition and achieved a similar status. Michael Bakunin, a wandering anarchist coming from the Russian aristocracy, lucidly recognized that the transition from the ruling classes to the radical left implied a willing déclassement. This philosophical and political break was inseparable from an anti-bourgeois ethos and inevitably meant a social metamorphosis. Possessing an evident autobiographical flavour, his words were the opposite of Marx's self-negation:

> If a man, born and raised in a bourgeois milieu, wishes sincerely and without nonsense to become the friend and brother of the workers, he must renounce all the conditions of his past existence, all his bourgeois customs, break all his ties of sentiment, vanity, and intellect with the bourgeois world and, turning his back on this world, become its enemy, declare outright war against it, throw himself entirely, without restriction or reserve, into the worker's world. If he does not discover a passion for justice in himself sufficient to inspire this resolution and courage, let him not fool himself or the workers; he will never become their friend.[43]

The conflict with Bakunin's anarchism was probably the main cause of Marx's denial of his status as an outcast. Committed to building a

---

43   Mikhail Bakunin, 'L'empire knouto-germanique et la révolution sociale', Œuvres (Paris: Stock, 1897), vol. 2, 370. Quoted by Robert Michels, *Political Parties: A Sociological Study of the Oligarchical Tendencies of Modern Democracy* (New York: Free Press, 1968), 313–14.

mass political movement, he believed that socialism could not prevail without breaking with the anarchist image of revolutionaries as nihilists and conspirators. True socialists had nothing in common with fanatical young terrorists like Nechaev and Karakozov. In 1872, the split of the anarchists from the International Workingmen's Association pushed Marx and Engels to write an extremely violent pamphlet against Bakunin, whom they depicted as the inspirer of the political skulduggeries of a sect of déclassés. In a footnote of the 1874 German edition, Engels explained this concept in disparaging terms that reflected the conservative prejudice of his time:

> In French, the *déclassés* are people of the propertied classes who were ousted or who broke away from that class without thereby becoming proletarians, such as business adventurers, rogues and gamblers, most of them professional literati or politicians, etc. The proletariat, too, has its déclassé elements; they make up the *lumpen-proletariat*.[44]

The most eloquent expression of this déclassé politics was *The Catechism of a Revolutionary* (1869), the apocalyptic programme of Nechaev that announced the moral and political duty of any revolutionary to destroy the entire civilized order. The text proclaimed a new 'science of destruction' based on the assimilation by the revolutionists of all significant accomplishments in the fields of 'mechanics, physics, chemistry, and perhaps medicine', which must be used with the exclusive purpose of destroying the establishment.[45] According to Marx and

---

44   Karl Marx, 'The Alliance of Socialist Democracy and the International Working Men's Association' (1873), *MECW*, vol. 23, 454. Peter Stallybrass observed that Marx and Engels 'sometimes used lumpen-proletariat as a racial category, and in this they simply repeated one of the commonplaces of bourgeois social analysis in the nineteenth century: the depiction of the poor as a nomadic tribe, innately depraved.' See Peter Stallybrass, 'Marx and Heterogeneity: Thinking the *Lumpenproletariat*', *Representations*, 31 (1990): 70. On Marx's contempt for the lumpen-proletariat, see also Gianluca Solla, *Memoria dei senzanome. Breve storia dell'infimo e dell'infame* (Verona: Ombre corte, 2013), 26–43.

45   Sergey Nechaev, 'Catechism of the Revolutionist' (1869), in Walter Laqueur (ed.), *Voices of Terror* (New York: Reed Press, 2004), 71. See also Franco Venturi, *Roots of Revolution: A History of the Populist and Socialist Movements in Nineteenth*

Sergei Nechaev, end of the 1860s.

Mikhail Bakunin (1860), portrait by Nadar.

Engels, this kind of nihilistic project that, with the pretext of abolishing any authority, simply pushed 'bourgeois immorality to the limit', was the ideology around which Bakunin had built an international sect. In Italy, where it did not have a proletarian character, the anarchist movement was successful in assembling 'a rabble of déclassés.' Its leaders, they went on, were 'lawyers without clients, doctors with neither patients nor medical knowledge, students of billiards, commercial travellers and other tradespeople, and principally journalists from small papers with a more or less dubious reputation'.[46]

For the proponents of historical materialism, science was a productive force and socialism had to be grounded in the achievements of a previous social formation. Revolution had to be prepared by building a labour movement conscious of its historical tasks and ready to reorganize both science and production along collectivist lines; it could not be *triggered* by incendiary bombs and destructive devices. The suppression of Tsarism had to be accomplished by a social and political revolution and should not be confused with the assassination of the tsar. Elevating socialism from utopia to science, according to Engels's famous formula, did not mean providing the workers with dynamite sticks. The discrepancy between Marxism and anarchism in the early 1870s was clear. The violence of Marx's criticism, however, is extreme and sounds like a ritual of exorcism. Whereas there are plenty of passages in Marx's letters complaining bitterly about his poverty and lack of resources, he never depicted himself as a bohemian or a déclassé.

Quoting the words of Bakunin in his famous study on mass political parties, Robert Michels nuanced the concept of déclassement and distinguished two kinds of 'intellectual proletariat': on the one hand, those who had failed in achieving a respectable profession within the state apparatus or a leading position in the institutions; on the other

Century Russia (London: Weidenfeld and Nicolson, 1960), 365. The best study on the nihilistic spirit of Russian terrorism is Claudia Verhoeven, *The Odd Man Karakozov: Imperial Russia, Modernity, and the Birth of Terrorism* (Ithaca, NY: Cornell University Press, 2009). On this debate, see also Tariq Ali, *The Dilemmas of Lenin: Terrorism, War, Empire, Love, Revolution* (London, New York: Verso, 2017), notably Chapter 2: 'Terrorism Versus Absolutism', 27–58.

46   Marx, 'The Alliance of Socialist Democracy', 504.

Carlo Cafiero (1878).

hand, the 'sworn enemies of the state', the 'eternally restless spirits' who became the leaders of the revolutionary movements. The theoretician of the 'iron law of oligarchy' and the circulation of the elites no longer believed in democracy, but he knew what he was talking about. During his time within the labour movement, this talented scholar had himself been a representative of this 'intellectual proletariat': before becoming a fascist and pursuing a brilliant career in the Italian university system, he had been excluded from the German academy because of his political commitment. This background explains his vision of intellectual déclassement not as a 'historical fact' but rather as a 'psychological postulate of the effective socialist action of those who were not proletarians by birth'. In the case of Carlo Cafiero, whom Marx contemptuously stigmatized as a déclassé during his sharp polemics within the First International, Michels observed that this Italian anarchist of aristocratic origins deserved respect: it was with a 'spirit of self-sacrifice and for the invincible firmness of his convictions' that he had 'placed the whole of his considerable fortune at the disposal of the party, whilst himself leading the life of a poor bohemian'.[47] Similar considerations could be extended to Bakunin,

47   Michels, *Political Parties*, 315.

who never worried about respectability, orderliness and etiquette, to the point of considering them as a sort of anathema. In his auto-biography, Alexander Herzen sketched this portrait of the Russian anarchist in the 1860s:

> At fifty he was still the same wandering student, the same homeless bohemian of the rue de Bourgogne, caring nothing for the morrow, despising money, scattering it on all sides when he had it, borrowing indiscriminately when he had none, with the same simplicity with which children take from their parents and never think of repayment, with the same simplicity with which he himself was prepared to give to anyone his last penny, reserving for himself only what was necessary for cigarettes and tea. He was never embarrassed by this mode of life; he was born to be the great wanderer, the great outcast.[48]

It is significant that the only Marxist thinker who seriously analysed the nature and function of intellectuals in modern society did not really overcome this self-negation. Several sections of Antonio Gramsci's *Prison Notebooks* (1929–35) are devoted to this topic, which he approached from a historical point of view. He defined the intellectuals not as ideologues but primarily as cultural organizers who elaborated the world vision of social classes. Suggesting a dichotomy that has since been canonized, Gramsci distinguishes between 'traditional' and 'organic' intellectuals.[49] The former belong to premodern societies and their typical representatives were clergymen and lawyers, who had codified the *Weltanschauung* of feudalism and absolutism, thus legitimizing the power of aristocracy. Their most popular embodiment, however, were writers, philosophers and artists, the agents of humanistic culture. The latter belong to modern societies, in which they defend values, fix ideological frameworks and outline the political projects of the ruling classes. They are not only men of law and

---

48   Quoted in E. H. Carr, *The Romantic Exiles* (London: Serif, 2007 [1933]), 194.

49   Antonio Gramsci, *Prison Notebooks*, ed. Joseph Buttigieg (New York: Columbia University Press, 1996), vol. 2, 199–210 (texts from 1932).

philosophers but also scholars, technicians, economists, managers, etc. Since their role consists in 'organizing the hegemony of a social group' within civil society, they cannot ignore politics. Intellectuals are not reducible to the large sector of technicians and professionals engendered by the social division of labour: hegemony means the control and guidance of superstructures, which are their allotted realm. Gramsci calls them the 'functionaries' of the ruling class. In as much as all class societies generate their own intellectuals, the subaltern classes can neither conquer political power nor transform the relations of production without establishing their own cultural hegemony. This means that the organic intellectuals of the proletariat emerge from the factory. In Gramsci's view, the factory is the domain of industrial labour and the paradigm of a new society grounded in productive rationality. The organic intellectuals of socialism are the technicians and the producers of a collective factory. Transcending the limits of the classical humanistic literati, they will participate in the creation of new forms of life and accomplish practical tasks as 'constructors' and 'organizers'. The success of the socialist weekly L'Ordine Nuovo, which played a crucial role in the occupation of Turin's factories in 1920, depended precisely on its capacity to 'develop certain forms of new intellectualism'.[50]

Nonetheless, between the 'traditional' intellectuals of the past and the 'organic' intellectuals of the socialist future prefigured by the Russian soviets and the workers' councils of Turin, the revolutionary intellectuals of the present still remained a mysterious and unthinkable object. Where did the founders of L'Ordine Nuovo come from? Gramsci did not seem very interested in applying his own definition of the intellectual to himself. In a bid to answer this question, one might observe that he came from the clash between tradition and modernity, between the 'traditional' and the 'organic' intellectuals of Italian society at the beginning of the twentieth century: he was born in Sardinia, a rural and economically backward island, to a family of small clerks and landowners, attended a traditional high school and discovered socialism as a student at the university of Turin, the

---

50   Ibid., 243.

Antonio Gramsci in the 1920s.

most industrialized city on the peninsula. Working as a journalist and literary critic for a socialist newspaper, he was neither a clerk nor a producer, neither a teacher nor a technician. For the conservatives, he was a dangerous political agitator, whereas university scholars regarded him as a proletarian intellectual or a déclassé.

Maps I: West

Eric Hobsbawm's observation that Marxist intellectuals were 'rare birds west of Vienna' before 1914 could probably be extended into the 1920s, even if some minorities had achieved a bigger visibility.[51] A general survey shows that, at the end of the Great War, European culture was dominated by nationalism. In Germany, it was the variegated constellation of the 'conservative revolution' that occupied the foreground. After the collapse of the Hohenzollern, the literary best-sellers were Ernst Jünger's war memoir, *Storm of Steel* (1920), and Oswald Spengler's *The Decline of the West* (1918–22), followed by a spate of reactionary and anti-Semitic essays by Moller van der Bruck, Werner Sombart, Hans Freyer, Leopold Ziegler and a galaxy

---

51   Eric Hobsbawm, 'Intellectuals and Communism', *Revolutionaries* (London: Weidenfeld and Nicolson, 1973), 25.

of less brilliant writers. Academia remained a bastion of the 'German mandarins', whence emerged the figures of two Catholic scholars: the juridical thinker Carl Schmitt and the young philosopher Martin Heidegger. Besides this conservative tendency, there were the 'republicans by reason' (*Vernunftrepublikaner*) such as Ernst Robert Curtius, Max Weber and Karl Jaspers: nationalists who resigned themselves to supporting the Weimar Republic but remained nostalgic for the Prussian empire in their hearts (some of them would change their mind in the following decade). Most scholars who accepted democracy and even those who, like Albert Einstein, joined social democracy, were openly anti-communist. As Peter Gay has convincingly argued, what is nowadays commonly called 'Weimar culture', identified with Bertolt Brecht's pieces, Fritz Lang's movies, Walter Gropius's Bauhaus and Walter Benjamin's literary criticism, was in fact the exceptionally creative outburst of a minority, a 'dance on the edge of a volcano' performed by a group of artists and writers who found their destiny in exile.[52]

In Italy, many writers, artists, and intellectuals joined fascism even before the consolidation of Mussolini's regime. The nationalist commitment of Gabriele D'Annunzio, a poet who discovered his political charisma during the war, became a model for Mussolini himself. The most significant aesthetic avant-garde of the time, futurism, enthusiastically supported the fascist movement, as well as revolutionary syndicalism and several currents of prewar nationalism. The intellectual opposition was embodied by representatives of classical liberalism like the philosopher Benedetto Croce, whose anti-fascist petition of 1925 was quickly answered by a fascist 'manifesto' inspired by Giovanni Gentile. The most famous intellectuals who chose exile were a Catholic priest, Luigi Sturzo, and a socialist historian, Gaetano Salvemini.[53] Left-wing intellectuals could be counted on the fingers of one hand.

---

52   Peter Gay, *Weimar Culture: The Outsider as Insider* (New York: Norton & Company, 2001 [1968]), xiv.

53   See Giovanni Belardelli, *Il ventennio degli intellettuali. Cultura, politica, ideologia nell'Italia fascista* (Rome: Laterza, 2005), and Ruth Ben-Ghiat, *Fascist Modernities: Italy 1922–1945* (Berkeley: University of California Press, 2001).

In France, Louis Aragon, the future official poet of the Communist Party, in 1917 depicted the October Revolution as 'a vague ministerial crisis'.[54] In the 1920s, French culture was still pervaded by the spirit of *Union sacrée* that during the war had united the Action Française with most Dreyfusard intellectuals, from Henri Bergson to Charles Péguy, from Émile Durkheim to Marc Bloch. The most popular newspaper of the decade was *Candide*, close to the nationalist and anti-Semitic ideas of Charles Maurras, which was a model for the fascist magazines of the 1930s like *Je suis partout!* and *Gringoire*. This is the context in which many nationalist intellectuals – Robert Brasillach, Marcel Déat, Lucien Rebatet and Pierre Drieu La Rochelle, and then nihilist writers like Louis Ferdinand Céline or Catholic poets like Paul Claudel – tried to create a native form of French fascism.[55]

So, who were the revolutionary intellectuals at the end of the First World War? Not so many from west of Vienna, even if their ranks began to swell in the wake of the October Revolution. Gathering them into a broad and approximate typology, we might distinguish some general categories: Jews from the multinational empires of Eastern and Central Europe, anti-war anarchists and socialists, avant-garde writers and artists such as surrealists and expressionists, American bohemians, feminists, and anti-imperialist intellectuals from the colonial world. The first and the last were certainly the most significant groups of this heterogeneous constellation.

Before looking more closely at these currents, the historical context deserves a preliminary observation. The anarchists and socialists who criticized the nationalist wave in 1914 were small minorities. The consequences of the collapse of the Second International, whose sections almost unanimously voted for war credits, became apparent after 1918. Many intellectuals, however, were turned into revolutionaries by their moral rejection of war. The evolution of Georg Lukács epitomizes a broader tendency. He writes that he decided to join the Hungarian Communist party for 'ethical considerations', but quickly

---

54   Quoted in Maurice Nadeau, *The History of Surrealism* (New York: Macmillan, 1965), 101.

55   See Zeev Sternhell, *Neither Right nor Left: The Fascist Ideology in France* (Princeton: Princeton University Press, 1986).

understood that this political choice, transcending by far the 'abstract moral imperatives of the Kantian school', amounted to a philosophical doctrine and a political project that entailed action. Revolution had become 'the incarnation of the ethics of the fighting proletariat'.[56]

In Russia, the crucial year 1917 marks the triumph of Turgenev's 'grandsons', the generation of rebellious students, writers, journalists and conspirators that had already emerged from the margins in 1905, when they encountered the labour movement and took leadership during the first mass uprising against the Tsarist regime. They occupy the stage in 1917, exiting from imperial jails and returning to Petrograd and Moscow from Western exile. The Bolsheviks, Mensheviks and Mezrayonka (Trotsky's group), were very influential in the soviets of workers, peasants and soldiers, but their leadership was composed of young intellectuals. The oldest of them – Lenin, Martov and Fyodor Dan – were in their forties. The first Soviet government that was formed on 8 November with Lenin as chairman, Trotsky as People's Commissar for Foreign Affairs, Vladimir Antonov-Ovseyenko for the army, and Anatoli Lunacharsky for Education, included seventeen members who (except for the twenty-five-year-old executive officer, Nikolai Gorbunov), had all experienced long periods of prison, Siberian exile and emigration to Western Europe. Most of them came back after the February Revolution. And many of them were Jews, as the propaganda of White Guards and Western anti-Bolsheviks eagerly emphasized in their pamphlets and posters. In 1917, they represented between one-fourth and one-third of the Central Committee of both the Menshevik and the Bolshevik parties,[57] and therefore they appeared as the true 'malignancy' responsible for the fall of tsarism and the Russian Revolution. As with most legends, the myth of Judeo-Bolshevism – the vision of revolution as a Jewish conspiracy – built an imaginary narrative starting from actual circumstances: in a year of mass turmoil, Soviet power was the result of a revolutionary process led by the *intelligenty*, a social layer in which the Jews, the most excluded and persecuted minority within the Tsarist empire,

56   Lukács, *History and Class Consciousness*, 39, 42.

57   Oleg Budnitskii, *Russian Jews Between the Reds and the Whites 1917–1920* (Philadelphia: University of Pennsylvania Press, 2012), 55.

were overrepresented. Trotsky as a Semitic monster with small glasses, surrounded by an Asiatic horde, is obviously a mythical depiction, but Trotsky was the charismatic leader of the Red Army.[58]

Cosmopolitanism was one of the most distinguishing features of this revolutionary intelligentsia. After his imprisonment and Siberian exile in the years that followed the foundation of the Russian social-democracy, Lenin lived in Western emigration from 1900 to 1917 – in Munich, London, Geneva, Krakow, Paris and Zurich successively. Trotsky similarly alternated between prisons, Siberian exile and Western emigration, moving from Geneva to London, Munich, Vienna, Paris and New York. Karl Radek (Karol Sobelsohn), was born in Lemberg, the capital of Habsburg Galicia, and grew up between its Austrian and Polish cultures. Before moving to Petrograd in 1917 and becoming vice-commissar for Foreign Affairs, and in this capacity participating with Trotsky in the Brest-Litovsk peace negotiations of March 1918, he was deeply involved in the political life of both tsarist Poland and Germany, notably in Bremen, where he led the anti-war socialist left after 1914. In Berlin in 1919, he took part in the Spartacist insurrection and, after being arrested, he transformed his cell into an annex of the Soviet embassy, where he received high functionaries of the German government. In the following years he became the secretary of the Comintern, organized the failed communist insurrection of 1923 in Germany and, as part of the Left Opposition within the Bolshevik party, in 1925 was excluded from any political responsibility. He was appointed provost of the Sun Yat-Sen University, an institution created in Moscow to educate Chinese students at the time of the alliance between the Kuomintang and Chinese communism. A polyglot, Radek wrote and spoke in Polish, German and Russian.

---

58   See Paul Hanebrink, *A Specter Haunting Europe: The Myth of Judeo-Bolshevism* (Cambridge, MA: Belknap Press, 2018). Hanebrink is certainly right in defining 'Judeo-Bolshevism' as an 'ideal construct' that distorts reality, since the Bolsheviks were a minority among the Jews; but he seems indifferent to the fact that the Jews were overrepresented among the Bolsheviks. In other words, rejecting an anti-Semitic trope is not a good reason to ignore the historical fact of the mutual attraction between the Jews and revolution in Eastern and Central Europe at the turn of the twentieth century. I have analysed this topic in *The Jewish Question: History of a Marxist Debate* (Leiden: Brill, 2018), chapter 2.

Karl Radek (ca. 1925).

His biographer Warren Lerner pertinently depicts him as a *vaterland-slos*, which means both unpatriotic and stateless. Even more than for Lenin and Trotsky, who considered themselves to be Russian, it is by no means rhetorical to say that Radek's fatherland was revolution: a political project, a doctrine, a goal, a concrete experience, and a way of life that shaped his entire existence.[59]

Cosmopolitanism was one of the matrixes of this revolutionary thought. Luxemburg's, Bukharin's and Lenin's theories of imperialism considered the accumulation of capital as an international process and focused on the entanglement between financial capital, colonialism and militarism. Trotsky's analysis of the 'uneven and combined development' of the world economy, which posited a dialectical relationship between developed and backward countries, was the basis of his theory of permanent revolution. This called into question the old 'stageist' vision of socialism, as a mechanical consequence of the growth of productive forces, and suggested the possibility of a global socialist transformation that could start from the weakest and less advanced countries like Russia and, from the 1920s onwards, the

---

59   Warren Lerner, *Karl Radek: The Last Internationalist* (Stanford: Stanford University Press, 1970), viii, 174.

colonial world. In the midst of a world war that had whipped up a wave of nationalism everywhere and devastated an entire continent, this cosmopolitan intelligentsia clearly adopted a post-national perspective. The nation, Trotsky wrote in *The War and the International* (1914), 'must continue to exist as a cultural, ideologic and psychological fact, but its economic foundation has been pulled from under its feet.'[60] In such historical circumstances, he concluded, the proletariat should not defend 'the outlived and antiquated national fatherland'; its task was rather 'to create a far more powerful fatherland, with far greater power of resistance: the United States of Europe as the foundation of the United States of the World'.[61]

This cosmopolitanism was also the premise of a new and powerful 'universalism from below' in the age of colonial empires.[62] In his memoirs, Manabendra Nath Roy describes as follows the Second World Congress of the Communist International that took place in Moscow in the early summer of 1920:

> For the first time, brown and yellow men met white men who were not overbearing imperialists but friends and comrades, eager to make amends for the evils of colonialism. There were a few Negroes also; some from the USA and a couple of them came from South Africa. For them, it was a novel experience to mix freely with white men, to the extent of dancing in public with white women without running the risk of being lynched. As a matter of fact, Negroes seemed to have the strongest attraction for Russian women. Perhaps it was a case of the harmony of contrasts.[63]

The Jews of Central Europe – especially those belonging to the *Bildungsbürgertum*, which was politically oriented towards classical

---

60   Leon Trotsky, *The Bolsheviks and World Peace* (New York: Boni & Liveright, 1918), 21 (this American translation was released after the Russian Revolution, but Trotsky was not a Bolshevik yet when he published his booklet in German with the title *Der Krieg und die Internationale*).

61   Ibid., 28.

62   On 'universalism from below' see Susan Buck-Morss, *Hegel, Haiti, and Universal History* (Pittsburgh: University of Pittsburgh Press, 2009), 106.

63   M. N. Roy, *Memoirs* (Bombay: Allied Publishers, 1964), 348.

liberalism and had been strongly nationalistic in 1914 – were no more attracted to Bolshevism than their fellow citizens, but the Jewish intelligentsia warmly welcomed the message sent by the soviets of Petrograd. Revolutionaries were a small minority amongst the Jews, but the Jews were a very significant and often leading minority amongst the revolutionaries. In Germany, the Spartacist insurrection of January 1919 was led by Rosa Luxemburg, a Jewish Marxist thinker who had emigrated to Berlin from Poland (the other charismatic figure of the Spartakus League was Karl Liebknecht). During the early 1920s, most of the leaders of German communism were Jewish intellectuals such as Paul Levi, Ruth Fischer (Elfriede Eisler), Arkadi Maslow (Isaak Efimovich Chemerinsky), and Karl Radek (Sobelsohn). Jewish intellectuals were also the major figures of the revolutions in Munich and Budapest in 1919. Kurt Eisner, the president of Bavaria between November 1918 and February 1919, was a left-wing socialist and journalist outside the academy. His assassination by anti-Semitic far-right nationalists was followed, very briefly, by an authentic bohemian government led by the expressionist playwright Ernst Toller, surrounded by anarchist writers like Gustav Landauer and Erich Mühsam. They opened the prisons, abolished money, and appointed a Jew to reform education, an area that had always been monopolized by Catholicism. Farcically, the commissar for foreign affairs, Dr Franz Lipp, declared war on Switzerland after it refused to loan sixty locomotives to the Bavarian republic under threat from the Freikorps. The leader of the third Soviet government was a communist, Eugen Leviné, who created a Red Army of 20,000 soldiers, mostly unemployed workers, to struggle against the Freikorps and the official army that finally crushed the Republic in May. All the Bavarian revolutionists were arrested and many, like Landauer, executed. In the Hungarian Soviet Republic that ran from March to August 1919, eighteen out of twenty-nine people's commissars were Jewish, from its chairman, Bela Kun, to the people's commissar for culture, Georg Lukács. According to several scholars, intellectuals formed the leadership of the revolution and the overwhelming majority of them (between 70 and 95 per cent) were Jewish.[64]

64   Istvan Deak, 'Budapest and the Hungarian Revolution', *Slavonic and Eastern European Review*, 46/106 (1968): 138. The best study on the political

Isaac Deutscher (ca. 1957). International
Institute of Social History, Amsterdam.

Isaac Deutscher coined a memorable definition – which was also
a self-portrait – to depict this generation of Eastern and Central
European revolutionary intellectuals: they were 'non-Jewish Jews'.
'The Jewish heretic who transcends Jewry belongs to a Jewish tradition', he wrote, mentioning Spinoza, Heine, Marx, Luxemburg and
Trotsky.[65] These Jewish intellectuals had broken with their religion
and traditional culture, but recognized themselves as Jewish because of
anti-Semitism, by assuming a history of persecutions and a present of
exclusion and stigmatization. In the modern world, especially after the
Emancipation, Judaism seemed to them 'too narrow, too archaic and
too constricting'. The universalistic core of the Jewish tradition could
be developed only beyond Judaism itself. The 'non-Jewish Jew' is a
dialectical figure that implies secularization, but includes both atheism
and Judaism. In other words, this figure transcends Judaism instead
of rejecting it. Inscribed in this 'tradition' of anti-conformism, heresy,
and critical thought, these outsiders stood in a peculiar position: both
severed from Judaism, which they perceived as a form of religious

radicalization of the Jewish intelligentsia in Central Europe is Michael Löwy,
Redemption and Utopia: Jewish Libertarian Thought in Central Europe (London,
New York: Verso, 2017 [1987]).

65   Isaac Deutscher, *The Non-Jewish Jew and Other Essays* (London, New
York: Verso, 2017 [1968]), 26.

obscurantism, and excluded from the institutions, respectability, and public careers of the established order. They could emerge as a leading group in exceptional historical circumstances, such as the collapse of the central empires at the end of the Great War, but Deutscher lucidly pointed out their vulnerable position. They were the ideal scapegoats of all social and political crises:

> All these great revolutionaries were extremely vulnerable. They were, as Jews, rootless, in a sense; but they were so only in some respects, for they had the deepest roots in intellectual tradition and in the noblest aspirations of their times. Yet, whenever religious intolerance or nationalist emotion was on the ascendant, whenever dogmatic narrow-mindedness and fanaticism triumphed, they were the first victims. They were excommunicated by Jewish rabbis; they were persecuted by Christian priests; they were hunted down by the gendarmes of absolute rulers and by the *soldateska*; they were hated by pseudo-democratic philistines; and they were expelled by their own parties. Nearly all of them were exiled from their countries; and the writings of all were burned at the stake at one time or another.[66]

In most Western European countries, where the Jews were usually well integrated in state institutions, revolutionary intellectuals belonged in the main to other marginalized groups. In Italy, where this tradition was historically embodied by anarchism, the only significant intellectual group to join the communist party was the already mentioned editorial board of *L'Ordine Nuovo*, created in Turin by four young journalists: Antonio Gramsci, Angelo Tasca, Palmiro Togliatti and Umberto Terracini. All of them had studied at the University of Turin and commenced their political activities by writing for the socialist press. They were less than thirty years old when they founded *L'Ordine Nuovo*, which quickly became the rallying point of the factory councils during the occupation of the Fiat plants by the workers in 1920.[67]

---

66 Ibid., 33–4.

67 See Paolo Spriano, '*L'Ordine nuovo' e i consigli di fabbrica* (Turin: Einaudi, 1971), notably the Introduction, 13–145.

L'Ordine Nuovo, 11–18 December 1920.

In France, the dogma of *Union sacrée* was unanimous; nobody opposed it apart from scattered and marginal socialist internationalists, such as the historian of Russian origin Boris Souvarine and the anarcho-syndicalists gathered around the journal *La Vie ouvrière*, led by Pierre Monatte and Alfred Rosmer. Epitomized by Romain Rolland's *Au-dessus de la mêlée* (1915) and Henri Barbusse's *Under Fire* (1916), the pacifist literary world did not oppose nationalism but simply denounced the inhumanity of war.[68] The deputies of the socialist party (SFIO) who, like Marcel Cachin and Ludovic-Oscar Frossard, participated in the foundation of the communist party at the congress of Tours in 1920, had voted in favour of war credits six years earlier. For Frossard, Bolshevism was an inheritor of 1789: Lenin and Trotsky had conquered power enlightened by the lessons of their forebears of 1793. Trotsky, who had spent several years of exile in Paris during the war, strongly criticized the nationalist tendencies of the French section of the Communist International.[69]

---

68   See Christophe Prochasson and Anne Rasmussen, *Au nom de la patrie. Les intellectuels et la Première Guerre Mondiale 1910–1919* (Paris: La Découverte, 1996), 144–50.

69   See Stéphane Courtois and Marc Lazar, *Histoire du Parti communiste français* (Paris: PUF, 1995), Chapter 2, 71–115. See the writings gathered in the first and second parts of Leon Trotsky, *Le movement communiste en France* (Paris: Éditions de Minuit, 1967).

La Révolution surréaliste, 1 December 1926.

During the 1920s, this atmosphere of republican nationalism was broken by avant-garde currents animated by young intellectuals. *Clarté*, a journal created by Barbusse in 1919, quickly became the organ of the intellectual revolutionary left. It published contributions by communist critics like Boris Souvarine, Pierre Naville and Marcel Fournier, as well as the Sorelian writer Édouard Berth, and explicitly claimed an anti-republican, anti-capitalist, anti-nationalist, anticolonial and 'anti-humanitarian' orientation. In 1924, it celebrated the death of Anatole France with a special issue titled 'Un cadavre', a corpse. *Clarté* was also a crossroads between communism and the most significant avant-garde current that appeared in France after the war: surrealism. This movement, created by André Breton, sought to merge the social and political revolution represented by Bolshevism with the liberation of a subversive unconscious and of the aesthetic creations directed at re-enchanting existence. Radically nonconformist and faithful to Rimbaud's injunction to 'change life', surrealism rejected any kind of classicism and academism. Breton and his friends wished to combine communism with psychoanalysis and anarchism. According to Walter Benjamin, surrealism had rediscovered a 'radical concept of freedom', something Europe had not had since Bakunin; however, 'to win the energies of intoxication for revolution' was not enough. Focusing exclusively on this task, he warned, meant 'to subordinate the methodical and disciplinary preparation for revolution entirely to a praxis oscillating between fitness exercises and celebration in advance'.[70] In short, what Benjamin reproached in this kind of 'Gothic Marxism' was its bohemian penchant. These arguments are at the core of Pierre Naville's *La Révolution et les intellectuels* (1926), an essay written with the aim of pushing Breton and his associates towards Bolshevism. Their movement expressed a highly 'subversive posture of the mind (*attitude de l'esprit*)', implying 'a belief in the destruction of the current state of things', he observed, but the nature of this belief was not yet clear, since surrealism swung 'between an absolutely anarchist attitude and a revolutionary Marxist conduct'.[71] The fact remains that, vigorously mobilized against the Rif War and the Colonial Exhibition of 1931, surrealism transcended the limits of purely aesthetic commitment and engaged in a political action that, in those years, inevitably overlapped with communism.

In both Germany and France, Marxist university scholars were, more than 'rare birds', virtually inexistent. During the Weimar Republic, the exception was the philosopher Karl Korsch, the author of *Marxism and Philosophy* (1923) and a pathbreaker of Western Marxism, who received a full professorship at the University of Jena in 1924, just before being elected to the Reichstag as a deputy of the KPD. The Institute for Social Research, which did not hide its Marxist orientation, was attached to the University of Frankfurt, but it benefited from an independent endowment provided by Felix Weil, a student from a wealthy family of Argentinian landowners and grain merchants. Close to communism during its first years (1923–30), when it was directed by the Austrian professor of law Carl Grünberg and aspired to become the German equivalent of the Marx-Engels Institute created in Moscow by David Riazanov in 1919, the Frankfurt School

---

70   Walter Benjamin, 'Surrealism: The Last Snapshot of the European Intelligentsia' (1929), *WBSW*, vol. 2/1, 216.

71   Pierre Naville, 'La révolution et les intellectuels' (1926), *La révolution et les intellectuels* (Paris: Gallimard, 1975), 58. See also Michael Löwy, 'The Revolution and the Intellectuals: Pierre Naville's Revolutionary Pessimism', *Morning Star: Surrealism, Marxism, Anarchism, Situationism, Utopia* (Austin: University of Texas Press, 2009), 43–64.

housed several communist activists or fellow-travellers including Franz
Borkenau, Henryk Grossman, Herbert Marcuse, Friedrich Pollock
and Karl Wittfogel. After the appointment of Max Horkheimer as its
director in 1930, however, the institute carefully avoided any political
commitment, further reinforcing this position during the years of its
American exile when, according to Herbert Marcuse, politics was
'strictly forbidden'.[72] In France, though the French university was far
from excluding Jewish scholars, many revolutionary intellectuals had
an academic training but worked as journalists or high-school teachers. This was the case for communist philosophers and essayists such
as Georges Friedmann, Henri Lefebvre, Pierre Naville, Paul Nizan
and Georges Politzer. Some of them would not start their university
careers until after the Second World War. Paul Nizan overtly casti-
gated the indifference of established scholars towards the condition
of the working classes. In *Les chiens de garde* (1932), he criticized the
'abdication' and the 'shameful absence' of the Sorbonne philosophers
who enclosed themselves in a realm of abstract values. 'Not a single
PhD dissertation', he wrote, 'expresses the class struggle carried out
by the bourgeoisie, the industrial slavery, the hate, fear and anger that
the rulers feel towards the proletariat.'[73]

Even in America, Bohemia was the environment most sensitive to the
appeal coming from Bolshevik Russia. Beside the dominant milieus of
immigrant socialism – the first secretary of the American communist
party was Louis C. Fraina (Luigi Fraina), an Italian-born, self-educated
journalist and Marxist essayist – the only intellectual group in which
the October Revolution became truly popular was the bohemia of
New York's Village. Its organ was the magazine *The Masses*, founded
in 1911 by Max Eastman, John Reed and Louise Bryant, who became
communists in 1917. The spirit of *The Masses* is well summarized by
John Reed's introduction:

72　Quoted in Thomas Wheatland, *The Frankfurt School in Exile* (Minneapolis:
University of Minnesota Press, 2009), 73.

73　Paul Nizan, *Les Chiens de garde* (Paris: Rieder, 1932), 91. See also Michel
Winock, *Le siècle des intellectuels* (Paris: Seuil, 1997), 257.

This magazine is owned and published cooperatively by its editors. It has no dividends to pay, and nobody is trying to make money out of it. A revolutionary and not a reform magazine; a magazine with a sense of humor and no respect for the respectable: frank, arrogant, impertinent, searching for the true causes; a magazine directed against rigidity and dogma wherever it is found; printing what is too naked or true for a money-making press; a magazine whose final policy is to do as it pleases and conciliate nobody, not even its readers – there is a field for this publication in America.[74]

With the entry of the United States into the war, *The Masses* was banned. It reappeared as *Liberator*, which quickly became a communist magazine, but the nonconformist attitude and aesthetic modernism of many older collaborators clashed with its newly orthodox orientation. Mike Gold, who became a representative of American 'proletarian literature' with *Jews Without Money* (1930), did not like the dogmatism, sectarianism, and puritanism of *The Liberator*, whereas Joseph Freeman openly deplored 'the bourgeois cult of the ego' so widespread amongst the radical bohemians.[75] The revolutionary commitments of New York's bohemia were consistently mirrored in the life of John Reed, a journalist who was imprisoned several times in the United States for his support of workers' strikes and who described the Mexican Revolution in a thrilling piece of reportage, *Insurgent Mexico* (1914). He wrote the most popular account of the Russian Revolution, *Ten Days That Shook the World* (1919), published just one year before his death in Moscow.[76] The bohemians of *The Masses* and *Liberator* paved the way for a new generation of New York intellectuals – the vast majority Jewish – which created new journals, notably *Partisan Review*, and affirmed its attachment to communism

---

74 Quoted in Daniel Aaron, *Writers on the Left: Episodes in American Communism*, preface by Alan Wald (New York: Columbia University Press, 1992 [1961]), 21.

75 Ibid., 97, 103.

76 See Robert A. Rosenstone, *Romantic Revolutionary: A Biography of John Reed* (New York: Knopf, 1975).

Thomas Hart Benton, *America Today* (1931). Egg tempera. Detail
with a Portrait of Max Eastman. Metropolitan Museum, New York.

and often Trotskyism until the Cold War and the advent of
McCarthyism.[77]

The Red Scare of the 1920s possessed a strong xenophobic dimension,
leading to the expulsion of many socialist and anarchist immigrants.
The climax of this nationalist campaign was the execution of Nicola

---

77   See Alan Wald, *The New York Intellectuals: The Rise and Decline of the
Anti-Stalinist Left from the 1930s to the 1980s* (Chapel Hill: University of North
Carolina Press, 1987).

Sacco and Bartolomeo Vanzetti in 1927, following the National Origins Act. Shaped by a clear racist and anti-Semitic, not to say proto-fascist character, this nationalist wave certainly targeted the left-wing intellectuals, but did not reach the paroxysmal forms taken by neoconservatism and the Nazi movement in Germany. It is interesting, from this point of view, to compare August Sander's photograph of Erich Mühsam, mentioned above, with the portrait of Max Eastman that Thomas Hart Benton included in his sumptuous mural, 'America Today', painted for the New School in 1931.[78] Offering a sweeping image of America in the 1920s with its industrial work, its technological accomplishments, its skyscrapers, its jazz orchestras, and its intense urban life, Benton's pictorial project presented some analogies with Sander's *Antlitz der Zeit*. In these works, however, Mühsam's and Eastman's inscription in their respective social spaces are almost antipodal: whereas the German anarchist appears on edge and unsettled as the archetype of the outcast, Eastman looks at home in his urban environment. Seated in a carriage of the New York subway in front of an elegant young lady and beside an African-American traveller, he is immersed in his thoughts, indifferent to the people who surround him. He looks to be a distinguished man who, as an intellectual, naturally belongs to this landscape of exciting modernism. Benton suggests that the revolutionary intellectual is one of the actors of this dynamic portrait of capitalist America, in which both social and political conflicts are absorbed by a Promethean enthusiasm for the future.

Radical Feminism

The appeal to liberation launched by the October Revolution had a significant impact on feminism, which saw Bolshevik Russia as a laboratory of women's emancipation. As we saw in Chapter Two, Alexandra Kollontai not only theorized sexual liberation and free love but made concrete moves, as a people's commissar for social welfare, to establish gender equality. In her view, a socialist future meant the end of the patriarchal family as the fundamental core of

---

78   Randall Griffey and Elizabeth Mankin Kornhauser, *Thomas Hart Benton's America Today* (New York: Metropolitan Museum of Art, 2015).

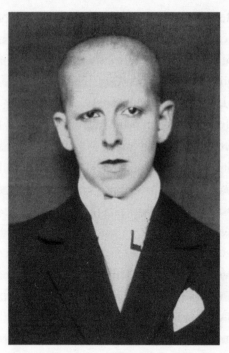

Claude Cahun, *Self-Portrait as a Young Man*
(1920). Museum of Modern Art, New York.

social structures. Many feminists joined communism, such as Clara
Zetkin in Germany, Henriette Roland-Holst in the Netherlands, and
Sylvia Pankhurst in the United Kingdom. It is probably in France
that feminism produced the most interesting figure of the revolutionary intellectual, Claude Cahun (Lucie Schwob). 'Artists are often
outsiders and transgressors', writes Michael Löwy, 'but few of them
embody as many boundary-defying qualities as Claude Cahun: lesbian
surrealist, dissident Marxist, non-Jewish Jew, photographer, poet,
critic and Resistance activist.'[79] Claude Cahun was an 'heiress', in
Bourdieu's sense of the word, since she had bourgeois origins – her
father was an established publisher and her uncle, the literary critic
Marcel Schwob – and started her career by writing for the respected
journal *Mercure de France*. Her entry into the avant-garde, however,
marked a radical break in her existential and intellectual itinerary.
She ditched all sexual conventions by assuming her lesbianism and
claiming a queer identity (stressed by her new first name, Claude,

79 Löwy, 'Claude Cahun: The Extreme Point of the Needle', *Morning Star*, 65.

both male and female in French), and she also adopted a clear aesthetic and political commitment within surrealism. In short, she was no longer part of the establishment; she had become an outsider. She combined her photographic work with writings against colonialism and fascism, and she embraced her marginality even during the war, when she transformed surrealism into a practice of Resistance and recovered, under the German occupation, her Jewish identity.[80]

But we cannot ignore the fact that Claude Cahun was an exception. The encounter between communism and feminism was ephemeral, contradictory, and often ambiguous, as we already saw. In 1922, the founder of Zhenodtel, the women's section of the Bolshevik party, was sent abroad as a diplomat and her feminist commitment was confined to a series of autobiographical writings. Most women who played a leading role in the communist movement, from Rosa Luxemburg to Angelica Balabanova, from Inessa Armand to Ruth Fischer, from Dolores Ibárruri to Henriette Roland-Holst, did not foreground their gender identity. In the 1920s, the heroic time of civil war and political upheavals, the military paradigm of the Bolsheviks as soldiers of a revolutionary army inevitably celebrated many qualities, from physical strength to courage and boldness, that are conventionally identified with maleness. This tendency was not completely new – think of the picture of Louise Michel in uniform during the Paris Commune[81] – but was strongly reinforced by the Great War. In the 1930s, the restoration of familial and hierarchical gender codes fixed women

---

80 See Jennifer L. Shaw, *Exist Otherwise: The Life and Works of Claude Cahun* (London: Reaktion Books, 2017).

81 See Marie Marmo Mullaney, 'Sexual Politics in the Career and Legend of Louise Michel', *Signs*, 15/2 (1990): 300–22. Being a teacher, Louise Michel participated in a project to reform the city educational system, then joined in the defence of the Paris Commune wearing the uniform of the National Guard and carrying a rifle. This was used as an evidence during the trial that condemned her to deportation. See Louise Michel, *The Red Virgin: Memoirs of Louise Michel*, eds Bullit Lowry and Elizabeth Ellington Gunter (Tuscaloosa: University of Alabama Press, 1981 [1886]), 85–6. On the myth of Louise Michel and the metamorphoses of her image over a century and a half (anarchist, 'pétroleuse', republican, soldier, 'red virgin', feminist, and queer revolutionary), see Sidonie Verhaeghe, *Vive Louise Michel. Célébrité et postérité d'une figure anarchiste* (Paris: Éditions du Croquant, 2021).

Eugène Appert, *Prison Portrait*
of Louise Michel (1871).

Portrait of Louise Michel wearing
the uniform of the Garde Nationale,
Berliner Illustrierte Zeitung, 1904.

in a subaltern position. As Brigitte Studer points out, a political ideology strongly grounded in class struggle deliberately marginalized
all issues related to gender domination and oppression, thus leaving
no place for the representation – even symbolic – of revolutionary
women except as proletarians.[82] Women were workers and peasants
and bore arms beside their fellow militiamen in the defence of Petrograd – as they appear in many Soviet posters – but they only existed
as members of their class. Once female workers, peasants and soldiers
were opposed to the traditional symbolization of motherhood, no
room remained for representing women as intellectuals (except as
androgynous outcasts, like the surrealist Cahun). This means that the
archetypal revolutionary intellectual was conventionally *male*: female
revolutionaries obviously existed, and could play a significant role,
but this implied the denial of their gender: the hierarchical structure
of the revolutionary movement gave them a subaltern position. In the

---

82   Brigitte Studer, *The Transnational World of the Cominternians* (London:
Palgrave, 2015), 40–58.

USSR, women led two important universities – Klavdiia Kirsanova the Leninist Institute and Maria Frumkina the University of Western National Minorities – but they were strongly underrepresented in the politburo of the Bolshevik party. In the Comintern, Studer explains, they were mostly used as secretaries, typists and translators.[83] Their position is reflected in their representation – or lack thereof – in the official iconography. A group photograph of the first congress of the Communist International in 1919 shows about fifty tightly packed delegates, amongst whom only two women can be made out. The portraits of the fourth congress in 1922 show many more individuals of colour, but the number of women does not change. There is a 1924 canvas by Isaak Brodsky, already painted in the style of socialist realism, illustrating the inauguration of the second congress of the Comintern in Petrograd's Tauride Palace. Gigantic, the picture shows the feverish atmosphere of such an event, with many leaders clearly recognizable. Lenin is speaking at the tribune, beside Karl Radek, and behind him, on a higher stand, are Alfred Rosmer, Clara Zetkin, Grigory Zinoviev and Leon Trotsky. Many other leaders are scattered among the international audience in the vast and crowded assembly room. Frequent 'exotic' costumes catch the eye, but women form a very small minority. Just under Lenin's tribune, six young women sit at a large desk, concentrated on writing or translating the minutes of the congress.[84] Feminism and intersectionality were still a long way away.

Maps II: Colonial World

The October Revolution marked a turning point in the colonial world, where it precipitated the emergence of a new generation of revolutionary intellectuals. Before 1914, the latter had been even more 'rare birds' there than in the West. In the age of 'early globalization',

---

83   Ibid., 64.

84   On the subaltern position of Comintern's women, which reproduced the gender hierarchies of society, see Brigitte Studer, *Reisende der Revolution. Eine Globalgeschichte der Kommunistischen Internationale* (Frankfurt: Suhrkamp, 2020), 84–6.

Moscow, First Congress of the Communist International (1919).

Isaac Izrailevich Brodsky, *The Festive Opening of the Second Congress of the Communist International* (1924). State History Museum, Moscow.

Lenin speaking at the second congress of the Communist International, July 1920. Humbert-Droz Archives. Brodsky based his painting on this photograph.

according to the magisterial study of Benedict Anderson on the Filipino leader José Rizal, their political radicalization took place under the triple flag of anti-imperialism, anarchism, and national liberation.[85] Coming from a rural world, they did not have Marx's prejudices against the peasantry, which they were more inclined to consider as a revolutionary subject. Marx's vision of the peasants derived from the French experience of 1848, when they became one of the pillars of Bonapartism. Differently from Marxism, which defined socialism as a product of the development of productive forces and regarded the nascent industrial proletariat as the main vector of a social and political transformation, anarchists were not disposed to postpone liberation until after the industrialization of the colonial world, and saw peasants as a reservoir of rebellion. Whereas Marx's intellectual milieu was basically a triangular area delimited by Berlin, Paris and London, with some exceptional extensions to Saint-Petersburg and New York, anarchists based their actions in Eastern and Southern Europe, mostly the Russian Empire, France, Italy and Spain, and simultaneously established organic connections with Latin America. Their cosmopolitanism was certainly comparable to that of the second generation of Marxist intellectuals. According to Anderson, Filipino leaders of Rizal's time were at ease in a multilingual world in which they 'wrote to Austrians in German, to Japanese in English, to each other in French, or Spanish, or Tagalog, with liberal interventions in the last beautiful international language, Latin'.[86]

Anarchist action, however, was based above all on 'factual propaganda' or 'propaganda by the deed', usually culminating in the assassination of kings and statesmen – a specialty invented by Dmitry Karakozov and mostly practiced by Russian and Italian anarchist terrorists. After the October Revolution, young intellectuals from the colonies provided the leadership for mass movements on an incomparably larger scale. The Bolshevik appeal for a world revolution – and the material support the Soviet Union gave to this project – was the premise for their shift from anarchism and nationalism to Marxism.

---

85   Benedict Anderson, *Under Three Flags: Anarchism and the Anticolonial Imagination* (London, New York: Verso, 2005).

86   Ibid., 5.

The first to answer this appeal were students, young journalists, nationalist exiles and immigrants who lived or travelled in several Western metropoles. Some examples can illustrate this process.

Manabendra Nath Roy, the 'Comintern Brahmin', and Ho Chi Minh, the father of Vietnamese independence, followed parallel paths. Roy was born in Calcutta, West Bengal, in 1887, and Ho Chi Minh in a village of French Indochina, three years later. Both of them had been educated in colonial schools, had worked for the British and French administrations, and became nationalists in their own countries before travelling to the West. Trying to get German support for Indian nationalism during the First World War, Roy faced a British crackdown and fled first to Japan, then to New York, where he discovered Marxism. Hunted by British agents, he moved to Mexico, where he began to write for the socialist magazine *El Pueblo* and participated in the foundation of the Mexican Communist Party in 1919. In Moscow the following year he attended the second congress of the Comintern, where he presented his famous 'Theses on the National and Colonial Question', which criticized Lenin's idea of a necessary coalition including the working class, the peasantry and the national bourgeoisie against imperialism.[87] Between 1911 and 1918, Ho Chi Minh lived in New York and London working menial jobs while writing anticolonial articles. Established in France between 1919 and 1925, he participated in the foundation of the French Communist Party in Tours, in 1920, and created the organ of the Intercolonial Union, *Le Paria*, a monthly magazine to which he was the principal contributor.[88] Both Roy and Ho Chi Minh wrote petitions to Woodrow Wilson in 1918, when the American president appeared as the harbinger of the right of peoples to self-determination, and finally concluded that independence had

---

87   See Roy's *Memoirs* quoted above and Kris Manjapra, who defines Roy as a 'non-Indian Indian', *M.N. Roy: Marxism and Colonial Cosmopolitanism* (New Delhi: Routledge, 2010), 115–17.

88   On Ho Chi Minh in Paris, then still named Nguyen An Ninh, and the production of the journal *Le Paria*, see Michael Goebel, *Anti-Imperial Metropolis: Interwar Paris and the Seeds of Third World Nationalism* (New York: Cambridge University Press, 2015), 190–4.

to be conquered through an anti-imperialist struggle. In the 1920s, both men were deeply involved in the activities of the Comintern. In 1927 he was in Canton, China, at the moment of the failed communist uprising. Allied to Bukharin in the struggle within the Soviet Union, he discovered in Berlin, two years later, that he had been expelled from the Comintern. He therefore decided to go back to India to pursue his political action. Differently from Ta Thu Thâu, who became an influential Vietnamese Trotskyist and was moreover executed by the Viet Minh, Ho Chi Minh did not criticize Stalinism. After travelling in China, where he too experienced the defeat of the communist insurrections of Shanghai and Canton, Ho Chi Minh founded the Vietnamese Communist Party in Hong Kong, in 1930. Involved in the war against Japan, he became familiar with the theory and practice of guerrilla warfare, which he successfully introduced into Vietnam following the French defeat of 1940.[89]

In China, the birth of communism was the result of the political evolution of a small cohort of intellectuals who had participated in the revolution of 1911 and significantly enlarged their influence amongst the youth after the student movement of May 1919, the first experience of 'elitism engaged in anti-elitism'.[90] Both Chen Duxiu and Li Dazhao, the main ideologues of the Communist party at the moment of its foundation in 1921, had discovered Marxism as students at Tokyo University. Of the leaders of the party, only Mao Zedong had not travelled abroad. Both Zhou Enlai and Deng Xiaoping, the youngest of the group, had become communists during their emigration in France. With the exception of Chen, born to a family of mandarins, they came from the lower layers of the administration and had studied at the universities of Beijing and Shanghai. All of them were radical Westernizers. It was after drawing the lessons of the defeat of the worker insurrections of 1925 and 1927 in Shanghai and Canton that Mao, breaking with the Western revolutionary paradigm, took the leadership of the Communist Party and imposed a new strategy

---

89   See William J. Duiker, *Ho Chi Minh* (New York: Hyperion, 2000).

90   Hung-Yok Ip, *Intellectuals in Revolutionary China 1921–49: Leaders, Heroes, and Sophisticates* (London: Routledge, 2005), 42.

based on peasant guerrilla warfare. This would provoke at least ten years of tension and conflict with the Comintern.[91]

Whereas the introduction of Marxism in China expressed both the powerful attraction of European modernity and a critical reassessment of Confucian culture, in Dutch Indonesia it reflected a new relationship between nationalism, anti-imperialism, and the Islamic tradition amongst a young generation of intellectuals who, like their Chinese comrades, had experienced both Japanese and Western emigration. This was the case of Tan Malaka (Ibrahim Gelar Datuk Sutan Malaka), a teacher from Sumatra who studied in the Netherlands from 1913 to 1919, where he was introduced to Marxism by Henk Sneevliet, one of the leaders of Dutch socialism and a founder of the Indonesian Communist Party. During the 1920s, Malaka travelled throughout the East, from China to Thailand, from the Philippines to Singapore, as an agent of the Communist International, being arrested several times. Whereas the strategic debates within Chinese communism focused on the conflictual relationship with the Kuomintang, in Indonesia 'bourgeois nationalism' was embodied by Sarekat Islam, with which both Sneevliet and Malaka called for an organic alliance. Elaborating an original interpretation of Islam, Malaka merged it with Marxism by highlighting a continuity between the two. In Indonesia, he argued, Marxism could become the leading ideology of a liberation movement only by assuming the legacy of Islam, just as in the West it had come out of radical Enlightenment. During the Second World War, he coined the concept of 'Madilog' (acronym for materialism, dialectics and logic), which stressed the relevance of the rationalistic legacy of Islam for building a modern Indonesia:

> Islam brought Greek philosophy to Christianity which had hitherto been based purely on dogma and faith. A physician and philosopher, Ibn Rushd, famous in the West under the name Averroes, a pupil of the great Aristotle … was viewed by the Christian West of the Middle Ages just as Marxism is viewed by the capitalist world today. Christian students who returned home to Western

---

91   See Gregor Benton, *Mao Zedong and the Chinese Revolution* (London: Routledge, 2008).

or Northern Europe from Spain with diplomas from their Arabic teachers of philosophy, were regarded as revolutionaries by the Christian priests. Three Averroist universities in Italy developed 'rationalism' as Islam's left wing in Europe.[92]

This was the philosophical background of both Malaka's support for the pan-Islamic movement and his opposition, in the 1930s, to Stalinist 'dogma and faith'. Without grounding it on philosophical and theological bases, Sneevliet shared the political outcomes of this vision. Malaka became one of the fathers of independent Indonesia; Sneevliet, who had spent many years in Asia and participated in the foundation of both Indonesian and Chinese communism, was deeply involved in the Dutch Resistance and was executed by the Nazis in Amsterdam in 1942.

Something of the mind and life of these Asian revolutionary intellectuals, torn between tradition and modernity, their home country and the West, theory and action, was captured by André Malraux in his novel *Man's Fate* (1933), which fictionalizes the communist insurrection of Shanghai in 1925. Kyo, the novel's hero, is surrounded by Katow and Chen. Katow is a Russian who had already participated in both the 1905 and 1917 revolutions, had joined the Chinese communist movement in the name of 'universal fraternity', and is ready to sacrifice himself for the cause. Chen is an inheritor of nineteenth-century terrorism, insofar as he is 'incapable of living by an ideology which does not immediately become transformed into action'.[93] Kyo is 'a half-breed, an outcast, despised by the white men and even more by the white women'.[94] His father is a French Marxist scholar from the university of Beijing; his mother is Japanese. May, his wife, is German. More than a critical theory, Kyo's Marxism is a programme for action, a posture reflected by his aspect: the features of his father, who resembles an 'ascetic abbot', are no longer recognizable in his

---

92   Quoted in Rudolf Mrazek, 'Tan Malaka: A Political Personality's Structure of Experience', *Indonesia*, 14 (1972): 31.

93   André Malraux, *Man's Fate*, trans. Haakon M. Chevalier (New York: Vintage, 1990), 64.

94   Ibid., 65.

'samurai's face'.[95] For Kyo, ideas 'have not to be thought, but lived' and this gives meaning to his life: revolution is the way to conquer dignity for 'these men whom famine, at this very moment, is killing off like a slow plague'.[96] Malraux's novel mirrors the despair of an insurrection doomed to failure, a state of mind which was certainly widespread in Shanghai in 1925, but did not correspond with the hopes of a generation that, despite this tragic experience, would lead the process of decolonization.

In Latin America, anarchism and socialism were essentially products imported from Europe, before the formation of an autochthonous intellectual layer at the turn of the twentieth century. There too, however, a striking dichotomy can be observed between 'fathers and sons', and even grandsons. In Argentina, Horacio Tarcus has distinguished several generations of Marx's interpreters: the French exiles after the Paris Commune in the 1870s; the 'scientific socialism' of the German émigrés of the 1880s; a third generation, more specifically Argentinian, of the 1890s – among them university scholars like José Ingenieros (Giuseppe Ingegnieri) and Juan B. Justo, the first Spanish translator (from German) of Marx's *Capital* in 1898 – and a more radical younger generation, born in the late 1880s and 1890s, that founded the communist parties of the 1920s.[97] The movement for university reform that swept the continent from 1919 onwards politicized a layer of students who participated in the struggle against their domestic authoritarian regimes. The trajectory of Julio Antonio Mella is emblematic of this group: a student of law of the University of Havana, he became a leader of the protest movement against the dictatorship of Gerardo Machado and was forced to flee to Central America and then Mexico. There he founded the Cuban Communist Party – the first to be recognized by Moscow – in 1925.

---

95   Ibid., 39.

96   Ibid., 65.

97   Horacio Tarcus, *Marx en la Argentina: Sus primeros lectores obreros, intelectuales y científicos* (Buenos Aires: Siglo XXI, 2007). On the sociological background of the formation of revolutionary intellectuals in Argentina, see also Tarcus's methodological observations in *El marxismo olvidado en la Argentina: Silvio Frondizi y Milcíades Peña* (Buenos Aires: El cielo por asalto, 1996), 36–40.

Despite evident differences, some crucial analogies remain between Asia and Latin America, a continent that tried to forge its own identity by cutting its umbilical cord with Europe, a legacy made of both colonialism and immigration. In both continents, Marxism could not become a hegemonic political culture without merging with the indigenous cultures that permeated many national contexts (thus being torn, according to Michael Löwy, between the two 'antipodal temptations' of 'Indigenism' and Europeanism).[98] In both continents, the working class was a minority in overwhelmingly rural societies and socialism faced the emergence of anti-imperialist national movements. Their archetypal expression was the American Popular Revolutionary Alliance (APRA), founded in Lima by Víctor Raúl Haya de la Torre in 1924. These dilemmas lie at the heart of the work of José Carlos Mariátegui, the author of *Seven Interpretive Essays of Peruvian Reality* (1928), today recognized as one of the leading figures of twentieth-century Latin American culture.

In a letter to the Argentinian literary critic Samuel Glusberg of January 1927, Mariátegui introduced himself with the following words:

I was born in '95. At 14 years of age I got into a newspaper as an assistant. Until 1919 I worked in daily journalism, first in *La Prensa*, later in *El Tiempo*, and lastly in *La Razón*. In this last daily we promoted the university reform movement. From 1918, nauseated by Creole politics, I turned resolutely toward socialism, breaking with my first attempts at being a literato full of *fin-de-siècle* decadence and Byzantinism, then in full bloom. From late 1919 to mid-1923 I travelled through Europe. I lived more than two years in Italy, where I married a woman and some ideas. I travelled through France, Germany, Austria, and other countries. My wife and child prevented me from reaching Russia. From Europe I joined with some Peruvians for socialist action. My articles from that period mark the steps of my socialist orientation. Upon my return to Peru, in 1923, in reports, in lectures at the Student Federation, in the People's University, in articles, etc., I explained the European situation

---

98   See Michael Löwy's Introduction to *Marxism in Latin America from 1909 to the Present: An Anthology* (Atlantic Highlands: Humanities Press, 1992).

and began my work of investigating national reality following the Marxist method. In 1924 I came, as I have already told you, close to losing my life. I lost a leg and was left in very poor health. I would surely have already recovered entirely with a tranquil existence. But, neither my poverty nor my spiritual restlessness [*inquietud intellectual*], permit it. I have not published any more books than those you already know. I have two ready and, in progress, two more. That is my life in a few words. ... I forgot: I am self-taught [*autodidacto*]. I once enrolled in Letters in Lima, but was only interested in taking a Latin course on Augustine. And, in Europe I freely attended some courses, but without ever deciding to lose my extra-collegiate, and perhaps anti-collegiate, status. In 1925, the Student Federation nominated me to the University as an instructor in the field that is my specialty; but the Rector's ill-will and, probably, my state of health, frustrated that initiative.[99]

The pretext with which he had not been allowed to teach at the university of Lima was precisely his status of being self-taught: he had started working for the Lima newspaper *La Prensa* at fifteen and published his first article at twenty. In the same year 1927, he launched the journal *Amauta* and, targeted by a campaign that depicted him as the architect of a communist 'conspiracy', answered by explaining in several articles the difference between a conspiracy and a revolution. As he wrote in his letter, he had travelled in Europe, where he had discovered a continent devastated by the Great War. His reports for the Peruvian press are an extraordinary portrait of the cataclysms and cultural transformations that had affected the Old World: the Versailles Conference; D'Annunzio, Marinetti, futurism and fascism in Italy; dadaism, surrealism, Bergson and Sorel in France; Grosz and expressionism in Germany; Stefan Zweig in Austria; Tolstoy, Aleksander Blok, Trotsky and Lunacharsky in Russia, etc. In Italy, Mariátegui attended the foundational congress of the Communist Party in 1921 and established solid contacts with both Gramsci and Togliatti.

---

99   José Carlos Mariátegui to Samuel Glusberg, 10 January 1927, in Horacio Tarcus (ed.), *Mariátegui en la Argentina o las políticas culturales de Samuel Glusberg* (Buenos Aires: El cielo por asalto, 2001), 135.

José Carlos Mariátegui, Lima 1928. Photograph taken by the Argentinian
painter José Malanca. Archivo José Carlos Mariátegui, Lima.

Amauta was modelled on *Clarté*, the French journal of Barbusse
and Naville, but possessed a more explicit Marxist orientation. *Amauta*
is a Quechua word that means 'master' or 'sage', and designates the
teachers who transmitted memory in the Inca empire. According to
Mariátegui, a socialist revolution in Peru should find a solution to
two linked problems: the land and the status of the indigenous population. The abolition of capitalism along the coast and the 'feudal'
latifundia of the interior should coincide with the revitalization of
the indigenous pre-Columbian communities, based on the collective
use of land – building a modern nation by overcoming the dualism
between the *criollo* coast and the indigenous interior. Thus Mariátegui advocated a form of revolutionary 'indigenism' that had nothing
to do with the romantic idealization of an archaic past. In certain
historical circumstances, he wrote in 1925, the idea of nation could
'embody the spirit of freedom'. In Western Europe it was outdated – a
fact incontestably proven by the First World War – but in the past it
had played a revolutionary role. Now, it played a similar role in the
countries oppressed by imperialism.[100]

---

100   See José Carlos Mariátegui, *Seven Interpretive Essays on Peruvian Reality*
(Austin: University of Texas Press, 1988 [1928]).

Mariátegui's presentation of *Clarté* to Peruvian readers involved a critical assessment of the relationship between the intelligentsia and revolution:

> Intellectuals are usually refractory to discipline, programmes and systems. Their psychology is individualistic and their thought heterodox. First of all, their individualistic feeling is excessive and boundless. The intellectuals' individuality always claims to be above common rules. Moreover, they very often despise politics, which seems to them an activity for bureaucrats and pettifoggers. They forget that if it is so in ordinary times, it is not so in revolutionary times, the turbulent and restless times that herald a new social state and new political forms. In such times, politics is no longer the monotonous business of a professional caste. In these times, politics transcends usual standards and seizes all dimensions of life and humanity.[101]

Sensitive and creative spirits could not remain indifferent to such transformations, simply because 'politics is life'. In such times, Mariátegui concluded, claiming a kind of aesthetic rejection of politics was a pose that masked a conservative mind.

According to the historian Cedric Robinson, nationalism emerged in the Caribbean at the beginning of the twentieth century within a black intelligentsia that was positioned between the overwhelming majority of the population – the descendants of slaves – and the ruling minority of the white bourgeoisie.[102] It was a marginalized intelligentsia, both excluded from white society and detached from its own cultural roots. Educated in colonial institutions and moulded by Western literature and values, its representatives took the path of national liberation by rejecting the dogma of assimilation. The first step towards radical anticolonialism was the visit to London, Paris, or

---

101 José Carlos Mariátegui, 'La revolución y la inteligencia: El grupo *Clarté*' (1925), *La escena contemporánea* (Lima: Amauta, 1988), 154.

102 Cedric J. Robinson, *Black Marxism: The Making of the Black Radical Tradition* (Bloomington: University of North Carolina Press, 2000 [1983]), 254–7.

C. L. R. James in 1939.

New York, where they discovered pan-Africanism and elaborated the idea of black identity. In 1963, C. L. R. James summarized as follows the trajectory of his generation:

> The first step to freedom was to go abroad. Before they could begin to see themselves as a free and independent people they had to clear from their minds the stigma that anything African was inherently inferior and degraded. The road to West Indian national identity laid through Africa.[103]

This is the road followed by two young intellectuals from Trinidad: George Padmore, who emigrated to the United States in the mid-1920s, where he joined the communist party, and James himself, who became a Marxist in London in 1934. One year later, both men were deeply involved in the international campaign against the Ethiopian War. James wrote that he had become a Marxist after reading Trotsky's *History of the Russian Revolution* (1932) and Oswald Spengler's *The Decline of the West* (1918).[104] Whereas Spengler's manifesto of German

---

103   C. L. R. James, 'Appendix' (1962), *The Black Jacobins: Toussaint L'Ouverture and the San Domingo* Revolution (New York: Vintage, 1989), 402.

104   See Alan MacKenzie, 'Radical Pan-Africanism in the 1930s: A Discussion with C. L. R. James', *Radical History Review*, 24 (1980): 74. On the intellectual formation of James, see Paul Buhle, *C. L. R. James: The Artist as Revolutionary* (London: Verso, 1988).

conservatism depicted the exhaustion of bourgeois civilization, an 'organism' that had completed its life cycle and whose present agonies created an apocalyptic atmosphere, Trotsky's account of the October Revolution announced an era of liberation. In Paris, Aimé Césaire, a student from Martinique, created the Negritude movement with the Senegalese poet Léopold Sédar Senghor. Césaire was close to sur- realism and joined the French Communist Party. In 1935 he created the journal *L'Étudiant noir*, in which he published a radical critique of 'assimilationism' and claimed his black identity as a form of racial pride. 'Servitude and assimilation resemble one another', he wrote: they were both 'forms of passivity' to which he opposed the way of 'emancipation', which meant 'action and creation'.[105] Black iden- tity signified also rediscovering a forgotten or occluded tradition of liberation struggles. In 1938, James published *The Black Jacobins*, a book that reconstitutes and interprets the Haitian Revolution: 'the transformation of slaves, trembling in hundreds before a single white man, into a people able to organize themselves and defeat the most powerful European nations of their day.'[106]

The three flags of colonial revolution evoked by Benedict Anderson – socialism, anti-imperialism and national liberation – could not be permanently woven together. Sometimes their coexistence was a source of tensions and conflicts. Considering these potential antinomies, a typology of revolutionary intellectuals from the South could include three different groups: rooted cosmopolitans, telluric revolutionaries, and rootless internationalists. Of course, these tendencies are 'ideal- types' that could very well intermingle within a single movement or even constitute different steps in the existential and political trajectory of the same revolutionary intellectual. There are many examples of this complex dialectic between internationalism and nationalism, the universal and the particular.

Coined by Mitchell Cohen, the concept of 'rooted cosmopolitanism' captures very well the status of many intellectuals who participated

---

105   Aimé Césaire, 'Jeunesse noire et assimilation', *L'Étudiant noir*, 1 (1935): 3. Quoted in Goebel, *Anti-Imperial Metropolis*, 227.

106   James, *The Black Jacobins*, ix.

Ho Chi Minh at the foundation congress of the French
Communist Party, Tours, December 1920.

in several revolutionary movements, wrote in several languages, and
experienced more or less extended periods of exile without losing a
deep link with their native country.[107] Ho Chi Minh, for example, spent
almost thirty years in various different countries and continents but
finally played a leading role in the Vietnamese Revolution. Between
1911 and 1941, Ho Chi Minh lived in Paris, New York, London,
Moscow, Canton, Shanghai, Whampoa, and Hong Kong, but after the
French defeat he was able to come back to Vietnam and take leadership of the armed struggle against the Japanese occupation. Within
a few years he achieved the status of a national hero, far beyond the
charisma of a successful military strategist. His itinerary suggests
that rooted cosmopolitan revolutionaries can also possess a 'telluric'
character.[108] According to Carl Schmitt, partisans have a strong relationship with the population and the territory in which their political
action occurs. They want to be hosted and nourished by peasants that

---

107   Mitchell Cohen, 'Rooted Cosmopolitanism', *Dissent*, 39/4 (1992): 478–83.
See also Sidney Tarrow, 'Cosmopolites enracinés et militants transnationaux', *Lien
social et politiques*, 75 (2016) : 202–17.

108   Carl Schmitt, *The Theory of the Partisan: A Commentary/Remark on the
Concept of the Political* (Candor, NY: Telos Press, 2007).

support their guerrilla movement, or protected by urban people who hide 'technical' sabotage operations. Revolutionary intellectuals did not fear exclusion, marginality, and exile, but completely uprooted rebels could not lead a mass movement or a struggle for national liberation. They needed a haven in which to cease their 'free-floating' circulation and fix their action.

Besides these rooted cosmopolitans, however, some revolutionary intellectuals presented an almost exclusively telluric character. The classical examples of this group are Stalin and Mao Zedong. Stalin was based in Georgia before 1917, and then he remained in Moscow until his death. He never experienced external exile, and left the Tsarist empire only on rare occasions to attend the conferences of the Bolshevik party in Western Europe. He spent one month in Vienna, in 1913, where he wrote an essay on Marxism and the national question, helped by Bukharin who provided him with some fundamental sources. He did not speak any foreign languages. According to many historians, his 'telluric' and anti-cosmopolitan disposition – a trait that in the 1930s turned into a form of Great-Russian nationalism – played a crucial role in elaborating his theory of 'socialism in one country', which replaced the Comintern's strategy of world revolution. Orlando Figes suggests that this new vision found great support among the second generation of intellectuals, executives and managers who had joined the Bolshevik party in 1917, whereas cosmopolitanism was a shared feature of the generation that made the revolution and was finally exterminated during the Moscow Trials and in the gulags.[109]

The other major example of a 'telluric' revolutionary thinker is Mao Zedong, whose familiarity with a country as large and diverse as China contrasts with his total lack of any direct knowledge of either the West or the rest of Asia. This peculiarity also set him apart from many other leading members of Chinese communism, who had studied in Japan and Western Europe or experienced periods of ideological and military training in Moscow. It was Mao who, strategically reflecting on the defeats of the urban revolutions of the mid-1920s,

---

109   Orlando Figes, *A People's Tragedy: The Russian Revolution, 1891–1924* (London: Penguin, 1997), 296.

decided first to create a Soviet Republic in Jiangxi (1929–34), and then to organize the epic Long March (1934–35), which allowed the communists to preserve their military organization and established the premises for both the anti-Japanese struggle and the revolution of 1949. This withdrawal to the countryside, which had initially been conceived as a temporary expedient after the tragic failure of the urban uprisings of 1925–27, became a strategic reorientation towards a peasant revolution. This was the 'kernel' of the discrepancy between Russian and Chinese communism. The Bolsheviks, Schmitt points out by quoting the former leader of the KPD, Ruth Fischer, were 'led by a group of theorists the majority of whom were emigrants'.[110] The Chinese communist party had certainly been created in an intellectual and proletarian urban milieu, but it prevailed by inscribing its theory and action within the peasantry. The observations of an insightful analyst like Isaac Deutscher on the peculiarities of Maoism deserve to be quoted:

> One hesitates to say it, yet it is true that the Chinese revolution, which in its scope is the greatest of all revolutions in history, was led by the most provincial-minded and 'insular' of revolutionary parties. This paradox throws into all the sharper relief the inherent power of the revolution itself.[111]

Telluric and cosmopolitan revolutionaries were not necessarily antipodal: the symbolic procession of a column of mounted soldiers of the Zapatista army at the funerals of Leon Trotsky in Mexico City, in 1940, gives a visual representation of their virtual alliance. But there was also a third group that had its own peculiarities and was far from negligible in a century of wars and revolutions: a group of 'rootless cosmopolitans'. Used pejoratively by both Stalinism and fascism – which gave it clearly xenophobic and anti-Semitic connotation – this label designated a really existing cluster nonetheless.

---

110   Schmitt, *Theory of the Partisan*, 40–1.
111   Isaac Deutscher, 'Maoism: Its Origins and Outlook' (1964), *Marxism, Wars, and Revolutions*, 182.

Manabendra Nath Roy, Moscow 1924. Roy is recognizable at
the centre of the picture. From left to right are also recognizable
Radek, Bukharin, Lenin, Gorky, Zimoviev and Stalin.

Manabendra N. Roy's trajectory runs parallel to that of Ho Chi
Minh, but their outcomes are very different. Between 1914 and 1931,
Roy lived in Kobe, Palo Alto, New York, Mexico City, Moscow,
Tashkent, Canton and Berlin, but when he came back to Bombay,
he did not find a synthesis between his revolutionary transnational
experience and the path of Indian national liberation. In 1935, at
the time of Ethiopian War, anticolonialism and anti-fascism went
together harmoniously. During the Second World War, his anti-
fascism led him to defer the goal of independence from Britain. He
did not become the Indian Ho Chi Minh. During the war years, he was
regarded as a 'Europhile' and even accused, slanderously, of being
a 'British spy'.

C. L. R. James is the wonderful historian of the 'Black Jacobins' of
Saint-Domingue and, after his expulsion from the United States – he
spent a year on Ellis Island under McCarthyism, where he wrote an
outstanding book on Melville's *Moby Dick* – he became an inspirer
of pan-Africanism, but after leaving Trinidad he never headed a mass

movement. And he never received a university post, instead living in London as a marginal, 'rootless cosmopolitan'. The equilibrium between rootedness and cosmopolitanism is complex, often unstable or transitional. When revolutions are defeated, many intellectuals who had restlessly struggled for decades either abandon their radicalism or return to their original, peripheral roles as outsiders. Telluric cosmopolitans are a rare dialectical species.

We do not need to adopt a nationalist cult of the earth and the dead in order to recognize that a 'telluric character' cannot be artificially created. From this point of view, the trajectory of Che Guevara is very instructive. The Argentinian physician, having travelled around Latin America in his twenties, had become an ardent anti-imperialist activist after the Guatemalan coup of 1954 and his meeting with Fidel Castro in Mexico City the following year. He was a cosmopolitan intellectual who chose to join the national liberation movement of a country which, seen from Buenos Aires, might appear exotic. He not only participated in the Cuban Revolution of 1958 but served as one of its leaders and merged his life with that of the Caribbean island. Romantic rebel, bohemian, statesman, and international harbinger of anti-imperialism, he was also a thinker who drew the lessons of his revolutionary experience in a famous essay: *Guerrilla Warfare: A Method* (1963). His strategy was grounded in a set of structural premises: in Latin America, endemic poverty, mass exploitation, and economic under-development were intermingled with an oligarchic power that ruled through military dictatorships and could not be overthrown by peaceful means. In his view, guerrilla warfare could win only as a mass movement, not by the action of a fighting minority; but he also believed that the objective conditions for a general uprising combining rural and urban masses could be created by the *guerrilleros* themselves. Here was the theory of the so-called *foco*, according to which a small nucleus of *guerrilleros* could succeed by 'either unleashing a counterattack or weathering the storm'.[112] Thus, Guevara did not conceive of partisan war as a simple technique but

---

112   Ernesto 'Che' Guevara, 'Guerrilla Warfare: A Method' (1963), *Che Guevara Speaks: Selected Speeches and Writings*, ed. George Lavan (New York: Merit Publishers, 1967), 87. For an excellent synthesis, see Michael Löwy, *The*

rather as a revolutionary strategy. His illusion consisted in thinking that a forest fire could spread out from a *foco*, from a spark ignited by a small group of (foreign) fighters. In 1967, the catastrophic conclusion of his guerrilla adventure in Bolivia, where a small group of fighters was hunted and dismantled by the CIA and the local armed forces, proved that he had dramatically underestimated the telluric dimension of a successful revolutionary movement. In Bolivia, a country with a strong tradition of workers' and urban struggles led by trade-unions and political parties, the conditions for a peasant guerrilla did not exist. On the one hand, rootless cosmopolitanism produced the most powerful icon of revolutionary martyrdom; on the other, it demonstrated its insuperable limits.

Conscious Pariahs

Certainly not exhaustive, the landscape surveyed above sketches the outlines of a global revolutionary map – rough and incomplete, but meaningful nonetheless – that covers the span from 1848 to the Second World War. Despite their ideological discrepancies, this colourful army of anarchist, socialist and communist rebels share a hatred of capitalism, conformist values, the established order, despotism and the bourgeois state. Most of them also share a social condition of marginality originating in their exclusion from academia and other state institutions, as well as in their general stigmatization in the public sphere. Most of them accord quite well with the definition of 'pariah' suggested by Max Weber in *Economy and Society* (1921) and elaborated by Hannah Arendt in a famous essay on the Jewish condition written in 1944.[113]

In his sociological treaty, Weber used the concept of 'intellectualism' as a synonym of both rationalization and secularism, a mental habitus and a world view opposed to any kind of mythology: intellectualism overcomes 'religious belief' (*Glaubensfrommigkeit*), which implies a

---

Marxism of Che Guevara: Philosophy, Economy, Revolutionary Warfare (Lanham: Roman & Littlefield, 2007 [1973]), notably Part 3, on guerrilla warfare.

113   For an interesting reconstruction of the history of the notion of 'pariah', see Eleni Varikas, *Les rebuts du monde. Figures du paria* (Paris: Stock, 2007).

'sacrifice of intellect'.[114] But the noun 'intellectual', which appears rarely in this work, mostly to describe figures of modern society like writers and journalists, is sometimes accompanied by the adjective 'pariah'. In *Ancient Judaism* (1917), Weber defined the Jews of pre-modern Europe as a 'pariah people' (*Pariavolk*) – a kind of Indian 'caste' in a casteless world – that exhibited some peculiar features: they lived among different nations with the status of foreigners, maintained a 'ritualistic' separation from other people, did not engage in agriculture due to their essentially urban character, and practised a kind of 'double morality': one internal to their own community and the other reserved for the broader environment.[115] In *Economy and Society*, the representatives of 'pariah intellectualism' do not have a solid social status and do not belong to the established social hierarchies; they live without strong material grounds and observe the world from the margins. Among several examples of 'pariah intellectuals', Weber indicated the English Puritans of the seventeenth century, the autodidactic peasants and decaying nobility in Tsarist Russia, the Western European anarchist and revolutionary ideologues and, last but not least, the Jewish intellectuals of Eastern and Central Europe, notably in Germany.[116]

For Arendt, 'pariah Judaism' was a 'hidden tradition' in which she included Heinrich Heine, Bernard Lazare, Charlie Chaplin and Kafka. She had been particularly struck by Lazare, the French anarchist and

114 Max Weber, *Economy and Society: An Outline of Interpretive Sociology*, eds Guenther Roth and Claus Wittich (Berkeley: University of California Press, 1978), 567.

115 Max Weber, *Ancient Judaism*, ed. Hans H. Gerth (New York: Free Press, 1952), 3. On Weber's concept of 'pariah people', see Ephraim Shmueli, 'The "Pariah-People" and Its Charismatic Leadership: A Reevaluation of Max Weber's Ancient Judaism', *Proceedings of the American Academy for Jewish Research*, 36 (1968): 167–247; also Arnaldo Momigliano, 'A Note on Max Weber's Definition of Judaism as a Pariah-Religion', *On Pagans, Jews, and Christians* (Middleton: Wesleyan University Press, 1987), 231–7. On the Jewish revolutionary intellectual as pariah, see the third chapter of Michael Löwy, *Redemption and Utopia: Jewish Libertarian Thought in Central Europe* (London, New York: Verso, 2017); also Enzo Traverso, 'The Jew as Pariah', *The Jews and Germany: From the 'Judeo-German Symbiosis' to the Memory of Auschwitz* (Lincoln: Nebraska University Press, 1995), 45–64.

116 Weber, *Economy and Society*, 514–15.

defender of Dreyfus, the author of *Job's Dungheap* (written in the 1890s, posthumously published in 1929), who depicted the Jewish pariah as a rebel. Before Lazare, the word 'pariah' had been used in a purely aesthetic, literary or moral sense: it defined an excluded and miserable people, objects of compassion and pity. In 1944, when she was living in New York as a refugee, Arendt reformulated this concept by giving it a strong new political meaning: the pariah has become nationless, stateless, and an exile.[117] In short, a person excluded from citizenship or, as she writes in *The Origins of Totalitarianism* (1951), a person who 'does not have the right to have rights'.[118] According to Arendt, the 'pariah people' formed a new category of human beings arising from the European crisis at the end of the Great War and the geopolitical transformations of the continent. They were stateless people, excluded from the nation-states created after the collapse of Europe's multinational empires and the first in line for ethnic cleansing. Thus they embodied a paradoxical contradiction: on the one hand, they were the authentic representatives of 'humanity' in its most universal meaning, since they epitomized the abstract definition of humanity postulated by the Enlightenment; on the other, they were precisely excluded from humanity, whose existence supposes political rights. In a letter to Karl Jaspers, Arendt defined pariahs as individuals who, excluded from any established political and juridical community, claimed values such as humanity, friendship, or solidarity. Affection, she pointed out, is important for people without any property.[119]

In other words, for Arendt the pariah condition was *historical* rather than ontological. The pariah who embraces his or her conditions of exclusion, she also suggested in the wake of Bernard Lazare, becomes a 'conscious pariah' and a rebel. Being a pariah is not only a condition

---

117   Hannah Arendt, 'The Jew as Pariah: A Hidden Tradition' (1944), *The Jewish Writings*, eds Jerome Kohn and Ron H. Feldman (New York: Schocken Books 2007), 275–97. See Bernard Lazare, *Job's Dungheap: Essays on Jewish Nationalism and Social Revolution* (New York: Schocken Books, 1948).

118   Hannah Arendt, *The Origins of Totalitarianism* (New York: Harvest Books, 1976), 298.

119   Hannah Arendt to Karl Jaspers, 7 September 1952, in Hannah Arendt and Karl Jaspers, *Correspondence 1926–1969* (New York: Harcourt, Brace, Jovanovich, 1992), 200.

Le Paria, Paris, 1922–26.

that is undergone, it can also be chosen. Considering the revolutionary intellectuals of Eastern and Central European Jewry, the colonial world and the Caribbean, their pariah condition was both suffered and chosen. It was, at the same time, a subaltern status and a consciously assumed political stance. They belonged to a stigmatized minority and represented, as an intellectual and political avant-garde, the dominated majority. Their exclusion from academia and respectability, their mobility and their déclassement reinforced by prison and exile: all these elements radicalized their political orientation and sharpened their epistemological position. They observed the world from the margins, escaping the cultural, political, mental, and even psychological prejudices of the countries in which they lived. They were 'strangers' in Georg Simmel's sense – they assimilated and merged different cultures – and 'free-floating' in Karl Mannheim's sense – deprived of any solid social attachment – but this status helped them to develop a critical gaze on history, society and politics.[120] Maybe it is not by chance that young communist intellectuals from North and West Africa, Asia and the Caribbean who lived in Paris in the 1920s decided to publish a journal named *Le Paria*, as mentioned above. This title perfectly summarized their status.

---

120   Georg Simmel, 'The Stranger' (1908) *The Sociology of Georg Simmel*, ed. Kurt H. Wolff (New York: Free Press, 1950), 402–8; Karl Mannheim, *Ideologie und Utopie* (Frankfurt/Main: Klostermann, 1985 [1929]), 73. The concept of 'free-floating' intelligentsia is blurred in the English translation: *Ideology and Utopia* (New York: Harvest, 1936).

Conservative Anti-Intellectualism

Déclassé rebels permanently involved in actions against the established order arouse feelings of contempt and fear, even hatred, amongst the defenders of bourgeois respectability. Very soon, revolutionary intellectuals became a prime target for conservative thinkers and ideologues who warned against the public danger they posed. Most of them looked at the revolutionary intelligentsia with moral aversion and physical repugnance. A gallery of quotations from conservative scholars, high ecclesiastical dignitaries, nationalists, fascists, and Nazis can be, if not pleasant, interesting and significative.

The portrait of Blanqui sketched by Tocqueville, a proud representative of the French aristocracy, in a private text like his *Recollections* (1851), starts the series by epitomizing a genuine and intense dislike:

> It was then that I saw appear, in his turn, in the tribune a man whom I have never seen since, but the recollection of whom has always filled me with horror and disgust. He had wan, emaciated cheeks, white lips, a sickly, wicked and repulsive expression, a dirty pallor, the appearance of a mouldy corpse; he wore no visible linen; an old black frock-coat tightly covered his lean, withered limbs; he seemed to have passed his life in a sewer, and to have just left it. I was told it was Blanqui.[121]

In the second half of the nineteenth century, when the rise of positivism and the emergence of new social sciences like criminal anthropology provided analytical categories that reinterpreted revolutions as pathologies of the social body, Jacobin, socialist and anarchist intellectuals were commonly depicted as 'degenerate'. In the writings of Hippolyte Taine, who studied the history of France after 1789 like a doctor looking into an ailing body devastated by syphilis, revolutionaries were the carriers of dangerous diseases which he described with a medical lexicon: cholera, typhus, malaria, alcoholism, cancer, etc.[122] We saw in Chapter Two the 'hyenas' and 'gorillas' of the Paris

---

121   Alexis Tocqueville, *Recollections* (New York: Macmillan, 1896), 163.

122   See Daniel Pick, *Faces of Degeneration: A European Disorder 1848–1918* (New York: Cambridge University Press, 1989), notably Chapter 2.

Auguste Blanqui. Portrait by his wife, Amélie Serre
(ca. 1835). Musée Carnavalet, Paris.

Commune, very popular in *fin-de-siècle* French political literature. With a more nuanced approach, Cesare Lombroso, the founder of criminal anthropology, distinguished between the terrorist killer and the nihilist who inspired him. The former was mostly a 'criminal born', a depraved individual who hated humanity, had no ethical values, and embodied illnesses like 'political epilepsy and hysteria'. The latter was usually an intellectual who, unlike the practitioner of violence whose degeneration was written on his face and clearly detectable from the form of his skull, could also exhibit a 'very beautiful physiognomy'. Rather than a 'criminal born', he or she was a political criminal 'by passion' who revealed forms of neurosis, fanaticism and mysticism 'by inheritance', to the point of replacing generosity with martyrdom.[123] Thus, Lombroso's taxonomy separated 'criminals and semi-insane' revolutionaries like Louise Michel and Giovanni Passanante, the Italian anarchist who tried to kill King Umberto I in 1878, from revolutionaries who were 'political criminals by passion' like Bakunin, Chernyshevsky and Zasulich.[124]

---

123   Cesare Lombroso, *Gli anarchici* (Milan: La vita felice, 2009 [1894]), 63–70.
124   Cesare Lombroso, *Il delitto politico e le rivoluzioni* (Turin: Bocca, 1890), 586–7. On this topic, see Daniel Pick, 'The Faces of Anarchy: Lombroso and

'Revolutionaries and Political Criminals', plates from
Cesare Lombroso, *Il Delitto politico e le rivoluzioni* (1890).

Max Nordau, an enthusiastic admirer of Lombroso, similarly
thought that 'the writings and acts of revolutionists and anarchists
are attributable to degeneracy.' Anarchists were affected by 'fervent
philanthropy' and the desire to eliminate injustice from humankind,
but as 'degenerated' beings, meaning individuals incapable of adapting
to existing circumstances and revealing an 'organic weakness of will',
they were pushed to crime by their 'absurdity and monstrous ignorance
of all real relations'.[125] Therefore, revolutionary intellectuals were
an additional example of the degeneration of modern life, alongside
other manifestations already visible in the big cities of the West:
shops selling commodities to satisfy depraved desires, the unchecked
spread of drug dealing and sexual perversion, suicide, madness and
murder because of urban noise, and boulevards invaded by the

---

the Politics of Criminal Science in Post-Unification Italy', *History Workshop*, 21
(1986): 60–81, and Patricia Bass, 'Cesare Lombroso and the Anarchists', *Journal
for the Study of Radicalism*, 13/1 (2019): 19–42.

125   Max Nordau, *Degeneration*, Introduction by George L. Mosse (Lincoln:
University of Nebraska Press, 1993 [1892]), 22.

unconventionally gendered smoking cigars. Revolutionary intellectuals were the equivalent, in theory and politics, of Baudelaire, Ibsen,
Oscar Wilde and Nietzsche in literature and philosophy.

In *The Secret Agent* (1907), Joseph Conrad amusingly fictionalizes
the image of the déclassé anarchist intelligentsia widespread in the
public opinion of the turn of the twentieth century. The small group
of conspirators who organize a terrorist attack at the Greenwich
Observatory is composed of fanatics, sociopaths and outcasts, whose
otherness is revealed by their physical traits and a general conduct that
is as hideous as it is grotesque. All of them belong to an underclass
of eternal students, sectarian ideologues and subversive thinkers.
Yundt, the oldest of this congregation, is 'old and bald, with a narrow,
snow-white wisp of a goatee hanging limply from his chin'. Though
his interventions are simply pathetic, 'an extraordinary expression
of underhand malevolence survived in his extinguished eyes.' His
gestures recall 'the effort of a moribund murderer summoning all
his remaining strength for a last stab'.[126] He has spent his entire life
in underground meetings and terrorist conspiracies, but when he
speaks 'the shadow of his evil gift' still clings to him 'like the smell
of a deadly drug in an old vial of poison'.[127] Ossipon, the author of
the group's leaflets, is a tall and robust ex-medical student without a
degree. His 'red, freckled face' is topped by 'a bush of crinkly yellow
hair', and his gaze projected by almond-shaped eyes, whereas his
nose and mouth are 'cast in the rough mould of the negro type'. An
admirer of Lombroso, he perfectly fits the criminologist's portrait of
'degenerate' and criminal men. During group discussions, his emotions
accentuate 'the negro type of his face'.[128] The 'Professor' – he is known
only by his nickname – was born to a poor family and inherited his
mental habitus from his father, the 'itinerant and rousing preacher'
of a Christian sect. Haunted by the dream of 'destroying public faith
in legality', he is a fanatic and has specialized in making bombs, 'the
supreme guarantee of his sinister freedom'.[129] Finally, Michaelis, 'the

---

126 Joseph Conrad, *The Secret Agente* (London: Penguin, 2007), 34.
127 Ibid., 39.
128 Ibid., 40.
129 Ibid., 65.

ticket-of-leave apostle', has spent several years in jail from which he emerged morbidly obese, 'round like a tub'.[130]

Undoubtedly, Conrad's portraits caricature the terrorist archetype of his time, probably merging several well-known anarchist figures. Except for their physical features, these grotesque conspirators recall Nechaev, whom Bakunin enthusiastically depicted as the representative of a generation of 'magnificent young fanatics, believers without gods',[131] and their projected attack could also evoke Peter Kropotkin or Errico Malatesta, respectively a scientist and a medical student, the spokespersons of 'propaganda by the deed'. But it is significant that, differently from both Kropotkin and Malatesta, who had aristocratic and wealthy origins, Conrad preferred to make his characters marginals from the dregs of society.

After the Russian Revolution, the archetype of the revolutionary intellectual shifted from the anarchist terrorist to the Bolshevik, the new spectre haunting Europe. In his famous lecture 'Politics as a Vocation' (1919), Max Weber sketched this latest figure by distinguishing him from other social actors like the bourgeois, the scholar or the responsible politician. Unlike these, who embodied an 'ethics of responsibility' (*Verantwortungsethik*) related to both the rationality of their profession and the capacity to foresee the consequences of their actions, intellectuals were the most unreliable and unpredictable social subjects. The bourgeois interiorizes the Protestant work ethic, which is based on a form of terrestrial asceticism oriented towards a rationally organized system of production and profit-making. The scholar is a man of science: his knowledge is objective and axiologically neutral, which allows him to achieve a critical distance free of any emotional interference. Like the artist, the responsible politician – who accomplishes his vocation for politics – escapes the rules of rationalization and is not

---

130   Ibid., 33. Contextualizing Conrad's novel, David Mulry points out that his 'gross caricatural representation and conflation of anarchist types' was quite common at the turn of the twentieth century (for instance in Zola's *Germinal*): 'The Anarchist in the House: The Politics of Conrad's *The Secret Agent*', *The Conradian*, 32/1 (2007): 1–12.

131   Nechaev, twenty-two and freshly escaped from a Russian prison, appeared this way to Bakunin in Switzerland in 1869: quoted in James Joll, *The Anarchists* (Cambridge, MA: Harvard University Press, 1980), 76.

subject to a hierarchical order, but does not ignore the superior interests of his country. The intellectual, on the other hand, does not belong to a class or an 'order' (*Stand*) and does not occupy a stable position in the structure of society or the economy. Whereas both classes and 'orders' – think respectively of the bourgeoisie and the clergy – have a coherent and highly developed worldview, intellectuals are socially uprooted and politically free-floating, an unstable condition that pushes them almost naturally towards anti-conformism and the critique of established powers. Resistant and refractory by nature to all ruling institutions, they become a source of chaos. In times of social and political unrest, they are apt to join revolutionary movements. They are mostly uprooted, strangers, emigrants, and frequently journalists. At the end of the First World War, they were attracted to extreme and demagogic postures, exposed to contingent passions and irresistibly susceptible to messianic dreams. These were the Bolsheviks, romantic intellectuals who, 'emotionally unfit for everyday life or averse to it and its demands', inevitably 'hunger and thirst after the great revolutionary miracle'.[132] This was the 'sterile excitement' of 'a particular type of intellectual', the member of a 'pariah-caste' – both Russian and German – who had played a crucial role in 'this carnival which is being graced with the proud name of a revolution'.[133] This was the deplorable result, Weber concluded, of a political action grounded in a total lack of 'clairvoyance' (*Augenmaß*) and responsibility.

Demagogy combined with political extremism produced a new form of messianism, the secular ersatz for a faith engulfed in modern rationality but still nostalgically remembered, still yearned for. Evoking implicitly Georg Lukács and Ernst Bloch, two young philosophers who had attended his circle at Heidelberg before the war and later supported the Russian revolution with a fervour coloured by mysticism, Weber stigmatized the propensity of some 'modern intellectuals to furnish their souls with, so to speak, guaranteed genuine antiques'. The new religion was called Bolshevism and its prophet was Leon Trotsky, an

---

132   Max Weber, 'Socialism' (1918), *Political Writings*, eds Peter Lassman and Ronald Speirs (Cambridge: Cambridge University Press, 1994), 298.

133   Max Weber, 'The Profession and Vocation of Politics' (1918), *Political Writings*, 331, 353.

intellectual who, 'not content to carry out this experiment in his own house', wished to export it and promoted 'unrivalled propaganda for socialism throughout the whole world'. 'With the typical vanity of the Russian *littérateur*', Weber emphasized, he hoped to provoke a civil war in Germany 'by means of wars of words'.[134] His followers were 'coffee-house intellectuals' who had invented a 'politics of the street', not to pressure governments but rather to call into question the state itself. As hubs of a public sphere antipodal to parliamentary politics, the coffee-houses acted as magnets for a multitude of uprooted intellectuals, as well as political activists external to the established parties and lacking a solid social status. Among these Weber included the leaders of the Spartacist uprising and the Bavarian Revolution of 1919 – Rosa Luxemburg, Karl Liebknecht and Kurt Eisner – whom he sneeringly described as 'a handful of street dictators'.[135]

In the same year as Weber's lecture in Munich, Eugenio Pacelli, the future Pope Pius XII, was papal nuncio in the Bavarian capital and sent his reports to the Vatican. One of them, written in April, describes Max Levien, the Soviet agent who tried to reorganize the revolutionary power threatened by the Freikorps, in frightening terms. His aide had visited the headquarters of the Soviet government and had been struck by the presence of numerous women who seemed comfortable with their male comrades. They were 'a gang of young women, of dubious appearance, Jewish like all the rest of them'. 'The boss of this female rabble', he continued, 'was Levien's mistress, a young Russian woman, a Jew and a divorcée.' As for Levien, he was particularly hideous: 'This Levien is a young man of about thirty or thirty-five, also Russian and Jew. Pale, dirty, with drugged eyes, hoarse voice, vulgar, repulsive, with a face that is both intelligent and sly.'[136] These outcast intellectuals, Pacelli's words suggested, perfectly fitted a pornographic picture of sexual debauchery as well as the conspirators of *The Protocols of the Elders of Zion*.

---

134   Weber, 'Socialism', 299–300. In the biography of her husband, Marianne Weber depicts Lukács and Bloch as 'messianic young men ... moved by eschatological hopes of a new emissary of the transcendent God': *Max Weber: A Biography*, trans. Harry Zohn (New York: Wiley, 1975 [1926]), 466.
135   Weber, 'Profession and Vocation of Politics', 350.
136   Quoted in Hanebrink, *A Specter Haunting Europe*, 12.

Ten years later, fascist anti-intellectualism combined an anti-Semitic with a homophobic tune, depicting intellectuals as the opposite of manly. 'Intellectualism', Mino Maccari wrote in *Il Selvaggio* in 1933, 'is a kind of unfruitful intelligence, an intelligence without virility.' Intellectualism 'is a pathological International, like that of homosexuals [*gli invertiti del sesso*] or that of anarchists. … They play a female role, but in the worst sense, because their womanhood does not mean maternity.'[137]

The anti-intellectualism of German nationalists – particularly the Nazis – was even stronger than that of their Italian partners, since the latter form of fascism tolerated the aesthetic avant-garde and tried to corrupt rather than persecute the intellectuals. However, under the Weimar Republic, attacking 'coffee-house intellectuals' was routine for right-wing newspapers and quickly became a specialty of nationalist ideologues, a crowded cohort that Theodor W. Adorno called the 'anti-intellectual intellectuals'.[138] The most prestigious of their journals, *Die Tat*, depicted Bolshevism as an 'artificial construction' built by a group of 'uprooted, rationalists, theoreticians and intellectuals', usually more attuned to breweries. The great target of this propaganda was 'cultural Bolshevism' (*Kulturbolschewismus*), a plague afflicting Germany. In Nazi publications, Bolsheviks, intellectuals and Jews were used at this time as synonyms. The Jews embodied a cosmopolitan, rationalistic, anti-German spirit that found favourable soil in the big cities and was dangerously carried out by their agents, the revolutionary intellectuals. In his speech delivered in Berlin in front of the Humboldt University, on 1 May 1933, just before the students of the Hitler Youth started the auto-da-fé of 'degenerate' books, Joseph Goebbels solemnly announced that 'the time of extremely sharp intellectualism [*überspitzen Intellektualismus*] was over.'[139] The National Socialist revolution was salvation for a Germany which 'the

---

137   Mino Maccari, *Il Selvaggio*, X/8 (1933): 58, quoted in Sandro Bellassai, *L'invenzione della virilità: Politica e immaginario maschile nell'Italia contemporanea* (Roma: Carocci, 2011), 77.

138   Theodor W. Adorno, *The Jargon of Authenticity* (London: Routledge, 2003), 1.

139   Speech of 8 May 1933, in Joseph Goebbels, *Reden*, ed. Helmut Heider (Düsseldorf: Droste, 1971), vol. 1, 108.

forces of sub-humanity [*Untermenschentums*]' had thrown into chaos at the end of the war by 'conquering the political arena'. They had inundated German libraries with a despicable 'asphalt literature', and these massive book-burning actions took a more than symbolic purifying character.[140]

Usually, the Nazis described intellectuals as 'cold' and 'bloodless' minds; Goebbels was accustomed to stigmatizing any 'intellectual agitator' who had found in Marxism his inspiration. 'The magnificent specimen of this human decadence', he clarified, was the Jew.[141] Jewish Bolshevism was a major threat for Western civilization, insofar as it sealed the alliance between a revolutionary ideology like Marxism and the Slavic soul, behind which lurked the racial 'sub-humanity' of the Eastern world: the Jewish intellectual – the true brain of the Soviet Union – was the maleficent mixer of this explosive cocktail. According to Alfred Rosenberg, 'Bolshevism [was] the last product of the combination of a Jewish-cosmopolitan intellectualism with a passionate oriental religious fervour.' And the origin of this dangerous nihilistic ideology could be detected with the help of racial biology: 'In order to understand the phenomenon of Bolshevism in its historical context', he explained in 1935, 'one must first accept the notion that parasites exist not only in the world of flora and fauna but, to put it in pedestrian scientific terms, also in the world of human beings.'[142] In other words, Bolshevism was the ideological expression of *parasitism*, 'a characteristic feature of the Jew's blood'. As for Hitler, in 1933 he simply identified the proletarian dictatorship with 'the dictatorship of Jewish intellectualism' and denounced the 'Jewish-intellectual leadership of world revolution'.[143]

---

140   Ibid., 109.

141   Joseph Goebbels, *Der Angriff*, 10 August 1931, quoted in Dietz Bering, *Die Intellektuellen: Geschichte eines Schimpfwortes* (Stuttgart: Klett-Cotta 1978), 123. Bering offers a general survey of the nationalist uses of the word 'intellectual' in Weimar and Nazi Germany, 94–147. Goebbels summarized his views in an editorial titled 'Die Intellektuellen', published on 11 February 1939 by the official Nazi newspaper *Völkischer Beobachter*.

142   Alfred Rosenberg, 'Bolshevism: The Work of an Alien Race' (1935), in Anson Rabinbach and Sander L. Gilman (eds), *The Third Reich Sourcebook* (Berkeley: University of California Press, 2013), 199–200.

143   Quoted in Bering, *Die Intellektuellen*, 122, 366.

Hall of the exhibition *Der ewige Jude*, Munich 1937.

Werner Scholem (ca. 1930).

On 28 November 1937, Joseph Goebbels inaugurated in Munich, hosted by the library of the German Museum, an exhibition titled *Der ewige Jude* ('The Eternal Jew'), which was devoted to illustrating the pernicious role historically played by the Jews in domestic and international politics by unveiling their racial background. In the exhibition hall, a gigantic panel displayed several portraits of Jewish personalities with a Jewish social-democrat, Rudolf Hilferding, and the Bolshevik Karl Radek, in the centre. Under these portraits the visitors could admire a life mask of Werner Scholem, a Jewish communist deputy of the Reichstag (and brother of the historian of Kabbala, Gershom

Scholem). Beside this life mask were displayed enlarged moulds of his ears, nose and mouth, which had been made in Dachau, the concentration camp where he had been deported. He died in Buchenwald the following year. For this exhibition, the Nazis had exhumed the tradition of life masks, popular at the end of the nineteenth century to document the racial features of the populations of German colonies. Scholem's mask was topped by the caption: 'They have typical physical characteristics' [*Sie haben typische äussere Merkmale*]. According to the Nazi paper *Völkischer Beobachter*, Goebbels was delighted by this exhibition, finding it 'exquisite'.[144]

'Fellow Travellers'

Revolutionary intellectuals should not be confused with the 'fellow travellers' of communism. Of course, this distinction is not always obvious: the line between the two was narrow and shifting, but it existed nonetheless. The notion itself of 'fellow traveller' is quite vague. It appears in Trotsky's *Literature and Revolution* (1924), first mentioned as a label coined within the milieu of German social democracy at the end of the nineteenth century. Now, he applied it to an ensemble of young Russian novelists and poets who had tumbled into the maelstrom of revolution without formally joining the ranks of Bolshevism. 'Between bourgeois art, which is wasting away either in repetitions or in silences and the new art which is as yet unborn', Trotsky argued, 'there is being created a transitional art which is more or less organically connected with the Revolution, but which is not at the same time the art of the Revolution.'[145] Its representatives, including remarkable figures such as Sergei Yesenin and Boris Pilnyak, still remained halfway across the river dividing committed Bolsheviks from everyone else. Trotsky stressed that their horizon had been fixed by the Revolution, and they had accepted it, each in his own way. 'But in these individual acceptances', he added, 'there is

---

144   The story of Werner Scholem's 'participation' in the Munich exhibition of 1937 is related by Mirjam Zadoff, *Werner Scholem: A German Life* (Philadelphia: University of Pennsylvania Press, 2018), 275–8.

145   Leon Trotsky, *Literature and Revolution* (Chicago: Haymarket, 2005), 61.

one common trait which sharply divides them from communism, and always threatens to put them in opposition to it. They do not grasp the Revolution as a whole and the communist ideal is foreign to them.' Therefore, he concluded, they were not the artists of the proletarian revolution, but rather its 'fellow travellers' (*paputchiki*).[146] In other words, the Bolsheviks regarded them with sympathy and considered them friends, but could not avoid a certain caution. They could share a part of the journey, but the point was to know until where.

The current meaning of this label, however, appeared in the 1930s and was definitively fixed during the Cold War, when it entered several Western languages to indicate a large category of scholars, writers and artists related to the communist parties (*compagnons de route*, *compagni di strada*, *Mitläufer*). Jean-Paul Sartre was never a member of the PCF – he sometimes criticized it – but shared a 'stretch of road' with the communists, as did Pablo Picasso. Dating the birth of the communist 'fellow traveller' is not difficult. He appeared when the Comintern abandoned the sectarian and extremist politics of the so-called 'third period' – when social-democracy was called 'social-fascism' – and adopted the strategy of Popular Fronts grounded in an alliance with socialist parties and a broad mobilization against fascism.

This political turn took place in France after the events of 6 February 1934, when a far-right demonstration threatened to march on the Palais-Bourbon, the seat of government, and the clashes that followed, at the place de la Concorde, left fourteen dead and hundreds wounded. After the rise to power of Hitler in Germany, fascism was spreading in Europe and the French left spontaneously created a united front between the socialist and the communist parties – the SFIO and the PCF – thus avoiding the divisions that had favoured the rise of the Nazi movement under the Weimar Republic. The architects of this turn were three scholars – the philosopher Alain, the physicist Paul Langevin, and the ethnologist Paul Rivet – who founded the Vigilance Committee of Anti-Fascist Intellectuals (*Comité de vigilance des intellectuels antifascistes*). This mobilization reached its apogee during the Spanish Civil War, when artists and writers from around

---

146   Ibid., 80–3, 86.

the world went to Spain to fight for the Republic.[147] In May 1935, the French-Soviet treaty of mutual assistance had reinforced the turn towards the Popular Front, which went on to win the elections of the following spring. Under the leadership of Maurice Thorez, the PCF endorsed the principle of 'national defence' by claiming the legacy of Jacobinism. It was in Paris that, in June 1935, the first International Writers' Congress for the Defence of Culture took place, chaired by André Malraux and André Gide and masterminded by Ilya Ehrenburg.[148] In the political context of the 1930s, sharing a stretch of road with communism did not necessarily mean joining a revolutionary movement; this choice was rather felt and lived as an ineluctable necessity in the struggle against fascism. And this wave involved scholars and public intellectuals who had never been seduced by the October Revolution. Think of Gide and Malraux in France, Heinrich Mann and Lion Feuchtwanger in Germany, or representatives of left-wing liberalism like Harold Laski, George Bernard Shaw, and Sidney Webb (1st Baron Passfield and founder of the London School of Economics) in the United Kingdom. In 1935, Sidney and his wife, Beatrice, published a quite shameful apology of Stalinism – *Soviet Communism: A New Civilization?* – that celebrated the accomplishments of Soviet industrialization. This was the immoral dimension of a general commitment to a just cause: anti-fascism was an *ethos* and a moral duty rather than a political strategy or a revolutionary commitment.[149] In *Moscow 1937*, Feuchtwanger went further by explicitly endorsing the indictments pronounced by the Soviet prosecutor, Andrey Vyshinsky.[150] But their relationship with the USSR – whether obsequious or critical,

147 On the mobilization of French intellectuals after the events of February 1934, see Winock, *Le siècle des intellectuels*, Chapter 26, 298–311.

148 See Herbert R. Lottman, *The Left Bank: Writers, Artists, and Politics from the Popular Front to the Cold War* (Chicago: The University of Chicago Press, 1982), Chapter 11, 83–98.

149 Sidney Webb and Beatrice Webb, *Soviet Communism: A New Civilization?* (London: Scribner's, 1936). See Anson Rabinbach, 'Legacies of Anti-Fascism', *New German Critique*, 67 (1996): 7. I developed this aspect of anti-fascism in *Fire and Blood: The European Civil War 1914–1945* (London, New York: Verso, 2016), Chapter 8.

150 Lion Feuchtwanger, *Moscow 1937: My Visit Described for My Friends* (London: Victor Gollancz, 1937). On Feuchtwanger's visit and meeting with Stalin, see Karl Schlögel, *Moscow 1937* (Cambridge: Polity Press, 2012), Chapter 5, 81–94.

as in the case of André Gide's *Back from the USSR* (1937)[151] – was external and not tied to any material aid or constraint. Unlike the revolutionary intellectuals, whom Stalinism placed before a tragic but simple dilemma – submission or persecution – many 'fellow travellers' were afforded the luxury of privately expressing their scepticism. In his conversations with Walter Benjamin in Skovbostrand, Denmark, in 1938, Bertolt Brecht defined the USSR as a 'workers' monarchy' and compared it to 'a grotesque natural phenomenon', like the emergence of 'horned fish or other monsters of the deep'; but publicly he remained a fellow traveller, and in 1949 he moved to East Berlin.[152] In 1929, Romain Rolland wrote to Panait Istrati that his criticism of the USSR had opened his eyes, but begged him not to publish his text, which would merely reinforce international reaction.[153] Six years later, he went to Moscow to interview Stalin.

Fundamentally, both the Bolsheviks and their 'fellow travellers' were conscious of their differences, even if they publicly showed a unanimous façade. The former needed the support of the Western intelligentsia to prove that they were the harbingers of progress and humanism. Unlike the universities and military schools intended to educate a generation of professional revolutionaries on a global scale, the All-Union Society for Cultural Ties Abroad (VOKS) regularly invited foreign intellectuals willing to promote the image of the USSR in the West. Its directors, first Olga Kameneva – wife of Lev Kamenev and sister of Trotsky, fired in 1929 – then Aleksander Arosev, between 1931 and 1937, had lived in exile and truly admired many of the scholars and writers they invited. Their goal was building a network of communist fellow travellers and friends of the USSR.[154]

151   André Gide, *Back from the USSR* (London: Secker & Warburg, 1937).

152   Walter Benjamin, *Understanding Brecht* (London: Verso, 2003), 121; and Erdmut Wizisla, *Walter Benjamin and Bertolt Brecht: The Story of a Friendship* (New Haven: Yale University Press, 2009), xxi.

153   Romain Rolland to Panait Istrati, 29 May 1929, quoted in Sophie Cœuré, *La grande lueur à l'Est. Les Français et l'Union Soviétique 1917–1939* (Paris: Seuil, 1999), 255.

154   See Ludmila Stern, *Western Intellectuals and the Soviet Union, 1920–40: From Red Square to the Left Bank* (New York: Routledge 2007), notably Chapters 5–7 devoted to the history of VOKS.

With hindsight, the enthusiastic chronicles and testimonies that these illustrious visitors brought back from their travels did not say anything new or original about Soviet society, but open a very interesting window on their own mental world, often stuffed with prejudice and incomprehension. They were tourists in a foreign country they did not really understand.

Whereas the Bolsheviks considered Russia a revolutionary bridge between West and East, many fellow travellers viewed the Soviet experiment through a benevolent Orientalist prism. Russia appeared to them as a backward, almost Asiatic country, inhabited by peasants whose ruthless but 'childlike' innocence possessed the charm of Noble Savages, and led by revolutionary intellectuals whose radical utopianism was the product of this social primitivity. In his *Moscow Diary* (1927), Theodore Dreiser described the 'exotic' character of the Soviet population, 'a mixture of Europeans and Asians' who reminded him of the 'Negroes' of the less developed parts of the United States.[155] In January 1933, three years before his famously disappointing visit and critical essay, André Gide expressed in his journal a sincere support for the Soviet experiment, which he 'wished wholeheartedly to be successful', while honestly admitting that this extraordinary experience was valuable for Russia but not the West. He did not believe that 'the social state' the Bolsheviks were building 'would be desirable for our people'.[156]

The already mentioned Paris Congress of 1935 decided to start an international association whose board included, beside Barbusse, Gide and Malraux, personalities such as Julien Benda, Ilya Ehrenburg, Aldous Huxley, Sinclair Lewis, Thomas Mann, Gaetano Salvemini and George Bernard Shaw. The common goal that united this motley band of writers and essayists was not revolution; it was the defence

---

155   Theodore Dreiser, *Dreiser's Russian Diary*, eds Tommaso Riggio and James L. W. West III (Philadelphia: Pennsylvania University Press, 1996), entries of 8 November and 4 December 1927, 59, 182. The Orientalist dimension of this fellow traveller's gaze is pointed out by Michael David-Fox, 'The Fellow-Travelers Revisited: The "Cultured West" through Soviet Eyes', *Journal of Modern History*, 75/2 (2003): 300–35, on Dreiser 316–17.

156   André Gide's journal, 4 January 1933, quoted in Cœuré, *La grande lueur*, 260.

of culture and civilization. In the face of fascism, many intellectuals who had hitherto regarded Bolshevism as a form of quasi-Asiatic anarchism suddenly became enthusiastic supporters of the USSR, a social and political creation in which they discerned a modern version of the Enlightenment. They wished to reaffirm the values of progress, democracy, freedom, equality and peace.[157] Did they ingenuously fall into the trap set by Soviet totalitarianism, as some conservative historians suggest? François Furet is right in observing that 'through antifascism, communism had recovered the trophy of democracy' and had 'reinvented itself as freedom by default' at the time of the Soviet Great Terror,[158] but his assessment must be qualified. It plainly disregards the fact that anti-fascism was a very large and heterogeneous movement including socialists, liberals, Trotskyists, anarchists, and even religious thinkers like Jacques Maritain, Luigi Sturzo and Paul Tillich. In most cases, they admitted their discrepancies with communism and the alliance was not as harmonious as many of them publicly pretended. During the Paris conference of 1935, the conflict between revolutionary intellectuals and Stalinism broke out within the ranks of the 'fellow travellers' when André Breton called for the liberation of Victor Serge (who had been deported to a Soviet gulag) and was banned from the proceedings after a violent confrontation with Ehrenburg (his speech was read by the poet Paul Eluard at midnight, when most of the audience had already left the Maison de la Mutualité).[159]

Antifascism was a transitional experience. It gathered the multiple heirs of the Enlightenment – from classical liberalism to revolutionary Marxism – into a common front against the forces of irrationalism, anti-humanism, vitalism, racism, anti-Semitism, authoritarianism and nationalism. When fascist Europe appeared as the consummation of the long trajectory of a counterrevolution running from 1789 to Hitler, Mathiez's idea of a historical continuity linking Jacobinism

---

157   This is the thesis convincingly argued by David Caute, *The Fellow-Travelers: Intellectual Friends of Communism* (New Haven: Yale University Press, 1988), 7, 264–81.

158   François Furet, *The Passing of an Illusion: The Idea of Communism in the Twentieth Century* (Chicago: University of Chicago Press, 1999), 224.

159   Lottman, *The Left Bank*, 92–6.

André Breton. Photo by
Henri Manuel (1927).

Victor Serge (1920s).

to Bolshevism was widely accepted. The two antipodal souls of the
Enlightenment would separate after 1945, when the united front had
become useless. Soviet communism and liberal democracy could share
a stretch of the road; this was the premise for the emergence of the
communist fellow travellers, but also for the confrontation between
the latter and the revolutionary intellectuals. In this respect, democratic writers who supported the USSR could even play a decisive
role as intermediaries between heretic and orthodox communists as
occurred in 1935, when Gide and Malraux interceded for the liberation
of Serge. This anti-fascist alliance lasted at least until the outbreak of
the Cold War, with a short but traumatic interruption between 1939
and 1941, the time of the German–Soviet Pact, which many intellectuals denounced as a betrayal.

Thomas Mann's Allegories

There is a literary masterpiece that astonishingly foreshadows this
conflictive but mutually accepted encounter between revolutionary
intellectuals and communist 'fellow travellers'; or, put differently, this
temporary compromise between revolution and liberal-democracy,
messianism and rationalism, emancipatory upheavals and linear

progress. It is, of course, Thomas Mann's novel *The Magic Mountain* (1923). Among the characters of the small community of sick men who haunt the sanatorium of Davos, in the Swiss mountains, on the eve of the Great War, we find Naphta, a fascinating figuration of the anarcho-communist Jewish intellectual, and Settembrini, the archetypal *Zivilisationsliterat*, who intransigently defends the principles of rationalism. Naphta and Settembrini stubbornly disagree on almost everything, but they are good friends. Naphta is an intriguing figure of the stranger, a marginal man. He is a Jew from Volinya, in Eastern Europe. His father was a ritual butcher, for whom to slaughter animals – Naphta had been familiar with the spectacle of blood since childhood – was the accomplishment of a religious duty. He was killed during a pogrom and Naphta recalls him with affection. Settembrini is a caricature of the Enlightener. Italian, inheritor of Risorgimento, he believes in progress, democracy and the rights of man. Like all democratic thinkers of the nineteenth century, he believes that social, economic, technological and moral progress are a single, entwined process. Progress is the law of history and its victory is ineluctable.

Naphta is an outcast. He has Jewish origins but converted to Catholicism and studied in a Jesuit college. He is a romantic, a conservative and a revolutionary at the same time, an apologist of theocracy and the Middle Ages and a propagandist of Bolshevism and international revolution. His arguments seem those of a conservative radical, until suddenly he adopts a communist posture. His ideal of communism is located in the past, as a form of classless, stateless, communitarian and egalitarian society. Mann depicts him this way:

> He was small, skinny, clean-shaven man, and so ugly – caustically, one could almost say, corrosively, ugly – that the cousins were astonished. Somehow everything about him was caustic: the aquiline nose dominating the face; the small, pursed mouth; the pale gray eyes behind thick lenses in the light frames of his glasses; even his studied silence, from which it was clear that his words would be caustic and logical.[160]

---

160   Thomas Mann, *The Magic Mountain*, trans. John E. Woods (New York: Knopf, 2005), 442.

Ernst Bloch (ca. 1920).

Georg Lukács as People's
Commissar of the Hungarian
Soviet Republic in 1919.

Naphta is an ambiguous figure of the apocalyptic rebel. Several scholars suggest that his portrait was inspired by Ernst Bloch or Georg
Lukács, a German and a Hungarian, two young Jewish intellectuals
whom Thomas Mann had known before the war.[161] At that time, both
of them were oriented towards romantic anti-capitalism and messianic
hopes: Lukács became People's Commissar of Culture under the
Hungarian Soviet Republic of Bela Kun in 1919; Bloch had devoted
many pages to the Middle Ages in *The Spirit of Utopia* (1918). As for
Settembrini, he is a parody of Thomas Mann's brother, Heinrich, who
embodied in Germany the ideas of the French Dreyfusards. Settembrini
believes in the principles of Enlightenment; in his view, two antipodal
forces struggle to conquer the world: despotism and law, tyranny and
freedom, superstition and science. But he is deeply convinced that the
march of history is unequivocally advancing towards universal fraternity grounded in the alliance between reason, science and law. Despite

---

161   See the entire second section of Judith Marcus, *Georg Lukács and Thomas
Mann: A Study in the Sociology of Literature* (Amherst: University of Massachusetts
Press, 1987); and Michael Löwy, 'Naphta or Settembrini? Lukács and Romantic
Anti-Capitalism', *New German Critique*, 42 (1987): 17–31.

the anachronism and naïvety of this contemporary Voltaire – the novel finishes with the outbreak of the Great War – Settembrini possesses something appealing and noble. He is a 'delicate man with brown hair and a black moustache twirled at the ends', wearing 'pastel checked trousers' and 'a wide-lapelled, double-breasted coat' that 'hung much too long', while his high collar are 'rough from frequent laundering'. His social condition is certainly modest, but his gestures are elegant, his voice 'precise and melodious', speaking perfectly German with an Italian accent. When he stops, he strikes 'a graceful pose' by 'propping himself on his cane and crossing his ankles'.[162] Although he wears second-hand, unfashionable clothes, his interlocutors immediately understand they have a gentleman before them. His face is a strange 'mixture of shabbiness and charm'.[163]

In *Geist und Tat* (1911), Heinrich Mann had called for the intervention of writers and scholars in the public eye in order to defend the rights of man and to democratize Imperial Germany. In the 1930s, as mentioned above, he became a 'fellow traveller' of the USSR, notably after publishing his essay *The Hate* (1933).[164] Thomas Mann, who had been a voice of 'conservative revolution' in his *Reflections of a Non-Political Man* (1918), joined his brother in the 1930s, thus turning himself into a *Zivilisationsliterat*. In the face of fascism, even Naphta and Settembrini could share a stretch of road.

Comintern Intellectuals

Among the many reasons that make the October Revolution a Copernican turn in intellectual history, one stands out: with the birth of the USSR, the outcast rebels of all continents found a homeland. For many of them, it was, once again, a precarious haven, a transitional experience, and a terrible disillusion; for others, it became a powerful anchorage or even a permanent abode. For all of them, this meant

---

162 Mann, *The Magic Mountain*, 54.

163 Ibid.

164 Heinrich Mann, 'Geist und Tat' (1911), in *Deutsche Intellektuelle*, 34–40; Heinrich Mann, *Der Hass: Deutsche Zeitgeschichte* (Frankfurt/Main: Fischer, 1987 [1933]).

an existential change. Firstly, it deeply affected their material status. In the former Tsarist empire, a generation of banned and perse-cuted intellectual exiles suddenly became the political, economic, managerial, cultural, and even military elite of a new state that had to be forged in the middle of a civil war. Just a few months before becoming chairman of the first Soviet government, Lenin was an exile in Zurich. One year before leading the Soviet delegation that negotiated the peace treaty with Germany in Brest-Litovsk, Trotsky was in New York writing for the socialist newspapers of the Russian émigrés, and Karl Radek was being hunted by the Austrian police because of his anti-war propaganda. Georgy Chicherin, who replaced Trotsky as head of the Commissariat of Foreign Affairs, heard about the Russian Revolution in a London prison, where he was serving time for his status as an antiwar activist, while Lev Kamenev, Lenin's deputy chairman in the Soviet government, had been liberated from his Siberian exile by the February Revolution. In Hungary, Bela Kun moved straight from prison to being the head of the Soviet republic. The list could be easily extended. For those intellectuals who joined the communist parties, Moscow became the new world capital. There they found material support, had strategic discussions, and met repre-sentatives of revolutionary movements from all continents. Outcasts in their own countries, they established an organic link with a political apparatus and a state institution which several anarchists found even more authoritarian than Marx's communism as criticized by Bakunin in the 1870s. In a certain way, it would not be wrong to say that the Bolsheviks – following in the footsteps of their French predecessors – put in power a sort of collective 'philosopher king', which quickly understood that, instead of instituting an ideal polis, it had to fight for survival. There is something paradoxical in this new dependence: since the end of the eighteenth century, philosophers and *hommes de lettres* had struggled to emancipate themselves – materially, ideologically and psychologically – from the patronage of the aristocratic courts; in the twentieth century, their most radical heirs accepted submission to a new court that they themselves had helped to build. And just like a century earlier, at the dawn of modern capitalism, those who did not accept this dependence found some spaces of freedom at the edges of a reified public sphere and in the culture industry of bourgeois countries. The 'world republic of letters' saved them.

Thus, many marginal intellectuals became 'professional revolutionaries', with a regular income, and some turned into apparatchiks. Anatoli Lunacharsky, the minister of education, who in 1917 was living precariously in Switzerland after having been expelled from France, exemplifies this metamorphosis. It certainly entailed a significant improvement of their material conditions and, of course, a dramatic reversal of their symbolic status, but this change does not fit into the canonical dichotomy between outsiders and established.[165] First, because there were almost no outsiders against whom the newly established could self-identify; and second, because the 'iron law of oligarchy' would appear later, under the form of what the Bolshevik diplomat (and former guest of Romanian prisons) Christian Rakovsky called 'the professional dangers of power'.[166] And even in the 1930s, a time in which social hierarchies had been restored and the high functionaries of the USSR benefited from real privileges, these advantages still remained quite relative when compared with those of the capitalist world. In the 1920s, high-ranking officials of the Soviet government lived in hotels and former aristocratic palaces converted into dormitories: a transitional arrangement in a time of egalitarian expectations positing the death of domesticity.[167] Things changed in the following decades. According to Yuri Slezkine, who has extensively investigated the life of the inhabitants of the 'house of government' – a massive ten-story building in the heart of Moscow with 500 apartments reserved for the Soviet nomenklatura from 1931 onwards – the living standards of most of them were definitely modest. In a letter written in 1936 during his travels in the Netherlands, Nikolai Bukharin, a former Soviet minister, expressed astonishment at the

---

165   Norbert Elias, *The Established and the Outsiders: A Sociological Enquiry into Community Problems* (London: F. Cass, 1965).

166   Christian Rakovsky, 'The "Professional Dangers" of Power' (1928), *Selected Writings on Opposition in the USSR 1923–1930*, ed. Gus Fagan (London: Allison & Busby, 1980), 126. On the 'iron law' of oligarchy, see Michels, *Political Parties*, 224–34.

167   Yuri Slezkine, *The House of Government: A Saga of the Russian Revolution* (Princeton: Princeton University Press, 2017), 318.

luxury of Dutch houses, a standard of living he had never encountered in Russia – 'all the rooms are large and spacious, and there is lots of storage space' – and the hotels: 'We have been put up in a terrific hotel. I have never lived in a hotel like this.'[168]

Joining the Party, however, was incontestably 'life-changing', according to the testimony of Eric Hobsbawm. He quotes the Italian communist leader Giorgio Amendola, the author of a beautiful auto-biography titled 'A Life Choice' (*Una scelta di vita*),[169] a choice that brought him nothing comfortable at all. It was rather the election of a life of sacrifice and constraint, in which bohemian freedoms and nonconformist behaviour coexisted with, but could also, very often, be replaced by discipline and a rigorous form of 'worldly asceticism'[170]. The true communist was not far different from the nineteenth-century Russian revolutionary depicted by Hans Magnus Enzensberger as 'rather a puritan than an epicurean', who 'led an extremely strict life, conscious, scrupulous, and marvellously modest'.[171] For most men and women, to accept this option meant more than renouncing an academic career or a respectable profession: it meant renouncing a family life. The moral rules of these 'revolutionary professionals' were, in many respects, much more strict and repressive than those of the bourgeois society they opposed: many women sent abroad on a political mission might find themselves separated from their young children for years. This pattern of conduct transformed the outsiders of the bourgeois world into complete insiders of a communism – whether the party or the Comintern – that possessed many features of a 'total institution'. But this was a peculiar type of 'open' total institution, 'both entry and exit being voluntary', where the submission to a superior power implied

---

168   Ibid., 494–5.

169   Eric Hobsbawm, *Interesting Times: A Twentieth-Century Life* (London: Allen Lane, 2002), 129. He refers to the first volume of the autobiography by the leader of the Italian communist party Giorgio Amendola, *Una scelta di vita* (Milan: Rizzoli, 1978).

170   This permanent swing between bohemianism and asceticism is well explained, giving several examples of female agents of the Comintern, by Brigitte Studer, *Reisende der Weltrevolution*, 211–20.

171   Hans Magnus Enzensberger, *Dreamers of the Absolute: Essays on Politics, Crime, and Culture* (Santa Fe: Radius Books, 1988), 160.

a set of internalized rules and a specific 'technology of the self'.[172] As many former communists explain, the CP appeared to its members as a kind of 'counter-society', a mixture of school, church, tribunal, barracks, and, for the 'revolutionary professionals',[173] international corporation. The Party, Edgar Morin wrote in his autobiography, ran a 'hierarchical universe as extraordinary and sacred as that of the Catholic Church, with its rituals, feasts, fervors, evils, customs, hypocrisies, and secrets'.[174] The Party had journals, newspapers and publishing houses to educate its members, as well as its own schools (the USSR created several universities for foreign communists, notably the Moscow International Lenin Institute). Its ideology cemented a community of believers gathered around the dogmas of a doctrine – Marxism-Leninism – supervised by an orthodox clerisy, which also administered justice through an iron law. As soldiers of a revolutionary army, communist activists submitted to a hierarchical system that implied discipline and, where appropriate, severe sanctions. In *History and Class Consciousness* (1923), Lukács defined discipline, far beyond its technical and practical aspects, as a dialectical synthesis between freedom and solidarity realized by the revolutionary organization: 'the discipline of the Communist Party, the unconditional absorption of the total personality in the praxis of the movement, was the only

---

172   Brigitte Studer, 'Communism as Existential Choice', in Silvio Pons and Stephen Smith (eds), *The Cambridge History of Communism* (Cambridge: Cambridge University Press, 2017), 506, 521. Studer refers to Erwing Goffman, *Asylums: Essays on the Social Situation of Mental Patients and Other Inmates* (Garden City, NY: Anchor Books, 1961), and to Michel Foucault, 'Technologies of the Self' (1984), *The Essential Works of Michel Foucault*, ed. Paul Rabinow (New York: The New Press, 1997), vol. 1, 223–51.

173   This definition, forged by the former guardian of the ideological orthodoxy of the PCF, Annie Kriegel, was mostly used during the Cold War to depict communist functionaries as agents of a Moscow conspiracy, but it possesses some heuristic value nevertheless. See Annie Kriegel, *Les communistes français* (Paris: Seuil, 1968). Many former communist intellectuals would transfer into anti-communism the mental habitus they achieved as party apparatchiks. On the former Stalinist intellectuals who became rabid anti-communists, see Deutscher, 'The Ex-Communist's Conscience' (1950), *Marxism, Wars, and Revolutions*, 49–59.

174   Edgar Morin, 'Préface' (1991), *Autocritique* (Paris: Seuil, 1991 [1959]), 10.

possible way of bringing about an authentic freedom.'[175] Lewis A.
Coser defined Bolshevism as a religious sect in the sociological sense
of Max Weber: an 'ecclesia pura' that operated as 'an exclusive body of
special religious performers'.[176] Considering the life of revolutionary
intellectuals such as Willi Münzenberg – the wandering organizer of
Comintern propaganda – Felix Dzerzhinsky – the inflexible chief
of the Cheka – or Larissa Reissner – whom Trotsky depicted as an
'Olympian goddess' who 'combined a subtle and ironical mind with
the courage of a warrior' – one could conclude that, ironically, they
rather matched the profile of the nihilist drawn by Nechaev in 1869:

> The revolutionary is a lost man; he has no interests of his own, no
> cause of his own, no feelings, no habits, no belongings; he does
> not even have a name. Everything in him is absorbed by a single,
> exclusive interest, a single thought, a single passion: the revolution.[177]

And communism became a transnational institution whose brain,
located in Moscow, organized missions all over the world. But unlike
in the 1920s, when internationalism meant coordinated liberation
struggles, over the following decade it largely meant the defence of
the USSR and the subordination of the action of all communist parties
to the prior interests of Soviet foreign policy.

Wondering about the consequences of possible membership of the
Communist Party, in January 1927 – when in Moscow he met the heads
of Soviet cultural institutions and daily visited his beloved Asja Lācis,
who worked for the Soviet theatre – Walter Benjamin evaluated the
pros and cons of a choice that would have put an end to his 'illegal
incognito among bourgeois authors'. He did not exclude this option,
but was aware of the obstacles that it could create for his research and
intellectual independence. On the one hand, it meant 'a solid position,
a mandate, even if only by implication', and an 'organized, guaranteed
contact with other people'; on the other, it also meant 'giving up your

---

175   Lukács, *History and Class Consciousness*, 320.

176   Lewis A. Coser, *Men of Ideas: A Sociologist's View* (New York: Free
Press, 1997 [1965]), 162.

177   Venturi, *Roots of Revolution*, 365.

private independence' and 'being able to project your own thoughts into something like a pre-established field of forces.'[178] In the end, he did not join the KPD, just as he never seriously considered the option of learning Hebrew and joining his friend Gershom Scholem in Jerusalem.

This existential microcosm was not the natural outcome of Marxist theory or Lenin's conspiratorial obsessions, even if Bolshevik centralism obviously played a role in building such an awful system. This was not the product of a malignant ideology, according to the fantasies of an anti-communist scholarship that brings to mind the anti-Semitic myth of an international Jewish plot. This was the final outcome of a militarization of the revolution that struggled to survive and build the USSR as an effective actor in the midst of an international civil war. Like Saturn, revolutions devour their children, and the intellectuals had a foremost place among the victims of Stalinism.

Needless to say, for a generation of intellectuals that had adopted Marxism as a revolutionary theory, this transformation brought an overwhelming spiritual impoverishment. As Hobsbawm reminds us in his autobiography, in the 1930s Marxism quickly became 'Dialectical and Historical Materialism', that is, a set of 'pedagogical simplifications' that turned it into a 'scientific' worldview 'in a rather nineteenth-century sense'.[179] In the interwar years, Western Marxism (Gramsci, Lukács, Korsch, and the Frankfurt School) as well as the most creative forms of anti-colonial Marxism (C. L. R. James or Mao Zedong) were produced outside of the control of the Comintern and the USSR. With very few exceptions – most notably Lukács – creative intellectuals could not think within the compelling structures of these 'total' institutions. In the 1930s, the paths of most revolutionary intellectuals dramatically divided: some accepted Stalinism, some embraced a form of heretical communism, some decided to stay outside the party to preserve their independence of thought, and some became anti-communists (a first wave in 1939, after the Soviet-German pact, and a second, much larger, wave with the Cold War). As for the

---

178   Walter Benjamin, *Moscow Diary*, ed. Gary Smith (Cambridge: Harvard University Press, 1986), 73.

179   Hobsbawm, *Interesting Times*, 96.

Russian and Eastern European revolutionary intellectuals, most of them perished between 1936 and 1938 in the purges. Six out of eight members of the first politburo of the Bolshevik Party created in November 1917 – Lev Kamenev, Nikolay Krestinsky, Leon Trotsky, Grigory Zinoviev, Andrei Bubnov, and Grigori Sokolnikov – were killed by Stalin between 1936 and 1941; only Lenin and Stalin himself died natural deaths.

In the 1930s, the Moscow trials became a breathtaking mirror of the conflicting tendencies and moral dilemmas that tore apart an entire generation of Bolsheviks and, indirectly, of revolutionary intellectuals on a global scale. Defending a communist ideal that transcended individual interests, their moral commitment was permanently threatened by two distinct drifts. The first was ethical extremism, which posited absolute values in the name of which any social, political, and even human consequence could be considered as minor and acceptable and any compromise as betrayal and a despicable form of realpolitik.[180] Bakunin and Nechaev had fixed its rules in a sort of revolutionary law:

> Hard toward himself, he [the revolutionary] must be hard toward others also. All the tender and effeminate emotions of kinship, friendship, love, gratitude, and even honor, must be stifled in him by a cold and single-minded passion for the revolutionary cause. There exists for him only one delight, one consolation, one reward and one gratification: the success of the revolution. Night and day, he must have but one thought, one aim: merciless destruction. In cold-blooded and tireless pursuit of this aim, he must be prepared both to die himself and to destroy with his own hands everything that stands in the way of its achievement.[181]

The second drift was a form of self-alienation in regards to a party viewed as the embodiment of revolutionary ethics. After 1917, this tendency prevailed and increasingly overwhelmed any realm of

---

180   According to Max Weber, this corresponded with the 'ethics of the Sermon of the Mount' that he attributed to Karl Liebknecht and the Spartakus League. See 'The Profession and Vocation of Politics', 357.

181   Nechaev, 'Catechism of the Revolutionist', 72. See also Venturi, *Roots of Revolution*, 365; Joll, *The Anarchists*, 77–8.

individual autonomy. According to Lukács, 'the true strength of the party is moral.'[182] The frightful spectacle of the Moscow trials, with a generation of brilliant, valuable, generous and often courageous revolutionary intellectuals 'confessing' to the most appalling imaginary crimes, depicting themselves as traitors, sheds light not only on the destruction of communist ethics by Stalinism but also on the extreme consequences of a dangerous philosophical and political theory that viewed the communist party as the embodiment of ethics itself. Confronted with the tragic outcomes of this practice of self-alienation, several communists rediscovered the virtues of radical humanism. Victor Serge's autobiography contains this sentence:

> Defense of Man. Respect for Man. Man must be given his rights, his security, his value. Without these, there is no socialism. Without these, all is false, bankrupt, and spoiled. I mean: man, whoever he is, be he the meanest of men – 'class enemy', son or grandson of a bourgeois, I do not care. It must never be forgotten that a human being is a human being. Every day, everywhere, before my very eyes this is being forgotten, and it is the most revolting and anti-socialist thing that could happen.[183]

Conclusion: An Ideal-Type

Across a century and a half, the revolutionary intellectual type underwent many changes by constantly swinging between bohemianism and partisanship. This is why, conveniently revised, Carl Schmitt's definition of the 'partisan' could help in drawing its portrait, even if this inevitably remains an approximate and unsatisfactory ideal-type. His *Theory of the Partisan* (1963) does not deal with the question of the intelligentsia, but it carefully analyses the writings of several thinkers and explicitly includes revolutions in its scrutiny by mentioning 'civil

---

182   Lukács, *History and Class Consciousness*, 42. On Lukács's 'ethical extremism', see Michael Löwy, *Georg Lukacs: From Romanticism to Bolshevism* (London: Verso, 1979), Chapter 3.

183   Victor Serge, *Memoirs of a Revolutionary*, foreword by Adam Hochschild (New York: New York Review of Books Editions, 2012 [1946]), 327.

war as a class struggle', a situation in which the main goal of the rebels is 'the elimination of the government of the enemy state'.[184] In other words, partisan warfare is a conflict in which the core of the political – the absolute clash between friend and enemy – finds its most complete expression, exactly analogous to the confrontation between revolution and counterrevolution. Significantly, Schmitt's essay also refers to Lenin as the archetype of the 'professional revolutionary' who establishes the 'alliance of philosophy with the partisan'.[185]

The partisans appear during a civil war, an anomic conflict that does not respect any rules, in which the laws of war are abandoned and the combatants try to destroy each other. When they are captured, they do not expect to be treated as military prisoners: they may be executed as criminals. Partisan warfare clearly expresses the conflict between legality and legitimacy: for the legal power, the opponents are bandits and criminals; for the partisans, the legal authority has lost all legitimacy and simply usurps its power. In a civil war, the belligerents do not consider each other as legitimate adversaries, rather as irreducible enemies: the *iustus hostis* has been replaced by the *inimicus*. Revolutionary intellectuals do not seek to compromise or regulate peaceful relationships with capitalism; they work to destroy capitalism. If they negotiate peace treaties or truces – as the Bolsheviks did at Brest-Litovsk – this is only one step in a long-term war. And even many avant-garde artists – we saw this in Chapter Two when considering Diego Rivera's guerrilla warfare against capitalist patronage – depict themselves as aesthetic partisans.

Thus, a portrait of the revolutionary intellectual should summarize some essential but not always coexisting and sometimes conflictual features: an intense ideological and political commitment; an anti-capitalist ethos; a free-floating condition of bohemian déclassement; and a cosmopolitan behaviour often combined with a telluric character. Let me describe each more closely.

Ideological commitment. Revolutionary intellectuals elaborated critical ideas for a radical transformation of society and the overthrow

---

184   Schmitt, *Theory of the Partisan*, 21.

185   Ibid., 36. See Carl Schmitt, *The Concept of the Political*, ed. George Schwab (Chicago: University of Chicago Press, 2007).

of the state. They dealt with different realms of knowledge – from economy to politics, from philosophy and history to aesthetics – but were not 'free thinkers' or isolated nonconformist writers, since their ideas were consciously committed to a political project of liberation: anarchism, socialism, communism; gender, racial or national emancipation.

Utopianism. This ideological and political commitment had a strong utopian dimension that could transform their movements into messianic communities. Critical thought provided arguments for building an alternative society and nourished an imagination projected towards the future. This utopian drift also coloured their approach to the past and propitiated a vision of history as a long march of emancipatory struggles. This made the intellectuals the guardians of revolutionary tradition and the carriers of a collective memory of rebellion.

Moral commitment. This ideological and political choice was grounded in an anti-capitalist ethos that could take either a hedonistic or a sacrificial form. It merged free love and 'worldly asceticism', the radical rejection of all bourgeois conventions of respectability and a puritanism that identified revolution with a monastic way of life, bohemian communitarianism and a sacrificial condition of discipline and self-denial. The rift between the oppressed and the rulers corresponded with the ethical dichotomy between good and evil, virtue and selfishness. A revolutionary life was antipodal to established customs and dominant values, perceived as an organized system of injustice. It enacted a specific relationship between the ethics of conviction and those of responsibility. The ethics of conviction accepted – or even prescribed – the use of violence as a tool of emancipation, and the ethics of responsibility subordinated individual interests to a superior collective concern.

Bohemian marginality. Just as the partisan is an irregular combatant who does not belong to a formal army and does not wear a uniform, so too the revolutionary intellectual did not belong to academia, did not seek institutional recognition, and rejected the symbolic markers of a conventional career. Regardless of social origins, he or she was a déclassé or bohemian thinker, writer or polemicist. Revolutionary intellectuals tended to live a precarious life with no regular income,

sometimes writing for periodicals on the margins of the culture industry, more frequently collaborating with the publications of the socialist
and revolutionary movements. In most cases, the material support
they received from the USSR did not render them 'established'. Revolution always attracted all kinds of outcasts: feminists, Jews, blacks,
avant-garde artists and writers.

Mobility. The mobility of revolutionary intellectuals followed the
circulation of avant-garde and critical ideas rather than an academic
map. Its tropism was not the evolution of the university job market
but rather the dynamic of class struggle. Mobility resulted from both
a lack of solid social attachments – what Karl Mannheim called the
'free-floating' status of intellectuals (*freischwebende Intelligenz*)[186] – and
state repression, which forced them into long periods of exile. Whether
chosen or suffered, this mobility was a source of cosmopolitanism that
led revolutionary intellectuals to think beyond national boundaries.

Cosmopolitanism. Distinguishing so many anarchist, socialist and
communist intellectuals from 1848 to the Cuban Revolution, cosmopolitanism very often merged with or was replaced by a political
commitment rooted in a national context. The case of Ho Chi Minh
shows that cosmopolitan rebels could reveal a profound telluric character, and the death of Trotsky in his Mexican exile equally demonstrates
that a bohemian transformed into the charismatic chief of the Red
Army could return to his original status of rootless cosmopolitan.
From Blanqui to Lenin, doctrinaires tried to tailor uncomfortable
uniforms that in many cases did not fit the existential trajectories of
free spirits passionately attached to the independence of their critical
thought. Legend has it that, in 1956, when Soviet tanks overthrew the
council government in Budapest, an officer asked Georg Lukács to
hand over his weapon and the latter gave him his pen. The old revolutionary philosopher who had endured the repression of Admiral
Horthy and the Moscow trials had kept his sense of humour, but his
gesture had a deeper symbolic meaning. Revolutionary intellectuals
are troublemakers.

---

186   Mannheim, *Ideologie und Utopie*, 135.

The Revolutionary Intellectual

Intense ideological and political commitment

Anarchism / Socialism / Communism

Utopianism

Poles of Anti-capitalist Ethos:

Free love versus *Worldly asceticism*

Rejection of bourgeois values versus *Party discipline*

Unconventionality versus *Sacrificial vocation*

Ethics of conviction versus *Ethics of responsibility*

Individualism versus *Collectivism*

Independence of thinking versus *Orthodoxy*

Bohemianism:

Déclassé status and social precarity

Pariah status: Blackness / Coloniality / Feminism / Jewishness

Anti-academicism: dichotomy outsiders / established

Cosmopolitanism:

Mobility: emigration, exile

Rooted cosmopolitanism / Telluric character / Rootless cosmopolitanism

Revolutionary Intellectuals
Nineteenth Century (Generations 1800s–50s)

	High School	University	Teaching	Journalism	Prison	Exile	Revolution	Power	Killed
M. Bakunin 1814		•		•	•	•	•		
A. Blanqui 1805		•		•	•	•	•		
C. Cafiero 1846		•		•	•	•			
D. De Leon 1852		•	•	•					
F. Engels 1820		•		•	•	•	•		
V. Figner 1852		•			•	•	•		
J. Guesde 1845		•		•	•	•			
A. Herzen 1812		•		•		•			
S. Katayama 1859		•		•	•	•			
K. Kautsky 1854		•	•	•		•	•		
P. Kropotkin 1842		•		•	•	•			
An. Labriola 1843		•	•	•					
P. Lafargue 1842		•		•	•	•	•		
F. Lassalle 1825		•		•	•		•		
P. Lavrov 1823		•		•	•	•	•		
Léo 1824				•		•	•		
E. Malatesta 1853		•		•	•	•			
K. Marx 1818		•		•	•	•	•		
F. Mehring 1846		•	•	•			•		
L. Michel 1830		•		•	•	•	•	•	
W. Morris 1834		•	•	•					
S. Nechaev 1847		•			•				•
G. Plekhanov 1856		•		•	•	•	•		
P.-J. Proudhon 1809		•		•	•		•		
J.-E. Reclus 1830		•	•	•	•	•	•		
J. Rizal 1861		•		•	•				•
G. Sorel 1847		•		•					
K. Shusui 1871		•		•	•	•			•
F. Tristan 1803		•	•			•			
J. Vallès 1832			•	•	•	•	•	•	
V. Zasulich 1851		•		•	•	•	•		
C. Zetkin 1857		•		•	•	•	•		

Revolutionary Intellectuals
Twentieth Century (Tsarist Empire: Generation 1870s–90s)

	University	Teaching	Journalism	Prison	Exile	Revolution	Power	Killed
A. Bogdanov 1873	•	•	•	•	•	•		
N. Bukharin 1888	•	•	•	•	•	•	•	•
V. Chernov 1873	•	•	•		•	•	•	
F. Dzerzhinsky 1877	•		•	•	•	•	•	
L. Jogiches 1867	•		•	•	•	•		•
L. Kamenev 1883	•		•	•	•	•	•	•
A. Kollontai 1872	•		•	•	•	•	•	
V. Lenin 1870	•		•	•	•	•	•	
A. Lunacharsky 1875	•	•	•	•	•	•	•	
J. Martov 1873	•		•	•	•	•		
K. Radek 1885	•	•	•	•	•	•	•	•
D. Riazanov 1870	•	•	•	•	•	•		•
J. Stalin 1878	•		•	•	•	•	•	
I. Rubin 1886	•	•	•	•	•	•		•
B. Savinkov 1879	•		•	•	•	•	•	•
Y. Sverdlov 1885	•		•	•	•	•	•	
L. Trotsky 1879	•		•	•	•	•	•	•
Volin 1882	•		•	•	•	•		
G. Zinoviev 1883	•		•	•	•	•	•	•

Revolutionary Intellectuals
Twentieth Century (Central Europe: Generation 1870s–90s)

	University	Teaching	Journalist	Prison	Exile	Revolution	Power	Killed
M. Adler 1873	•	•	•		•	•		
O. Bauer 1881	•		•		•	•		
E. Bloch 1885	•	•	•		•	•		
R. Fischer 1895	•		•		•	•		
P. Frölich 1884	•		•	•	•	•		
H. Grossmann 1881	•	•	•		•	•		
K. Korsch 1886	•	•			•	•		
B. Kun 1886	•		•	•	•	•	•	•
G. Landauer 1870	•		•	•		•		•
P. Levi 1883	•		•			•		
E. Leviné 1883	•		•			•	•	•
K. Liebknecht 1871	•		•			•		•
G. Lukács 1885	•	•	•	•	•	•	•	
R. Luxemburg 1871	•		•	•		•		
H. Marcuse 1898	•	•			•	•		
W. Münzenberg 1889	•		•		•	•		•
E. Mühsam 1878	•		•	•		•	•	•
F. Pfemfert 1879	•		•		•	•		
W. Reich 1897	•	•			•	•		
R. Rosdolsky 1898	•	•	•		•	•		
W. Scholem 1895	•		•	•		•		•
A. Thalheimer 1884	•	•	•		•	•	•	
E. Varga 1879	•	•	•		•	•	•	

Revolutionary Intellectuals
Twentieth Century (Western Europe: Generation 1880s–1900s)

	University	Teaching	Journalism	Prison	Exile	Revolution	Power	Killed
L. Aragon 1897	•		•					
A. Bordiga 1889	•		•	•				
A. Breton 1896	•		•		•			
C. Cahun 1894	•		•	•				
G. Friedmann 1902	•	•	•					
A. Gramsci 1891	•		•	•				
D. Guérin 1904	•		•	•				
H. Lefebvre 1901	•	•	•					
P. Naville 1904	•	•	•	•				
A. Nin 1892	•		•			•		•
P. Nizan 1905	•		•					
S. Pankhurst 1882	•		•	•	•			
A. Pannekoek 1873	•	•	•					
P. Pascal 1890	•	•	•					
B. Péret 1899	•		•		•			
G. Politzer	•	•	•	•	•			•
H. Roland-Holst 1888	•		•		•			
A. Rosmer 1877			•					
V. Serge 1890			•	•	•	•		
P. Togliatti 1893	•		•	•	•		•	

	University	Teaching	Journalism	Prison	Exile	Revolution	Power	Killed
A. Berkman, 1870	•		•	•	•			
L. B. Boudin 1874	•		•					
L. Bryant 1885	•		•					
J. Burnham 1905	•	•	•					
M. Eastman 1883	•		•					
L. Fraina 1892	•		•					
S. Frondizi 1907	•	•	•					•
A. Giovannitti 1884	•		•	•				
M. Gold 1894	•		•					
E. Goldman 1869	•		•	•		•		
J. Ingenieros 1877	•	•	•					
J. C. Mariátegui 1894			•					
J. A. Mella 1903	•		•	•	•			•
An. Ponce 1898	•	•	•		•			
Ph. Rahv 1908	•	•	•					
J. Reed 1887	•		•	•		•		

Revolutionary Intellectuals
Twentieth Century (Colonial World: Generations 1880s–1900s)

	High School	University	Teaching	Journalism	Prison	Exile	Revolution	Power	Killed
A. Césaire 1913		•		•					
Chen Duxiu 1880		•		•	•		•		
Deng Xiaoping 1904		•					•	•	
C. L. R. James 1901		•		•	•	•			
Ho Chi Minh 1890		•		•	•	•	•	•	
Mao Zedong 1893		•		•			•	•	
T. Malaka 1897		•		•	•	•	•		•
C. McKay 1889		•		•		•			
G. Padmore 1903		•		•					
Li Dazhao 1889		•	•	•			•		•
La. Senghor 1889				•					
M. N. Roy 1887		•		•	•	•			
Ta Thu Thao 1906		•		•	•	•	•		•
Zhou Enlai 1898		•					•	•	

Chapter 5

Between Freedom and Liberation

Revolution is the war of liberty against its enemies.
> Robespierre, 'On the Principles of
> Revolutionary Government' (1793)

Freedom only for the supporters of the government, only for the members of one party – however numerous they may be – is no freedom at all. Freedom is always and exclusively freedom for the one who thinks differently. Not because of any fanatical concept of 'justice' but because all that is instructive, wholesome and purifying in political freedom depends on this essential characteristic, and its effectiveness vanishes when 'freedom' becomes a special privilege.
> Rosa Luxemburg, *The Russian Revolution* (1918)

Genealogies

Thinking freedom (what political philosophy has been doing for centuries) and historicizing it (which means interpreting concrete historical experiences) are not exactly the same thing, and the relationship between freedom and revolution – a liberating action – may underscore this discrepancy. There are many genealogies of freedom, and this not only because of its different paths but also because of the plurality of its conceptions. Viewed from a Marxist or a classical liberal perspective, the paths of freedom dramatically diverge. In fact, freedom is undoubtedly one of the most ambiguous and polysemic words of our political lexicon. Everybody utters it, but nobody gives it the same meaning. Since the time of Enlightenment, freedom is an almost universally accepted ideal, but its definitions are highly diverse – in many cases incompatible – and its conceptual field is full of paradoxes. In his *Considerations on France* (1797), Joseph de Maistre, the darkest apologist of the Old Regime whom we already met in a previous chapter, suggested a legitimist definition: liberty, he wrote, 'is the action of free beings under a divine hand. Freely slaves.'[1] For three centuries, the slave trade between Africa, Europe, and the Americas was carried out by ships that defiantly displayed names such as 'Friendship', 'Brotherhood' and … 'Liberty'.[2] And things did not change in the twentieth century. In their famous essay, 'The Doctrine of Fascism' (1932), Giovanni Gentile and Benito Mussolini defined liberty as a synonym of totalitarianism. 'Fascism stands for liberty,' they wrote, 'and for the only liberty worth having, the liberty of the state and of the individual within the State.'[3] Therefore, fascism understood as a totalitarian state was the only true accomplishment of liberty. In fascism, they explained, individuals were deprived of 'all useless and possibly harmful freedoms', but their fundamental liberty was preserved since, they concluded, 'the deciding power in this question cannot be the individual, but the State alone.'[4]

Freedom was also inscribed in the USSR Constitution of 1936, the year of the first Moscow Trial, where it was identified with the power of the communist party. In *The Revolution Betrayed* (1937), Leon Trotsky observed that the new charter 'guaranteed' many 'freedoms' – of speech, press, assembly, and street marches – but in fact these 'freedoms' took the form 'either of a heavy muzzle or of shackles upon the hands and feet'. Thus, the true meaning of the Soviet law was exactly the opposite of its formal assessment. Prefiguring George Orwell's *1984*, Trotsky pointed out that freedom of the press meant

---

1 Joseph de Maistre, *Considerations on France*, ed. Richard A. Lebrun (Cambridge: Cambridge University Press, 1994), 3.

2 Vincent Harding, *There is a River: The Black Struggle for Freedom in America* (New York: Vintage, 1981), 3.

3 Benito Mussolini, 'The Doctrine of Fascism', *Fascism: Doctrine and Institutions* (Rome: Ardita, 1935), 11.

4 Ibid.

'a continuation of the fierce advance-censorship whose chains are held by the Secretariat of a Central Committee whom nobody has elected', freedom of thinking 'the crude and ignorant command of science, literature and art', and freedom of assembly 'the obligation of certain groups of the population to appear at meetings summoned by the authorities for the adoption of resolutions prepared in advance.' The result was that, under the new constitution, thousands of people were put 'in prisons and concentration camps for crimes against the dogma of infallibility'.[5] The meaning of freedom in Stalin's Constitution was, Trotsky concluded, saturated through and through 'with the spirit of usurpation and cynicism'.[6] But Stalin was only the paroxysmal expression of a general tendency and his efforts to reinterpret freedom found many worthy competitors. One of the most powerful international agencies of conservative propaganda in the postwar years was called the 'Congress for Cultural Freedom'.[7] It was in the name of the 'free world' and the defence against the threat of communism that the State Department of the United States organized or supported putsches and military dictatorships in Iran (1953), Guatemala (1954), Indonesia (1965) and Chile (1973), just to name a few examples.

Most handbooks of political philosophy start with the canonical distinction fixed by Benjamin Constant in 1819 between the liberty of the ancients compared with that of the moderns, which Isaiah Berlin reformulated as 'positive' and 'negative' liberties: liberty *to* versus liberty *from*.[8] The first was collective and made of active participation in public life: liberty to decide the future of the state. The second was individual and grounded in the capacity of citizens to organize their own life without external interference, free from all coercion. The first supposed a political community, the second a society of atomized individuals – a market society. Understood as the opposite

---

5   Leon Trotsky, *The Revolution Betrayed: What Is the Soviet Union and Where Is it Going?* (New York: Pathfinder Press, 1972), 224.

6   Ibid., 232.

7   See Peter Coleman, *The Liberal Conspiracy: The Congress for Cultural Freedom and the Struggle for the Mind in Postwar Europe* (New York: Free Press, 1989).

8   Isaiah Berlin, *Four Essays on Liberty* (New York: Oxford University Press, 1970).

of collectivism, negative liberty does not need democracy. According to Constant, the aim of representative institutions was not to embody popular sovereignty but rather to favour the free development of individual initiative and entrepreneurship. As he explained at the end of his essay, the 'representative system' was

> nothing but an organization by means of which a nation charges a few individuals to do what it can't or doesn't want to do itself. ... The representative system is a mandate given to a certain number of men by the mass of the people who want their interests to be defended but don't have the time to defend them constantly themselves.[9]

According to this vision, the freedom of owners clearly prevails over the democracy of citizens. In his neoliberal manifesto, *The Road to Serfdom* (1944), Friedrich A. Hayek wrote that 'the system of private property is the most important guarantee of freedom'[10] and explained that, long before Hitler, the germ of totalitarianism had been introduced by socialism, a political current whose hostility to private property threatened all modern liberties. In his view, freedom meant property and totalitarianism was the most accomplished form of collectivism. In his introduction, he stressed that 'the rise of fascism and Nazism was not a reaction against the socialist trends of the preceding period but a necessary outcome of those tendencies.'[11] Democracy, he added, 'is essentially a means, a utilitarian device for safeguarding internal peace and individual freedom'.[12] As such, it was certainly not 'infallible' and could become 'as oppressive as the worst dictatorship'.[13] Insofar as 'distributive democracy' was the high road to serfdom, an effective antitotalitarian struggle meant first of all the defence

---

9 Benjamin Constant, 'The Liberty of the Ancients Compared with That of the Moderns', *Political Writings*, ed. Biancamaria Fontana (Cambridge: Cambridge University Press, 1988), 325.

10 Friedrich A. Hayek, *The Road to Serfdom* (Chicago: Chicago University Press, 1944), 103.

11 Ibid., 3–4.

12 Ibid., 70.

13 Ibid.

of civilization, or 'men's submission to the impersonal forces of the market'.[14] Thus, fighting the Axis powers was not enough: Hayek suggested also fighting against 'the totalitarians in our midst', people who, like John Maynard Keynes, prescribed dangerous measures of state intervention in the economy.[15] Based on such premises, the history of freedom would become a triumphal march of property and market competition, finally inscribed into the mental habitus and conduct of life of the neoliberal *homo economicus*. Drawing on such a genealogy, freedom has today triumphed with the World Bank and the IMF.

But there is also a radically different genealogy of freedom that rejects property. Its starting point was probably Rousseau's *Discourse on Inequality* (1754), whose second part started with a famous incipit:

> The first man who, having enclosed a piece of ground, thought of saying 'This is mine', and found people simple enough to believe him, was the true founder of civil society. How many crimes, wars, murders; how much misery and horror the human race would have been spared if someone had pulled up the stakes and filled in the ditch and cried out to his fellow men: 'Beware of listening to this impostor. You are lost if you forget that the fruits of the earth belong to everyone and that the earth itself belongs to no one!'[16]

The conception of freedom grounded in the criticism of property found its most significant moments under modern capitalism. In 1842, the young Karl Marx wrote several articles for the *Rheinische Zeitung* devoted to enclosures in the Rhineland: for centuries, deadwood in the forests had been freely available as a common material and the peasants had taken it for their own needs, but with the conversion of the forests into private property they had suddenly become 'thieves'. Property had destroyed an ancestral freedom on which peasants had built their collective life. Marx's arguments were compelling but hardly

---

14   Ibid., 204.

15   Ibid., Chapter 13.

16   Jean-Jacques Rousseau, *A Discourse on Inequality*, ed. Maurice Cranston (London: Penguin, 1984), 109.

new, since his critique of property had illustrious ancestors, from the Levellers – who had discussed the issue in their Putney debates[17] – to the Jacobins: the conflict between property and the 'right to existence' was at the heart of the drafting of the French Constitution of 1793. Marx strongly opposed the Rhineland law, which in the name of private property had transformed the gathering of fallen wood into theft. He demanded 'for the poor a *customary right*' that should be universally extended as an elementary human right, aiming to protect the 'lowest, propertyless and elemental mass'.[18]

As the French philosopher Daniel Bensaïd has pointed out regarding these debates, there are some striking analogies between the past and the present.[19] The enclosures of the end of the eighteenth century in the United Kingdom and the early 1840s in Germany are astonishingly similar to the growing destruction of the 'commons' (of both nature and culture) through its privatization and subjection to the law of the market economy since the end of the twentieth century. Today, a natural resource like water has been appropriated and has become a commodity sold by private companies. Biotechnologies, genomics, patent rights, and different forms of intellectual property are means to the dispossession of human beings, exactly as the enclosures of two centuries ago marked a crucial moment in the process of the accumulation of capital. As Karl Polanyi explained in *The Great Transformation* (1944), far from being 'neutral' or 'natural', market society was built as a planned dismantling of commonalities that had their own forms of freedom. Reversing Hayek's arguments, Polanyi emphasized that so-called nineteenth-century civilization had not been destroyed by the joint attacks of right- or left-wing barbarians obsessed by the idea of a planned economy. In his view, fascism was the final product of

---

17   See Ellen Meiksins Wood, *Liberty & Property: A Social History of Western Political Thought from Renaissance to Enlightenment* (London, New York: Verso, 2012), 231–240.

18   Karl Marx, 'Debates on the Law on Thefts of Wood' (1842), *MECW*, 1: 230.

19   See Daniel Bensaïd, *The Dispossessed: Karl Marx's Debates on Wood Theft and the Right of the Poor*, ed. Robert Nichols (Minneapolis: University of Minnesota Press, 2021), Chapter III.

the illusion of a self-regulated market society that, having entered into an insuperable conflict with democracy, decided to resolve the contradiction by destroying democracy itself. Preserving 'freedom in a complex society' – this was the conclusion of his essay – meant questioning the dogma of free-market capitalism: 'For the origins of the cataclysm [the Second World War and fascism] we must turn to the rise and fall of the market economy.'[20] Abandoned to its own demons, capitalism ineluctably put freedom in danger.

Many scholars have stressed the 'unique twin birth' of classical liberalism and racial slavery.[21] Insofar as property was its ultimate substratum, liberty was not incompatible with either colonialism or slavery: colonialism meant the appropriation of land belonging to no one (*terra nullius*) and slavery transformed black forced labourers into the property of slave owners.[22] As Susan Buck-Morss has observed, most Enlightenment thinkers considered slavery as a useful metaphor to depict coercion as opposed to freedom, but for them it was a purely discursive form.[23] Understood as a rhetorical figure borrowed from Antiquity, it did not conflict with a historical reality made of slave trade and slave labour. John Locke prized freedom and condemned slavery as a 'vile and miserable estate of man', but he had no qualms about being a shareholder of the Royal African Company, a British agency involved in the enslavement of black Africans to labour on Virginia plantations.[24] It is also significant that the abolition of slavery did not result in the financial compensations of its victims but rather in reparation agreements with the slaveholders. It is obvious that a

---

20   Karl Polanyi, *The Great Transformation: The Political and Economic Origins of Our Time* (Boston: Beacon Press, 1957), 29.

21   See the second chapter of Domenico Losurdo, *Liberalism: A Counter-History* (London, New York: Verso, 2011).

22   See Ellen Meiksins Wood, *Empire of Capital* (London, New York: Verso, 2003), 96–8.

23   See Susan Buck-Morss, *Hegel, Haiti, and Universal History* (Pittsburgh: Pittsburgh University Press, 2009), 21–6, and also David B. Davis, *Problems of Slavery in the Age of Revolution* (Ithaca, NY: Cornell University Press, 1975), 263.

24   The best study on the topic is Matthieu Renault, *L'Amérique de John Locke. L'expansion coloniale de la politique européenne* (Paris: Éditions Amsterdam, 2014). See also Buck-Morss, *Hegel, Haiti, and Universal History*, 28.

genealogy of freedom written from the perspective of both slaves and colonized peoples would put into question many of the general assumptions of classical liberalism.

Unveiling the hypocrisy and deception of capitalist freedom was, throughout the nineteenth century, one of the topoi of left-wing radicalism. One of its targets – a powerful visual representation of freedom as capitalist prosperity – was the Statue of Liberty, whose unveiling took place on Liberty Island, New York, in 1886. This was the time, at the end of Reconstruction and the enforcement of segregation laws by the US Supreme Court, when lynching in the Southern states reached its peak. The black-owned *Cleveland Gazette* covered the ceremony of dedication of the Statue with a sarcastic editorial arguing that, installed in the country of the Ku Klux Klan and racial hatred, this symbol of liberty 'enlightening the world' was 'ridiculous in the extreme'.[25] During the Great War, the event that announced the end of the nineteenth-century wave of European immigration and the emergence of the United States as the hegemonic world power, Alexandra Kollontai, the famous Russian socialist then exiled in New York, described the statue as an anachronistic survival of the past, 'an old and forgotten legend'. This symbol had come too late, when the American myth was exhausted:

> For our grandfathers and great-grandfathers, the New World was truly the land of freedom. Here, whatever they had been in ageing Europe, they felt themselves to be the sons and equal citizens of a free country. Here they could pray to their God according to their own beloved rites. Here they could still believe that a man could forge his own happiness, wealth and destiny, with his own hands. Here the fairy of success still freely beckoned to unsettled lands and fruitful plains, to barren mountains concealing gold.[26]

---

25 Quoted in Edward Berenson, *The Statue of Liberty: A Transatlantic Story* (New Haven: Yale University Press, 2012), 98.

26 Alexandra Kollontai, 'The Statue of Liberty' (1916), *Selected Articles and Speeches* (Moscow: Progress, 1984).

But the tale of American freedom was over and now the statue appeared small and meaningless against the imposing New York skyline. The realm of freedom had become the land of capital:

> The skyscrapers have robbed her of her halo, and now it is no longer she who soars above the bay of this international city, no longer she who lights the way into the international port, into the New World. Millions of lights from the windows of the fifty-storey skyscraper office-blocks eclipse the light of the goddess of Liberty. The grey giants look out derisively over the narrow New York streets which, jammed with businessmen and their clerks, thread their way far below like canyon streams between cliff walls. And it is these solid walls of stone, the safe refuge of the kings of American capital, which now more completely express the 'spirit' that reigns over the continent of Columbus than the pitiful, shrunken, green statue that seems to be embarrassed.[27]

Representations

The tension between freedom and liberation was one of the most significant features of nineteenth-century culture, the age of 'bourgeois revolutions'. Carried out by the 'People' – the popular classes of early industrial capitalism – these upheavals had brought the bourgeoisie to power as the new ruling class in Europe. But, in this time of the 'persistence of the Old Regime', neither the industrial and financial elites nor their intellectual and political representatives participated in the uprisings or erected barricades.[28] In the first half of 1830, François Guizot, the future embodiment of the French July Monarchy, was still pondering how to reform the kingdom of Charles X. He passively observed the sudden and unexpected revolutionary wave that

---

27   Ibid. On the symbolic metamorphosis of this monument, see Rudolph Vecoli, 'The Lady and the Huddled Masses: The Statue of Liberty as a Symbol of Immigration', in Wilton S. Dillon and Neil G. Kotler (eds), *The Statue of Liberty Revisited*, (Washington, DC: Smithsonian Institution Press, 1994).

28   See Ellen Meiksins Wood, *The Origin of Capitalism: A Longer View* (London, New York: Verso, 2002), 116–21.

established bourgeois liberal institutions. The actors of the 'three glorious days' of 27–29 July 1830 were skilled workers who formed the Parisian people: craftsmen, carpenters, locksmiths, cobblers, stonemasons, print workers, etc. A small number of students were involved in the movement as it grew, as well as a significant section of the National Guard that gradually shifted to the side of the insurgents, without however playing a leading role. Once solidly installed in power, the bourgeoisie faced the difficult task of appropriating symbolically an event it had neither inspired nor led. The July Column on place de la Bastille, built between 1835 and 1840, finally merged with the innumerable monuments to national glory scattered across the French capital; its crowning statue, Augustin Dumont's 'Spirit of Freedom', is remarkably 'neutral' in both appearance and meaning.

This contradiction between a domesticated bourgeois freedom and the memory of a liberation movement – or, to put it differently, this transition from the July Revolution to the July monarchy – found a significant expression in Eugène Delacroix's famous painting *Liberty Leading the People*. The object of divergent interpretations, its intrinsic ambiguity probably explains why, after being exhibited at the Salon of 1831 and purchased by King Louis-Philippe, it was quickly withdrawn from public display and remained hidden until 1848, before being canonized under the Third Republic, which transferred it to the Louvre Museum. Described by its author as an 'actual allegory' (*allégorie réelle*),[29] this imposing painting is dominated by the figure of Liberty, a bare-breasted woman who leads the insurgent people across the remains of a barricade. She holds a gun and the tricolour, the flag that during the July uprising had reappeared and replaced the white banner of the Bourbon dynasty. Beyond her lie the corpses of three insurgents, an almost naked worker and two soldiers, while a third young rebel kneels before her with a gesture of imploring devotion. Behind her the battle is raging. She is surrounded by three other actors of the uprising: an adolescent wielding a pair of pistols and two ordinary workingmen. Whereas one is brandishing a sword and is still in his work clothes, the other, armed with a gun, is a young

29   Cf. Hélène Toussaint, *La Liberté guidant le peuple de Delacroix* (Paris: Éditions de la Réunion des Musées Nationaux, 1982), 57.

Eugène Delacroix, *Liberty Leading the People*
(1831). Canvas. Musée du Louvre, Paris.

craftsman wearing a jacket, a top hat, and a tie. On the ground, a
student is recognizable from his cocked hat. Most of these figures have
been diversely interpreted, starting of course with Liberty herself.
Half-naked and imposing by her size, she certainly belongs to a larger
pictorial tradition of allegorical representations – exactly like the
Republic – and it is highly doubtful that she could be taken for a
symbol of sexual emancipation, but she certainly appears as a woman
from the people.[30] As many exegetes of this painting have pointed out,
Delacroix drew inspiration from Auguste Barbier's *La Curée* (*The
Bandwagon*), a poem written just after the insurrection, where Liberty
is evoked as 'a strong woman, stout-bosomed', who 'strides forward
with confidence, rejoicing in the clamour of the people.'[31] Balzac too,

---

30   According to Maurice Agulhon, Delacroix's canvas belongs to the long
tradition of pictorial allegories of the female body: 'On Political Allegory: A Reply
to Eric Hobsbawm', *History Workshop*, 8 (1979): 167–73. On the contrary, the
novelty of this allegory based on the popular character of Delacroix's representation of Liberty is emphasized by Eric Hobsbawm, 'Man and Woman in Socialist
Iconography', *History Workshop*, 6 (1978), now included in Eric Hobsbawm,
Uncommon People: Resistance, Rebellion and Jazz (London: Abacus, 1998), 129.

31   Auguste Barbier, 'La Curée', *Revue de Paris*, 18 (1830): 140. Quoted by
Nicos Hadjinicolau, 'La Liberté guidant le peuple de Delacroix devant son premier

who admired Delacroix's canvas at the Salon of 1831, mentions it in his novel *The Peasants* (1855) where Liberty is portrayed as Catherine, a woman from the lower classes:

> Catherine, a strong, tall creature, in every point like the young women whom sculptors and painters take for the model of Liberty, as the Republic used to do, fascinated the youth of the valley of the Avonne by the same exuberance of bosom, the same muscular legs, the same figure, robust and flexible at once, the plump arms, the eyes enlivened by a spark of fire; by the haughty air, the hair twisted in great braids, the masculine brow, the red mouth with the lips curved by a quasi-ferocious smile, which both Eugène Delacroix and David d'Angers have so successfully grasped and reproduced. A living image of the common people, the dark-skinned, ardent Catherine flashed insurrection from her bright, tawny eyes, piercing eyes, and soldier-like in their insolence. She inherited from her father such a violent temper that the whole family at the wine-shop feared her.[32]

In Delacroix's painting, this female warrior leads a popular insurrection. As several art critics have pointed out, the young insurgent wielding a gun is not a bourgeois: top hat and tie were quite common among city craftsmen and his modest social status is clearly revealed by his pants and belt. Therefore, the canvas does not illustrate the class 'alliance' between the proletariat and a still revolutionary bourgeoisie. No one among the critics and commentators of 1830 considered this young rebel as bourgeois. Charles Farcy, a conservative, viewed him as 'an equivocal figure, half-bourgeois and half-worker.'[33] All of them were unanimous in considering Delacroix's canvas as a representation

---

public', *Actes de la Recherche en Sciences Sociales*, 28 (1979): 14, and T. J. Clark, *The Absolute Bourgeois: Artists and Politics in France 1848–1851* (London: Thames & Hudson, 1973), 17–18.

32   Honoré de Balzac, *The Peasants*, trans. George B. Ives (Philadelphia: George Barrie and Son, 1899), 268–9.

33   Hadjinicolau, 'La Liberté guidant le peuple', 20–1. See also Toussaint, *La Liberté guidant le peuple*, 43–4, 49. These careful investigations call into question T. J. Clark's interpretation according to which Delacroix painted the 'alliance of bourgeois and People ... point by point', *The Absolute Bourgeois*, 19.

of the popular insurrection: a movement embodied by the labouring classes of Paris, workers and craftsmen, supported by some déclassé bourgeois. This is why the Orleanist newspapers were so disappointed: the liberal bourgeoisie, the true winner of the 1830 insurrection and the new ruling class in the July Monarchy, is simply missing from this painting. With very opposed motivations, both legitimists and republicans appreciated Delacroix's aesthetic accomplishment. Whereas the former viewed it as a portrait of the mob, the populace, the rabble, the *canaille*, and a warning against the barbarians of the French capital – several critics emphasized the roughness of this disgraceful woman, even remarking on her hairy armpits – the latter hailed a work of art that recognized the people as a political actor.

Liberty Leading the People is a tangle of paradoxical elements. The people undoubtedly appear as its hero, evidence that explains the enthusiasm of the republican visitors to the Salon in 1831. From this point of view, this canvas also reveals the radicalism of its young artist, who twenty years later would paint the Galerie d'Apollon in the Louvre to celebrate the crushing of the June insurrection of 1848. But other features display the ambiguity of this painting. On the right, the contours of Notre-Dame cathedral lend a religious character to the allegorical figure of Liberty. Despite the barricade, which is barely recognizable, the composition reproduces a very conservative aesthetic canon: Liberty holding a tricolour is an explicit reference to *Augereau on the bridge at Arcole* (1798), a canvas by the neoclassicist painter Charles Thévenin that celebrates the heroism of a Napoleonic general. In 1830, Thévenin was famous as a painter of the battles of the French Revolution and the First Empire and, by choosing this aesthetic model, Delacroix clearly gave the tricolour of Liberty a Bonapartist dimension.[34] Furthermore, considering that in 1830 the July Revolution coincided with the first Algerian war, this allegory of freedom already announced the ambiguities of French republicanism:

---

34   On Thévenin as the aesthetic model for Delacroix, see Jörg Träger, Aude Viray-Wallon, 'L'épiphanie de la liberté. La Révolution vue par Eugène Delacroix', *Revue de l'Art*, 98 (1992): 24. On the political meaning of this aesthetic model, see Pierre Gaudibert, 'Delacroix et le romantisme révolutionnaire', *Europe* (April 1963): 4–21.

the entanglement between universalism and nationalism, freedom as a revolutionary conquest and the goal of a colonial 'civilizing mission'.

This portrait of liberty as a majestic, fighting woman with a flag and a gun is nevertheless quite unusual. Allegorical female figures were typically innocent and unarmed, whereas the iconic images of liberation were strongly gendered, with the accent on male physical strength.[35] And this tendency would last for more than a century. As we already saw in a previous chapter, in the communist propaganda of the early 1920s world revolution frequently appeared as a vigorous, muscled, masculine proletarian smashing the shackles of imperialism. But this peculiarity should not hide some affinities. Despite their different gender connotations, ideological orientations, and cultural backgrounds, both Delacroix's painting and later Soviet posters depict freedom as a goal to be conquered through liberating action. From the French Revolution onwards, freedom cannot be dissociated from liberation, that is from the representation of human beings breaking the chains of oppression, demolishing the walls of despotism and going to the barricades. That is why, since the beginning of the nineteenth century, freedom has been the object of multiple attempts at domestication, either by reducing it to a mere metaphor or by describing it as a gift from a providential and enlightened power. This is the core of the discourse on slavery that shaped the rise of abolitionism in both Europe and the Americas. Liberty and justice, Frantz Fanon observed in *Black Skin, White Masks* (1952), were always 'white liberty and white justice', enjoyment and respite generously granted to the slaves by their masters. 'The black man contented himself with thanking the white man', he wrote, 'and the most forceful proof of the fact is the impressive number of statues erected all over France and the colonies to show white France stroking the kinky hair of this nice Negro whose chains had just been broken.'[36] As the art historian Hugh Honour has persuasively argued, throughout the nineteenth century the representations of the abolition of slavery were unfailingly

---

35   See the entire previously-quoted article by Hobsbawm, 'Man and Woman in Socialist Iconography', 125–49.

36   Frantz Fanon, *Black Skin, White Masks*, trans. Charles L. Markmann, forewords by Ziauddin Sardar and Homi Bhabha (London: Pluto Press, 1986), 220–21.

François Auguste Biard, *Proclamation of the Abolition of Slavery in the French Colonies* (1849). Canvas. Chateau de Versailles, France.

inspired by a strong paternalism – think of the paintings and statues of Victor Schoelcher or Abraham Lincoln – while the images of naked African warriors illustrated the mythical view of black savagery and the civilizing work of European colonizers.[37] An eloquent mirror of this ideology is Jean-François Biard's *Proclamation of the Abolition of Slavery in the French Colonies* (1849). A slave couple embrace each other, the man exhibiting his broken chains, in front of a white representative of the French Republic speaking beside a tricolour. They are surrounded by bare-breasted black women on their knees before the French flag, expressing their gratitude to two benevolent white ladies.

The idea of the 'civilizing mission' of the Europeans towards the coloured populations of the colonial world was deeply rooted in the culture of Enlightenment, as testified by the works of most eighteenth-century philosophers as well as the public statements of the French and British abolitionist associations that appeared in the 1780s.[38] The

---

37   See Hugh Honour, 'Philanthropic Conquest', in David Bindman and Henry Louis Gates Jr. (eds), *The Image of the Black in Western Art*, vol. 4: *From the American Revolution to World War I* (Cambridge: Harvard University Press, 1989).

38   See Robin Blackburn, *The Overthrow of Colonial Slavery 1776–1848* (London: Verso, 1988). The French debates on Black Emancipation are well summarized in Jonathan Israel, *Revolutionary Ideas: An Intellectual History of the French Revolution from The Rights of Man to Robespierre* (Princeton: Princeton University Press, 2014), Chapter 15, 396–419.

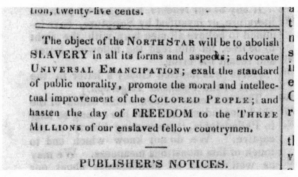

The North Star, 22 February 1850.

Black Jacobins overthrew slavery in Saint-Domingue but – except for a short moment during the French Revolution that coincided with the first abolition of slavery by the Convention in 1794[39] – they were not able to vanquish this widespread prejudice. The nineteenth century would be the golden age of racism codified as a scientific discourse.

It was against this paternalistic mentality and ideological disposition – the liberated slaves as passive recipients of rights bestowed by an external power – that many representatives of black radicalism stressed an alternative vision of the abolition of slavery, as a process of self-emancipation. This idea was clearly formulated in the statement of *North Star*, the abolitionist weekly published in Rochester by Frederick Douglass between 1847 and 1851: 'The object of the North Star will be to abolish slavery in all its forms and aspects; advocate universal emancipation; exalt the standard of public morality, promote the moral and intellectual improvement of the colored people; and hasten the

---

39   A significant testimony of this exceptional moment is the famous portrait of the black deputy Jean-Baptiste Belley by Anne-Louis Girodet de Roussy-Trioson. In this painting, the representative of Saint-Domingue at the Convention in 1794 appears as a figure of dignity beside the bust of Guillaume-Thomas Raynal, the most important defender of abolition in the eighteenth century: their heads are at the same level – there is no hierarchy between them – and Belley's gaze is directed towards his island rather than the statue behind him. For an interesting interpretation of this portrait, see Helen D. Weston, 'Representing the Right to Represent: The "Portrait of Citizen Belley, Ex-Representative of the Colonies"', *Anthropology and Aesthetics*, 26 (1994): 83–99. Christopher A. Bayly mentions this canvas to illustrate the birth of 'hybrid political identities' in the nineteenth century: *The Birth of the Modern World 1780–1914: Global Connections and Comparisons* (Malden, MA: Blackwell, 2004), 375.

day of freedom to the three millions of our enslaved fellow country-men.'[40] A similar position – in which the memory of the revolution of Saint-Domingue can still be recognized – was endorsed by the black abolitionist movement, which solemnly declared in its Cleveland Convention of 1854:

> That no oppressed people have ever obtained their rights by vol-untary acts of generosity on the part of their oppressors. That it is futile hope on our part to expect such results through the agency of moral goodness on the part of our white American oppressors. That if we desire liberty, it can only be obtained at the price which others have paid for it.[41]

The American Civil War was an entanglement of conflicts that involved actors whose aims could certainly converge but belonged to different cultures and expressed heterogeneous motivations. The clash between the rising industrial capitalism of the North-Eastern states and the Southern cotton economy, already integrated in the world market but still ruled by premodern slaveowners, had become inevitable. Whereas white abolitionism was inspired by the values of honour and the morality of a WASP bourgeoisie both aware of its roots and concerned with the American future, black abolitionism was the struggle of slaves – an oppressed racial minority – for their libera-tion.[42] For them, taking up arms was a moment of self-emancipation. Thus, Lincoln's Proclamation in 1862 was the crossing point of two distinct genealogies of freedom: the first extended the principles of the American Revolution, which had created the premises of a pros-perous society grounded in the free market and political democracy; the second was a new step in a process of self-emancipation that had begun with the Saint-Domingue Revolution and had unfolded, first, with the abolition of the slave trade in 1807, then with the emancipa-tion of the slaves in the British and French empires, in 1833 and 1848

---

40   Quoted in L. Diane Barnes, *Frederick Douglass: Reformer and Statesman* (New York: Routledge, 2013), 60.

41   Quoted in Harding, *There Is a River*, 191.

42   Ibid., 126.

respectively. In other words, the American Civil War was a step in what C. L. R. James called the history of 'pan-African revolt'.[43]

Ontology

If the concept of freedom is ambiguous and polysemic, its genealogy requires us to distinguish between its *politico-philosophical* and its *historical* definition: freedom as a juridical and political status is a goal to conquer or a condition to be used. As Herbert Marcuse pointed out, calling for freedom under oppression has emancipatory and critical potentialities; doing so in a free society tends to become empty rhetoric or a justification for conformist postures. Think of real socialism: the meaning of freedom was clear for the workers who demonstrated in the streets of East Berlin in June 1953, for those who tore down the statue of Stalin in Budapest in November 1956, for the actors of the Prague Spring in 1968 or those who created Solidarność in Poland in 1980. Today, however, the word 'freedom' adorns the name of many Central European far-right movements.

By explaining the dialectic of Enlightenment, Marcuse stressed that freedom could become an empty shell or a fallacious façade hiding new forms of oppression. In his view, the metamorphosis of reason from an emancipatory tool into a blind, instrumental rationality corresponded with the emergence of an illusory freedom in a completely reified society. Totalitarianism, as in the destruction of freedom by violence and terror, was only one among many possible forms of domination, and perhaps 'already obsolete'.[44] In affluent societies, Marcuse wrote in *One-Dimensional Man* (1964), the satisfaction of pleasure becomes a form of 'repressive desublimation' or 'repressive tolerance' – the 'pleasure principle' being reduced insofar as the range of socially admitted and oriented enjoyments is enlarged – which generates submission. 'Under the rule of a repressive whole,' he concluded, 'liberty can be made into a powerful instrument of domination.'[45] Modern

---

43 C. L. R. James, *A History of Pan-African Revolt* (London: Merlin Press, 2012 [1938]), 58.

44 Herbert Marcuse, *Five Lectures* (Boston: Beacon Press, 1970), 4.

45 Herbert Marcuse, *One-Dimensional Man* (New York: Routledge, 2002), 7.

Jean-Paul Sartre (1945).

oppression is based on three pillars: alienation, or the repression of 'sensual drives that want only pleasure and gratification'; division of labour, which inscribes our lives into complex networks of legal rights and duties; and technology, which means the mastery of nature. Classical liberalism combines all three in a philosophical conception of freedom: moral freedom based on 'renunciation' and self-control within the boundaries of 'socially accepted pleasure' (alienation); political freedom as the margins of autonomy conferred on us by the law (the duties corresponding to the division of labour); and intellectual freedom, or our capacity to change the world through human reason (technology). The 'psychic substance common to these three aspects of freedom' is 'rational unfreedom' or 'rational domination'.[46] In other words, what we call freedom is nothing but alienation, state power, and a growing separation between human beings and their natural background.

The ontological definition of freedom is at the core of Sartre's *Being and Nothingness* (1943), the first great work of the French thinker published under Nazi occupation. This impressive philosophical treaty in which the influence of Descartes, Hegel, and above all Heidegger is clearly perceptible, was not unanimously acclaimed. In 1944, in the electric atmosphere of French Liberation, it was enthusiastically received, according to Sartre's biographer Annie Cohen-Solal, as

---

46   Herbert Marcuse, *Five Lectures*, 12.

a superb appeal to freedom and 'individual anarchism'.[47] But other reviewers, including Marcuse, pointed out its problematic and highly ambiguous character. In the wake of Heidegger's concept of 'authenticity' (*Eigentlichkeit*), Sartre posited an insuperable discrepancy between reality and subjectivity, between the concrete and mundane condition of the individual's *être-en-soi* (Being-in-itself) and his *être-pour-soi* (Being-for-itself), a permanent source of anxiety and, at the same time, of an irrepressible desire for liberty. Claiming the supremacy of consciousness over the external and contingent conditions of existence, Sartre gave multiple examples of this ontological liberty irreducible to any historical form of alienation, domination, and oppression, from wage labour and slavery to anti-Semitic persecution. The Jewish condition under National Socialism simply illustrated this fundamental fracture between the reality of persecution and this indestructible subjective freedom. To be Jewish, Sartre explained, means 'being Jewish' in the eyes of the anti-Semite. Of course, this defines 'the external objective limit of the situation', but the Jewish person can choose to abstract themselves from this external constraint and, by forgetting their 'being Jewish', can rediscover their ontological status of free subject. If, Sartre argued, 'it pleases me to consider the anti-Semites as pure *objects*, then my being-a-Jew disappears immediately to give place to the simple consciousness (of) being a free, unqualifiable transcendence.'[48] A human being can be alienated, oppressed, and offended, but she will remain free to rebel and her wish for freedom cannot be destroyed, thus proving its supremacy over any objective circumstances.

Sartre probably did not know, when his book was released in the Parisian bookshops, that the gas chambers were functioning at full power in Auschwitz and Treblinka. Writing his review of *Being and Nothingness* in 1948, Marcuse was aware of this distasteful coincidence, that he assumed as a mirror of the ambiguities of Sartrean existentialism:

---

47   Annie Cohen-Solal, *Sartre: A Life* (New York: Pantheon Books, 1987), 188.

48   Jean-Paul Sartre, *Being and Nothingness: An Essay on Phenomenological Ontology*, trans. Hazel E. Barnes (London: Routledge, 2003), 527.

If philosophy, by virtue of its existential-ontological concepts of man or freedom, is capable of demonstrating that the persecuted Jew and the victim of the executioner are and remain absolutely free and masters of a self-responsible choice, then these philosophical concepts have declined to the level of a mere ideology, an ideology which offers itself as a most handy justification for the persecutors and executioners, themselves an important part of the *réalité humaine.*[49]

Marcuse stigmatized Sartre's position as an idealism that ignored history by casting it as a purely contingent feature of individual subjectivity. This meant considering freedom as the very structure of human beings, something that cannot be annihilated by external factors. Sartre treated historical events as useful examples to illustrate his philosophical – in the last analysis metaphysical – conception of freedom: 'The essential freedom of man, as Sartre sees it, remains the same before, during, and after the totalitarian enslavement of man.'[50] Sartre's radicalism, Marcuse concluded, remained outside of his philosophy; it could find a place in the style of his work, not in its content.[51]

By a significant coincidence, *Being and Nothingness* was released in French bookshops in June 1943, just a few weeks after the crushing of the Warsaw Ghetto Uprising by the soldiers of the SS commander Jürgen Stroop. It is highly improbable that, in such a landscape of desolation and death, the starving Jews were possessed by any feeling

---

49   Herbert Marcuse, 'Sartre's Existentialism' (1948), *The Essential Marcuse: Selected Writings*, eds Andrew Feenberg and William Leiss (Boston: Beacon Press, 2007), 143.

50   Ibid., 131.

51   This was the conclusion of Marcuse's review in 1948 (*Philosophy and Phenomenological Research*, III, 3, 1948, 335). He changed the last paragraph when he republished his essay in *Kultur und Gesellschaft* (Frankfurt: Suhrkamp, 1967, vol. 2), almost twenty years later, by recognizing that in the later works of Sartre, notably his preface to Fanon's *Wretched of the Earth* (1961), 'pure ontology and phenomenology' had been replaced by politics. The French philosopher had abandoned his early abstract thought, to introduce history, assimilate Marxism and adopt dialectic. He had thus 'fulfilled his promise of a morality of liberation': Marcuse, 'Sartre's Existentialism', 158.

Herbert Marcuse (ca. 1945).

Mordechai Anielewicz.
Passport photo,
Poland, late 1930s.

of being a 'free, unqualifiable transcendence'. Not only was the ghetto
the most radical negation of freedom, but freedom had deserted its
inhabitants' existential horizon altogether. The Ghetto Uprising has
a special place in the history of insurrections insofar as it was not a
liberation movement. Unlike the Warsaw Uprising that took place
one year later and whose main goal was to liberate the city before the
arrival of the Red Army, the few hundreds of young Jewish fighters
who, very poorly armed, fiercely resisted the German troops, did
not expect freedom. They certainly struggled against oppression, but
liberation was simply impossible. They had chosen to die by fighting
and their choice was an affirmation of human dignity. Describing the
death of Mordechai Anielewicz, the twenty-four-year-old leader of
the uprising, Emanuel Ringelblum, chronicler of the Warsaw Ghetto,
emphasized that the dominant feeling amongst the youth was the search
for an 'honorable death'. They did not try to survive by escaping, by
arranging 'Aryan' papers or getting a hideout on the other side of the
ghetto walls: 'Their only worry was about the most honorable death,
the kind of death that a two-thousand-year-old people deserves.'[52]
This choice was not purely nihilistic, because Anielewicz's struggle
contained a message that transcended the boundaries of the ghetto. He

---

52 Quoted in Samuel D. Kassow, *Who Will Write Our History? Emanuel
Ringelblum, the Warsaw Ghetto, and the Oyneg Shabes Archive* (Bloomington:
Indiana University Press, 2007), 371.

was a member of the Hashomer Hatzair, a Marxist Zionist movement, and Ringelblum stressed that he believed in 'the world revolution'.[53] As Jean Améry suggested, the insurrection in the Jewish ghetto of Warsaw, as well as those in the extermination camps of Sobibor and Treblinka, was not a struggle for survival or freedom; they were examples of 'human redemption' through 'voluntary death' (*die Freiheit des Zum-Tod-Seins*): death by fighting as opposed to death imposed by the ruler. It was by this 'voluntary death' that they affirmed their universalism and joined an international liberation movement.[54]

Foucault, Arendt and Fanon

The conceptual distinctions between freedom and liberation go beyond the canonical conflict between liberalism and socialism. According to Michel Foucault, freedom is not an ontological realm but rather a socially produced form of life and, as such, it is not opposed to but rather inscribed within power through multiple tensions and practices. There are 'practices of liberty' that transform social relationships, modify consolidated hierarchies and affect the structures of ruling state apparatuses, thus acting inside the 'microphysics' of a diffused, rhizomorphic, and all-compassing power.[55] If power is a whole of relations and networks that shape and build us, both disciplining our bodies and caring for our lives as a 'shepherd protects his flock', then the opposition between power and freedom does not make sense, insofar as the former cannot be destroyed through a 'liberating' action. In Foucault's view, liberation as a violent confrontation between a sovereign state and an insurgent subject was a mythical narrative that

---

53   Ibid., 372.

54   Jean Améry, 'Im Warteraum des Todes' (1969), *Widersprüche* (Stuttgart: Klett-Cotta, 1971), 122.

55   On the concept of 'practices of freedom', see 'L'éthique du souci de soi comme pratique de la liberté' (1984), in Michel Foucault, *Dits et Écrits*, eds François Ewald and Daniel Defert (Paris: Gallimard, 1994), vol. 4, 709–12. On the concept of power as a complex network of 'power relations', see the texts gathered in Michel Foucault, *Power* (*The Essential Work of Michel Foucault 1954–1984*, vol. 3), eds Paul Rabinow and James Faubion, trans. Robert Hurley (New York: The New Press, 2003).

Michel Foucault (1970s).

depicted freedom as a kind of original substratum covered, hidden and enchained by political authority. Freedom cannot be 'conquered', it has to be built by introducing practices of resistance within the relations of power; it is the result of a process, the outcome of building new subjectivities. For instance, sexuality cannot be 'liberated' but rather reshaped by proper 'technologies of the self', in other words by new practices of existence – made of desires, force, resistance, and movements – through which subjects may constitute themselves.[56]

This Foucauldian distinction between liberty and liberation is both fruitful and problematic. It is a valuable reminder that a 'realm of liberty' cannot simply be proclaimed or established by an act of will: all revolutions have been caught up in the legacy of the past, a fact that has deeply shaped any attempt at building a new society. But Foucault was not altogether original in criticizing the fetishism of liberation: from the mid-nineteenth century, Marx warned against both Bakunin's illusion of achieving freedom by 'abolishing' the state and Blanqui's temptation to reduce revolution to a kind of insurrectional technique. The point is that by criticizing such a naïve conception of freedom Foucault simply evacuates the question of liberation.

---

56   See Michel Foucault, *Technologies of the Self: A Seminar with Michel Foucault*, eds Luther H. Martin, Huck Gutman and Patrick H. Hutton (Amherst: University of Massachusetts Press, 1988).

Foucault's remarks deserve to be seriously meditated upon, and his committed opposition to the carceral condition of the 1970s is evidence that his 'practices of liberty' were not an empty formula. Nevertheless, his rejection of liberation in the name of freedom elicits a legitimate scepticism. Of course, the link between them is not teleological and does not draw a linear, ascending curve to chart a continuous and irreversible expansion of capacities and enjoyment, such as that described by Condorcet in his famous *Sketch for a Historical Picture of the Progress of the Human Mind* (1795).[57] Freedom is not the result of a providential and ineluctable self-fulfilment. At the end of the twentieth century, Eric Hobsbawm no longer believed in this teleological narrative. In the early 1960s he had started his tetralogy on the history of the nineteenth and twentieth centuries as a succession of emancipatory waves: 1789, 1848, the Paris Commune in 1871, then the Russian Revolution and finally, from the Second World War onwards, the revolutions of Asia and Latin America, from China to Cuba and Vietnam. History had a telos, and freedom was its natural horizon. It meant progress, and the labour movement was its tool. After 1989 and the collapse of real socialism, Hobsbawm recognized that this periodization did not reflect any deterministic causality and did not depict a linear trajectory; but the experiences of liberation running through his historical narrative had existed, nonetheless. Under the Old Regime, liberty meant a set of concrete 'liberties': exemptions, permissions and privileges allowed to certain groups. The Atlantic Revolutions established a new, universal idea of freedom, inscribed in both natural rights and positive laws, which built up in the collective imagination and mobilized a powerful symbolism for more than two centuries.[58] The revolutionary breaks investigated by Hobsbawm in his tetralogy on the nineteenth and twentieth centuries prove that this universal idea had a performative character.

Foucault crafted his dichotomy between freedom and liberation in the 1980s, the final step of his intellectual trajectory, a time when,

---

57   Condorcet, 'The Sketch' (1795), *Political Writings*, eds Steven Lukes and Nadia Urbinati (New York: Cambridge University Press, 2012), 1–148.

58   See Mona Ozouf, 'Liberté', in François Furet and Mona Ozouf (eds), *Dictionnaire critique de la Révolution française. Idées* (Paris: Flammarion, 1992), 253–5.

according to many critics, he expressed an open penchant for individualism and neoliberalism. In some marginal texts he admittedly did not exclude uprisings from the practices of liberty – 'People rise up', he wrote, 'that is the way subjectivity (not that of great men but that of everyone) enters history and gives it its breath'[59] – but they were exceptions. Nowhere does his work express any interest in revolutions, neither the classic ones nor those of his own time (with the strange exception of the Iranian revolution, which he agreed to chronicle for the Italian newspaper *Corriere della Sera*). A fruitful use of Foucault would consist, perhaps, in re-historicizing his vision of freedom, thus reconnecting it with liberation. It is debatable that, in the nineteenth century, the advent of a new biopolitical power – what he called 'governmentality' – finally replaced older forms of sovereignty: the management of bodies, populations and territories instead of 'the right to decide life and death'.[60] Governmentality reshaped sovereignty without exhausting it. The history of the twentieth century, with its total wars and revolutions, presents the apocalyptic hubris of sovereign power. Many Foucauldian categories are useless to historians if they are not connected with those of Marx, Weber and Schmitt.[61] Historically understood, freedom has emerged as a constituent power that came up against and dismissed a previous sovereign power.

59   Foucault, 'Inutile de se soulever?' (1979), *Dits et Écrits*, vol. 2, 790.

60   Michel Foucault, 'The Right of Death and the Power over Life', *History of Sexuality, Vol. I: An Introduction*, trans. Robert Hurley (New York: Penguin, 1978), 135. According to Foucault, biopolitics meant 'a new mechanism of power which had very specific procedures, completely new instruments, and very different equipment'. In his view, this biopolitical power was 'absolutely incompatible with relations of sovereignty'. See Michel Foucault, *Society Must Be Defended: Lectures at the Collège de France, 1975–1976*, ed. Mauro Bertani and Alessandro Fontana, trans. David Macey (New York: Picador, 2003), 35. This supposed incompatibility between biopolitics and sovereignty was criticized by Roberto Esposito, *Bios: Biopolitics and Philosophy*, trans. Timothy Campbell (Minneapolis: University of Minnesota Press, 2008), 13–38.

61   Rather than reconciliation or an impossible synthesis between Marx and Foucault, this would mean working with them by assuming their 'disjunction'. See Étienne Balibar, 'L'anti-Marx de Michel Foucault', in Christian Laval, Luca Paltrinieri and Ferhat Taylan (eds), *Marx & Foucault. Lectures, usages, confrontations* (Paris: La Découverte, 2015), 85–102. See also Enzo Traverso, 'Biopotere e violenza. Sugli usi storiografici di Foucault e Agamben', *Contemporanea*, 3 (2009): 523–30.

Hannah Arendt (1963).

Analogously to Foucault, even if starting from different philosophical premises, Hannah Arendt drew a line between liberation and freedom. In her famous essay *On Revolution* (1963), she depicted liberation as an act of voluntarism – by definition transitional and ephemeral – that may create freedom but also engender despotism, whereas freedom, she pointed out, is a permanent status that requires a republican political system. Freedom allows human beings to interact as citizens, that is to participate as equal subjects in a common public sphere. She was interested in revolution exclusively as a foundational moment of republican freedom, as a *constitutio libertatis*. On this basis, she compared the American and French Revolutions as two antipodal models. She did not seek to compare two historical experiences but rather to juxtapose two conflicting ideal-types. And her conclusion was clear: whereas the American Revolution was successful in establishing Republican freedom, the French Revolution failed because of its ambition of combining the conquest of freedom with social emancipation. Beyond freedom, it pretended to liberate society from exploitation and necessity. But this implied authoritarian interventions into the social body, and since it was unable to preserve the autonomy of the political field, it produced authoritarianism, despotism and finally totalitarianism. 'The American Revolution remained committed to the foundation of freedom and the establishments of lasting institutions', she wrote, whereas the French Revolution 'was determined by the exigencies of liberation not from tyranny but from necessity'.[62] Radically separating politics from society as two irreconcilable realms, Arendt considered it both 'futile' and 'dangerous' to 'liberate humankind from poverty by political means', and therefore considered the French Revolution a global failure: the result, she wrote, 'was that necessity invaded the political realm, the only realm where men can be truly free'.[63] Curiously, her essay does not analyse the Russian Revolution, which consciously pursued the goal of changing society's bases themselves by abolishing capitalism.

In *The Origins of Totalitarianism* (1951), Arendt devoted several pages to Edmund Burke, the first conservative critic of the philosophy of human rights, depicting him as a precursor of totalitarian rule.[64] Ten years later, she prized Burke as a lucid detractor of the French Revolution. In her view, Burke's criticism of the Rights of Man was 'neither obsolete nor reactionary', since he had understood that the French enlighteners reproached the Old Regime for depriving human beings, not of freedom and citizenship but rather of their 'rights of life and nature'.[65] *On Revolution* is a contradictory text. On the one hand, it defends a conception of freedom that is close to anarchism, notably in its vision of the republic as a form of direct democracy epitomized by the Paris Commune, the soviets of 1917, and the Hungarian Revolution of 1956. On the other hand, its criticism of the French Revolution reproduces many of the commonplaces of conservative liberalism, which always disparaged Rousseau's radical democratic utopianism as a premise of totalitarianism. This contradiction deserves to be explored.

---

62 Hannah Arendt, *On Revolution* (New York: Penguin, 2006), 82.

63 Ibid., 104. Arendt's opposition of the American and French Revolutions was not new. As Antonio Negri points out, its first thinker was Friedrich von Gentz, in his introduction to the German translation of Edmund Burke's *Reflections on the Revolution in France*, which had then been popularized by John Adams's supporters against Jefferson during the presidential campaign of 1800. See Antonio Negri, *Insurgencies: Constituent Power and the Modern State* (Minneapolis: University of Minnesota Press, 1999) 25–6.

64 Hannah Arendt, *The Origins of Totalitarianism* (New York: Harcourt, Brace & Co., 1976), 175–6.

65 Arendt, *On Revolution*, 98–9.

According to Arendt, freedom implies direct, active participation in public life; it is an 'agonal' or 'ocular' form of democracy, which rejects the principle of representation; it is a realm of action in which 'Being and Appearing coincide'.[66] It does not designate democratic pluralism as a multiplicity of political parties represented in a Parliament; it rather means a public sphere animated by the interaction of free citizens. In her vision, politics is the realm of *infra*, which is a reformulation of the Heideggerian concept of being (*Sein*) as 'being with' (*Mitsein*).[67] In her earlier work *The Human Condition* (1956), she had distinguished between three major forms of human existence: *labour*, which means a primary, almost metabolic exchange between human beings and nature; *work*, which creates the material world and our social environment; and *action*, the realm of freedom that is not subjected to any dialectic between means and ends, because it is its own end.[68] In other words, freedom, the highest and noblest form of politics, is an autonomous realm radically separate from society, any interference in which risks engendering despotism. Therefore, Arendt's Republic lacks all social content: freedom does not mean emancipation from economic and social oppression, it means free citizens free-floating in a social vacuum.

Arendt's radical distinction between freedom and necessity implicitly excludes from politics all those whose primary concern is to satisfy their vital needs before participating in the public sphere, and simply ignores those who do not do so for lack of time, knowledge, education, etc. But revolutions are precisely the moments in which the excluded are no longer voiceless and clamour to be heard. Marx

---

66   Hannah Arendt, *The Life of the Mind* (New York: Harcourt, Brace & Jovanovich, 1978), 19. See also *The Human Condition* (Chicago: University of Chicago Press, 1958), 50. On Arendt's 'agonal' concept of politics, see Seyla Benhabib, *The Reluctant Modernism of Hannah Arendt* (Lanham: Rowman & Littlefield, 2000), 125–6, 199–200.

67   Hannah Arendt, 'Introduction into Politics' (1950), *The Promise of Politics*, ed. Jerome Kohn (New York: Schocken Books, 2005), 93–199. On Arendt's concept of politics as a critical reassessment of the Heideggerian ontology of *Being and Time* (1927), see in particular Benhabib, *The Reluctant Modernism of Hannah Arendt*, 51–7.

68   Arendt, *The Human Condition*.

defined communism as a 'realm of freedom' that could be established beyond the field of production. Arendt was hostile towards social revolutions, which appeared to her as either pre-political or anti-political. In her view, the ultimate responsibility for this tragic misunderstanding belonged to Marx, a thinker whose 'place in the history of human freedom will always remain equivocal', since, she concluded, 'the abdication of freedom before the dictate of necessity' had found in him 'its theorist'.[69] Criticizing her concept of revolution, Eric Hobsbawm remarked that, as a historian, he could not enter into dialogue with her. They spoke different languages, like theologians and astronomers in early modern Europe (and one can imagine who, in this analogy, embodied Galileo and who the Inquisition).[70]

This conflict simply goes back to the original aporia of modern liberty: the internal contradiction between man and citizen that shapes the entire culture of the Enlightenment and that the young Marx had analysed in 1842 in his writings on the Rhineland enclosures. The richest and the poorest are 'equal' as citizens but certainly not as 'private individuals', meaning as possessors of property, which is the core of freedom as defined by classical liberalism. The French Constitution of 1793 had tried to overcome this dichotomy between man and citizen: all human beings (embodying universal and inalienable rights) were citizens (enjoying positive, instituted and effective rights), and property was subordinated to the 'right to existence.' In other words, freedom and equality went together; their link was not established by individual property but rather by the needs of the community. Étienne Balibar describes this union with the concept of *equaliberty*.[71]

In comparing the American and French revolutions, Tocqueville was probably more lucid than Arendt. Whereas the American Revolution was directed against an external power and did not mean to destroy any economic and social structure inherited from the past, the French

---

69   Arendt, *On Revolution*, 51.

70   Eric Hobsbawm, 'Hannah Arendt on Revolution' (1965), *Revolutionaries* (New York: The New Press, 2001 [1973]), 239–47.

71   See in particular the first three chapters of Étienne Balibar, *Equaliberty: Political Essays*, trans. James Ingram (Durham: Duke University Press, 2014).

Revolution was directed against the Old Regime; its political emancipation could not take place without destroying the entire edifice of
Absolutism, a system of power that had ruled for centuries moulding
mentalities, cultures and behaviours.[72] It could not separate political
and social emancipation; it was forced to invent a new society in order
to replace the old. The American Revolution resolved the social
question through the Frontier: space was the horizon of its freedom
and democracy was conceived of as a conquest, with the creation of
settlers and landowners. The Frontier was an inexhaustible horizon
of appropriation.[73] In order to idealize the American Revolution,
Arendt was compelled to neglect its original stigmas: the genocide
of the indigenous people and the acceptance of slavery. One century
later, however, the American Civil War was as violent and lethal as
the Terror had been or would be during the French and the Russian
revolutions. Arendt defended a strange concept of freedom, swinging
between Rosa Luxemburg and Tocqueville, another great admirer of
the American democracy.

In a famous and controversial article on Little Rock written in 1957,
at the time of the battle for civil rights in the United States, Arendt
vigorously denounced any form of legal discrimination against African
Americans; but she considered their social segregation as an inevitable and finally acceptable fact that could not be resolved by political
measures. 'The question', she wrote in 1959, 'is not how to abolish
discrimination, but how to keep it confined within the social sphere,
where it is legitimate, and prevent its trespassing on the political and
the personal sphere, where it is destructive.'[74] One could observe

---

72   See Alexis de Tocqueville, *The Old Regime and The Revolution* (Chicago:
University of Chicago Press, 1998).

73   After enthusiastically approving Arendt's vision of revolution as the
expression of the autonomy of politics – a 'constituent power' that, as an 'expansive
principle', creates the political 'from nothingness' (*Insurgencies*, 25–30) – Antonio
Negri gives a socio-historical interpretation of the American Revolution as a
'frontier' of freedom in which 'space founds power because it is conceived as
appropriation, as expansion' (ibid., Chapter 4).

74   Hannah Arendt, 'Reflections on Little Rock', *Dissent*, 1 (1959): 51. For a
careful criticism of Arendt's position on the struggle against black segregation in
the United States in the 1950s, see Kathryn T. Gines, *Hannah Arendt and the Negro
Question* (Bloomington: Indiana University Press, 2014).

that the exclusion of the social question from the political sphere is precisely the argument by which classical liberalism always tried to legitimate the privileges and powers related to property. In the nineteenth century, democracy was seen as the 'trespassing of the social question on the political sphere', a dangerous system that the most prominent thinkers of liberalism, from John Stuart Mill to Benjamin Constant, rejected by linking the right to vote with property. It is true that Arendt's blindness towards the social question did not come from the philosophical tradition of classical liberalism but rather from an existentialist conception of the 'autonomy' of the political.[75] The upshot, however, remains the same: either by sacralizing property (Constant and Mill) or ignoring it (Arendt), all of them excluded the poor from the realm of politics.

How are we to explain Arendt's controversial vision of freedom? As she wrote on several occasions, she had discovered politics through the 'Jewish question', being the question of a minority that was politically discriminated against and persecuted but socially integrated. She wrote powerful and illuminating pages on how anti-Semitism had transformed the Jews into pariahs, stateless people deprived of citizenship and therefore of any juridical and political existence; she viewed them as the mirror of both the internal contradictions of the Enlightenment – the unresolved divide between human beings and citizens – and the crisis of the nation-state in the twentieth century. The fact is that black segregation in the United States had its own history and could not be interpreted through a Jewish prism.[76] When the Nazis promulgated the Nuremberg laws in 1935, the Jewish ghettos had ceased to exist in Germany for over a century. Abolishing legal discrimination was certainly progress, but it did not put an end to either the racism or the social oppression that practically voided legal emancipation itself.

---

75   On the existentialist roots of Arendt's concept of the political, see Martin Jay, 'The Political Existentialism of Hannah Arendt', *Permanent Exiles: Essays on the Intellectual Migration from Germany to America* (New York: Columbia University Press, 1986), 237–56.

76   See Enzo Traverso, 'Between Two Epochs: Jewishness and Politics in Hannah Arendt', *The End of Jewish Modernity* (London: Pluto Press, 2016), 60–81.

More broadly speaking, Hannah Arendt was indifferent to any form of anticolonial revolution. As David Scott observed, 'for Arendt there are only two eighteenth-century revolutions, the French and the American', whereas the Haitian Revolution was simply unthinkable.[77] In her essay titled *On Violence* (1970), she pointed out 'the rarity of slave rebellions and of uprisings among the disinherited and the downtrodden', adding that 'when they occurred', it was 'mad fury' that 'turned dreams into nightmares for everybody'.[78] The violence of the colonized was worse than the oppression they suffered, she wrote against Sartre, since it was a pre-political 'volcanic explosion' that could not produce anything fruitful, beyond replacing leaders without changing the world. The 'Third World' was 'not a reality but an ideology' and its unity was a myth as dangerous as Marx's appeal to the unity of proletarians regardless of their nationhood.[79] Instead of the leaders of a revolutionary process of decolonization, Mao, Castro, Che Guevara and Ho Chi Minh were the 'saviours' of 'pseudo-religious incantations' of students disillusioned by both East and West, the two opposed blocs of the Cold War, while Black Power was predicated on the illusion of creating an alliance between African Americans and this mythical 'Third World' (in other words, a potentially racist anti-white movement). To write this in 1970 was neither simply inaccurate nor distastefully contemptuous; it was the expression of an astonishing intellectual blindness, not to say a clearly Eurocentric and Orientalist prejudice.

By de-historicizing revolution, Arendt espoused conservative clichés regarding the barbarism of lower races and backward continents.

---

77   David Scott, *Conscripts of Modernity: The Tragedy of Colonial Enlightenment* (Durham: Duke University Press, 2004), 217. The adjective 'unthinkable' should be understood in the sense given to it by Michel-Rolph Trouillot: the Haitian Revolution was 'unthinkable' in the framework of Western thought. See Michel-Rolph Trouillot, *Silencing the Past: Power and the Production of History* (Boston: Beacon Press, 1995), 82.

78   Hannah Arendt, 'On Violence', *The Crisis of the Republic* (New York: Harcourt, Brace & Jovanovich, 1972), 123.

79   Ibid., 123–4. On Arendt's 'pervasive Eurocentrism', see Judith Butler, *Parting Ways: Jewishness and the Critique of Zionism* (New York: Columbia University Press, 2012), 139–40.

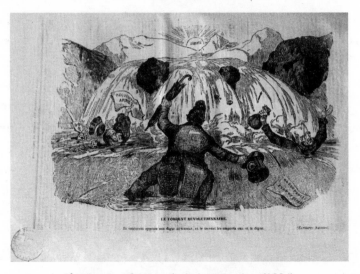

Charivari, *The Revolutionary Torrent* (1834).

In fact, extreme violence was far from being an exclusive feature of colonial revolutions. By executing the king, the English, French and Russian Revolutions tried to channel and control a spontaneous wave of violence coming from below. According to Arno J. Mayer, the great historian of Terror in the French and Russian Revolutions, violence was consubstantial to them, two 'furies' that overthrew any order or ruling power.[80] In 1834, the French satirical magazine *Charivari* depicted revolution as a 'torrent' that flooded everything with irresistible, elemental force. Revolutions often follow an autonomous dynamic, as uncontrolled spirals that aim at obliterating the past and inventing the future from a *tabula rasa*. And since their constituent power violently clashes with the old sovereignty, they need to destroy its symbols. There is no freedom without the execution of the king. As we already saw, revolutions display a spectacular iconoclastic charge that turns liberation into a visible and tangible accomplishment. The Fourteenth of July designates the storming of the Bastille, which was systematically demolished. The Paris Commune too needed its symbolic iconoclastic act, which took place with the demolition of the Vendôme Column. Insurrections are moments of collective effervescence in which ordinary people feel an irrepressible desire

---

80   Arno J. Mayer, *The Furies: Violence and Terror in the French and Russian Revolutions* (Princeton: Princeton University Press, 2000).

Pere Català Pic, *Antifascism* (1938). Museu
Nacional d'Art de Catalunya, Barcelona.

to invade the streets, occupy the sites of power, exhibit their own
strength, if necessary take up arms, and celebrate liberation through
manifestations of fraternity and happiness. According to Lenin, one
of its most austere thinkers, revolution is a 'festival of the oppressed'.
Aware that revolutionary memory needs powerful iconic landmarks,
Sergei Eisenstein opened *October* (1927) with the image of the insurgent crowd destroying the statue of the Tsar. In July 1936, at the
outbreak of the Spanish Civil War, freedom also meant the struggle
against fascism, always represented as the act of smashing its symbols.
Thus, the violence of anticolonial struggle held nothing exceptional.
Analysing the burning of plantations during the slave revolution in
Saint-Domingue, C. L. R. James compared it to several analogous
European practices: 'The slaves destroyed tirelessly. Like the peasants
in the Jacquerie or the Luddite wreckers, they were seeking their salvation in the most obvious way, the destruction of what they knew
was the cause of their suffering; and if they destroyed much it was
because they had suffered much.'[81]

---

81   C. L. R. James, *The Black Jacobins: Toussaint L'Ouverture and the San
Domingo Revolution* (New York: Vintage Books, 1963 [1938]), 88.

Frantz Fanon (1960).

It is almost impossible to read Arendt's words on anticolonial violence – 'mad fury' and 'nightmares' – without thinking of the famous chapter on violence in Frantz Fanon's *The Wretched of the Earth* (1961). The contrast is impressive. Arendt's categorical separation between freedom and necessity recalls Fanon's portrait of the dichotomic colonial city, where in fact two separate cities coexisted: the white and the coloured; the first European and 'civilized', the second 'primitive', dominated by elementary worries and usually described with a zoological lexicon: colours, smells, promiscuity, dirt, disorder, noise, etc. Fanon focused on the bodily symptoms of this alienation, which he depicted as a kind of 'muscular spasm' or 'tetany'. It expressed an internalized aggressiveness that could turn to 'self-destruction', a behaviour that many Western observers interpreted as indigenous 'hysteria'.[82]

What Arendt called 'mad fury' was for Fanon a regenerating violence. In his view, violence was a necessary means of liberation that 'detoxified' and 'rehumanized' the oppressed: 'The colonized man liberates himself with and through violence.'[83] Born as a counterviolence, it became a crucial step in the dialectic process of liberation

---

82 Frantz Fanon, *The Wretched of the Earth*, trans. Richard Philcox (New York: Grove Press, 2004), 19, 217.

83 Ibid., 44.

where it played the role, in Hegelian terms, of the 'negation of the negation': not an illusory 'reconciliation' (the harmful perspective of 'humanizing' colonialism) but a radical suppression of both rulers and ruled. The subject–object relation established by colonialism was broken: the object had become a subject. Revolutionary violence could not be interpreted as a struggle for recognition; it was a struggle to destroy the colonial order and, in this sense, its disorder was 'both a symptom and a cure'.[84]

Of course, this conceptual metamorphosis of Arendtian 'mad fury' into Fanonian redemptive violence implies an *epistemic displacement*: viewing colonialism through the eyes of the colonized and adopting a non-Western observation point. Arendt was incapable of such a change of perspective. It is interesting to observe that Jean Améry (Hans Mayer), an Austrian Jew who had been deported to Auschwitz and supported the FLN during the Algerian War, admired Fanon and defended his vision of violence. Fanon, he pointed out, 'was no longer in the closed circuit of hatred, contempt, and resentment'.[85] His vision was political and had nothing in common with mythical, nihilistic or mystical glorifications of violence such as could be found in the writings of Georges Sorel, the young Walter Benjamin ('divine violence'), or Georges Bataille (suffering as a sensualist accession to the sacred). Violence and oppression were not an inescapable destiny; their immemorial chain could be broken. In *At the Mind's Limits* (1967), his testimony on war and deportation, Améry recalled that when being tortured as a Resistance member in Fort Breendonk in Belgium, he longed to be able to give 'concrete social form to [his] dignity by punching a human face'.[86] According to Améry, Fanon's conception of violence was at the same time existential and historical. It was undoubtedly provided with 'patently messianic-chiliastic aspects', but this simply reinforced its legitimacy: 'Freedom and dignity must be attained by way of violence, in order to be freedom and

---

84   Ibid., 217.

85   Jean Améry, 'The Birth of Man from the Spirit of Violence: Frantz Fanon the Revolutionary' (1969), *Wasafiri*, 20/44 (2005): 14.

86   Jean Améry, *At the Mind's Limits: Contemplations by a Survivor on Auschwitz and Its Realities* (Bloomington: Indiana University Press, 1980), 91.

dignity'.[87] It is not as an existentialist philosopher (Sartre had prefaced *The Wretched of the Earth*) that Améry defended Fanon's view; he did as a Jewish survivor of the Nazi camps. Revolutionary violence, he wrote, 'is not just the midwife of history, but the midwife of the human being discovering and fashioning himself in history'.[88]

In *The Origins of Totalitarianism* Arendt had grasped the genetic link that connected nineteenth-century imperialism with National Socialism and its extermination policies, but she abandoned this powerful intuition in her later works and, in the last instance, her approach to politics remained deeply Eurocentric. Her essay on revolution did not mention the Haitian Revolution. The overthrow of colonialism by a self-emancipatory movement of enslaved peoples was 'unthinkable' within her category of freedom. Despite her fruitful intuitions at the end of the Second World War, she ultimately rejoined the Eurocentric mainstream.

As Domenico Losurdo observes, in the nineteenth century freedom was restrained by powerful class, race and gender boundaries: only property allowed complete citizenship to white males, whereas proletarians, colonized people and women did not have the right to vote.[89] Thereafter, a genealogy of freedom should be viewed as a process connecting three forms of liberation that historically took the names of socialism, anticolonialism, and feminism.

Freedom, Bread and Roses

In fact, the link between freedom and social emancipation is far from being a peculiarity of the French Revolution. In 1848, the German radicals pointed out that the 'freedom to read' (*Pressenfreiheit*) could not be truly enjoyed without the 'freedom to feed' (*Fressenfreiheit*), an aphorism that Bertolt Brecht would reformulate as 'first comes food, then morality'. In February 1917, the Russian Revolution started with a demonstration of women in Saint-Petersburg demanding bread; a few months later, the Bolsheviks took power by promising peace, the

---

87 Jean Améry, 'The Birth of Man from the Spirit of Violence', 16.
88 Ibid.
89 Losurdo, *Liberalism: A Counter-History*.

factories to the workers, and the land to the peasants. The meaning of this link between political freedom and social emancipation was well captured by the textile workers involved in the 1912 strike in Lawrence, Massachusetts, when they coined the slogan: 'Bread for all, and roses too'.[90]

In fact, most experiences of liberation mean the invention of new practices that merge not only social emancipation and political freedom but also a deep transformation in cultural, aesthetic, sexual and many other realms of collective life. In April 1871, during the Paris Commune, the Federation of Artists led by Gustave Courbet published a Manifesto that summarized this aspiration in the concept of 'communal luxury'.[91] As Kristin Ross explains, this meant neither state collectivism nor a mimicry of bourgeois luxury but rather 'equality in action' and the socialization of all enriching and enjoyable human activities. As the communard geographer Élisée Reclus wrote several years later, the Commune had set up for the future

a society in which there are no masters by birth, title or wealth, and no slaves by origins, caste or salary. Everywhere the word 'commune' was understood in the largest sense, as referring to a new humanity, made up of free and equal companions, oblivious to the existence of old boundaries, helping each other in peace from one end of the world to the other.[92]

Similar aspirations emerged in many other revolutionary experiences. During the first years of Soviet Russia, between 1918 and 1922, Chagall, Lissitzky and Malevich created in Vitebsk the People's Art School. Despite its poor material conditions and the conflict between

---

90 See Bruce Watson, *Bread and Roses: Mills, Migrants, and the Struggle for the American Dream* (New York: Penguin, 2005). On the feminist dimension of this slogan, see Sheila Rowbotham, *Women, Resistance and Revolution: A History of Women and Revolution in the Modern World* (London, New York: Verso, 2014 [1974]), Chapter 5 (on the Lawrence strike, 111–12). In 2004 Ken Loach's *Bread and Roses* came out, a beautiful film on the strikes of immigrant workers in Los Angeles.

91 Quoted in Kristin Ross, *Communal Luxury: The Political Imaginary of the Paris Commune* (London, New York: Verso, 2015), 38.

92 Ibid., 5.

its different pictorial currents – figurative painting, cubism, futurism, and suprematism – this institution aimed at transforming everyday life and reshaping the urban landscape with new aesthetic forms. Its artists created posters and magazines, designed tramway tickets and food stamps, decorated building façades, squares and streets.[93] This was the time in which Alexandra Kollontai led the Zhenotdel, the 'Women's Department' of the Soviet government, and theorized free love and sexual liberation in a society where human relations were no longer property relations. 'A jealous and proprietary attitude to the person loved', she wrote in 1921, 'must be replaced by a comradely understanding of the other and an acceptance of his or her freedom.'[94]

In *Homage to Catalonia* (1938), George Orwell gives a striking portrait of Barcelona during the first months of the Spanish Civil War, when the city was transformed by the invention of new practices of liberty. His description of the Catalan capital as he discovered it in December 1936 deserves to be quoted:

The aspect of Barcelona was something startling and overwhelming. … Every shop and café had an inscription saying that it had been collectivized; even the bootblacks had been collectivized and their boxes painted red and black. Waiters and shop-walkers looked you in the face and treated you as an equal. Servile and even ceremonial forms of speech had temporarily disappeared. … There were no private motor-cars, they had all been commandeered, and all the trams and taxis and much of the other transport were painted red and black. The revolutionary posters were everywhere, flaming from the walls in clean reds and blues that made the few remaining advertisements look like daubs of mud. … In outward appearance it was a town in which the wealthy classes had practically ceased to exist. Except for a small number of women and foreigners there were no 'well-dressed' people at all. Practically everyone wore

93   See the essays edited by Angela Lampe, *Chagall, Lissitzky, Malevitch: L'Avant-garde russe à Vitebsk 1918–1922* (Paris: Éditions du Centre Pompidou, 2018).

94   Alexandra Kollontai, 'Theses on Communist Morality in the Sphere of Marital Relations' (1921), *Selected Writings*, ed. Alix Holt (London: Allison and Busby, 1977), 231.

rough working-class clothes, or blue overalls, or some variant of the
militia uniform. All this was queer and moving. There was much
in it that I did not understand, but I recognized it immediately as a
state of affairs worth fighting for.[95]

Barcelona 1936, Hotel Ritz transformed into a popular
'Gastronomic Hotel' by the CNT Anarchists.

This passage illustrates the emotional dimension of liberation that
transcends the pathos of rhetorical formulas and makes for a new
intensity of life, the discovery of new human relationships between
people themselves and with the world. Freedom fixed as a juridical
status and a form of social justice implies the transcription of rights
into codified rules, which are permanent and regulate collective life.
Building a new society is a hard and often painful process. A liberating
action is more ephemeral but also very exciting. It is a moment of
self-emancipation, when ordinary people become historical subjects,
which is joyful and pleasant: it usually involves both souls and bodies,
as many images show.

But behind these liberating emotions a material substratum still
remains. In 1936 the CNT, the Spanish anarchist trade-union, created
a short film on the Hotel Ritz, once one of the most luxurious hotels
in Barcelona, now turned into a militia barracks and its famous res-
taurant become a lunchroom.[96] This movie materializes the concept
of 'communal luxury' – enjoyment grounded in the suppression of

95   George Orwell, *Homage to Catalonia*, Introduction by Lionel Trilling
(New York: Harvest Books, 1980), 4–5.

96   I am grateful to Julián Casanova for drawing my attention to this film.

social hierarchies and privileges – by focusing on food: liberation meant eating one's fill and gastronomy was no longer reserved for a wealthy caste. No freedom without social justice, a principle that could also be translated as no freedom without food – or, in more hedonistic terms, bread for all but also good wine and a delicious dessert. Freedom and liberation may be conceptually distinguishable but they are not historically understandable without considering their symbiotic relationship. There is no freedom without liberation from necessity, in other words without social emancipation. Otherwise, freedom simply means privilege, exactly as it was conceived of in the nineteenth century, when it was opposed to democracy (viewed in turn as Terror and plebeian despotism). The entanglement between liberty and equality structures the identity of the Left, and defines the divide between the left-wing and the right-wing conceptions of liberty.

It is probably true that, in the same way in which classical liberalism sacralized property, the radical left fetishized liberation by neglecting the political and juridical system of norms required for establishing freedom as a durable order. This was the meaning of the severe criticism that Rosa Luxemburg directed toward the Bolsheviks, a few months after the birth of the Soviet government and the dissolution of the Russian Constituent Assembly. Writing from a German prison, she emphasized the historical relevance of the October Revolution, a step in the process of proletarian emancipation that she unconditionally supported against conservatism and reaction, but she did not hide her disagreement with several measures taken by the Bolsheviks and also, more profoundly, with their conception of power. Proletarian dictatorship, she pointed out, was a *class*, not a *party* dictatorship, and by consequence it should mean 'the most active, unlimited participation of the mass of the people, or unlimited democracy'. Addressing Lenin and Trotsky's claim that the Bolsheviks had 'never been idol-worshippers of formal democracy', she felt necessary to clarify:

We have always distinguished the social kernel from the political form of *bourgeois* democracy; we have always revealed the hard kernel of social inequality and lack of freedom hidden under the sweet shell of formal equality and freedom – not in order to reject the latter but to spur the working class into not being satisfied with the shell, but rather, by conquering political power, to create a socialist democracy to replace bourgeois democracy – not to eliminate democracy altogether.[97]

Rosa Luxemburg (ca. 1900).

Dictatorship, Luxemburg concluded, 'consists in the *manner of applying democracy*, not in its *elimination*'.[98]

Liberation of Time

According to Marx, human emancipation means, in the last analysis, the liberation of time. The history of capitalism can be retraced as a large and violent process of mastering time by submitting human beings to the constraints of a production system that possesses its own temporality. Many scholars have described the advent of modernity as the rationalization of time: the dissemination of clocks, the progressive

---

97 Rosa Luxemburg, 'The Russian Revolution' (1918), *The Rosa Luxemburg Reader*, eds Peter Hudis and Kevin B. Anderson (New York: Monthly Review Press, 2014), 308.
98 Ibid.

synchronization of social life between the cities and the country and between nations and continents, and the development of the division of labour as a whole of temporarily connected activities.[99] This meant the emergence of a productive time more and more disconnected from nature: a mechanical time that triumphed with the industrial revolution. The presence of clocks on the façades of public buildings, the introduction of chronometers in factories, and the spread of watches whose aesthetic form was increasingly sacrificed to precision and functionality, beat the time of modern capitalism. For millions of people whose entire life – both work and leisure – was organized according to the cyclical cadence of nature – the progression of the seasons, the variation of day and night, of sun, rain and snow – the industrial rationalization of time did not mean the mastering of nature but rather their own submission to the impersonal Moloch of mechanical production. Their customs, rituals and cultural practices – their inherited 'liberties', speaking with Edmund Burke – were ruthlessly supplanted by a new labour process whose rationality was purely mechanical and productive, disconnected from both the external changes of nature and the psycho-physical needs of human bodies. Gradually but inexorably the nineteenth century unified the lived time of people whose customs had been moulded by a rural world with the measured time of the industrial revolution. Sundials were progressively replaced by clock towers.[100] The rationalization of time was much more than an admirable technological accomplishment: it was, as Edward P. Thompson pointed out, the advent of a new 'time-sense' intimately related to 'time-measurement as a means of labour exploitation'.[101] As both Thompson and Foucault have meticulously explained, this historical change corresponded with a broad process of disciplining

99   See Jürgen Osterhammel, *The Transformation of the World: A Global History of the Nineteenth Century* (Princeton: Princeton University Press, 2014), Chapter 2: 45–76.

100   See Alain Corbin, 'The Daily Arithmetic of the Nineteenth Century', *Time, Desire and Horror: Towards a History of the Senses* (Cambridge: Polity, 1995), 1–12.

101   Edward P. Thompson, 'Time, Work-Discipline and Industrial Capitalism' (1967), *Customs in Common: Studies in Traditional Popular Culture* (New York: The New Press, 1992), 382.

that affected all dimensions of social life: from elementary schools to barracks and factories, people learned the disciplining of bodies and the compelling rules of capitalist time. The 'iron cage' that Max Weber described as the ineluctable result of human life phagocytized by the demons of rationality was also a time-cage. Far from embodying an anachronistic form of technological nihilism – according to a frequent but mistaken depiction – the Luddite machine-breakers were simply expressing their radical rejection of the capitalist organization of time.

In Europe, this metamorphosis of social time ran from the industrial revolution to the Great War, an event that could well be described as a powerful step in the denaturalization of human life. When millions of peasants in uniform discovered the sinister spectacle of total war, with nights lit up by flares and blasts and bodies constantly imperilled by tanks, bombings and the fire of machine guns, time was organized by a murderous apparatus that had lost any human or natural aspect. Walter Benjamin described the Great War as the symbolic end of the storyteller. For a generation that was born in a rural world and had realized the fragility of human bodies on fields of mechanical and serialized extermination, experience had become an empty and meaningless word. Experience, the substance of any storyteller's narration, implies a transmissible memory which industrial war had annihilated.[102] Like the workers in a Fordist factory, the soldiers of modern armies executed mechanical tasks for which any inherited knowledge or practical culture was utterly useless.

Marx's analysis of the historical process of capital accumulation does not ignore its inner time-structure. The first volume of *Capital* describes the linear, homogeneous and abstract time of production; the second deals with the cyclical time of the expanded reproduction of capital and the circulation of its exchange values; and the third merges the time of production and that of circulation into a single movement (*Gesamtkapital*).[103] Far from being a homogeneous or harmonious path,

---

102   Walter Benjamin, 'The Storyteller: Observations on the Works of Nikolai Leskov' (1936), *WBSW*, vol. 3, 143–4.

103   See Stavros Tombazos, *Time in Marx: The Categories of Time in Marx's Capital* (Leiden: Brill, 2014).

this also means periodic spasms that break the continuity of the process itself and, combined with extra-economic factors, transform it into a sequence of expanding and retracting waves. Thus, the premise of capitalism is not only the separation of the workers from their means of production but also the expropriation of their life-time, which is now 'rationalized' and measured according to the production of commodities. Once transformed into 'abstract' work – a change related to the advent of 'labour power' already mentioned in the first chapter of this book – the worker's activity is disconnected from natural time. And abstract work means the reification of the labouring subject. Differently from a craftsman who creates use values by mastering the labour process and fixing its time according to his own needs and decisions, the factory worker produces commodities: exchange values. Not only do such workers not possess the tools of their labour, they do not even control the labour process in which they are involved and their time is calculated according to external criteria.[104] The abstract work of capitalist production means the alienation of the producers, the imprisonment of their lives inside the time walls of work discipline and organized production. In his economic manuscripts of 1857–58, Marx considers the abolition of capitalism as the restitution of time to human accomplishment and happiness. Instead of being the condition for capital accumulation, the development of the productive forces should create free time and transform the producers into free subjects: with the end of alienation, abstract work is replaced by the creation of a common, socialized wealth, and the measure of progress is no longer work but *free time*.

> Real economizing – saving – consists in the saving of labour time. ... But this saving is identical with the development of the productive power. Hence in no way renunciation of enjoyment but development of *power*, of the capacity to produce and hence of both the capacity for and the means of enjoyment. The capacity for enjoyment is a condition for it, and hence the basic means for it, and this capacity

---

104   The best study on this topic remains Harry Braverman, *Labour and Monopoly Capital: The Degradation of Work in the Twentieth Century* (New York: Monthly Review Press, 1998).

is created by the development of an individual disposition, productive power. The saving of labour time is equivalent to the increase
of free time, i.e. time for the full development of the individual,
which itself, as the greatest productive force, in turn reacts upon
the productive power of labour. … It is self-evident that immediate
labour time itself cannot remain in abstract antithesis to free time, as
it appears to do from the standpoint of bourgeois political economy.
… Free time – which is both leisure and time for higher activity
– has naturally transformed its possessor into another subject.[105]

In the third volume of *Capital*, Marx describes socialism as the transition from the realm of necessity to the realm of true freedom,
meaning a creative organization of life no longer subjected to material constraints. In fact, he writes, 'the realm of freedom actually
begins only where labour, which is determined by necessity and
mundane considerations, ceases.' When the satisfaction of human
needs are disconnected from the imperative of increasing the forces
of production, then socialized human beings will be effectively free.
It is beyond the 'realm of necessity' that 'begins that development of
human energy which is an end in itself, the true realm of freedom'.
In other words, socialism means free time: 'The shortening of the
working day is its basic prerequisite.'[106] Even while criticizing Fourier,
who depicted the transformation of labour into a pleasant game, Marx
prized the French utopian thinker for his capacity to imagine a society
of conscious subjects inspired by the search for collective happiness,
the opposite of alienated workers involved in an economic system
based on profit. Herbert Marcuse, one of the first thinkers to stress
the relevance of the passage quoted above from Marx's *Grundrisse*,
drew a clear conclusion:

Freedom is living without toil, without anxiety: the play of human
faculties. The realization of freedom is a problem of *time*: reduction of the working day to the minimum which turns quantity

---

105   Karl Marx, 'Economic Manuscripts of 1857–1858', *MECW*, vol. 29, 97.
106   Karl Marx, 'Capital, volume III', *MECW*, vol. 37, 807.

into quality. A socialist society is a society in which free time, not labour time is the social measure of wealth and the dimension of the individual existence.[107]

From this point of view – the pleasure principle as motor of human agency and the foundation of a free society – there is a remarkable continuity between Fourier's utopian socialism and Marxism. According to Paul Lafargue, author of the provocative essay *The Right to Be Lazy* (1883), socialism was the radical antithesis of Protestant asceticism and its work ethic. In a century in which the average factory workday was fourteen hours, he claimed its reduction to three hours as a reasonable goal. With a romantic anti-capitalist posture that sarcastically mocked both philanthropists and admirers of technical progress, he stigmatized capitalism as inhumanity. 'Far better were it to scatter pestilence and to poison the springs', he wrote, 'than to erect a capitalist factory in the midst of a rural population. Introduce factory work, and farewell joy, health and liberty; farewell to all that makes life beautiful and worth living.'[108] Socialism, he continued, meant the end of 'the prejudices of Christian ethics, economic ethics and free-thought ethics'. It meant the rediscovery by the proletariat of its 'natural instincts', which consist in proclaiming 'the Rights of Laziness, a thousand times more noble and more sacred than the anaemic Rights of Man concocted by the metaphysical lawyers of the bourgeois revolution.' The proletariat, he concluded, 'must accustom itself to working but three hours a day, reserving the rest of the day and night for leisure and feasting'.[109]

Borrowing the words of Marx's famous preface to his *Contribution to the Critique of Political Economy* (1859), one might call the liberation of time the end of the 'prehistory of human society' and the

---

107 Herbert Marcuse, 'Preface' (1957) to Raya Dunayevskaya, *Marxism and Freedom: From 1776 Until Today* (Amherst, NY: Humanities Books, 2000), xxiii.

108 Paul Lafargue, *The Right to Be Lazy and Other Studies* (Chicago: Charles H. Kerr, 1907), 22.

109 Ibid., 29. On the history of this pamphlet, see Leslie Derfler, *Paul Lafargue and the Founding of French Marxism 1842–1882* (Cambridge, MA: Harvard University Press, 1991), 177–84.

Paul Lafargue (1871).

beginning of its true history.[110] This transition, however, could be interpreted in two different ways, both suggested by Marx's writings themselves. On the one hand, liberation of time could be viewed as the accomplishment of the development of productive forces within the framework of a social organization no longer oriented towards profit and exploitation, but still opposed to any premodern form of creative work. This approach was implicit in Marx's vision of Asia as an immutable and stagnant social system – a world of 'unchange-ableness' – that only the external blows of colonialism could shake and finally destroy.[111] Lenin defended a similarly apologetic view of the West as the time of progress opposed to the backward and slow time of Eastern Europe: exhuming an old metaphor, he accused the partisans of Jewish socialism of 'turning back the wheel of history', which rolled from St Petersburg to Berlin, London and New York rather than in the opposite direction.[112] On the other hand, Marx's emphasis on the abolition of capitalism as the end of the reification of the social world and of the alienation of human labour depicts the

---

110   Karl Marx, 'A Contribution to the Critique of Political Economy' (1859), *MECW*, 29: 264.

111   Karl Marx, 'Capital', *MECW*, vol. 35, 363–4.

112   Lenin, 'Critical Remarks on the National Question' (1913), *LCW*, vol. 20, 29.

transition from 'prehistory' to the true history of humankind as the advent of a new, liberated, and qualitatively different organization of time. The time of free human beings was not that of instrumental rationality, of the calculated beat of production and the frenetic dance of commodities: liberated time was the *negation* of capitalist time.[113]

Benjamin's Messianic Time

Liberation as the negation of capitalist time is the core of Walter Benjamin's theory of revolution, which he identified with the theological category of *messianic time*. Messianic Judaism imbued his interpretation of Marxism with an apocalyptic and eschatological dimension: the social and political liberation through class struggle and socialist revolution posited by classical Marxism coincided with messianic redemption. Instead of being the end point of a historical trajectory – the run of civilization from the Stone Age to a liberated and affluent society – socialism meant the cataclysmic advent of a post-historical age, of a new messianic time that radically broke with previous history and civilization. In 1921, probably influenced by the writings of Rosenzweig and Sorel, Benjamin wrote an enigmatic text on violence clearly oriented towards nihilistic anarchism. Describing history as a continuous display of oppressive violence, he imagined the irruption of a 'divine violence' in the realm of history that would destroy any political order based on law and create its own legitimacy.[114] A few years later, this vision of redemptive violence – as radical as it is abstract, not to say metaphysical – took a new formulation through the language of Marxism. 'Divine violence' became the proletarian revolution, rooted in a social and historical subject.

It is in his famous theses 'On the Concept of History', a highly cryptic text, that Benjamin's attempt to find a synthesis between

---

113   This interpretation is convincingly developed by Sergio Tischler Visquerra, 'Tiempo de reificación y tiempo de insubordinación', *Memoria, tiempo y sujeto* (Puebla: BUAP, G&G Editores, 2005), 151–74. See also Antonio Negri, *Marx Beyond Marx: Lessons on the Grundrisse*, trans. Michael Ryan, Mauricio Viano and Harry Cleaver (New York: Autonomedia, 1989), Chapter 8, in particular 165.

114   Walter Benjamin, 'Critique of Violence', *WBSW*, vol. 1, 236–52.

messianic Judaism and secular Marxism reached its most accomplished form. In the prolegomena to this text, he pointed out that Marx had 'secularized the idea of messianic time [*messianische Zeit*]' in his vision of the 'classless society'. Unlike more widespread forms of romantic nationalism or religious conservatism, whose nostalgia harked back to supposedly organic social hierarchies and authoritarian political institutions, Benjamin's critique of modernity did not aim at restoring the past. His wistfulness for bygone times was rather a detour through the past looking towards the future. Far from rehabilitating absolutism or feudalism, his romantic anti-capitalism was eminently utopian, directed at overcoming the bourgeois order and moving toward socialism. In his essay 'Paris, Capital of the Nineteenth Century' (1935), he described a dialectical tension between the image of the classless community of a forgotten past and the future of an emancipated society. The most ancient age survived in the 'dream images' (*Wunschbilder*) of human beings, where they joined utopian expectations:

> Corresponding to the form of the new means of production, which in the beginning is still ruled by the form of the old (Marx), are images in the collective consciousness in which the new is permeated with the old. These images are wish images …. In the dream in which each epoch entertains images of its successor, the latter appears wedded to elements of primal history [*Urgeschichte*] – that is, to elements of a classless society. And the experiences of such a society – as stored in the unconscious of the collective – engender, through interpenetration with what is new, the utopia that has left its trace in a thousand configurations of life, from enduring edifices to passing fashions.[115]

Benjamin's conception of history was radically opposed to *historicism* (that is, in his lexicon, a form of positivism he identified with scholars like Leopold Ranke and Numa Denis Fustel de Coulanges). For historicism, the past was a closed continent and a definitively consummated process; it simply meant the accumulation of dead stuff ready to be

---

115   Walter Benjamin, 'Paris, Capital of the Nineteenth Century', *WBSW*, vol. 3, 33–4.

Walter Benjamin (1929).

chronologically ordered, archived and put into a museum. To this conception he opposed a vision of history as an open temporality. According to Benjamin, the past was at the same time permanently threatened and never altogether lost; it haunted the present, and could be reactivated.

Historicism was a form of 'empathy with the victors' based on the 'indolence of the heart'.[116] Against this approach that accepted the victory of the rulers as ineluctable, he defended a dialectical and redemptive relationship with the past, which could be brought back by working through the contradictions of the present. Benjamin called 'recollection' or 'remembrance' (*Eingedenken*) this process of reactivation of an unfinished past. Of course, rescuing history did not mean going back and remaking it; it meant rather changing the present. In other words, in order to salvage the past, human beings should rebirth and realize the hopes of the vanquished, to give new life to their wishes and expectations. Whereas historicism defended a purely linear and chronological vision of history as *khronos*, a 'homogeneous and empty time', historical materialism advocated a dialectical conception of history as *kairos*, that is, an open, restless, and changeful temporality.

---

116   Walter Benjamin, 'On the Concept of History' (1940), *WBSW*, vol. 4, 391.

Benjamin portrayed social democracy as the political equivalent of historicism. Its ineffectiveness was rooted in a vision of history as a quantitative accumulation of productive forces according to which economic growth meant social progress, and the advent of socialism appeared as the ineluctable outcome of civilization. In the culture and practice of social democracy, progress was not a potentiality of science and technology, it was its necessary and irreversible result: 'something that automatically pursued a straight or spiral course.' Nothing, he observed, had 'corrupted the German working class so much as the notion that it was moving with the current'.[117] This conception was antipodal to Marx's theory, Benjamin explained, which did not view the 'oppressed class' as the harbinger of material progress but rather as 'the avenger that completes the task of liberation in the name of generations of the downtrodden.'[118]

Rescuing the past meant seizing its emergence in what Benjamin called 'now-time' or 'actualization' (*Jetzt-Zeit*), the dialectic link between a bygone time and the utopian future: 'what has been [*Gewesene*] comes together in a flash with the now [*Jetzt*]] to form a constellation.'[119] This meeting of past and present condensed itself into ephemeral but intense images. Thus, the concept of 'now-time' designated the disruptive moment in which the continuum of chronological time broke up and the past suddenly emerged in the present. The concepts of 'now-time' and 'recollection' suppose a symbiotic relationship between history and memory. In this sense, according to Benjamin, history was not only a 'science' but also, and perhaps above all, 'a form of recollection' (*Eingedenken*). Conceived of in this way, it resulted in a montage of 'dialectical images' (*Denkbilder*) rather than in a linear narrative (typical of historicism).

In his fourteenth thesis of 1940, Benjamin defined revolution as 'a tiger's leap into the past' that took place in the realm of history, meaning in a given society with its antagonistic class relations and political conflicts: 'The same leap in the open air of history is the

---

117   Ibid., 393.

118   Ibid., 394.

119   Walter Benjamin, *The Arcades Project*, trans. Howard Leiland and Kevin Mclaughlin (Cambridge: Harvard University Press, 2002), 462.

dialectical one, which is how Marx understood the revolution.'[120] Revolution was a potentiality, not the automatic result of historical development. The alternative was fascism, which threatened both the present and the past, living human beings and their ancestors. In a passage that implicitly evoked Rosa Luxemburg's warning of 'socialism or barbarism', he pointed out that fascism 'had not ceased to be victorious' and, if it should ultimately win, 'even the dead will not be safe.'

As we saw in Chapter One, Marx's vision of revolutions as the 'locomotives of history' channelled a teleological philosophy of history against which Benjamin opposed his theological conception of revolution as a reactivation of the past triggered by the train's 'emergency brake'.[121] This view places Benjamin in a quite unique position in both the Marxist and the Jewish traditions. On the one hand, he rejected the teleological interpretations of historical materialism; on the other, he clearly departed from all inherited forms of messianic theology, which posited redemption as the irruption of God into history for which human beings should wait, not provoke or accomplish. For Benjamin, the messianic interruption of the linear course of history was the result of revolutionary action. As Herbert Marcuse has observed, this vision tried to overcome dialectically the traditional conflict between religious chiliasm and atheistic socialism in a synthesis in which 'redemption became a materialist political concept: the concept of revolution.'[122] In short, revolution was the core of a reinterpretation of Marxism built around three correlated themes: a critique of *historicism* (linear temporality), a critique of *deterministic causality* (automatic social change), and a critique of the *ideology of Progress* (both a teleological philosophy and a politics of impotence). Benjamin's Marxism was a theory of historical discontinuity and messianic breaks. Instead

---

120   Benjamin, 'On the Concept of History', 395.

121   Walter Benjamin, 'Prolegomena to On the Concept of History', *WBSW*, vol. 4, 402.

122   Herbert Marcuse, 'Revolution und Kritik der Gewalt. Zur Geschichtsphilosophie Walter Benjamins', in Peter Bulthaup (ed.), *Materialen zu Benjamin Thesen 'Über den Begriff der Geschichte'* (Frankfurt: Suhrkamp, 1975), 24. On Benjamin's Marxism, see Michael Löwy, *Fire Alarm: Reading Walter Benjamin's On the Concept of History* (London, New York: Verso, 2005).

of accelerating the current of history, socialism meant a change of civilization, which corresponded with the transition from a historical to a messianic temporality. In terms of political theology, this could be defined as messianic redemption: the passage from an earthly city (*civitas terrena*) to a heavenly city (*civitas celestis*).

In his theses 'On the Concept of History', Benjamin evoked the passage from historical to messianic time through a secular image: the insurgents of the July Revolution who, 'simultaneously and independently', at several locations in Paris, fired at the dials of clocktowers. They wished to replace the quantitative and 'rational' time of capitalism with the qualitative time of liberation, the joyful, non-instrumental and non-utilitarian time of a community created by the revolution itself. 'What characterizes revolutionary classes at their moment of action', Benjamin wrote, 'is the awareness that they are about to make the continuum of history explode.'[123] Another evidence of this search for a qualitative time not measurable by clocks, Benjamin added, was the new calendar introduced by the French Revolution: a representation of time grounded in historical consciousness; the remembrance of meaningful events instead of the regular, ineluctable, and desperately identical progression of hours, days, months and years.

Introduced by the Convention in 1793, the revolutionary calendar was abolished by the First French Empire in 1806. Despite claiming the legacy of revolution, Napoleon wished to re-establish the historical continuity of his rule with the Old Regime.[124] Like the festivals, rituals and symbols created by the Revolution, the new calendar meant the advent of a new age for a 'regenerated' society. It is interesting to observe that the Bolsheviks did not create a new calendar but simply abolished the Julian one and replaced it with the Gregorian, which Lenin called the 'Western European Calendar'. Of course, they introduced new national holidays – 22 January commemorated the 'Bloody Sunday' that started the 1905 Revolution; 18 March remembered the Paris Commune; 1 May was dedicated to the Haymarket martyrs and became the Day of the International; 7 November was the Day of

---

123   Benjamin, 'On the Concept of History', 395.

124   See Mona Ozouf, 'Calendrier', in Furet and Ozouf (eds), *Dictionnaire critique de la Révolution Française*, 91–106.

the Proletarian Revolution, etc. – but the primary goal of this Soviet reform was to join a standardized world time. A few decades after the start of modern globalization, this was a necessity, but it was also the faithful mirror of a theory of history and society elaborated by revolutionary Westernizers like Lenin and Trotsky. During the first years of the USSR, the invention of a new, qualitative and utopian (messianic) temporality was the affair of both aesthetics and politics: on the one hand, the creations of the futurist and suprematist avant-garde; on the other, the strategic preparations for world revolution by the Communist International. In the economic field, the Bolsheviks desperately fought to rebuild a devastated and impoverished country. The growth of productive forces was an inescapable imperative. This is the context in which the constructivist attempts to merge art and production coexisted with the discussion about a possible introduction of Taylorism in the Soviet factories. Like most uprisings of the twentieth century, the Bolshevik revolution took place in conditions of social and economic backwardness. It was the result, as Trotsky argued, of Russia's 'uneven and combined development', but its transformation into a permanent revolution was stopped in Berlin, Munich, Budapest and Vienna, the cities where, between 1919 and 1923, the outposts of a Western socialist revolution tragically failed. The true 'realm of freedom' remained, speaking with Benjamin, a *Wunschbild*, an 'image of desire'. Lenin and Trotsky realized what freedom meant during a civil war, with a form perhaps most akin to the definition once given by Saint-Just: 'Revolution is the war of freedom against its enemies.'[125]

---

125   Quoted in Ozouf, 'Liberté', 268.

Chapter 6

Historicizing Communism

Communism is for us not a *state of affairs* which is to be established, an *ideal* to which reality [will] have to adjust itself. We call communism the *real* movement which abolishes the present state of things.

Karl Marx, Friedrich Engels, *The German Ideology* (1845)

What has finished today is the monstrous step of a gigantic adventure to change the world.

Edgar Morin, 'Preface' (1991) to the
second edition of *Autocritique* (1959)

Periodization

At the conclusion of this study, let us try to recapitulate the general picture of modern revolutions. Three successive waves swept across the long nineteenth century. The first was that of the 'Revolutionary Atlantic', which started in America in 1776, ran through France in 1789, and finally reached the Caribbean where, on the first of January 1804, insurgent slaves proclaimed the independent state of Haiti.[1] The Revolutionary Atlantic was a political laboratory.

---

1   I borrow this definition from Jürgen Osterhammel, *The Transformation of the World: A Global History of the Nineteenth Century*, trans. Patrick Camiller (Princeton: Princeton University Press, 2014), 529. It is significant that, distinguishing the Atlantic Revolutions as a specific step in the history of revolutions,

It is during this 'saddle-period' (*Sattelzeit*) lasting from 1776 to 1804 that concepts such as freedom, equality, emancipation, and revolution itself appeared with their present meaning. They were inscribed in all the programmatic texts of that time, from the American Declaration of Independence (1776) to the French Declaration of the Rights of Man (1789); from the decree of the French National Convention abolishing slavery (1794) to Simón Bolívar's Angostura Address (1819), the manifesto of the struggles for national liberation in Latin America that drew inspiration from the Haitian Revolution.[2] The second wave took place in the middle of the century. It was wider than the first, but it did not have the same spatial and political unity. Its most significant moments – the European revolutions of 1848, the Taiping rebellion in imperial China (1850–64), the Indian rebellion of 1857, and the American Civil War (1861–65) – remained disconnected, without being able to merge in a common process. Their synchronization did not depend on their political affinities and did not correspond to a common dialectic between Europe, Asia and North America. Too many cultural, ideological and political discrepancies separated the Taiping rebels – inspired by a peculiar syncretism between Confucianism and evangelical Protestantism – from the sepoys who fought against British rule in the name of restoring precolonial India. The third wave included the Eurasian revolutions that broke out around the edges of the Great War. The uprising against the Tsarist Empire in Russia in 1905 had a strong impact on Asia and the Islamic world. As Lenin observed, it powerfully inspired the Constitutional Revolution in Iran (1905–11), the Young Turk Revolution in the Ottoman Empire (1908), and the movement of Sun Yat-sen that, putting an end to the Qing Dynasty, proclaimed the Republic of China in 1911.[3] This third wave joined the Americas with the Mexican Revolution

---

beside the religious heresies (fifteenth and sixteenth centuries) and the modern socialist revolutions (from 1848 onwards), Martin Malia only considers the English, American and French Revolutions, without devoting a single line to the Haitian Revolution. See Martin Malia, *History's Locomotives: Revolutions and the Making of the Modern World* (New Haven: Yale University Press, 2006).

2 Osterhammel, *Transformation of the World*, 543.

3 Lenin, 'Lecture on the 1905 Revolution' (1917), *LCW*, vol. 23, 236–53.

(1910–17), a peasant struggle for land and freedom that closed an old and opened a new cycle of revolutions, at the intersection of the nineteenth and the twentieth centuries. With the exceptions of Russia and Mexico, this third wave was made of 'revolutions from above'[4] carried out by intellectual and military elites. They recalled the Italian Risorgimento, a change accomplished without popular support or a limited, elite-fomented mass mobilization that Gramsci defined, in his *Prison Notebooks*, as a non-Jacobin or 'passive revolution'.[5] The Paris Commune, the most significant revolutionary experience of the nineteenth century for both its socialist goals and its durable memory, was, on the contrary, a revolution from below, but it was an isolated firework that could not be inscribed in any supranational wave. Of course, it followed the French upheavals of 1830 and 1848, from which it inherited its republicanism, its socialist egalitarianism, and also some of its inspirers like Auguste Blanqui. Nonetheless, its meteoric trajectory did not find any connections with similar movements elsewhere.

The revolutionary map of the twentieth century is as huge as it is diverse and fragmented: it includes socialist revolutions in the West and anticolonial revolutions in the South, which in many cases took a socialist character; revolutions from above in all continents and antibureaucratic revolutions in several countries of real socialism. The 'age of catastrophe', according to Eric Hobsbawm's striking definition, was not only a time of wars, fascism and genocide. It was also a time of high hopes in which socialism became a possible and concrete utopia. Socialist revolutions broke out in Eastern and Central Europe at the end of the Great War; in China in the mid-1920s; in Spain at the beginning of the Civil War in 1936; and in both Europe and Asia at the end of the Second World War: Yugoslavia, Greece, Indochina, and China between 1945 and 1949. To the east of the Danube and the Oder-Neisse line, capitalism was abolished from above through a process of structural assimilation to the USSR, a transformation quite similar to the destruction of feudalism

---

4   Osterhammel, *Transformation of the World*, 518.
5   Antonio Gramsci, *The Gramsci Reader: Selected Writings 1916–1935*, ed. David Forgcas (New York: New York University Press, 2000), 246–69.

accomplished in the same territories by the French army during the Napoleonic Wars (1792–1814).[6]

The Bolshevik hope of breaking the isolation of the USSR by extending the Russian Revolution to both Western Europe and Asia failed, and many of its defeats were tragic – Italy in 1922–26; China in 1925–27; Germany in 1933; Spain in 1939 – but ultimately it was the Red Army that changed the relations of force. In 1945, revolution had not won, but the USSR was no longer isolated. In the eyes of millions of people, the Red Army that planted a Soviet flag on the roof of a devastated Reichstag in May 1945 represented an ersatz revolution. The time of barricades was over; old-style uprisings had been replaced by a much more effective military force. In the postwar decades, the axis of revolution shifted from the West to the South: anticolonial and socialist revolutions broke out in Asia (China in 1949; Vietnam between 1954 and 1975); anti-imperialist and socialist revolutions in Latin America (Bolivia in 1951; Cuba in 1958; Chile in 1972–74; Nicaragua in 1979); antibureaucratic revolutions in Central Europe (Hungary in 1956; Czechoslovakia in 1968; Poland in 1980–81); and anticolonial revolutions in Africa (Algeria in 1954–62; Libya in 1969; Ethiopia in 1974; Angola and Mozambique in 1975). In some ways, the apogee of this second cycle was 1968, not really a revolution but rather a constellation of events which were in dialogue with each other. The lexicon of those years spoke of 'three sectors' of the world

---

6   Trotsky suggested this historical analogy in September 1939, just after the German-Soviet pact and the occupation of Poland: 'The first Bonaparte halted the revolution by means of a military dictatorship. However, when the French troops invaded Poland, Napoleon signed a decree: "Serfdom is abolished". This measure was dictated not by Napoleon's sympathies for the peasants, nor by democratic principles but rather by the fact that the Bonapartist dictatorship based itself not on feudal, but on bourgeois property relations. Inasmuch as Stalin's Bonapartist dictatorship bases itself not on private but on state property, the invasion of Poland by the Red Army should, in the nature of the case, result in the abolition of private capitalist property, so as thus to bring the regime of the occupied territories into accord with the regime of the USSR. This measure, revolutionary in character – "the expropriation of the expropriators" – is in this case achieved in a military bureaucratic fashion.' See Leon Trotsky, 'The USSR in War', *In Defense of Marxism* (New York: Pioneer Publishers, 1942), 18.

revolution – an expression coined by Ernest Mandel[7] – that needed to be anti-capitalist in the West, anti-Stalinist in the East, and anti-imperialist in the South. In 1968, with the Tet offensive in Vietnam, the Prague Spring and the barricades of Paris, these three dimensions merged into a single insurgent wave that was not only global but also *synchronic*. The feeling of participating in a world rebellion affected an entire generation across continents. Besides the world wars, the twentieth century did not witness any other similarly unified events.

Many of these revolutions were led by radical left-wing parties, others by national liberation movements, but with very few exceptions they all inscribed themselves within a socialist horizon. The Cuban Revolution, whose leadership was made up of Jacobin, democratic, and nationalist intellectuals, very quickly achieved a socialist character (this change was officially proclaimed by Fidel Castro in a famous speech of April 1961).[8] In the context of the Cold War this was almost inevitable. Most of the revolutions that did not take a socialist orientation failed or remained incomplete, as in Bolivia (1951–55) and Algeria (1954–65). While in many cases they had a socialist or communist leadership, they never had a purely proletarian dimension. Most of them recognized in Marx their inspirer, but the century of world revolution did not accomplish the outlook of *The Communist Manifesto*: the emergence of the proletariat as a class that, by emancipating itself, would liberate all mankind. In the age of Fordist capitalism and mass production, the industrial working class was the main actor in many crucial struggles – think of the US strikes of 1934–35, 1936 and 1968 in France, the 'hot autumn' of 1969 in Italy, the Argentinian *Cordobazo* in the same year, Chile's Unidad Popular in 1971–73, the Polish uprising of 1980, or the Korean

---

7   See Ernest Mandel, *Revolutionary Marxism Today* (London: New Left Books, 1979).

8   For a historiographical reassessment of the Cuban Revolution, driven to socialism initially from below (by popular mobilization) and then from above (by the choices of its leadership), see Samuel Farber, *The Origins of the Cuban Revolution Reconsidered* (Chapel Hill: North Carolina University Press, 2006). From the beginning, several analysts stressed the socialist dynamic of the Cuban Revolution. See Leo Huberman and Paul Sweezy, *Cuba: Anatomy of a Revolution* (New York: Monthly Review Press, 1960).

strikes of 1987–90, just to mention some significant moments – but it never carried out a revolution without creating a coalition with other social classes and groups. This was what had occurred in Russia in 1917, where the soviets also included soldiers and peasants, as well as in Yugoslavia in 1945. The German and Hungarian revolutions of 1919–20, which possessed a very pronounced proletarian character, resulted in calamitous defeats. The anticolonial revolutions were led by intellectual elites that claimed a socialist and a Marxist orientation, but their social base was made up of peasants.

In the first chapter of *History of the Russian Revolution*, Trotsky summarized his theory of uneven and combined development – initially elaborated to analyse the peculiarities of Russian history – in order to explain why socialist revolutions could take place in socially backward rather than in capitalist advanced countries:

> Unevenness, the most general law of the historic process, reveals itself most sharply and complexly in the destiny of the backward countries. Under the whip of external necessity their backward culture is compelled to make leaps. From the universal law of unevenness thus derives another law which, for the lack of a better name, we may call the law of *combined development* – by which we mean a drawing together of the different stages of the journey, a combining of the separate steps, an amalgam of archaic with more contemporary forms. Without this law, to be taken of course, in its whole material content, it is impossible to understand the history of Russia, and indeed of any country of the second, third or tenth cultural class.[9]

This was the first step of a theoretical reassessment that led to the abandonment of a Eurocentric view of revolution and the acknowledgment of its socially plural – today one would say 'intersectional' – rather than exclusively proletarian character. Therefore, the socialist revolutions of the twentieth century should be rethought in the same way in which the most recent historiography has revised the canonical

---

9   Leon Trotsky, *History of the Russian Revolution*, trans. Max Eastman (Chicago: Haymarket, 2008), 5.

interpretation of a nineteenth century built by a 'double' revolution, both economic and political: the English Industrial Revolution that transformed capitalism and the French Revolution that, culminating in the Napoleonic Wars, demolished the Old Regime in Europe.[10] If the nineteenth century was incontestably an age of modernization, such a process was neither rapid nor homogeneous: rather than the rise of the *bourgeois* state, it created hybrid forms of domination between an ascending bourgeoisie (not yet ruling politically) and a declining aristocracy that remained the core of a 'persistent' Old Regime. Analogously, the age of socialism resulted from a variety of hybrid revolutions in which, far from being the only actor, the proletarian classes interacted with other social layers, from the intelligentsia to the peasantry, and sometimes were even eclipsed by them. In the nineteenth century, socialism was viewed as the historical mission of the industrial working class: first accomplished in Western Europe, it would later be extended on a global scale. In the twentieth century, socialism was the horizon of world revolution. This major change was a product of the Russian Revolution, and this also explains why the twentieth-century revolutions were so deeply identified with communism.

Faces of Communism

The legacy of the October Revolution is torn between two antipodal interpretations. The rise to power of the Bolsheviks appeared, on the one hand, as the announcement of a global socialist transformation; on the other hand, as the event that set the stage for an epoch of totalitarianism. In 1927, Sergei Eisenstein shot *October*, a film that shaped the imagination of several generations in depicting revolution as an epic mass uprising. The historiographical equivalent of this work of art was Trotsky's *History of the Russian Revolution*, both a chronological and an analytical reconstruction of this event, in which the empathetic, colourful narration of the witness merged with the conceptual insight of the Marxist thinker, like an astonishing fusion of the styles of Jules

---

10   Eric J. Hobsbawm, *The Age of Revolution: 1789–1848* (New York: Vintage, 1996 [1962]). Osterhammel criticizes this approach in *Transformation of the World*, 543.

Michelet and Karl Marx. In a chapter of his biography of the head of the Red Army titled 'The Revolutionary as Historian', Isaac Deutscher stresses Trotsky's capacity to grasp the emotions of oppressed people suddenly transformed into political actors by combining this 'imaginative élan' with 'crystalline clarity'.[11] The result was a book written with both passion and thought. For decades, most of the left – far beyond official communist movements – perceived the October Revolution in a similar way: as both the iconic image of utopian aspirations and the irrefutable evidence of a teleological vision positing socialism as the natural end of history.

The contrary interpretation depicts the Bolsheviks as the embodiment of the totalitarian potentialities of modernity. After the consolidation of the USSR in the second half of the 1920s, the initial descriptions of a herd of baboons jumping around a field of ruins and skulls – according to Churchill's prose – were abandoned, but communism continued to be depicted as a dangerous pathology of modern societies. For many conservative thinkers, from Isaiah Berlin to Martin Malia, from Karl Popper to Richard Pipes, it was an 'ideocracy': the inevitable outcome of the coercive transformation of society according to an abstract and authoritarian model.[12] According to this right-wing wisdom, the will to create a community of equals engendered a society of slaves. François Furet, for his part, rejected the communist 'passion' along with its ideology, and connected both to the original madness of revolution itself, establishing a linear trajectory from Jacobin Terror to Soviet Gulag: 'Today, the Gulag is leading to a rethinking of the Terror precisely because the two undertakings are seen as identical.'[13]

---

11   Isaac Deutscher, *The Prophet Outcast: Trotsky 1929–1940* (London: Verso, 2003 [1954]), 189.

12   The latest of a long tradition, Martin Malia writes that 'for the world created by October we were never dealing in the first instance with a *society;* rather, we were always dealing with an ideocratic *regime*', *The Soviet Tragedy: A History of Socialism in Russia, 1917–1991* (New York: Free Press, 1994), 8. Richard Pipes attributes the revolution to the contamination of an ideological 'virus': *The Russian Revolution* (New York: Knopf, 1990), 132–3.

13   François Furet, *Interpreting the French Revolution* (New York: Cambridge University Press, 1981), 12.

The most radical versions of these opposed interpretations – official communism and Cold War anti-communism – also converge insofar as, for both of them, the Communist Party was a kind of demiurgic historical force. As Claudio S. Ingerflom ironically observed, most Cold Warrior scholars promulgated 'the anti-Bolshevik version of a "Bolshevized" history'.[14] As in the Soviet version, ideology indisputably dominated the landscape and the party appeared as its trustful instrument, even if now the road to paradise had become the road to hell. Thirty years after the end of the USSR and 'really existing socialism', only the first variant of this symmetrical representation has disappeared; the second one lives on, holding a strong – even if no longer hegemonic – position in scholarship, and deeply shaping the public uses of the past, from media vulgarizations to memory policies.

Historicizing the communist experience, therefore, means overcoming this dichotomy between two narratives – one idyllic, the other horrific – which are also fundamentally alike. Several decades after its exhaustion, the communist experience does not need to be defended, idealized or demonized; it deserves to be critically understood as a whole, as a dialectical totality shaped by internal tensions and contradictions, presenting multiple dimensions in a vast spectrum of shades, from redemptive élans to totalitarian violence, from participatory democracy and collective deliberation to blind oppression and mass extermination, from the most utopian imagination to the most bureaucratic domination – sometimes shifting from one to the other in a short span of time. In 1991, writing a new preface to the autobiographical account of his rupture with the French Communist Party, Edgar Morin proposed a definition of Stalinism that captures at the same time the complexity and the contradictory character of the communist experience: it was 'the monstrous step of a gigantic adventure to change the world'.[15] Inevitably, this nightmarish moment overshadowed the rest – in fact, it casts its shadow over the entire twentieth century – but this adventure had begun earlier and continued after the fall of real socialism. Thus, historicizing communism

---

14   Claudio Sergio Ingerflom, 'De la Russie à l'URSS', in Michel Dreyfus (ed.), *Le siècle des communismes*, (Paris: Éditions de l'Atelier, 2000), 121.

15   Edgar Morin, 'Préface', *Autocritique* (Paris: Éditions du Seuil, 1991 [1959]), 7.

means inscribing it into a 'gigantic adventure' as old as capitalism itself. Communism was a chameleon that could not be isolated as an insular experience or separated from its precursors and heirs.

Communism came out of the October Revolution, whose trajectory calls to mind in condensed form Gibbon's vision of the Roman Empire: it possessed origins, a rise, and a fall. Neither its emergence nor its conclusion was inevitable, despite its historical premises, and many of its turns resulted from unexpected circumstances. Far from being linear, its trajectory was fractured, marked by breaks and bifurcations. It includes insurgencies from below and radical changes 'from above', leaps and Thermidorian regressions that only a retrospective view could inscribe into a single historical sequence. Though Lenin and Stalin were not alike, Sheila Fitzpatrick emphasizes, they belonged to the same process: 'Napoleon's revolutionary wars can be included in our general concept of the French Revolution, even if we do not regard them as an embodiment of the spirit of 1789; and a similar approach seems legitimate in the case of the Russian Revolution.'[16] In her book, the Russian Revolution runs from February 1917 until the Great Purges of 1936–38. Believing in a possible 'regeneration' of its original spirit, Isaac Deutscher extended the process through the de-Stalinization of 1956. Today it is easy to see that his diagnosis was wrong, but his perception of an ongoing movement was shared by millions of people across the world. The binary vision of a revolutionary Bolshevism opposed to a Stalinist counterrevolution allows one to distinguish between emancipatory violence and totalitarian repression – which is crucial – but also hides the connections that unite them and avoids any interrogation about their genetic link. Equally sterile, the conservative interpretation of a substantial continuity from Lenin to Gorbachev, grounded in the ideological bases of the USSR, simply carries on the apologetic and 'immunizing' purpose of Cold War liberalism: market society and liberal democracy are the features of a natural order, and criticizing capitalism inevitably leads to totalitarianism.

---

16 Sheila Fitzpatrick, *The Russian Revolution* (New York: Oxford University Press, 1994), 3.

Understanding communism as a global historical experience requires one to distinguish between movements and regimes[17] without separating them: not only did movements shift into regimes, but the latter retained a symbiotic link with the former, orienting their projects and actions. The Bolshevik party before 1917, mostly composed of exiled and pariah intellectuals, seems a different universe from the gigantic bureaucratic apparatus that led the USSR in the following decades. They were two different worlds, but many threads connected them. This does not exclusively concern the history of Russian Bolshevism, but rather the history of communism as a whole, at least during its first decades. Whereas in the USSR Stalin decided to eliminate the Bolshevik old guard (half a million estimated executions in the second half of the 1930s), communists led Resistance movements against fascism in Western Europe, and organized one of the most epic revolutionary experiences of the twentieth century with the 'Long March' across China (1934–35).

Like many other 'isms' of our political and philosophical lexicon, communism is a polysemic and ultimately 'ambiguous' word. Historically understood, it is neither an ideal type nor really a concept, but rather, more prosaically, an umbrella covering multiple events and experiences. Its ambiguity does not lie exclusively in the discrepancy that separates the communist idea – elaborated by many utopian thinkers up through Marx – from its historical embodiments. It lies in the extreme diversity of its expressions. Not only because Russian, Chinese and Italian communism were different, but also because in the long run many communist movements underwent deep changes, despite keeping their leaders and their ideological references. Considering its historical trajectory as a world phenomenon, communism appears as a mosaic of *communisms*. Sketching its 'anatomy', one can distinguish at least four broad forms, interrelated and not necessarily opposed to each other, but different enough to be recognized on their own: communism as *revolution*; communism as *regime*; communism as *anticolonialism*; and finally, communism as a variant of *social democracy*.

---

17   The first scholar to suggest this distinction was Renzo De Felice in a famous interview with Michael A. Ledeen: *Fascism: An Informal Introduction to Its Theory and Practice* (New Brunswick: Transaction Books, 1976).

The October Revolution was their common matrix. This does not mean that all of them had a Russian origin, insofar as Bolshevism itself was a synthesis of several European ideas and experiences. But it does mean that all forms of twentieth-century communism were related to the Russian Revolution, the great historical turn in which they found a departure (and in many cases an epilogue, after the fall of the Berlin Wall and the repression in Tiananmen Square in 1989).

Revolution

Revolution is a process, Sheila Fitzpatrick explains, but the vision of communism as revolution mostly focuses on its inaugural moment and emphasizes its disruptive character. Revolution is the moment in which human beings make their own history; it is the moment in which the oppressed become historical subjects, turn the old social and political order upside-down and replace it with a new one. Revolution is a suspension of the course of history, when the linearity of a 'homogeneous and empty' time is violently broken, opening new horizons and projecting society into a future to be invented. We could call it the Eisensteinian stage of communism: *October* is not a historical reconstitution of the Russian Revolution; it is a masterpiece that captures its emancipatory élan. Revolution deals with power relations, tactics and strategy, movements and leaderships, and the art of insurrection; but it also concerns aspirations, rage, resentment, happiness, commonality, utopias, and memory. In short, it is a moment in which politics is suddenly flooded with feelings and emotions. It is an eruption of commonality absolutely antipodal to classical liberalism's model of a society of isolated individuals acting as competitors. In such historical circumstances, the leaders are pushed forward and oriented by these new forms of collective agency. They seem to be recording and formalizing the decisions of a constituent power rising from below.

It is important to remember the mood of the Russian Revolution, because it powerfully contributed to creating an iconic image that survived the misfortunes of the USSR and cast its shadow over the entire twentieth century. Its aura attracted millions of human beings across the world, and remained relatively well-preserved even when the aura of the communist regimes completely fell apart. In the 1960s and 1970s, it fuelled a new wave of political radicalization that not only claimed autonomy from the USSR and its allies, but also perceived them as enemies.

The Russian Revolution came out of the Great War. It was a product of the collapse of the 'long nineteenth century', the age of the 'hundred years' peace', to speak with Karl Polanyi, and the symbiotic link between war and revolution shaped the entire trajectory of twentieth-century communism. Emerging from the Franco-Prussian War of 1870, the Paris Commune had been a forerunner of militarized politics, as many Bolshevik thinkers emphasized, but the October Revolution amplified it to an incomparably larger scale: the National Guard was not the Red Army and the twenty districts of the French capital simply cannot be compared to the Tsarist Empire. The First World War transformed Bolshevism itself, altering many of its features: several canonical works of the communist tradition, like Lenin's *The Proletarian Revolution and the Renegade Kautsky* (1918) or Leon Trotsky's *Terrorism and Communism* (1920), simply could not be imagined before 1914. Just as 1789 introduced a new concept of revolution – no longer defined as an astronomical rotation but rather as a social and political break – October 1917 reframed it in military terms: a crisis of the old order, mass mobilization, dualism of power, armed insurrection, proletarian dictatorship, civil war, and a violent clash with counter-revolution. Lenin's *State and Revolution* (1917) formalized Bolshevism as both an ideology (an interpretation of Marx's ideas) and a unity of strategic precepts distinguishing it from social-democratic reformism, a politics belonging to the exhausted age of nineteenth-century liberalism. Bolshevism came out of a time of increasing brutalization, when war erupted into politics, changing its language and its practices. It was a product of the anthropological transformation that, speaking with George L. Mosse, shaped the old continent at the end of the Great War.[18] This genetic code of Bolshevism was visible everywhere,

---

18   On World War I as a matrix of violence in the 'European Civil War', see Enzo Traverso, *Fire and Blood: The European Civil War 1914–1945* (London: Verso, 2016). On the brutalization of politics, see George L. Mosse, *Fallen Soldiers:*

from texts to languages, from iconography to songs, from symbols to rituals. It outlasted the Second World War and continued to fuel the rebellious movements of the 1970s, whose slogans and liturgies obsessively emphasized the idea of a violent clash with the state. Bolshevism created a military paradigm of revolution that deeply shaped communist experiences throughout the planet. The European Resistance, as well as the socialist transformations in China, Korea, Vietnam and Cuba reproduced a similar symbiotic link between war and revolution. The international communist movement was therefore envisioned as a revolutionary army formed by millions of combatants, and this had inevitable consequences in terms of organization, authoritarianism, discipline, division of labour and, last but not least, gender hierarchies. In a movement of warriors, female leaders could only be exceptions. Even Gramsci, who tried to question this Bolshevik paradigm for the revolution in the West, could not avoid a military theoretical framework in which he distinguished between the 'war of movement' and the 'war of position'.[19]

The Bolsheviks were deeply convinced that they were acting in accordance with the 'laws of history'. The earthquake of 1917 was born from the entanglement of many factors, some set in the *longue durée* of Russian history and others more temporary, abruptly synchronized by the war: an extremely violent peasant uprising against the landed aristocracy, a revolt of the urban proletariat affected by the economic crisis, and finally the dislocation of the army, formed of peasant-soldiers who were exhausted after three years of a terrible conflict, which they neither understood nor perceived as nearing an end. If these were the premises of the Russian Revolution, it is difficult to grasp in it any supposed historical necessity. The Soviet experiment was fragile, precarious and unstable during its first years of existence. It was constantly threatened, and its survival required both inexhaustible energies and enormous sacrifices. A witness to

Reshaping the Memory of the World Wars (New York: Oxford University Press, 1990); and, for the Russian context, Peter Holquist, *Making War, Forging Revolution: Russia's Continuum of Crisis, 1914–1921* (Cambridge, MA: Harvard University Press, 2002).

19   *The Gramsci Reader*, 222–30.

those years, Victor Serge, wrote that in 1919 the Bolsheviks considered
the collapse of the Soviet regime likely, but instead of discourag-
ing them, this awareness multiplied their tenacity. The victory of
the counterrevolution would have been an immense bloodbath.[20]
Maybe their resistance was possible because they were animated by
the profound conviction of acting in accordance with the 'laws of
history', but, in reality, they did not follow any natural tendency;
they were inventing a new world, unable to know what would come
out of their endeavour, inspired by an astonishingly powerful utopian
imagination, and certainly incapable of imagining its totalitarian
outcome.

Despite their usual appeal to the positivistic lexicon of 'historical
laws', the Bolsheviks had inherited their military conception of revolution from the Great War. Soldiers formed the Petrograd Military
Revolutionary Committee that deposed the provisional government
on the night of 25 October 1917, and the terrible civil war that bled the
former tsarist empire between 1918 and 1921 was an extension of the
war that had broken out in the summer of 1914. During this military
clash, Peter Holquist explains, 'methods ... forged for external war
were turned inward, to domestic conflicts'[21]. In many cases its battles
were conducted by the same armies, the same generals and the same
soldiers. The Russian revolutionaries read Clausewitz and dealt with
the interminable controversies about the legacy of Blanquism and the
art of insurrection, but the violence of the Russian Revolution did not
arise from an ideological impulse; it stemmed from a society brutalized
by war. This genetic trauma had profound consequences. The war
had reshaped politics by changing its codes, introducing previously
unknown forms of authoritarianism. In 1917, chaos and spontaneity
still prevailed in a mass party composed mostly of new members and
directed by a group of exiles, but authoritarianism quickly consolidated
during the civil war. Lenin and Trotsky claimed the legacy of the Paris

---

20   Victor Serge, *Year One of the Russian Revolution* (London: Pluto Press,
1992).

21   Peter Holquist, 'Violent Russia, Deadly Marxism? Russia in the Epoch
of Violence, 1905–21', *Kritika: Explorations in Russian and Eurasian History*, 4/3
(2003): 637.

Commune of 1871, but Julius Martov was right when he pointed out that their true ancestor was the Jacobin Terror of 1793–94.[22]

The military paradigm of the revolution should not be mistaken, however, for a cult of violence. In *History of the Russian Revolution*, Trotsky put forward solid arguments against the thesis widely spread from the 1920s onwards of a Bolshevik 'coup'. Rejecting the ingenuity of the idyllic vision of the taking of the Winter Palace as a spontaneous popular uprising, he dedicated many pages to the methodical preparation of an insurrection that required, well beyond a rigorous and efficient military organization, an in-depth evaluation of its political conditions and a careful choice of its execution times. The result was the dismissal of the interim government and the arrest of its members – Kerensky had already escaped – practically without bloodshed. The disintegration of the old state apparatus and the construction of a new one was a painful process that lasted for more than three years of civil war. Of course, the insurrection required a technical preparation and was implemented by a minority, but this did not equate to a 'conspiracy'. In opposition to the pervasive view spread by Curzio Malaparte, a victorious insurrection, Trotsky wrote, 'is widely separated both in method and historical significance from a governmental overturn accomplished by conspirators acting in concealment from the masses'.[23] There is no doubt that the taking of the Winter Palace and the dismissal of the provisional government was a major turn within the revolutionary process: Lenin called it an 'overthrowing' or an 'uprising' (*perevorot*).[24] Nevertheless, most historians recognize that this twist

---

22   According to Martov, 'If Trotsky and Radek had shown a greater knowledge of the past, they would not have tried to tie the genealogy of the Soviets to the Commune of 1871 but to the Paris Commune of 1793–94, which was a center of revolutionary energy and power very similar to the institution of their own time.' See Julius Martov, 'Decomposition or the Conquest of the State' (1919), *The State and the Socialist Revolution* (New York: Socialist Review, 1938), 45.

23   Trotsky, *History of the Russian Revolution*, 740, and 833 for the allusion to Malaparte. See Curzio Malaparte, *Coup d'État: The Technique of Revolution* (New York: E. P. Dutton, 1932).

24   This was a common term used by the Bolsheviks to define the October Revolution. It would seem, therefore, too forced to translate it, as Robert Service does, with 'coup': *Lenin: A Biography* (New York: Belknap Press, 2002), 309.

took place in a period of extraordinary effervescence, characterized by a permanent mobilization of society and constant recourse to the use of force; in a paradoxical context in which Russia, while remaining involved in a world war (the peace treaty with Germany would not be signed at Brest-Litovsk until March 1918), was a state that no longer possessed the monopoly on the legitimate use of violence. The most tenacious Cold Warrior historians, such as Martin Malia and Richard Pipes, have written books on the history of the 'Russian Revolution', even if they interpret it as a 'coup'. One of the premises of October was the failed putsch of General Kornilov, in August 1917, which Trotsky analysed as the incarnation of an abortive form of Bonapartism. Vladimir Antonov-Ovseenko, the military chief of the seizure of the Winter Palace, was not a general but an intellectual who had returned to Russia in the spring of 1917 after years of exile.

Paradoxically, the thesis of the Bolshevik 'coup' is the crossing point between conservative and anarchist criticisms of the October Revolution. Their reasons were certainly different – not to say antipodal – but their conclusions converged: Lenin and Trotsky had established a dictatorship. Emma Goldman and Alexander Berkman, expelled from the United States in 1919 because of their enthusiastic support of the Russian Revolution, could not accept Bolshevik rule and, after the repression of the Kronstadt rebellion in March 1921, decided to leave the USSR. Emma Goldman published *My Disillusionment in Russia* (1923) and Alexander Berkman *The Bolshevik Myth* (1925), whose conclusion expressed a bitter and severe assessment:

> Gray are the passing days. One by one the embers of hope have died out. Terror and despotism have crushed the life born in October. The slogans of the Revolution are foresworn, its ideals stifled in the blood of the people. The breath of yesterday is dooming millions to death; the shadow of today hangs like a black pall over the country. Dictatorship is trampling the masses underfoot. The Revolution is dead; its spirit cries in the wilderness.[25]

---

25 Alexander Berkman, *The Bolshevik Myth: Diary 1920–1922*, Introduction by Nicolas Walter (London: Pluto Press, 1989), 319. See also Emma Goldman, *My Disillusionment in Russia* (London: C. W. Daniel, 1925). It seems that her earlier

Their criticism certainly deserves attention, since it came from inside the revolution itself. Their diagnostic was pitiless: the Bolsheviks had established a party dictatorship that ruled not only in name of the soviets but sometimes – as in Kronstadt – against them, and whose authoritarian features had becoming more and more suffocating. In fact, the Bolsheviks themselves did not contest this trenchant appraisal. In *Year One of the Russian Revolution* (1930), Victor Serge described the USSR during the Civil War in this way:

> At this moment, the party fulfilled within the working class the functions of a brain and of a nervous system. It saw, it felt, it knew, it thought, it willed for and through the masses; its consciousness, its organization were a makeweight for the weakness of the individual members of the mass. Without it, the mass would have been no more than a heap of human dust, experiencing confused aspirations shot through by flashes of intelligence – these, in the absence of a mechanism capable of leading to large-scale action, doomed to waste themselves – and experiencing more insistently the pangs of suffering. Through its incessant agitation and propaganda, always telling the unvarnished truth, the party raised the workers above their own narrow, individual horizon, and revealed to them the vast perspectives of history. After the winter of 1918–19, the revolution becomes the work of the Communist party.[26]

The Bolsheviks' eulogy of party dictatorship, their defence of the militarization of work and their violent language against any left-wing criticism – either social-democratic or anarchist – of their power, was certainly abhorrent and dangerous. It was during the Civil War that Stalinism found its premises. The fact remains that a left-wing alternative was not an easy option. As Serge himself lucidly recognized, the most probable alternative to Bolshevism was simply counterrevolutionary terror. As Alexander Rabinowitch bluntly put it, terror was

---

American publisher (Doubleday, Page & Co.) gave this title without her consent, since the original title was *My Two Years in Russia*.

26 Victor Serge, *Year One of the Russian Revolution*, trans. and ed. Peter Sedgwick (Chicago: Haymarket, 2015), 411.

'the price of survival'.[27] Without being a coup, the October Revolution meant the seizure of power by a party that represented a minority and which remained even more isolated after its decision to dissolve the Constituent Assembly. At the end of the Russian civil war, however, the Bolsheviks had conquered the majority, thus becoming the hegemonic force in a devastated country. This dramatic change did not happen because of the Cheka and state terror, as pitiless as it was, but because of the division of their enemies, the support of the working class and the passing over to their side of both the peasantry and the non-Russian nationalities. If the final outcome was the dictatorship of a revolutionary party, the alternative was not a democratic regime; the only alternative was a military dictatorship of Russian nationalists, aristocratic landowners and pogromists.[28]

Regime

The communist regime institutionalized the military dimension of revolution. It destroyed the creative, anarchistic and self-emancipatory spirit of 1917, but at the same time inscribed itself into the revolutionary process. The shift of the revolution toward the Soviet regime passed through different steps: the civil war (1918–21), the collectivization of agriculture (1930–33), and the political purges of the Moscow Trials (1936–38). Dissolving the Constituent Assembly, in December 1917, the Bolsheviks affirmed the superiority of Soviet democracy, but by the end of the civil war the latter was dying. During this atrocious and bloody conflict, the USSR introduced censorship, suppressed political pluralism to the point of finally abolishing any fraction within the Communist Party itself, militarized labour and created the first forced labour camps, and instituted a new political secret police (Cheka). In March 1921, the violent repression of Kronstadt symbolized the end

---

27   Alexander Rabinowitch, *The Bolsheviks in Power: The First Year of Soviet Rule in Petrograd* (Bloomington: Indiana University Press, 2007), Chapter 15.

28   See Ronald Grigor Suny, *Red Flag Unfurled: History, Historians, and the Russian Revolution* (London, New York: Verso, 2017), 295. For a historiographical balance sheet, see the entire Chapter 6: 'Breaking Eggs, Making Omelets: Violence and Terror in Russia's Civil War, 1918–1922'.

of Soviet democracy and the USSR emerged from the civil war as a single-party dictatorship. Ten years later, the collectivization of agriculture brutally ended the peasant revolution and invented new forms of totalitarian violence and bureaucratically centralized modernization of the country. In the second half of the 1930s, the political purges physically eliminated the vestiges of revolutionary Bolshevism and disciplined the entire society by establishing the rule of terror. For two decades, the USSR created a gigantic system of concentration camps. Between collectivization and the Moscow Trials, the cultural revolution that had flourished after 1917 was brutally smashed; the aesthetic avant-garde was brought to heel and socialist realism became the official Soviet doctrine in literature and the arts, while Russian nationalism was practically imposed in all non-Russian republics of the USSR. Stalinism resulted from these transformations.

From the mid-1930s, the USSR roughly corresponded with the classical definition of totalitarianism elaborated a few years later by many conservative political thinkers: a correlation of official ideology, charismatic leadership, single-party dictatorship, suppression of rule of law and political pluralism, monopoly of all means of communication through state propaganda, social and political terror backed by a system of concentration camps, and the suppression of free-market capitalism by a centralized economy.[29] This description, currently used to point out the similarities between communism and fascism, is not wrong but extremely superficial. Even if one overlooks the enormous differences that separated the communist and fascist ideologies, as well as the social and economic content of their political systems, the fact remains that such a canonical definition of totalitarianism does not grasp the internal dynamic of the Soviet regime. It is simply unable to inscribe it into the historical process of the Russian Revolution. It depicts the USSR as a static, monolithic system, whereas the advent of Stalinism meant a deep and protracted transformation of society and culture.

---

29 This was the classical definition of totalitarianism suggested by Carl J. Friedrich and Zbigniew Brzezinski, *Totalitarian Dictatorship and Autocracy* (Cambridge, MA: Harvard University Press, 1956). On this debate, see Enzo Traverso, 'The Uses of Totalitarianism', *The New Faces of Fascism: Populism and the Far Right* (London, New York: Verso, 2019), 151–82.

Equally unsatisfactory is the definition of Stalinism as a bureaucratic counterrevolution or a 'betrayed' revolution. Stalinism certainly
signified a radical departure from any idea of democracy and self-
emancipation, but it was not, properly speaking, a *counterrevolution*. A
comparison with the Napoleonic Empire is pertinent insofar as Stalinism consciously linked the transformations engendered by the Russian
Revolution to both the Enlightenment and the tradition of Russian
Empire, but Stalinism was not the restoration of the Old Regime,
neither politically or economically, nor even culturally. Stalinism
belonged to the process of the Russian Revolution, Stephen Kotkin
suggests, because its project was the building of a new civilization:

> Bolshevism must be seen not merely as a set of institutions, a group
> of personalities, or an ideology but as a cluster of powerful symbols
> and attitudes, a language and new forms of speech, new ways of
> behaving in public and private, even new styles of dress – in short,
> as an ongoing experience through which it was possible to imagine
> and strive to bring about a new civilization called socialism.

In the wake of Bolshevism, he continues, 'Stalinism was not just a
political system, let alone the rule of an individual. It was a set of
values, a social identity, a way of life.'[30] Far from restoring the power
of the old aristocracy, Stalinism created a completely new economic,
managerial, scientific and intellectual elite, recruited from the lower
classes of Soviet societies – notably the peasantry – and educated
by new communist institutions. This is the key to explaining why
Stalinism benefited from a social consensus, notwithstanding the
Terror and mass deportations.[31] According to Boris Groys, even in
the aesthetic field Stalinism spurred, despite its totalitarian forms, the
creative élan of revolution. Therefore, it would be wrong to reduce
socialist realism to a simple form of neoclassicism. Like the avant-
garde, Groys suggests,

---

30   Stephen Kotkin, *Magnetic Mountain: Stalinism as a Civilization* (Berkeley:
University of California Press, 1995), 23.
31   See Sheila Fitzpatrick, *Everyday Stalinism: Ordinary Life in Extraordinary
Times: Soviet Russia in the 1930s* (New York: Oxford University Press, 1999).

Stalinist culture continued to be oriented toward the future; it was prospective rather than mimetic, a visualization of the collective dream of the new world and the new humanity rather than the product of an individual artist's temperament; it did not retire to the museum, but aspired to exert an active influence upon life. In brief, it could not simply be regarded as 'regressive' or pre-avant-garde.[32]

Interpreting Stalinism as a step in the process of the Russian Revolution does not mean sketching a linear track. The first wave of terror – pertinently comparable to the Jacobin Terror of 1794 – took place during a civil war, when the existence of the USSR itself was threatened by an international coalition. The brutality of the White counterrevolution, the extreme violence of its propaganda and of its practices – pogroms and massacres – pushed the Bolsheviks to establish a pitiless dictatorship. Stalin initiated the second and third waves of terror during the 1930s – collectivization and the purges – in a pacified country whose borders had been internationally recognized and whose political power had been menaced neither by external nor by internal forces. Of course, the rise to power of Hitler in Germany clearly signalled the possibility of a new war in the medium term, but the massive, blind and irrational character of Stalin's violence significantly weakened the USSR instead of reinforcing and equipping it to face such dangers. Stalinism was a 'revolution from above', a paradoxical mixture of modernization and social regression, whose final result was mass deportation, a system of concentration camps, an ensemble of trials exhuming the fantasies of the Inquisition and a wave of mass executions that decapitated the state, the party, and the army. In rural areas, Stalinism meant, according to Bukharin, the return to a 'feudal exploitation' of the peasantry with catastrophic economic effects.[33] Thus, Eric Hobsbawm's apologetic vision of Stalin as a dictator adapted to the historical conditions of a peasantry

---

32 Boris Groys, *The Total Art of Stalinism: Avant-Garde, Aesthetic Dictatorship, and Beyond* (London: Verso, 2011), 113.

33 Nicolas Werth, 'A State Against Its People', in Stéphane Courtois (ed.), *The Black Book of Communism: Crimes, Terror, Repression* (Cambridge, MA: Harvard University Press, 1999), 144.

whose mentality recalled that of the Western plebeians of the eleventh century seems highly debatable.[34] At the same time as the kulaks were starving in Ukraine, the Soviet regime was transforming tens of thousands of peasants into technicians and engineers. In short, Soviet totalitarianism merged modernism and barbarism; it was a peculiar, frightening, Promethean trend. In the wake of Isaac Deutscher, Arno Mayer defines it as 'an uneven and unstable amalgam of monumental achievements and monstrous crimes'.[35] Of course, any left scholar or activist could easily share Victor Serge's assessment on the moral, philosophical and political line that radically separated Stalinism from authentic socialism, insofar as Stalin's USSR had become 'an absolute, castocratic totalitarian state, drunk with its own power, for which man does not count'; but this does not change the fact, recognized by Serge himself, that this red totalitarianism unfolded in and prolonged a historical process started by the October Revolution.[36] Avoiding any teleological approach, one could observe that this result was neither historically ineluctable nor coherently inscribed into a Marxist ideological pattern. The origins of Stalinism, nevertheless, cannot simply be imputed, as radical functionalism suggests, to the historical circumstances of war and the social backwardness of a gigantic country with an absolutist past, a country in which building socialism inevitably required reproducing the gruesomeness of 'primitive capital accumulation'.[37] Bolshevik ideology played a role during the Russian Civil War in this metamorphosis from democratic upsurge to ruthless, totalitarian dictatorship. Its normative vision of violence as the 'midwife of history' and its culpable indifference to the juridical framework of a revolutionary state, historically transitional and doomed to extinction, certainly favoured the emergence

---

34   Eric Hobsbawm, *Age of Extremes: A History of the World, 1914–1991* (New York: Vintage, 1994), 390.

35   Arno J. Mayer, *The Furies: Violence and Terror in the French and Russian Revolutions* (Princeton: Princeton University Press, 2000), 607.

36   Victor Serge, *Memoirs of a Revolutionary* (New York: New York Review of Books, 2012), 326.

37   In the early 1920s, Evgenii A. Preobrazhensky forged the concept of 'primitive socialist accumulation'. See his essays collected in *The Crisis of Soviet Industrialization*, Introduction by Richard B. Jay (London: Routledge, 2017).

of an authoritarian, single-party regime. Multiple threads run from revolution to Stalinism, as well as from the USSR to the communist movements acting across the world. Stalinism was both a totalitarian regime and, for several decades, the hegemonic current of the left on an international scale.

It is worthwhile, then, to stress the peculiar nature of Stalinism. The ways in which it disciplined the entirety of Soviet society and suffocated freedom and democracy undoubtedly constituted a form of totalitarianism, but this form displayed few affinities with fascism or National Socialism: despite superficial similarities and a shared opposition to liberal democracy, their social bases, their ideologies, and their objectives were antipodal. Considering both their economic structures (socialism versus capitalism) and their philosophical backgrounds (the Enlightenment versus *Gegenaufklärung* or reactionary modernism), to speak of a single totalitarian Janus with two opposite faces – communist and fascist – is meaningless. The Second World War was a significant test of the chasm that divided these societies and their political regimes. In February 1942, Isaac Deutscher, a Marxist Polish historian with an impeccable anti-Stalinist pedigree, wrote these words on the Nazi aggression against the USSR:

One fundamental truth about the German-Soviet war has to be understood: the heroic resistance of the Russian workers and peasants is proof of the vitality of revolutionary society. Soviet workers and peasants are defending all that, in spite of various deformations, has remained of the revolution: an economy without capitalists and landlords. They defend what they see as their socialist fatherland – and here the accent is on the adjective no less than on the noun. They defend it not because, but *in spite of* the privileges which the new bureaucracy has usurped for itself; not because, but in spite of the totalitarian regime with its GPU, concentration camps, cult of the leader, and the terrible purges.[38]

---

38 Isaac Deutscher, '22 June 1941', *Marxism, Wars & Revolutions: Essays from Four Decades*, Preface by Perry Anderson, Introduction by Tamara Deutscher (London: Verso, 1984), 19–20.

Scholars of fascism are quite unanimous in finding that the Italian entry into the war in 1940 was the beginning of the decline of Mussolini. When fascism fell, in the summer of 1943, a large section of Italian society had already deserted it, turned anti-fascist and gone to join the Resistance. In Germany, Stalingrad destroyed the myth of the 'Thousand-Year Reich' and yet the civilians supported Hitler's regime until its collapse, simply because of Nazi terror and the fear spread amongst the population by relentless Allied bombing. In the USSR, the Great Patriotic War was not merely a legend. Despite the exaggeration and lies of Stalinist propaganda, it mirrored a general mobilization of society against the invasion. One has to compare the war chronicles by Curzio Malaparte and Vasily Grossman, on opposite sides of the Eastern Front, to understand the antipodal meanings that the belligerents gave to their commitment – extermination and resistance – in a confrontation in which humanity itself was at stake.[39] One has to compare the attitude of artists and intellectuals in the two camps: on the one hand, the blend of cynicism, resignation and disgust with which, through metaphors and allusions, Carl Schmitt and Ernst Jünger described in their correspondence the 'nihilism' and the apocalyptic, Hieronymus Bosch-like landscape of the Nazi war in Ukraine in 1942;[40] on the other hand, the intense emotion and fighting spirit with which, in August 1942, in the middle of a starving city under siege, the Soviet citizens attended the 'Leningrad Symphony' of

---

39   See Curzio Malaparte, *Kaputt* (New York: New York Review of Books, 2005); and Vasily Grossman, *A Writer at War: Vasily Grossman with the Red Army, 1941–1945*, eds and trans. by Antony Beevor and Luba Vinogradova (New York: Pantheon Books, 2005). Malaparte's novel, originally published in Italian in 1944, describes the Wehrmacht atrocities on the Eastern Front and is based on his war chronicles (many of them censured) for *Corriere della Sera*. Grossman's reportages from the front line were the source for his famous novel *Life and Fate* (New York: Harper & Row, 1985).

40   See Ernst Jünger, Carl Schmitt, *Briefwechsel: Briefe 1930–1983*, ed. Helmut Kiesel (Stuttgart: Klett-Cotta, 1999), 151–3. On this correspondence, see Gopal Balakrishnan, 'Two on the Marble Cliffs', *New Left Review*, 1 (2000): 162–8. See also Ernst Jünger, 'Notes from the Caucasus', *A German Officer in Occupied Paris: The War Journals 1941–1945*, Foreword by Elliot Neaman (New York: Columbia University Press, 2019), 115–65.

Shostakovich.[41] According to Anne Applebaum, the war even raised a wave of patriotism among the Gulag prisoners. Many of them were allowed to join the Red Army while others were upset at their exclusion from front-line combat. In the Nazi camps, by contrast, news of the Allied bombings of German cities was received as a source of hope. As inhuman and lethal as it was, the Gulag was vastly different from Buchenwald or Auschwitz. Despite its great variety, it was not conceived of as a centre of extermination but rather as a realm of political re-education and forced labour. Anne Applebaum points out the 'peculiar paradox' of the Soviet camps that were 'slowly bringing "civilization" – if that is what it can be called – to the remote wilderness'.[42] Despite specifying that 'the Gulag was a penal institution first, and a productive institution second', Steven A. Barnes emphasizes that it played a crucial role in the social transformation of the country:

> The Gulag made a substantial, if costly, contribution to the Soviet economy from the 1930s through the 1950s. Gulag labourers completed such massive construction projects as the White Sea to Baltic Sea and Volga River to Moscow River canals, opened up gold mines along the far east's Kolyma River, built rail lines throughout the Soviet Union, felled timber in Siberia, produced oil and coal in places like Vorkuta, Noril'sk, and Karaganda, and operated large agricultural enterprises in Siberia and Karaganda.[43]

For twenty years, the prisoners of the Gulag built roads, railways, electric plants, factories, and even cities. Their oppression and exploitation were undoubtedly brutal – a modern form of slavery – but were not grounded on racial ideological premises and did not have extermination as a final goal. Even a lucid conservative such as Raymond Aron understood the difference between a totalitarian system that resulted in forced labour and racial domination that ended in the gas

---

41   See Brian Moynahan, *Leningrad: Siege and Symphony* (New York: Grove Atlantic, 2013).

42   Anne Applebaum, *Gulag: A History* (New York: Doubleday, 2003), 89–90.

43   Steven A. Barnes, *Death and Redemption: The Gulag and the Shaping of Soviet Society* (Princeton: University of Princeton Press, 2011), 39, 36.

chambers.[44] When the Gulag reached its apogee in the USSR, during the war years, the advance of the Red Army in Central Europe was perceived in the West – with the significant exception of Poland in 1944 – as a liberating march that heartened and encouraged the Resistance movements.

Stalinism was not a Russian Behemoth, 'a non-state, a chaos, a rule of lawlessness, disorder, and anarchy', according to the striking definition of Nazi Germany suggested by Franz Neumann in his eponymous work.[45] Its social roots were much more solid and deep, as its victory during the Second World War and its considerable duration have patently shown. However, it was so intimately contradictory and historically new that defining its nature is not an easy task, even retrospectively. Stalinism buried the October Revolution by extracting its social and economic strength from the profound changes introduced by the break of 1917 and it embodied, at least for a couple of decades, a message of liberation in the eyes of millions of people all over the world. In the 1930s and 1940s, its ruthless, violent and arbitrary power pushed to paroxysmal limits the attributes of Western sovereignty, which Foucault had summarized as the absolute capacity by the state to kill its subjects. At the same time, it transformed the USSR into a gigantic biopolitical laboratory in which a new society was built through population transfers, industrializing policies, the collectivization of agriculture, and forced labor in the Gulags. In the twentieth century, so many revolutions remained engulfed in the dark and cold waters of this chameleonic monster.

Anticolonialism

As we saw, the Bolsheviks were radical Westernizers.[46] Differently from Marx who, at the end of his life, had imagined the possibility of

---

44   Raymond Aron, *Démocratie et totalitarisme* (Paris: Gallimard, 1965), 298.

45   Franz Neumann, *Behemoth: The Structure and Practice of National Socialism 1933–1944* ((New York: Harper & Row, 1966), xii.

46   Karl Korsch, 'The Marxist Ideology in Russia' (1938), *Marxist Theory* (Austin: University of Texas Press, 2013), 158–64. Eric Hobsbawm pointed out 'the paradox of Russian Marxism', which inherited the revolutionary tradition of populism and, in the wake of the so-called 'Legal Marxists', used Marx's writings

a shift from the Russian peasant community (*obshchina*) to socialism, Trotsky saw 'Slavophilism' as nothing but the 'messianism of backwardness'.[47] Bolshevik literature was full of references to the French Revolution, 1848 and the Paris Commune, but it never mentioned the Haitian Revolution or the Mexican Revolution. For Trotsky and Lenin, who loved this metaphor, the 'wheel of history' rolled from Petrograd to Berlin, not from the boundless Russian countryside to the fields of Morelos or the Antillean plantations.

In a chapter of his *History of the Russian Revolution*, Trotsky underlined that 'civilization had made the peasantry its pack animal' and deplored the fact that peasants were usually ignored by the history books, just as theatre critics pay no attention to the workers who, behind the scenes, operate the curtains and change the scenery: 'The part played by the peasantry in past revolutions remains hardly cleared up to this day.'[48] In his own book, however, the peasants appear mostly as an anonymous mass. They are not neglected but are observed from afar, with analytical detachment rather than empathy. Trotsky had little experience of the peasant world, which remained a memory of his childhood in Ianovka, Ukraine. Viewed from Vienna, Paris and New York, the cities of his exile, the immense Russian countryside seemed distant to him. Therefore, this observation remained isolated in his book. At the heart of his great fresco were not peasants but the urban masses in action, and they were composed essentially of workers. The 'Black Jacobins' were slaves and the Mexican revolutionaries – including their leaders – were indigenous peasants. The Bolsheviks had started to question their vision of the peasantry – inherited from Marx's writings on French Bonapartism[49] – as a culturally backward

---

to prove that 'Russia had to pass through the stage of capitalism': 'The Influence of Marxism 1880–1914', *How to Change the World: Reflections on Marx and Marxism* (New Haven: Yale University Press, 2011), 220.

47   Trotsky, *History of the Russian Revolution*, 6. On discussions between Marx and Russian populists see Theodor Shanin (ed.), *Late Marx and the Russian Road: Marx and the Peripheries of Capitalism* (New York: Monthly Review Press, 1983).

48   Trotsky, *History of the Russian Revolution*, 617.

49   According to Marx, the cultural horizon of French peasants did not cross the borders of their own properties and, because of their ancestral prejudices, they were unable to act as a class. Instead of creating a political entity, he wrote

and politically conservative class, but their proletarian tropism was too strong to complete this revision. This was done, not without theoretical and strategic confrontations, by anticolonial communism in the years between the two world wars. Before the already mentioned historical work of C. L. R. James, *The Black Jacobins* (1938), the most significant examples of this reassessment came from China and Latin America.

In China, the communist turn towards the peasantry resulted from both the devastating defeat of the urban revolutions of the mid-1920s and the effort to inscribe Marxism into a national history and culture. After the bloody repression inflicted by the Kuomintang (GMD), the communist party cells had been almost completely dismantled in the cities, and its members imprisoned and persecuted. At the end of 1927, the Communist party had only 10,000 members, down from 60,000 one year earlier. Retreating into the country, where they found protection and could reorganize their movement, many communist leaders started looking at the peasantry with different eyes, abandoning their former Westernized gaze on Asian 'backwardness'. This strategic turn, the object of sharp controversies between the Communist International and its Chinese section during the 1930s, was claimed by Mao Zedong at the beginning of 1927, even before the massacres perpetrated by the GMD in Shanghai and Canton in April and December of that year.[50] Coming back to his native Hunan, Mao wrote a famous report in which he designated the peasantry – instead of the urban proletariat – as the driving force of the Chinese Revolution. The revolutionary character of the peasants was so evident that it did not need to be proven and, even if at that time he had not yet contested the alliance with the GMD, he was already hailing the

---

in *The Eighteenth Brumaire*, their union was purely mechanical: 'The great mass of the French nation is formed by simple addition of homologous magnitudes, much as potatoes in a sack form a sack of potatoes.' See Karl Marx, *Collected Works* (London: Lawrence & Wishart, 2010), vol. 11, 187. Therefore, peasants had to be represented by an external force, like the Church during the French Revolution or Louis Napoleon in 1848.

50   For a synthetic account of the revolutionary process in China, see Rebecca Karl, *Mao Zedong and China in the Twentieth-Century World* (Durham, NC: Duke University Press, 2010), Chapters 3–5.

importance of peasant leadership: 'Without the poor peasants there would be no revolution. To deny their role is to deny the revolution. To attack them is to attack the revolution.'[51] In Mao's view, peasants were 'clear-sighted' and able to establish their own power. Certainly, their revolution would be an outburst of violence, but its yardstick was the timeless brutality of the oppression inflicted by the landlords. In a later-canonized passage, he wrote:

A revolution is not a dinner party, or writing an essay, or painting a picture, or doing embroidery; it cannot be so refined, so leisurely and gentle, so temperate, kind, courteous, restrained and magnanimous. A revolution is an insurrection, an act of violence by which one class overthrows another. A rural revolution is a revolution by which the peasantry overthrows the power of the feudal landlord class. Without using the greatest force, the peasants cannot possibly overthrow the deep-rooted authority of the landlords which has lasted for thousands of years. The rural areas need a mighty revolutionary upsurge, for it alone can rouse the people in their millions to become a powerful force.[52]

Against the Moscow agents who conceived of peasant militias exclusively as triggers of urban uprisings, in 1931 Mao persisted in building a Soviet republic in Jiangxi. Without believing in the rural character of the Chinese Revolution, he could not have organized the Long March in order to resist the annihilation campaign launched by the GMD. Initially considered as a tragic defeat – only 8,000 soldiers arrived in Shaanxi in October 1935, out of 90,000 who had left Jiangxi one year earlier – this epic undertaking paved the way for a successful struggle in the following decade, first against the Japanese occupation and then against the GMD itself. Two years later, the initial size of the Red Army

---

51   Mao Zedong, 'Report on an Investigation of the Peasant Movement in Hunan' (1927), *Selected Works*, vol. 1 (Peking: Foreign Languages Press, 1965), 33.

52   Ibid., 28. It is interesting to observe that in 1932 Trotsky stressed the need to rebuild communist cells in the cities and expressed great scepticism towards the peasant Red Army created by Mao in Jiangxi. See Leon Trotsky, 'Peasant War in China and the Proletariat' (1932), *On China*, eds Les Evans and Russell Block, Introduction Peng Shu-tse (New York: Monad Press, 1976), 522–31.

Mao Zedong during the Long March (1934).

had been reconstituted, and in 1947, when the civil war with the GMD broke out, it numbered 2,700,000. The proclamation of the People's Republic of China in Beijing in 1949 was the result of a process that, from the uprisings of 1925 to the Long March and the anti-Japanese struggle, found one of its necessary premises in October 1917; but it was also the product of a strategic revision. There was a complex genetic link between the Chinese and the Russian Revolutions.[53]

The three major dimensions of communism analysed in this chapter – revolution, regime, and anticolonialism – emblematically merged in the Chinese Revolution. As a radical break with the traditional order, it was incontestably a revolution that heralded the end of centuries of oppression; as the conclusion of a civil war, it resulted in the conquest of power by a militarized party which, since the beginning, established its dictatorship in the most authoritarian forms. And as the conclusion of fifteen years of struggle, first against the Japanese occupation and then against the GMD – a nationalist force that had become the agent

53 According to Perry Anderson, 'the Chinese Revolution grew directly out of the Russian Revolution, and remained connected with it, as inspiration or admonition, down to their common moment of truth at the end of the eighties.' See Anderson, 'Two Revolutions: Rough Notes', *New Left Review*, 61 (2010): 60.

of Western great powers – the communist victory of 1949 marked not only the end of colonialism in China but also, on a broader scale, a significant moment in the global process of decolonization. Whereas, in Russia, the bureaucratization of the Bolshevik party and the end of Soviet democracy were a product of the civil war, in China the militarization of communism had started almost twenty years before its conquest of power, when a party of uprooted intellectuals left the cities and became the leadership of a peasant liberation movement.

Undoubtedly, this revolutionary process mobilized the entire Chinese society and experienced many heroic and epic moments, foremost among them the Long March – but it did not have the euphoric, utopian, almost anarchistic élan of October 1917. It changed the face of an immense country, but failed to produce any form of self-management or council democracy, any aesthetic avant-garde or debate on sexual emancipation, to mention only a few significant moments of the early Soviet Union. The mythic tale of popular insurrection created by Eisenstein in *October* could not be easily transposed to China, even less Gustav Landauer's definition of revolution as an abrupt interruption of the historical continuum in which 'everything happens incredibly quickly, just like in dreams in which people seem to be freed from gravity.'[54] The Chinese Revolution was not a social and political break that suddenly liberated the repressed energies and desires of society. It was the epilogue of twenty years of revolutionary wars. China was devastated and exhausted. Neither an emancipatory insurgency, like in 1917, nor a 'revolution from above', like the process of structural assimilation to the USSR that took place in the countries of Central Europe occupied by the Red Army in 1945, the Chinese Revolution was a singular osmosis of revolution from below, authoritarianism driven from above by a militarized party, and a powerful offensive against imperialism. The images of Mao Zedong proclaiming the People's Republic of China from Tiananmen Square in Beijing, on 1 October 1949, radiate the aura of a historical event, which is certainly not reducible to the routine march-past of a totalitarian

---

54 Gustav Landauer, 'Revolution' (1907), *Revolution and Other Writings: A Political Reader*, ed. Gabriel Kuhn, Preface Richard Day (Oakland: PM Press, 2010), 153.

regime. Nonetheless, they have little in common with the crazy chaos of Berlin in January 1919, when the city was paralysed by impromptu barricades, or the joyful excitement of the crowds that overran the streets of Havana in December 1958 to welcome the Rebel Army of Fidel Castro and Che Guevara. In China, the revolutionary process combined the liberation from Japanese rule with social emancipatory measures and the establishment of an extremely authoritarian power. While liberating the country from imperialism and emancipating the peasants from ancestral domination, the communist party installed its exclusive dictatorship by suffocating any democratic élan.

Maoism was a *sui generis* revolutionary movement, not a Chinese version of Russian Bolshevism. Mao prevailed in imposing his strategic line against the Comintern, whose orientation – strongly put forward by its agents – basically extended the Russian experience to China. Moscow imposed a similar path on Latin America. In the 1920s and 1930s, the Third International established its leadership in Buenos Aires. The choice of Argentina, the most European country of Latin America, clearly revealed a general disregard for the continental revolutionary traditions, only a few years after the Mexican Revolution, as well as for the subversive potential of the indigenous populations. The Brazilian rebellion led by Carlos Prestes, whose legendary column crossed the country between 1924 and 1928, and then organized an uprising in 1935 against Getúlio Vargas's rule, did not become the Latin American equivalent of the Chinese Long March. In the 1920s, the 'Bolshevization' of the communist parties consolidated the Russian control of their leaderships and, during the following decades, the international strategy of the Popular Front replaced anti-imperialism with anti-fascism, with the result that in 1958 the Cuban Revolution did not depart from the communist tradition.[55] In the 1920s and 1930s, however, Bolshevism reached Latin America and transformed its political landscape by introducing a new actor alongside nationalism, populism, and an exhausted liberalism. The continental revolutionary culture and imagination were deeply transformed, and Bolshevism

---

55   See Manuel Caballero, *Latin America and the Comintern* (Cambridge: Cambridge University Press, 1986).

Diego Rivera, *Distribution of Arms* (1926). Mural.
Secretaría de Educación Pública, Mexico City.

Tina Modotti, *Mexican Sombrero with Hammer and
Sickle*. Front page of *The Masses*, October 1928.

reformulated its aesthetic codes by merging European and indigenous
symbols. The October Revolution had become a universal paradigm.
Mexican artists painted canvases in which European forms of war were
translated into a Latin American context, like José Clemente Orozco's
'The Trench' (1926), and in which the Mexican Revolution – a peasant
war for land and power – was represented through the emblems of
Soviet communism, such as Diego Rivera's painting 'Distribution
of Arms' (1928) and Tina Modotti's photograph 'Mexican Sombrero
with Hammer and Sickle' (1928).

Whereas the Russian Revolution appeared as a kind of North Star for rebels across the Americas, an authentic form of Latin American Marxism could not but be created against the orthodoxy of the Comintern. The Peruvian José Carlos Mariátegui, the most important Latin American Marxist thinker in the first half of the twentieth century, refused to follow the instructions coming from Moscow. He believed that the history of pre-Columbian Mesoamerican civilizations could not be considered analogous to European feudalism. Socialism, in this region, could not simply be imported from the West but had to merge with the ancestral tradition of Inca communism, which he compared with that of the Russian rural community. In his view, the key to socialist revolution in Peru was in solving the land problem that corresponded with the oppression of indigenous people. For the Inca, land was the source of life, not an object to conquer and exploit:

> Faith in the renaissance of the Indian is not pinned to the material process of 'Westernizing' the Quechua country. The soul of the Indian is not raised by the white man's civilization or alphabet but by the myth, the idea, of the socialist revolution. The hope of the Indian is absolutely revolutionary. That same myth, that same idea, are the decisive agents in the awakening of other ancient peoples or races in ruin: the Hindus, the Chinese, et cetera. Universal history today tends as never before to chart its course with a common quadrant. Why should the Inca people, who constructed the most highly developed and harmonious communistic system, be the only ones unmoved by this worldwide emotion? The consanguinity of the Indian movement with world revolutionary currents is too evident to need documentation. I have said already that I reached an understanding and appreciation of the Indian through socialism.[56]

---

56   José Carlos Mariátegui, *Seven Interpretive Essays on Peruvian Reality*, trans. Marjory Urquidi, Introduction Jorge Basadre (Austin: University of Texas Press, 1971), 28–9. See Robert Paris, *La formación ideológica de José Carlos Mariátegui* (Mexico City: Pasado y Presente, 1981); and Michael Löwy's 'Introduction' to his edited anthology *Marxism in Latin America* (Atlantic Highlands, NJ: Humanities Press, 1992), xix–xxiv.

After the Russian Revolution, socialism crossed the boundaries of Europe and became an agenda item in the South and the colonial world. This is the new context in which both Mao and Mariátegui reconsidered the role of the peasantry as an insurgent force. Their theoretical and strategic reassessment took place once October 1917 had laid the premises of decolonization. Because of its intermediary position between Europe and Asia, with a gigantic territory extending across both continents, inhabited by a variety of national, religious and ethnic communities, the USSR became the locus of a new crossroads between the West and the colonial world. Bolshevism was able to speak equally to the proletarian classes of the industrialized countries and to the colonized peoples of the South. One needs to go back more than a century, with the symbiotic link between the French and the Haitian Revolutions, to find a historical event with a similar global impact. During the nineteenth century, anticolonialism was almost non-existent in the West, with the notable exception of the anarchist movement, whose activists and ideas widely circulated between Southern and Eastern Europe, Latin America, and different Asian countries. After Marx's death, socialism based its hopes and expectations on the growing strength of the industrial working class, mostly white and male, and was concentrated in the developed (mostly Protestant) capitalist countries of the West. Every mass socialist party included powerful currents defending the 'civilizing mission' of Europe throughout the world. The extreme violence of colonialism could be vigorously denounced – as it was after the extermination of the Herero in German Namibia in 1904 – without casting doubt on the historical right of European empires to rule Asia and Africa. Social-democratic parties – particularly those located in the biggest empires – postponed colonial liberation until after the socialist transformation of Europe and the US. In 1907, the Stuttgart congress of the Second International approved a resolution that upheld the principle of colonialism. Most socialist thinkers viewed it as a necessary civilizing mission, one that a socialist order would accomplish through peaceful means. This was the significance of a 'positive colonial policy', as the Belgian Émile Vandervelde defined it, which sought to avoid the violence and inhumanity of imperialism.[57] Three years earlier, at the Amsterdam congress, several American, Dutch, and Australian socialists had proposed a resolution that called for the restriction of immigration into developed countries for 'workingmen of inferior races', mentioning both 'Chinese and Negroes'. Daniel De Leon, the leader of the Socialist Labor Party of America – born in Curaçao to a Dutch Jewish family with Spanish and Portuguese origins – vigorously criticized this xenophobic and racist position:

> Where is the line that separates 'inferior' from 'superior' races? … To the native American proletariat, the Irish was made to appear an 'inferior' race; to the Irish, the German; to the German, the Italian; to the Italian – and so down the line through the Swedes, the Poles, the Jews, the Armenians, the Japanese, to the end of the gamut. Socialism knows not such insulting, iniquitous distinctions as 'inferior' and 'superior' races among the proletariat. It is for capitalism to fan the fires of such sentiments in its scheme to keep the proletariat divided.[58]

The Bolsheviks radically broke with such a tradition. The second congress of the Communist International, held in Moscow in July 1920, approved a programmatic document calling for colonial revolutions against imperialism: its goal was the creation of communist parties in the colonial world and the support of national liberation movements. The congress clearly affirmed a radical turn away from the old social-democratic views on colonialism. A couple of months later, the Bolsheviks organized a Congress of the Peoples of the East in Baku, Azerbaijan Soviet Socialist Republic, which convened almost 2,000 delegates from twenty-nine Asian nationalities, and which started with a spirited speech by Grigory Zinoviev appealing

---

57   See Georges Haupt, *La Deuxième Internationale et l'Orient* (Paris: Cujas, 1967), 25–34.

58   Daniel De Leon, 'Flashlights on the Amsterdam Congress', *Daily People*, 27 November 1904; quoted in David S. Herreshoff, *The Origins of American Marxism: From the Transcendentalists to De Leon* (New York: Monad Press, 1973), 169.

Grigory Zinoviev speaks at the Congress of the
Peoples of the East, Baku, 1 September 1920.

for a Jihad against imperialism.[59] In gathering intellectuals involved
in embryonic communist movements, leaders of trade-unions and
peasant associations, as well as representatives of several emerging
nationalist currents, this 'congress' was in fact a propaganda meeting
that fulfilled many purposes. In the middle of the Russian civil war,
it aimed to reinforce Soviet influence in Central Asia and also to
put pressure on Britain by forcing Lloyd George to negotiate with
the USSR lest it foment revolutionary movements within its own

---

59   See the stenographic report of Zinoviev's inaugural speech in John Riddell
(ed.), *To See the Down: Baku 1920 – First Congress of the Peoples of the East*, trans.
Brian Pearce (New York: Pathfinder Press, 2019), 88. Many interventions evoked
the 'holy war' against imperialism. Directed to the 'peoples of the East' who had
already 'marched under the green banner of the Prophet', the Manifesto of the
congress declared that all holy wars were 'fraudulent' and called for 'the first real
holy war, under the red banner of the Communist International': 'a holy war for
freedom, independence, and happiness for all the people of the East!' Ibid., 262.
See also Pierre Broué, *Histoire de l'Internationale Communiste 1919–1943* (Paris:
Fayard, 1997), 181–2; Serge Wolikow, *L'Internationale Communiste (1919–1943).*
Le Komintern ou le rêve déchu du parti mondial de la révolution (Paris: Éditions de
l'Atelier, 2010), 35–7; and Pierre Frank, *Histoire de l'Internationale Communiste*
1919–1943 (Paris: Éditions La Brèche, 1979), vol. 1, 104–7.

colonies.[60] M. N. Roy, the Indian Marxist who had discussed with Lenin the theses on the colonial question, refused to attend this meeting, which in his memoirs he qualified as 'Zinoviev's circus'.[61] According to several testimonies, the congress took place in an atmosphere of confusion and excitement, with delegates exhibiting their weapons and, in some cases, closing profitable business deals during their stay. Despite many ritual slogans against imperialism, the question of nationalism was not really discussed. Enver Pasha, one of the leaders of the Young Turk Revolution in 1908, was not allowed to attend but sent a long message that was read and applauded.[62] Although both Turks and Armenians were strongly represented – sending 235 and 157 delegates, respectively – the Armenian genocide was never mentioned in the debates. Alfred Rosmer, one of the few Western personalities who attended the congress, described in his memoirs an 'extremely picturesque' auditorium where 'all the Eastern costumes gathered together', making 'an astonishingly rich and colored picture.'[63]

Beyond its ideological confusion and propagandistic backdrop, however, the Baku congress expressed some significant changes in revolutionary culture. Despite their small number among the delegates, women played an important role in the discussions. The chairmanship was equal – two male and two female presidents – and the question of women's rights was put on the agenda. The Turkish feminist Najiye Hanum insisted that there was no national liberation without women's emancipation and claimed a complete civil and political equality for women in the East. Their struggle, she emphasized, went well beyond 'the right to walk in the street without wearing the chador'.[64] At a time when women still did not have the right to vote in most Western countries, Hanum set forth the following demands:

---

60   See Stephen White, 'Communism and the East: The Baku Congress, 1920', *Slavic Review*, 33/3 (1974): 492–514.

61   M. N. Roy, *Memoirs* (Bombay: Allied Publishers, 1964), 392.

62   See Enver Pasha's message in *To See the Dawn*, 138–42.

63   Alfred Rosmer, *Lenin's Moscow*, trans. Ian Birchall (Chicago: Haymarket, 2016 [1953]), 93.

64   See the proceedings of Session 7, held on 7 September 1920, devoted to 'Women of the East', in Joh, Riddell (ed.), *To See the Down*, 232.

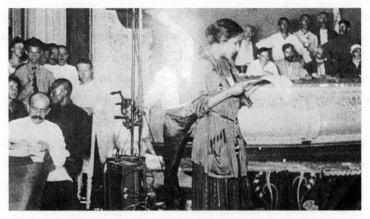

The Turkish Najiye Hanum speaks at the Congress
of the Peoples of the East, Baku, 7 September 1920.

1) Complete equality of rights. 2) Ensuring to women unconditional access to educational and vocational institutions established for men. 3) Equality of rights of both parties to marriage. Unconditional abolition of polygamy. 4) Unconditional admission of women to employment in legislative and administrative institutions. 5) Establishment of committees for the rights and protection of women everywhere, in cities, towns, and villages.[65]

As Brigitte Studer points out, the Baku congress was the first public event in which the communist movement tried, with its own language, to articulate the categories of class, gender and race within a single political discourse (thus prefiguring what today is called 'intersectionality').[66]

Echoes of the congress in the Western newspapers had a different taste. On 23 September, *The Times* dismissed the congress as 'the spectacle of two Jews [Zinoviev and Radek], one of them a convicted pickpocket, summoning the world of Islam to a new Jihad.'[67] Writing from Moscow as a British reporter, H. G. Wells mentioned 'a congress at Baku' in which 'Zinoviev and his associates' had convened 'white, black, brown, and yellow people, Asiatic customs and

---

65 Ibid., 234.
66 Brigitte Studer, *Reisende der Weltrevolution*, 125.
67 Quoted in White, 'Communism and the East', 502.

astonishing weapons' with the purpose of 'swearing undying hatred of capitalism and British imperialism'.[68] Behind these disparaging accounts, however, the British Cabinet considered the congress as a serious threat: in March 1921, one of the conditions it put on a trade agreement with the USSR was an end to its anti-British agitation in the East, epitomized by the Baku assembly.[69] Undoubtedly, political and strategic confusion, Soviet realpolitik, diplomatic goals, ambiguous partnerships and cultural paradoxes – appeals for women's emancipation alternating with encomiums to traditional Islam – shaped this event, whose immediate consequences were negligible. The Bolsheviks clearly led the dance, and the delegates followed their instructions; five years before the communist uprisings of Shanghai and Canton, the eight Chinese delegates did not play any role in the discussions. Nonetheless, a retrospective assessment cannot ignore the symbolic dimension of the Baku congress. In his inaugural speech, Zinoviev explicitly affirmed that the Communist International had broken with older social-democratic attitudes, according to which 'civilized Europe' could and must 'act as tutor to "barbarous" Asia'.[70] Revolution was no longer considered as the exclusive realm of 'white' European and American workers, and socialism could not be imagined without the liberation of colonized peoples:

We are mindful that in the world there are living not only people with white skins, not only the Europeans whom the Second International took particularly into account; in addition, there are also in the world hundreds of millions of people who live in Asia and Africa. We want to put an end to the rule of capital everywhere in the world. And this will become possible only when we have lit the fire of revolution not merely in Europe and America but throughout the world, and when behind us march all the working people of Asia and Africa.[71]

---

68 H. G. Wells, *Russia in the Shadows* (New York: George H. Doran Company, 1921), 96.

69 See White, 'Communism and the East', 493, 503.

70 *To See the Dawn*, 74.

71 Ibid, 54–5.

In his speech, Radek emphasized that 'nothing can stay the torrent of the workers of Persia, Turkey, India, if they unite with Soviet Russia ... Soviet Russia can produce arms and arm not only its own workers and peasants, but also the peasants of India, Persia, Anatolia, all the oppressed, and lead them in a common struggle and a common victory.' And he added that 'the Eastern policy of the Soviet government is no diplomatic manoeuvre ... We are bound to you by a common destiny.'[72] The conflicting relationships between communism and nationalism would be clarified in the following decades, but the October Revolution was the inaugural moment of global anticolonialism. In the 1920s, anticolonialism suddenly shifted from the realm of historical possibility to the field of political strategy and military organization. The Baku conference announced this historic change.[73]

Of course, this turn – both political and epistemological – had multiple dimensions. On the left, it meant the reconfiguration of the relationship between race and class, extending the conception of political agency to the colonized peoples. This change took place within the theoretical framework of Marxism and shaped the entire trajectory of twentieth-century communism as a new stage of radical Enlightenment: communism merged humanism, anticolonialism and universalism. On the right, it meant the racialization of Bolshevism itself. Since the Russian civil war and the revolutionary uprisings in Central Europe, nationalist propaganda had begun to depict the Bolsheviks as savages, as the embodiment of a dangerous form of 'Asiatic barbarism' that threatened the West.[74] Under the Weimar Republic, pan-Germanism cast the Slavic peoples as an inferior race and depicted the Bolsheviks as the leaders of a gigantic revolt of

---

72 Quoted in *The Communist International 1919–1943: Documents*, ed. Jane Degras (London: Oxford University Press, 1956), vol. 1, 105.

73 This corresponded with Lenin's move from a 'chrono-topic and evolutionary logic' towards a 'multilinear' view of the historical process, according to Matthieu Renault, who notwithstanding considers the Baku Congress to have been a meaningless event. See Matthieu Renault, *L'empire de la révolution: Lénine et les musulmans de Russie* (Paris: Syllepse, 2017).

74 For Hitler, Bolshevism was 'a human doctrine in Asian or barbaric garb'. Quoted in Ernst Nolte, *Streitpunkte: Heutige und künftige Kontroversen um den Nationalsozialismus* (Berlin: Propyläen, 1993), 371.

slaves, reminiscent of the prophecy made by Nietzsche. Racist stereo-
types – from the Asiatic origins of Lenin to the myth of a Chinese
Cheka[75] – saturated anti-communist literature. In the following decade,
National Socialism completed this picture by describing Bolshevism
as the coalition of a non-white sub-humanity led by a revolutionary
Jewish intelligentsia. In a famous speech delivered in Dusseldorf in
1932 before an audience of German industrialists, Hitler presented the
USSR as a major threat to the 'White race' and Western civilization.[76]
For several decades, colonialism, anti-Semitism and anti-communism
were essential dimensions of the political culture of Western conservatism, in a wide spectrum merging multiple currents and running
from Churchill to Hitler.

The alliance between communism and anticolonialism experienced
several moments of crisis and tension, related to both ideological
conflicts and the imperatives of the USSR's foreign policies. In the
1930s, the French Communist Party's anti-fascist turn took place as
a peculiar symbiosis of Stalinism and national-republicanism, which
inscribed the Russian Revolution into the tradition of Jacobinism
and socialist internationalism into its universal civilizing mission.
As a consequence, anticolonialism was put aside. At the end of the
Second World War, the PCF participated in a coalition government
that violently repressed anticolonial revolts in Algeria (1945) and
Madagascar (1947), and in the following decade it supported Prime
Minister Guy Mollet at the beginning of the Algerian War.[77] In India,
the communist movement was marginalized during the Second World
War because of its decision to suspend its anticolonial struggle and to

---

75   The origins of this myth – the 'rat cage' torture supposedly practiced by
a Chinese Cheka – go back to a White Guard pamphlet published by Sergei P.
Melgunov in 1924 and quickly translated into various Western languages: *The Red
Terror in Russia* (London: Dent, 1925). During the German historians' controversy
of the 1980s, it was exhumed by Ernst Nolte, *Der europäische Bürgerkrieg 1917–1945:
Nationalsozialismus und Bolschewismus* (Frankfurt: Ullstein, 1987), 115, and a long
footnote, 564. See Hans-Ulrich Wehler, *Entsorgung der deutschen Vergangenheit?
Ein polemischer Essay zum 'Historikerstreit'* (Munich: Beck, 1988), 147–54.

76   Quoted by Nolte, *Streitpunkte*, 356.

77   Jakob Moneta, *Le PCF et la question coloniale* (Paris: Maspero, 1971).

support the British Empire's involvement in a military alliance with the USSR against the Axis powers.

If these examples clearly show the contradictions of communist anticolonialism, they do not change the historical role played by the USSR as a rear base for many anticolonial revolutions. The entire process of decolonization took place in the context of the Cold War, within the relations of force established by the existence of the USSR. Retrospectively, decolonization appears as a historical experience in which the contradictory dimensions of communism previously mentioned – emancipation and authoritarianism, revolution and dictatorial power – permanently merged. In most cases, anticolonial struggles were conceived and organized like military campaigns carried out by liberation armies, and the political regimes they established were, from the beginning, one-party dictatorships. In Cambodia, at the end of a ferocious war, the military dimension of the anticolonial struggle completely suffocated any emancipatory impulse, and the conquest of power by the Khmer Rouge immediately resulted in the establishment of a genocidal power.[78] The happiness of insurgent Havana on the first of January 1959 and the terror of the Cambodian killing fields are the dialectical poles of communism as anticolonialism.

Social-Democratic Communism

The fourth dimension of twentieth-century communism is *social-democratic*: in certain countries and periods, communism played the role traditionally fulfilled by social democracy. This happened in some Western countries, mostly in the postwar decades, thanks to a set of circumstances related to international context, the foreign policy of the USSR, and the absence or weakness of classic social-democratic parties; and it also occurred in some countries born from decolonization. The most significant examples of this peculiar phenomenon are found in the US, at the time of the New Deal, in postwar France and Italy, as well as in India (Kerala and West Bengal). Of course,

---

78 See Ben Kiernan, *The Pol Pot Regime: Race, Power, and Genocide in Cambodia Under the Khmer Rouge, 1975–79* (New Haven: Yale University Press, 2008).

social-democratic communism was geographically and chronologically more circumscribed than its other forms, but it existed nonetheless. To a certain extent, the rebirth of social democracy itself after 1945 was a by-product of the October Revolution, which had changed the balance of power on a global scale and compelled capitalism to transform significantly, adopting a 'human face'.

Social-democratic communism is an oxymoronic definition that does not ignore the links of French, Italian or Indian communism with revolutions, Stalinism, and decolonization. It does not neglect these movements' capacity to lead insurgencies – notably during the Resistance against the Nazi occupation – or their organic connections with Moscow for several decades: their first open criticism of USSR foreign policy took place only in the 1960s, first with the Sino-Soviet split, then with the invasion of Czechoslovakia by Soviet tanks. Even their internal structure and organization was, at least until the end of the 1970s, much more Stalinist than social-democratic, as well as their culture, theoretical sources and political imagination. In spite of these clearly recognizable features, such parties played a typical social-democratic role: reforming capitalism, containing social inequalities, getting accessible healthcare, education and leisure to the largest number of people; in short, improving the living conditions of the labouring classes and giving them political representation. Their goal was not the abolition of capitalism, but rather a global, social reformation within the framework of capitalism itself. Their politics fundamentally corresponded with the theoretical 'revision' of classical Marxism proposed by Eduard Bernstein in his famous essay *Evolutionary Socialism* (1899), which envisaged a transformation of capitalism and a gradual road to socialism, even if no communist party ever acknowledged this connection. Bernstein's definition of socialism as 'universal citizenship' and his claim of a historical continuity between liberalism and socialism fit the programmes of social-democratic communism.[79] In his essay, Bernstein urged the German Social Democratic Party to 'find the courage to emancipate itself from a phraseology which is actually outworn' and 'to

---

79   Eduard Bernstein, *Evolutionary Socialism: A Criticism and Affirmation*, trans. Edith C. Carvey (New York: B.W. Huebsch, 1911), 148

Eduard Bernstein (1895).

appear what it is in reality today: a democratic, socialistic party of reform.'[80]

This conclusion did not differ very much from the orientation of the Italian Communist Party in the 1970s. Of course, its doctrinal armoury remained strong and compelling, but it tried to reform capitalism instead of destroying it. This created a specific form of 'revisionism' that consisted in conceptualizing its strategic orientation by reworking the canonical tradition. The publication of Gramsci's *Prison Notebooks* (1948–51) with his reflections on hegemony, national culture, historical bloc, Machiavelli, and the differences between the state in Russia and the West, was instrumental in legitimizing this social-democratic turn (and sterilizing at the same time the reception of Gramsci's work itself). A strategist of revolution in the West was reinterpreted as the pioneer of evolutionary socialism: 'hegemony' meant the abandonment of any revolutionary break in favour of a purely institutional politics; 'historical bloc' designated the alliance between the left and the conservative Christian Democracy; and the

---

80   Ibid., 197. For a reconstruction of this debate, see Peter Gay, *The Dilemma of Democratic Socialism: Eduard Bernstein's Challenge to Marx* (New York: Columbia University Press, 1952).

'war of position' was opposed to the 'war of manoeuvre' as a political action inscribed exclusively within the institutional framework
of liberal democracy.[81] In 1976, Enrico Berlinguer, Santiago Carrillo
and Georges Marchais, the leaders of the Italian, Spanish and French
communist parties, solemnly announced their abandonment of 'proletarian dictatorship'. This rereading of Gramsci allowed the Italian
communists to rejoin Bernstein without disavowing Lenin. The last
attempt to give a theoretical ground to this kind of reformism was,
in the mid-1970s, the idea of Eurocommunism, which some intellectuals elaborated by connecting it to the tradition of Austro-Marxism,
embodied in the first half of the twentieth century by thinkers like
Otto Bauer, Max Adler, Karl Renner and Rudolf Hilferding.[82] Both
Austro-Marxism and Eurocommunism, Donald Sassoon argues,
sought a 'third way' between Soviet-style communism and reformist
social democracy.[83] Like Otto Bauer, who defined his movement as
a synthesis between the social achievements of Red Vienna and the
heroic deeds of revolutionary socialism during the insurrection of
February 1934, the Italian Communist Party claimed the legacy of the
Resistance and proudly publicized the achievements of 'Red Bologna',
the city that it had administered since 1945.

Of course, one of the peculiar features of social-democratic communism was its exclusion from political power, except for a couple of
years between the end of WWII and the breakout of the Cold War (the
swansong of social-democratic communism took place in France at the
beginning of the 1980s, when the PCF participated in a left coalition
government under Mitterrand). Unlike the British Labour Party, the
German SPD, or Scandinavia's social democracies, it could not claim
paternity of the welfare state. In the US, the communist party was one
of the left pillars of the New Deal, along with the trade-unions, but

81   See Perry Anderson, *The Antinomies of Gramsci* (London, New York:
Verso, 2017).

82   On the trajectory of Italian communism, see Lucio Magri, *The Tailor of Ulm:
Communism in the Twentieth Century* (London: Verso, 2011). On Eurocommunism
as a global phenomenon, see Ernest Mandel, *From Stalinism to Eurocommunism:
The Bitter Fruits of 'Socialism in One Country'* (London: Verso, 1978).

83   Donald Sassoon, *One Hundred Years of Socialism: The West European Left
in the Twentieth Century* (New York: The New Press, 1996), 73.

it never entered the Roosevelt administration. It did not experience power, only the purges of McCarthyism. In France and Italy, the communist parties were strongly influential in the birth of postwar social policies simply because of their strength and their capacity to put pressure on governments. The arena of their social reformism was 'municipal socialism' in the cities they led as hegemonic strongholds, like Bologna, or the Parisian 'red belt' (*banlieue rouge*). In a much bigger country like India, the communist governments of Kerala and West Bengal could be considered equivalent forms of 'local', postcolonial welfare states. In Europe, social-democratic communism had two necessary premises: on the one hand, the Resistance that legitimized communist parties as democratic forces; on the other, the economic growth that followed the postwar reconstruction. By the 1980s, the time of social-democratic communism was over.

Therefore, the end of communism in 1989 throws a new light on the historical trajectory of social democracy itself. In the postwar years, its image was mostly linked to the establishment of the welfare state in the advanced capitalist countries of the West. This widespread identification, while by no means wrong, requires some explanation. Of course, in many countries socialist currents participated in the Resistance and contributed to the defeat of fascism. They re-established democracy and conquered substantial economic gains: the welfare state introduced by the Labour government of Clement Attlee in the United Kingdom; the programme of the National Council of the Resistance in France; or the Italian Constitution of 1946, prepared jointly by socialists, communists, and Christian democrats, to recall only the most significant examples. An accomplished form of the social-democratic welfare state only existed, however, in Scandinavia, where, according to Tony Judt, social democracy became almost a 'way of life'.[84] Elsewhere, the welfare state was much more the result of a capitalist self-reformation than a social-democratic conquest. The premises of this 'humanized' form of capitalism were announced in the famous 1942 report by William Beveridge in the United Kingdom. After 1947, the Marshall Plan fostered many welfare measures in the

---

84   Tony Judt, *Postwar: A History of Europe Since 1945* (New York: Penguin, 2005), 363.

realms of health, pensions, and education, as well as against occupational injuries and unemployment. In Germany, the welfare state was established by a politician as conservative as Konrad Adenauer; in France, by the coalition governments of the Fourth Republic; in Italy, the Christian Democratic governments introduced a weaker form of the welfare state by implementing many of the social institutions inherited from the fascist regime. At the end of the Second World War, in the midst of a continent in ruins, capitalism was unable to restart without powerful state intervention. Despite its obvious – and largely achieved – goal of defending the principle of the 'free market' against the Soviet economy, the Marshall Plan was, as its name indicated, a 'plan' that assured the transition from total war to peaceful reconstruction. Without such massive American help, many materially destroyed European countries would have been unable to recover quickly, and the United States worried that a new economic collapse might push entire countries towards communism.[85]

From this point of view, the postwar welfare state was an unexpected outcome of the complex and contradictory confrontation between communism and capitalism that had begun in 1917. Whatever the values, convictions, and commitments of its members and even its leaders, social democracy played a *rentier*'s role: it could defend freedom, democracy and the welfare state in the capitalist countries simply because the USSR existed, and capitalism had been compelled to transform itself in the context of the Cold War. In the final analysis, this confirms the dialectical relationship between reform and revolution that Rosa Luxemburg sketched at the end of the nineteenth century, when German socialism was shaken by the controversy over 'revisionism'. 'Work for reform', she wrote against Eduard Bernstein, 'does not contain its own force independent from revolution. … In each historic period, work for reforms is carried on only in the *framework* of the social form created by the last revolution. Here is the kernel of the problem.'[86]

---

85 Ibid., 90–9.

86 Rosa Luxemburg, 'Social Reform or Revolution' (1900), in *The Rosa Luxemburg Reader*, eds Peter Hudis and Kevin B. Anderson (New York: Monthly Review Press, 2004), 156.

The historic turn of 1989 confirmed this diagnostic. After 1989 and the end of real socialism, capitalism recovered its 'savage' face, rediscovered the élan of its heroic times and dismantled the welfare state almost everywhere. In most Western countries, social democracy turned to neoliberalism and became an essential tool of this transition. And alongside old-style social democracy, even social-democratic communism disappeared. The self-dissolution of the Italian Communist Party, in 1991, was the emblematic epilogue of this process: it did not turn into a classic social-democratic party but rather an advocate of centre-left liberalism, with the explicitly claimed model of the American Democratic Party. For decades, the PCI had embodied the hope of a new left-wing force capable of overcoming the historical split between communism and social democracy. This was the project of Giorgio Amendola, the communist leader who had suggested the reunification of the Italian left after the death of Palmiro Togliatti in 1964. In his view, the reasons for the schism engendered by the October Revolution no longer existed and times were ripe for creating a new unified left movement, as socialism had been before 1914.[87] His proposal was rejected, even if it laid the groundwork for Berlinguer's 'historic compromise' strategy ten years later. But the golden age of reformism was over: in the 1980s, communism disappeared, and social democracy went neoliberal.

Excluded from central power, postwar European communist parties tended to act like 'counter-societies' in which the entire existence of their members was reshaped, from their workday (where there were communist cells) to their cultural practices and imagination.[88] Communists had their own newspapers and magazines, publishing houses, movies, and music, their own leisure activities and their own

---

87 Giorgio Amendola, 'Il socialismo in Occidente' and 'Ipotesi sulla riunificazione', published by the communist weekly *Rinascita* on 7 and 28 November 1964. On this debate, see Franco Andreucci, *Da Gramsci a Occhetto: Nobiltà e miseria del PCI 1921–1991* (Pisa: Della Porta, 2014), 374–83, and Aldo Agosti, *Storia del Partito comunista italiano 1921–1991* (Roma-Bari: Laterza, 2012), 94–5, and also Sassoon, *One Hundred Years of Socialism*, 302–3.

88 See Annie Kriegel, *Les communistes français. Essai d'ethnographie politique* (Paris: Éditions du Seuil, 1968).

rituals. Communism was a kind of anthropological microcosm that enveloped daily life. As many testimonies emphasized, the communist parties simultaneously played the role of a church, as a community of faith; of an army, with its hierarchy and discipline; and of a school, with educational purposes. Joining the Party was experienced as a conversion and leaving it entailed apostasy and excommunication. Thus, social-democratic communism did not escape from the legacy of both communism-as-revolution and communism-as-regime: the revolution as a military organization for struggle and the regime as a monolithic system of power. The logic of the Cold War reinforced this pattern. Depicting communist movements in the West as foreign bodies and fifth columns inside liberal democracy, anti-communism reinforced their tendency to act as counter-societies, monolithic and impermeable to any external influence. Intellectuals and artists were mostly 'fellow travellers', insofar as party membership would prove an obstacle to their independence and creative activity.

The Heteronomies of Ilio Barontini

The four communist souls mentioned above – revolution, regime, anticolonialism, and social-democratic reformism – were distinct yet deeply entangled dimensions of the same phenomenon. Exceptionally, they could find a unique embodiment not only in the abstractions of political theory but also in the living trajectory of human beings. A figure usually neglected by communist scholarship – Ilio Barontini – was one of these singular incarnations. Without being a leader or a thinker, he played a significant role in the history of Italian and international communism.[89] His life shows how communism changed the existence of ordinary working-class people by transforming them into first-class political actors on a global scale. Of course, not all communist activists became a Barontini, but far from being fortuitous his path was emblematic.

---

89   See a biographical account in Fabio Baldassarri, *Ilio Barontini: Fuoriuscito, internazionalista e partigiano* (Turin: Robin Edizioni, 2013). On Barontini's activity within the Ethiopian Resistance, see Neelam Srivastava, 'Anticolonialism and the Italian Left: Resistances to the Fascist Invasion of Ethiopia', *Interventions*, 8/3 (2006): 413–29.

Ilio Barontini. Photograph from the
Fascist Police Archives (late 1920s).

Ilio Barontini in Ethiopia (1939). Biblioteca
Labronica Livorno (Fondo Barontini).

Born in 1890 to a peasant family in Cecina, Tuscany, he was still
an adolescent when he joined the socialist party. In 1921 he participated in the foundation of the Italian Communist Party in which, as
a railway worker, he took up trade-union responsibilities. Very soon,
he became an anti-fascist activist. After being arrested several times,
in 1931 he escaped the fascist police and ultimately emigrated to
France, the stronghold of Italian communist exile. He was forty-one
when the Communist International called him to Moscow, where he
was selected to attend the Frunze Military Academy. One year later

he was in Manchuria, freshly occupied by Japan, where he joined the communist guerrillas. We do not know how much time he spent in China. In 1936, at the outbreak of the Spanish Civil War, Barontini was appointed as an officer of the International Brigades and played an important role during the battle of Guadalajara. Thanks to his solid reputation as a military expert, in 1938 he was sent to Ethiopia, where the Comintern had decided to support Abyssinian guerrilla warfare against the Italian occupation. He lived there for two years. With two other communists, Anton Ukmar and Bruno Rolla, Barontini advised the Ethiopian Resistance and participated in the editorship of a bilingual – Aramaic and Italian – weekly: *La Voce degli Abissini*. Hunted by the fascist army, he left Africa and returned to France, where he became one of the leading members of the MOI (Main-d'œuvre immigrée) of Marseille. The MOI was the immigrant branch of the communist party, mostly composed of Eastern Jews, Italians, Spaniards and Armenians. Its main activity was organizing military attacks against the German occupation forces, notably by killing officers. After the fall of fascism in 1943 he came back to Italy, where he participated in the Resistance as a military expert. By the time of Liberation, Barontini had experienced the revolution of the early 1920s (in Italy, the factory occupations of 1919–20), the Stalinist USSR, anticolonialism in China and Ethiopia, and anti-fascism in Italy, Spain, France, and Italy again. In 1946 he was elected as a deputy in the first Parliament of the Italian Republic. Two years later, he used his authority and charisma to stop the spontaneous insurrection that followed the fascist attack against the secretary of the communist party, Palmiro Togliatti. Barontini, the former revolutionary and guerrilla fighter, had become a social-democratic communist. The last years of his life – he died in a car accident in 1951 – were quiet and peaceful. His itinerary emblematically mirrors the multiple roles played by communism during the first half of the twentieth century.

Epilogue

In 1989, the fall of communism closed the curtain on a play as epic as it was tragic, as exciting as it was terrifying, of the human 'gigantic adventure to change the world'. The time of decolonization and the welfare state was over, but the collapse of communism-as-regime also took with it communism-as-revolution. Instead of liberating new forces, the end of the USSR engendered a widespread awareness of the historical defeat of twentieth-century revolutions: paradoxically, the shipwreck of real socialism engulfed the communist utopia. The twenty-first-century left is compelled to reinvent itself, to distance itself from previous patterns. It is creating new models, new ideas and a new utopian imagination. This reconstruction is not an easy task, insofar as the fall of communism left the world without alternatives to capitalism and created a different mental landscape. A new generation has grown up in a neoliberal world in which capitalism has become a 'natural' form of life. The left rediscovered an ensemble of revolutionary traditions that had been suppressed or marginalized over the course of a century, anarchism foremost among them, and recognized a plurality of political subjects previously ignored or relegated to a secondary position. The experiences of the 'alter-globalization' movements, the Arab Spring, Occupy Wall Street, the Spanish *Indignados*, Syriza, the French *Nuit debout* and *gilets jaunes*, feminist and LGBT movements, and Black Lives Matter, are steps in the process of building a new revolutionary imagination, discontinuous, nourished by memory but at the same time severed from twentieth-century history and deprived of a usable legacy.

Born as an attempt at taking heaven by storm, twentieth-century communism became, with and against fascism, an expression of the dialectic of the Enlightenment. Ultimately, the Soviet-style industrial cities, five-year plans, agricultural collectivization, spacecraft, gulags converted into factories, nuclear weapons, and ecological catastrophes, were different forms of the triumph of instrumental reason. Was not communism the frightening face of a Promethean dream, of an idea of Progress that erased and destroyed any experience of self-emancipation? Was not Stalinism a storm 'piling wreckage upon wreckage' and which millions of people mistakenly called 'Progress'?[90] Fascism merged a set of conservative values inherited from the counter-Enlightenment with a modern cult of science, technology and mechanical strength. Stalinism combined a similar cult of technical modernity with a radical and authoritarian form of Enlightenment: socialism transformed into a 'cold utopia'. A new, global left will not succeed without 'working through' this historical experience. Extracting the emancipatory core of communism from this field of ruins is not an abstract, merely intellectual operation; it will require new battles, new constellations, in which all of a sudden the past will re-emerge and 'memory flash up'. Revolutions cannot be scheduled, they always come unexpectedly.

---

90   Walter Benjamin, 'On the Concept of History' (1940), *WBSW*, vol. 4, 392.

Illustration Credits

0.1 Théodore Géricault, *The Raft of the Medusa* (1819), oil on canvas. Musée du Louvre, Paris. © RMN–Grand Palais / Alamy New York. 0.2 V. Spassky, *To the Lighthouse of the Communist International* (1919). Soviet Poster. Lenin Library, Moscow. © Sputnik / Alamy Stock Photo. 1.7 Yury Pimenov, *Against Religion, For Industrial and Financial Plan, Complete Five-Year Plan in Four Years* (1930). Soviet Poster. © Sputnik / Alamy Stock Photo. 1.8 Soviet Poster (1939). © Heritage Image Partnership Ltd / Alamy Stock Photo. 1.9 The Ramp of Auschwitz. © Image Broker / Alamy Stock Photo. 2.1 Marc Chagall, *Forward, Forward!* (1918). Gouache. Musée National d'Art Moderne, Paris. © 2020 Artists Rights Society (ARS), New York / ADAGP, Paris. 2.3 *Bolshevism Brings War, Unemployment, and Starvation* (1920). Poster of the League for the Struggle Against Bolshevism, Berlin. © Hi-Story / Alamy Stock Photo. 2.5 Execution of Louis XVI, Paris, January 1793, Engraving. © RMN–Grand Palais / Alamy Stock Photo. 2.9 David, *The Tennis Court Oath* (1791). Canvas. Musée Carnavalet, Paris. © RMN–Grand Palais / Alamy Stock Photo. 2.11 Viktor Deni, *Capital*, Soviet Poster (1920). © Sputnik / Alamy Stock Photo. 3.2 Bruno Braquehais, *The Demolition of the Vendôme Column* (1871). Musée d'Orsay, Paris. © Alex Ramsay / Alamy Stock Photo. 3.6 Thibault, *Barricade of the rue Saint-Maur-Popincourt before the army assault*, 25 June 1848. © RMN–Grand Palais / Alamy Stock Photo. 3.7 Thibault, *Barricade of the rue Saint-Maur-Popincourt after the army assault*, 26 June 1848. © RMN–Grand Palais / Alamy Stock

Photo. 3.8 Ernest Meissonier, *La Barricade* (1851). Canvas. Musée du Louvre, Paris. © RMN–Grand Palais / Alamy Stock Photo. 3.9 Willy Römer, Berlin, January 11, 1919 (*Freiheit-Postkarte*). © dpa Picture Alliance / Alamy Stock Photo. 3.10 El Lissitzky, *Hit the Whites with the Red Wedge!* (1919), oil on canvas. © 2020 Artists Rights Society (ARS), New York. 3.11 Diego Rivera, *Man at the Crossroads* (1934). Mural. Palacio de Bellas Artes, Mexico City. © 2020 Banco de México Diego Rivera Frida Kahlo Museums Trust, Mexico, D.F. / Artists Rights Society (ARS), New York. 4.1 August Sander, *Revolutionaries* (Alois Lindner, Eric Mühsam, Guido Kopp). © Die Photographische Sammlung / SK Stiftung Kultur – August Sander Archiv, Cologne / ARS, NY 2020. 4.2 August Sander, *Communist Leader* (Paul Frölich), © Die Photographische Sammlung / SK Stiftung Kultur – August Sander Archiv, Cologne / ARS, NY 2020. 4.3 August Sander, *Proletarian Intellectuals*, (Else Lasker-Schüler, Tristan Rémy, Franz Wilhelm Seiwert, Gerd Arntz), © Die Photographische Sammlung / SK Stiftung Kultur – August Sander Archiv, Cologne / ARS, NY 2020. 4.4 Karl Marx (1875). Private Collection. © HIP / Alamy Stock Photo. 4.6 Mikhail Bakunin (1860), portrait by Nadar. Private Collection. © HIP / Alamy Stock Photo. 4.13 Thomas Hart Benton, *America Today* (1931). Egg tempera. Detail, with a portrait of Max Eastman. Metropolitan Museum, New York. © 2020 T. H. and R. P. Benton Testamentary Trusts / UMB Bank Trustee / Licensed by VAGA at Artists Rights Society (ARS), NY. 4.14 Claude Cahun, *Self-Portrait as a Young Man* (1920). © The Museum of Modern Art, New York licensed by Scala / Art Resource, New York. 4.15 Louise Michel, portrait by Eugène Appert, (1871). © Alamy Stock Photo. 4.16 Portrait of Louise Michel wearing the uniform of the Garde Nationale, *Berliner Illustrierte Zeitung*, 1904. © FLHC41 / Alamy Stock Photo. 4.18 Isaac Izrailevich Brodsky, *The Festive Opening of the Second Congress of the Communist International*, detail (1924). State History Museum, Moscow. © Alamy Stock Photo. 4.19 José Carlos Mariátegui, Lima 1928. Archivo José Carlos Mariátegui, Lima. © History and Art Collection/ Alamy Stock Photo. 4.21 Ho Chi Minh at the congress of the French Communist Party, Tours, 1920. 4.18 Manabendra Nath Roy, Moscow 1924. © Photo 12 / Alamy Stock Photo. 4.27 Hall of the exhibition *Der ewige Jude*, Munich 1937. © Sueddeutsche Zeitung Photo / Alamy Stock Photo. 5.1 Eugène Delacroix, *Liberty Leading the People* (1831), oil on canvas. © Alamy Stock Photo. 5.2 François Auguste Biard, *Proclamation of the Abolition of Slavery in the French Colonies* (1849. Canvas. Château de Versailles © Alamy Stock Photo. 6.2 Diego Rivera, *Distribution of Arms* (1926). Mural. Secretaría de Educación Pública, Mexico City. © 2020 Banco de México Diego Rivera Frida Kahlo Museums Trust, Mexico, D.F. / Artists Rights Society (ARS), New York. All other images are in the public domain.

Index